INDIGENOUS PEOPLES AND POLITICS

Edited by
Franke Wilmer
Montana State University

A ROUTLEDGE SERIES

Indigenous Peoples and Politics

Franke Wilmer, *General Editor*

CULTURAL INTERMARRIAGE IN
SOUTHERN APPALACHIA
*Cherokee Elements in Four Selected
Novels by Lee Smith*
Kateřina Prajnerová

STORIED VOICES IN NATIVE AMERICAN
TEXTS
*Harry Robinson, Thomas King,
James Welch, and Leslie Marmon Silko*
Blanca Schorcht

ON THE STREETS AND IN THE STATE
HOUSE
*American Indian and Hispanic Women
and Environmental Policymaking in
New Mexico*
Diane-Michele Prindeville

CHIEF JOSEPH, YELLOW WOLF, AND THE
CREATION OF NEZ PERCE HISTORY IN
THE PACIFIC NORTHWEST
Robert R. McCoy

NATIONAL IDENTITY AND THE
CONFLICT AT OKA
*Native Belonging and Myths of
Postcolonial Nationhood in Canada*
Amelia Kalant

NATIVE AMERICAN AND CHICANO/
A LITERATURE OF THE AMERICAN
SOUTHWEST
Intersections of Indigenous Literature
Christina M. Hebebrand

THE PRESENT POLITICS OF THE PAST
*Indigenous Legal Activism and
Resistance to (Neo)Liberal
Governmentality*
Seán Patrick Eudaily

THE ECOLOGICAL NATIVE
*Indigenous Peoples' Movements and
Eco-Governmentality in Colombia*
Astrid Ulloa

SPIRALING WEBS OF RELATION
*Movements Toward an Indigenist
Criticism*
Joanne R. DiNova

NEGOTIATING CLAIMS
*The Emergence of Indigenous Land
Claim Negotiation Policies in Australia,
Canada, New Zealand, and the
United States*
Christa Scholtz

COLLECTIVE RIGHTS OF INDIGENOUS
PEOPLES
*Identity-Based Movement of Plain
Indigenous in Taiwan*
Jolan Hsieh

THE STATE AND INDIGENOUS
MOVEMENTS
Keri E. Iyall Smith

SPEAKING WITH AUTHORITY
*The Emergence of the Vocabulary of
First Nations' Self Government*
Michael W. Posluns

MEDIA AND ETHNIC IDENTITY
*Hopi Views on Media, Identity, and
Communication*
Ritva Levo-Henriksson

THE STATE, REMOVAL AND INDIGENOUS
PEOPLES IN THE UNITED STATES AND
MEXICO, 1620–2000
Claudia B. Haake

THE STATE, REMOVAL AND INDIGENOUS PEOPLES IN THE UNITED STATES AND MEXICO, 1620–2000

Claudia B. Haake

Routledge
New York & London

Routledge
Taylor & Francis Group
270 Madison Avenue
New York, NY 10016

Routledge
Taylor & Francis Group
2 Park Square
Milton Park, Abingdon
Oxon OX14 4RN

© 2007 by Taylor & Francis Group, LLC
Routledge is an imprint of Taylor & Francis Group, an Informa business

Printed in the United States of America on acid-free paper
10 9 8 7 6 5 4 3 2 1

International Standard Book Number-10: 0-415-95860-1 (Hardcover)
International Standard Book Number-13: 978-0-415-95860-8 (Hardcover)

No part of this book may be reprinted, reproduced, transmitted, or utilized in any form by any electronic, mechanical, or other means, now known or hereafter invented, including photocopying, microfilming, and recording, or in any information storage or retrieval system, without written permission from the publishers.

Trademark Notice: Product or corporate names may be trademarks or registered trademarks, and are used only for identification and explanation without intent to infringe.

Library of Congress Cataloging-in-Publication Data

Haake, Claudia B.
   The state, removal and indigenous peoples in the United States and Mexico, 1620-2000 / by Claudia B. Haake.
      p. cm. -- (Indigenous peoples and politics)
   Includes bibliographical references and index.
   ISBN 0-415-95860-1
   1. Indians of North America--Relocation. 2. Indians of Mexico--Relocation. 3. Indians of North America--Government relations. 4. Indians of Mexico--Government relations. 5. North America--Ethnic relations. 6. Mexico--Ethnic relations. 7. North America--Race relations. 8. Mexico--Race relations. I. Title.

E98.R4H33 2007
305.897--dc22
                                          2007007585

Visit the Taylor & Francis Web site at
http://www.taylorandfrancis.com

and the Routledge Web site at
http://www.routledge.com

Contents

List of Maps   vii

Preface   ix

Acknowledgments   xi

Introduction
Removal and Identity   1

Chapter One
Indian Policy in the United States: Removal of Difference   11

Chapter Two
The Longest Removal   29

Chapter Three
'Loss of Independence Day'   41

Chapter Four
Identity (in) Crisis?: Delawares in the Cherokee Nation   61

Chapter Five
History Is Not Over Yet: The Delawares and the Law   79

Chapter Six
Indian Policy in Mexico: Removal of Indianness?   85

Chapter Seven
The Will to Endure — 107

Chapter Eight
Removal of the Yaquis: Out of *Yaquimi* — 121

Chapter Nine
Silences from Yucatán — 139

Chapter Ten
History Is Not Over Yet: The Yaquis and the Land — 157

Chapter Eleven
Removal in Comparative Perspective — 163

Chapter Twelve
Survival of the Fittest? — 179

Chapter Thirteen
Histories of Change and Survival — 199

Notes — 213

Bibliography — 269

Index — 289

List of Maps

Map 3–1: Map of the United States—Delaware Removal   41

Map 9–1: Map of Mexico—Removal of the Yaquis   139

Preface

Since the study at hand is a comparative project, I have opted to structure it in such a way as to make its parts as accessible as possible without requiring the reader to read the entire book. Readers with different interest and from different backgrounds will necessarily have varying knowledge of the backgrounds of these removals. While including chapters on the Indian policies of the United States and Mexico, I have attempted to make as much background information available in the chapters on the tribes. Unfortunately, this necessitates some overlap between chapters. I hope that those readers who dedicate themselves to the entire project will pardon this. (Those purely interested in the comparative chapters will find a summary of the two case studies in Chapter Eleven.)

I have opted to keep all quotes in the original language. Usually, such quotes are paraphrased in the sentence that follows or to lend credibility to a statement from the preceding one. My more literal translation of the original quote can then be found in the corresponding footnote. In a few instances, usually when I have included brief fragments only and where a literal translation was not possible, I have opted to include the translation in the text and kept the original in the footnote. All translations of primary sources are my own, unless otherwise indicated.

I use the terms 'Delawares' and 'Lenape' interchangeably and for variation. Traditionally, the Delawares referred to themselves as Lenape but have long been known by the outside world as Delawares. The latter is the name under which they were federally recognized. They carry both names in their seal.

Similarly, I use the terms 'Yaquis' and 'Yoeme' interchangeably and purely for reasons of variation. Traditionally, the Yaquis refer to themselves as Yoeme but have usually been called Yaquis by the outside world.

I use the terms Native Americans and American Indians interchangeably and for variation.

Acknowledgments

I am indebted to a multitude of people, but, most of all to Franklin Knight, who never ceased to support me, build me up, and offer help. I was fortunate to have him as my advisor and I know that this kind of support is not ordinarily given to doctoral students. Barbara Potthast, my advisor in Germany, had a great part in the finding of this topic for which I will always be indebted to her.

Others I need to thank profusely are Herman Bennett and Christof Mauch, as well as the Graduiertenkolleg 'Sozialgeschichte von Gruppen, Schichten, Klassen und Eliten' of the Universität Bielefeld / Germany. Additionally, I would like to say thanks to the German Historical Institute in Washington, DC, as well as to the employees of the National Archives and the Library of Congress of that city. In Mexico, the staff of the archives in Mexico, D.F., in Sonora and Yucatán greatly contributed to this work, especially Jorge Canto. I am also indebted to Raquel Padilla Ramos and Alfonso Torrúa Cienfuegos for temporarily housing me, a perfect stranger, and also for many an inspiring discussion about the Yaquis and Native Americans in general. Many times we were joined in these by the late Hernán Menéndez who greatly enriched these debates.

I also owe thanks to the British Academy and the AHRC for grants that enabled me to write and to present findings at conferences.

I also need to extend my gratitude to the *Yoeme* and the *Lenape*, for enduring so I could come along and write about them. I would especially like to thank Señor Matus from the Yaquis, who helped me all he could and never tired of telling me about his view of Yaqui history. And I owe the pleasure of having been introduced to him to Dr. Juan Liceaga, also a long-time supporter of the Yaqui people. From the Delaware tribe, Jim Rementer and Deborah Nichols need to be lauded for their incessant support and their patience in dealing with the never-ending stream of my questions. Everyone I met at the Delaware Tribal Headquarters was really interested in what I was doing and eager to help. I am especially thankful for this attitude since I had been expecting a much more negative one, considering what scientists of all areas had already done to them and other Native Americans. I also would have liked for the late Herbert Kraft to see this work, in which he expressed the kindest interest. I could not have written this without all the work he and a few others had already done on the Delawares.

My colleagues in at the University of Western Ontario in Canada and at the University of York in the United Kingdom were wonderful and have offered support when it was needed the most. I am especially grateful to Miles Taylor who made me persist in the face of adversity, to Louise Wannell for helping me through a difficult year, to Richard Bessel for edging me on, and especially to Shane O'Rourke who has been a great friend and a wonderful listener. Now, as I am about to leave York for a position at La Trobe in Melbourne, I realize how fortunate I have been and can only hope to find equally great colleagues and friends where I am about to go.

Donald Fixico has been amazingly supportive and has taken an interest in my work from a very early date for which I can never thank him enough. Discussions with Kiera Ladner, Peter d'Errico, Michael Green, and Tim Garrison, in person and on email, have enriched the study, as have conversations especially with the founding members of the Native Studies Network in the UK, as well as with friends I made at conferences, including Brian Collier and Laurie Arnold.

Franklin Knight, Jim Rementer, Wolfgang Gabbert, Ian Steele, Raquel Padilla and Carsten Haake read chapters and offered very useful suggestions, criticism, and encouragement. However, I claim responsibility for all the mistakes I have made.

Apart from the academic community, I have to express my deepest gratitude to a number of other people. You at times tend to get lonely when traveling foreign countries for such a long time and changing archives so frequently. Thanks to all those of you who made life so much brighter for me, especially the 'Hermosillo archive gang,' and also Carlos and Adelaida. And I would like to thank all my hosts, many of whom I have come to regard as family, especially since some of them would not allow me to pay rent and made me feel very welcome and like a true family member. Thanks to the Axilbunds, los Martínez, and to Marion Fein. I owe you.

There are many wonderful people whom I neglected to mention here. I have not forgotten you and fondly look back on all my experiences. I have always considered myself blessed by being fortunate enough to have met such great people.

I would also like to thank my grandparents, especially my maternal grandfather, for infusing me with a sense of and a love for history, as well as for playing *Cowboys and Indians* with me. You brought me onto the right track. And most of all I would like to express my gratitude to my family—my parents and my brother. You have been very understanding even though you had to endure many of my moods. I especially like to thank Cliff and Byron, who accompanied me on many a relaxing walk or went jogging with me in any kind of weather, while patiently listening to my problems. A couple of sentences here can never express what I feel for all of you and how much I owe you. Danke!

Introduction
Removal and Identity

> " ... *you mean he took it [the land] away from whoever was here before, Indians. . . . Well, I'm taking it away from him.*"
>
> Thomas Dunson (portrayed by
> John Wayne) in 'Red River' (1945)

This quote is from a western movie in which Native Americans figure only very marginally. Dunson and two friends, an old man and a boy, have come to Texas looking for land to start a ranch. When they finally find the right spot, the land turns out to belong to someone else already, a man who had received it as a gift from the Spanish king. To John Wayne, alias Thomas Dunson, this does not justify the possession of such a vast area. Thus, he shoots one of the two men representing the owner and sends the other one back to inform his employer that he, Dunson, is taking the land away from him, just as he and the Spanish king had taken it away from the Indians.

Coming from a Hollywood motion picture in which Indians do not even figure centrally, this quote could not be expected to reflect historic real-life attitudes towards Native Americans, but to my mind it does so perfectly specifically because it is uttered in such a casual and off-handed manner. It shows how little respect Indian ownership of land desired by non-Indians has received. While Dunson partly and implicitly justified taking the land by stating that the current owner had taken it from the Indians he did not make any effort to return it to the rightful owners, which, according to his own logic, should have been the Indians, but instead kept it for himself. By shooting the employee, Wayne/Dunson made clear that matters really came down to power. Power—or the lack thereof—was the reason the indigenous owners of the land had been deprived of it and power was the only reason John Wayne felt he needed to take it for himself.

Sadly, in this respect Hollywood emulates life as this holds true for real-life American Indians as much as for the colorfully painted, fake-tan ones made in Hollywood and encountered by and through John Wayne. But more often than not the real stories of the Native peoples who lost their lands remain hidden, just like they did in the movie where not even the name of the tribe in question was mentioned.

INDIAN POLICIES AND COVERT AGENDAS

Injustice comes in many forms, ranging from the taking of lands to being ignored or forgotten. Sometimes even the selection of the 'topic' of a study betrays a decidedly western or Eurocentric focus. Usually, it is the formidable opponents who are deemed worthy of the investigators' attention, be it because of their sheer numbers, 'civilized' achievements, or simply by virtue of military success. Other groups tend to be overlooked more easily. Some of this may be due to practical reasons, since more 'white' documents were produced in the dealings with the former, more 'warlike' peoples. Yet some of it may also be caused by a subconscious way of judging the worthiness of the societies in question, as Richard White has pointed out.[1] Furthermore, many Latin American Natives have received even less attention than those in the United States or Canada.[2] It thus is very easy to be simply overlooked so that the history of injustice continues—in yet another form.

Histories of injustices are all around us. Yet some are hidden better than others. United States Indian policy and especially removal are among the latter. Vine Deloria once said that "if the United States has rarely fulfilled the spirit of the law, it has nevertheless done better by its native people than other countries that faced this problem."[3] And Christian F. Feest, in his comparison of the Indian policies of the United States and Mexico, asserts that the removal of tribes in the United States was a measure of preservation, while the Mexicans' actions were designed to dissolve the tribal organizations.[4] While neither of these statements is devoid of truth I would not subscribe to either of them. By investigating the removal of Yaquis and Delawares, this study will show that the United States did not do any better by its Natives than its neighbor to the South. Even though the rhetoric of removal in the United States was one of benevolence, its practice and especially its consequences were dire. It has at times been asserted that at least some of the consequences were due to misguided good intentions and doubtlessly there is some truth in this. However, in my opinion the rhetoric of benevolence has often distracted from the more sinister elements of the policy and has thus shown the United States in a better light than deserved. I believe that these more sinister, exploitative, and greedy influences more often than not dominated the implementation of US Indian policy, no matter how well-intentioned it may have been at its inception. So the United States, I argue, did not necessarily do so much better by 'their' Natives than for instance Mexico. On the contrary, when removal in the United States is contrasted with the same policy in Mexico, it becomes obvious that essentially both nations were pursuing the same goal, the disappearance of the Natives. Yet Mexico in the case of the Yaquis came much closer to achieving this goal than the United States did with the Delawares. The Mexican government was not hindered by having to at least on the surface live up to a rhetoric of benevolence. Removal in Mexico also was not a nationwide program and therefore it was much easier there to custom-make rules for the Yaquis. In the case of the Delawares, the government to a certain extent was bound by the legal framework of the Indian Removal Act of 1830, as well as by other legislative measures. But in the end, I argue, it was the less benevolent elements within United States Indian policy which ultimately precluded the latter from reaching its goal of 'disappearing' the Indians. It was these forces that pushed a covert agenda of land acquisition which often came to take precedence over the official one of gradual assimilation. Instead of breaking up tribes, removal transplanted them as entire units, thus putting considerable stress on them but ultimately leaving their structures intact. And in the case of the Delawares, removal even helped to heal internal rifts within the tribe. The covert agenda of removal and other policies, land acquisition, thus ultimately also stood in its own way. In Mexico, where the Yaqui tribe was rigorously broken up until this policy was stopped by the outbreak of the Revolution, the measure came much closer to achieving its aim.

Partly through books like John Kenneth Turner's *Barbarous Mexico*, the latter country has acquired a poor reputation with regards to its treatment of indigenous peoples. Yet while the nation was by no means a shining example it was most certainly not significantly worse than the United States, who often have come out looking much better. This, I believe, falsely suggests to United States based tribes that much of the rhetoric of benevolence was true, that assimilation—a goal held to be beneficial for Natives—was what the government and its agencies strove to achieve. It thus diverts attention from both the United States' guilt and its responsibility, both of which continue well into the present.

THE CASE STUDIES

As sketched above, injustice comes in many forms, ranging from the taking of lands to being ignored or forgotten. Sometimes even the selection of the 'topic' of a study betrays a decidedly western or Eurocentric focus. Usually, it is the formidable opponents who are deemed worthy of the investigators' attention, be it because of their sheer numbers, 'civilized' achievements, or simply by virtue of military success. Others tend to be overlooked more easily. Some of this may be due to practical reasons, yet some of it may also be caused by a subconscious way of judging the worthiness of the societies in question.[5] The country in which the indigenous groups live also seems to have an impact. Latin American Natives have received even less attention than those in the United States or Canada.[6] It thus gets increasingly easy to be simply overlooked so that the history of injustice continues—in yet another form.

The Delawares are just one example for these concealed, forgotten, or denied histories and whose name is rarely remembered these days. This is extraordinarily strange and curious, since they were the first Native American nation to sign a treaty with the newly created United States of America.[7] Today, the general public knows of or about the tribe primarily through James Fenimore Cooper's *Leatherstocking Tales*. According to these books Uncas, the 'second-to-last Mohican,' was a 'prince' of the Delawares. The book, and especially the introduction to the 1851 edition, portrays Natives in general and the Delawares in particular as 'vanishing' peoples.[8] And while the tribe refused to vanish, the Delawares are also not commanding much attention these days even though their history has been especially turbulent since the 1970s and they lost their federal recognition as recently as 2005.

Indigenous peoples not based within the territorial confines of the United States generally receive even less attention than Natives who live there. For a non-US tribe, the Yaquis have received a comparatively great amount of attention from both Mexican and US-American historians and anthropologists, but scholarship on them still lags far behind that on the 'more advanced' societies like the Mayas or Aztecs / Mexica. To the general public the Yaquis are known even less. Carlos Castañeda introduced them to a wider audience only in the seventies through his *Teachings of Don Juan* and various follow-ups, focussing mainly on mysticism.

Neither of these two introductions served the Native groups well but instead supplied the general reader with a distorted picture of the tribes, their culture, and their history, portraying them either as vanishing peoples or as ancient societies later used to serve perceived new age needs. Matters are somewhat better when it comes to academic attention, even though that as well has been limited to a few authors. For the Delawares these most notably include Clinton A. Weslager and Herbert C. Kraft and for the Yaquis major writings have been produced by Edward H. Spicer, Evelyn Hu-DeHart and more recently and in Spanish by Raquel Padilla Ramos.

Still, aspects of the tribes' history so far have remained insufficiently investigated or not at all and so some of these will be explored in this study.

Subject peoples' responses to colonialism and imperialism cannot be predicted. Yet the experiences may be instructive as the parallel histories of the Delawares in the United States and the Yaquis in Mexico indicate very well. Both societies started out subsisting by farming, hunting, and gathering. Both were semi-sedentary and consisted of several partially independent villages. The first contacts with Europeans were established within a few years of each other.[9] But the similarities do not end there. Both peoples were missionized, the Yaquis by Jesuits, the Delawares by Moravian missionaries. Both had leaders who attempted to establish something like an independent Native American state.[10] Most importantly, both experienced removal at about the same time and specifically at a time that the respective states were attempting to build or re-build the nation-state. While the removal of the Delawares, although late in comparison with that of other US-American Indians, started in 1867, one year after its final arrangement by means of treaty, the mass deportations of the Yaquis originated in 1902 (although the measure as such had been introduced even earlier though on a smaller scale).[11]

Strictly speaking, the Delawares, also known as Lenape, were removed almost simultaneously with their first contacts with the European invaders.[12] Sometimes they were simply pushed back, crowded out, or fought back. On other occasions their removal was established by means of treaty.[13] Therefore, taken literally, to investigate 'the removal of Delaware Indians' as this study sets out to do, would imply a discussion of over three hundred years of removal history.[14] Even though I do supply an overview over that long a period of their history, I still had to limit the study's main focus to the first removal that was based on legislation passed by Congress, the Indian Removal Act of 1830. Its effects extended over the Delawares only in the 1850s, one of many factors that led to their removal to Indian Territory. The 'people of the first frontier,' the Delawares, as a consequence of contact with white societies and the pressure of their territorial advancement, were fragmented and split into many different groups.[15] Today, Delaware or Lenape communities can be found between Canada and Texas, making it hard if not impossible to include all of them, particularly in a transnational comparison. The study focuses on what could be termed the 'main body' of the Delawares, whose descendants now live principally in Oklahoma, as members of the Delaware Tribe which is currently fighting to regain its federal recognition.

The Yaquis, or Yoeme, spent some of their early post-contact history by 'commuting' to jobs outside of their territory.[16] First, they did so to the great exasperation of the Jesuits who tried to congregate them and keep them from going to mines and haciendas where they would be exposed to harmful 'white' influences and not have the benefit of Jesuit supervision. They even crossed the border to the neighboring United States of America. (Today there still is a Yaqui community in Arizona, which for the longest time had not come under the control of the Bureau of Indian Affairs (BIA) since they were not technically United States Indians.[17]) The Yaquis were removed on various occasions and to different places. In this study, I will concentrate on the pre-Revolutionary removals, initiated while Porfirio Díaz was President of the Republic of Mexico. This leaves out the removal conducted in the 1920s, ironically by a government which had earlier pointed out how much it detested this means. Furthermore, I will only look at the Yaquis removed to the Yucatán peninsula, mostly to the Mérida area. Others were deported to Oaxaca, and possibly also to other destinations but including these would have been beyond the scope of the study.[18]

As my investigation will show, starting out from a very similar pre-contact situation, the history of Delawares and Yaquis, while still sharing some key elements, developed in different directions. Yet with the onset of removal, both tribes found themselves in a very similar situation again, as will become evident especially in the concluding chapters of the study. These chapters also show some striking similarities in the motivations and objectives of the two nation-states in connection with the removal of Native Americans. In the past it has often been the differences which were emphasized by the (admittedly scarce) comparisons on the subject. Yet, as this study proves specifically through its adoption of the comparative method, at a basic level the similarities outweigh(ed) the dissimilarities.

THE NOTION OF IDENTITY

The study has a dual focus, centering on Indian policies in Mexico and the United States as well as on Native responses. As already indicated, United States Indian policy aimed at assimilation and land acquisition and, as the investigation of Delaware history reveals, these are the areas the tribe attempted to defend. Similarly, Native responses would have had at least some impact on how policies were carried out. Therefore, to point out the obvious, Indian policy and Indians were intricately connected, even though at times government agencies still betrayed an astounding ignorance of many matters Native American. Similarly, Yaqui behavior in the eyes of the Mexican government made the adoption of deportation necessary, and the tribe's reaction shaped the ways in which it was carried out.

As both nation states aimed to 'disappear' the Natives in their midst (be it by assimilation or eradication) and to open up Indian lands, identity and land were among the foremost matters that Natives tried to defend to the best of their abilities. Furthermore, in their eyes as well as in those of the government these issues often were connected. The Yaquis derived strength and endurance from their sense of place and the Delawares were very aware of the need for an unbroken settlement area and fertile lands to enable tribal life and to support themselves. And especially in the United States, depriving Natives of their legal/juridical identity could also have consequences on their ability to hold lands communally, thus once again linking identity and land.

Part of the investigation will thus specifically focus on the impact removal had on the two tribes, especially with respect to their identity. It determines that pre- as well as post-removal members of the Delawares and the Yaquis insisted on being and remaining separate from mainstream society. They resisted (admittedly half-hearted) attempts to assimilate them into the nation state and steadfastly defended their separate existence as a tribal society, rejecting all other options in the process.

The concept of identity has met with increasing criticism in recent years. Some of that criticism has not been without a valid foundation. For instance, the validity of the concept for non-Western cultures has been called into question. As Richard Handler has pointed out, notions of boundedness are absent in some non-Western cultures and that identity thus cannot be a meaningful concept for those societies.[19]

> "Groups are not bounded objects in the natural world. Rather, 'they' are symbolic processes that emerge and dissolve in particular contexts of action. Groups do not have essential identities; indeed, they ought not to be defined as things at all. For any imaginable social group—defined in terms of nationality, class, locality, or gender—there is no definitive way to specify 'who we are,' for 'who we are' is a communicative process that includes any voices and varying degrees of understanding and, importantly, misunderstanding."[20]

That, I believe, is a meaningful reservation and it is illustrated in this study for instance by the temporary split of the Delaware tribe when faced with the dire consequences of removal. However, it does not fully apply to the cases discussed here because of the prolonged contacts between the two tribes and the non-Native societies surrounding them. Originally, the concept of identity may have had limited validity within those societies but prolonged contact brought changes the groups could not escape. As Craig

Calhoun has pointed out, "identity turns on the interrelated problems of self-recognition and recognition by others."[21] Through prolonged contact both Delawares and Yaquis learned how to deal with European perceptions and expectations and thus to structure and frame their responses accordingly. Without wanting to deny Native agency, it is obvious that tribes were—and still are—forced to maneuver within a colonial framework and to respond to certain requirements from the dominant society. In order to protect what was meaningful to them the tribes thus learned to adopt terms and concepts that would be intelligible to the outside power. Thus the Delawares talked about nationality and referred to their separate identity as a tribe and the Yaquis, somewhat less vocal in their protest and objections, emphasized rootedness and primordial rights.

Then as well as now the use of the concept of identity, however framed or couched, has been to an extent strategic and thus had to make use of a language the dominant power would be able to comprehend and thus more likely to respond to. Yet over time these concepts and categories would also be increasingly internalized. This, I believe, is the logical continuation of what John R. Gillis hinted at when he stated that "identities and memories are not things we think *about*, but things we think *with*. As such they have no existence beyond our politics, our social relations, and our histories."[22] In that sense, identities, like nations, may well be imagined, yet they still were and are very real.

Besides the constructedness of identity, the belief in a common descent, claims to kinship, a common history, and to certain symbols capturing the core of the group's identity are often stressed in the scholarship, as well as the group's self-consciousness, originating from within or stemming from the outside and then being claimed by the group.[23] Identity has also been described as fluid, subject to change, and as something that can be manipulated. Stuart Hall has called it hybrid.[24] In the opinion of some, territory also plays a role in (ethnic) identity.[25] It is, at least to some extent, the result of the choice an individual makes and does not appear the same to everyone.[26] Therefore, identity can also be discarded or lost.

While most, if not indeed all, of these markers have some importance in the study of Delawares and Yaquis I still found them to be very abstract. Thus, for matters of illustration, I would like to use an allegory. I picture identity as a house, an old family home. A family has been living there for generations.[27] Some of the members have added to the house, and have made changes over time.[28] Its inhabitants have worked to maintain it, yet still there are some cracks in the house and some parts needed to be replaced or maybe even torn down. Very probably not everyone put the same amount of work into the place. Some individuals or groups may have

Introduction

left the house over time, possibly taking bits and pieces with them, to later return or to stay away forever, while others may have moved there from elsewhere.[29] And not everyone, the inhabitants, the neighbors, or strangers, perceive the house in exactly the same way. From the outside, some people may not even understand why anyone would chose to live in it and there would certainly have been pressure on the inhabitants to make their home more in keeping with the rapidly changing surroundings.

To the Delawares and the Yaquis, the old house that was their identity was always more attractive than any of the dwellings offered to them from the outside, no matter how many changes the structure underwent over time. They defended it for multiple reasons but referred to it in terms they believed the outside world would understand and accept. Within this rhetoric the Delawares focussed on the value and the usefulness of the house and the Yaquis on its age, location, and tradition, yet this does not mean that the reasons for their steadfast defenses of the home were necessarily limited to these aspects. However, these are the arguments that have survived.

THE LEGACY OF HISTORY

In his well known study *The Conquest of America: The Question of the Other*, historian Tzvetan Todorov states that it is not enough to damn the conquerors and to feel sorry for the Indians, "for conquests do not only belong to the past."[30] He concludes that one has to analyze the weapons of the conquerors to stop them from using these even today. The cases of the Delawares and the Yaquis prove this only too well. The Yoeme throughout the course of their history were only tolerated when they had something to offer the outside world, like their labor. That has changed little as their modern-day appeals to allow them to work the traditional lands show.

The connection is even clearer with the Lenape who to this day are fighting the legal consequences of their last removal. They are still forced to work within the legal framework created by the colonizer and which attempts to negate the successes they achieved in the past and in fighting to overcome the negative consequences of removal.[31]

Just as at the time of removal, matters today still evolve around land and diversity and in the end they still come down to power. John Wayne knew it all along.

Chapter One
Indian Policy in the United States: Removal of Difference

American Indians were and are very diverse peoples. That is the reason why it makes only limited sense to treat them as a uniform group. American Indian policy is a somewhat different matter because policymakers largely treated Native Americans as monolithic. Still, the same policy could turn out to be a very different experience for different tribes as to a considerable extent it would have been shaped by those actually carrying it out along with those who were forced to receive it, as well as by those who originally made the laws.

Yet even when taking all these dissimilarities into account, removal is one of the—if not indeed the—dominant theme of United States Indian Policy as it was present in a range of policies from treaties of land cession over allotment to termination and relocation. This chapter will show how removal has been a prevalent motif in any aspects of Indian policy as practiced in the United States.

THE COLONIAL LEGACY OF TREATY-MAKING

Upon their 'discovery' and under what has come to be called the 'doctrine of discovery,' Indians, while held to be inferior to Europeans, were generally recognized by most European nations as political entities capable to deal with Europeans by means of treaty. The reasons for this decision on the part of the Europeans would have been complex. While the European presence in what today is the United States was still comparatively weak, treaty-making was the easiest and probably the most secure way to deal with Native American nations. It also gave an air of legality and propriety to the dealings Europeans had with American Indian nations. Significantly, this would have lent strength to the claims Europeans laid to parts of the New World in particular against possible rival claims by

11

other Europeans. Had this not been the case it may have been easier and more convenient to simply adhere to Native traditions instead of written treaties which would be binding under European law as well and thus potentially inconvenient for the European party.

When the United States of America achieved independence, it adhered to this established pattern within Native-white relations and assumed the treaty-making powers earlier exercised by Great Britain and other European nations. This may partly have been because Native Americans were key actors during the American Revolution and hence needed to be catered to, and partly because the standard had already been established.[1] So in 1778, the newly created United States entered into its first (known) treaty with an Indian nation, the Lenape or Delawares.[2] While this was a treaty of friendship and thus reflective of the United States' need for allies, that was not necessarily the normal content of such documents. Among other things, treaties often arranged for a more or less orderly transfer of land-ownership from Indians to the United States. And so with each treaty signed the Indians lost more and more of their land base.

As becomes obvious when looking at treaties of land cession which suggested to the Indians that it would be beneficial for them to surrender their lands, "white America's policy from the beginning was a curious mixture of the benign and the malevolent."[3] At times it seemed like Europeans could not make up their minds if they wanted to help the Indians or eradicate them. Indeed, some policies seem to have aimed to do both and even the genuinely benevolent help given to Indians quite often turned out to ultimately be to the Natives' disadvantage. This curious fact has been reflected in many Indian policies, starting with the very earliest ones. For instance, during the first years of the nineteenth century, the United States of America followed a policy of assimilation. "Assimilation, the replacement of one culture by another, was considered the humane solution to the problem of peaceful coexistence of peoples from such different cultures as Indians and whites."[4] The underlying idea was that once Native Americans gave up hunting for subsistence they would not need the traditional amount of land, which were vast to European eyes, and thus could probably be induced to give them up to the newcomers. (From George Washington on, American presidents, following John Locke's ideas about property as the basis for prosperity, ignored the agricultural elements of many Native societies.) And as the white culture was generally considered to be vastly superior to the American Indian one, assimilation—removal of their aboriginal culture and way of life—was also viewed as being ultimately beneficial for the Natives.

REMOVAL ANTECEDENTS

However, most Natives did not share this conviction and would refuse to be assimilated, leaving their European neighbors at a loss for what to do to still achieve their goal of land acquisition. In 1803, President Thomas Jefferson bought Louisiana from France, and with this purchase, the idea of physical removal was born. The Indians were to be removed to the newly acquired 'Great American Desert,' which was presumed to be unfit for farming, thus freeing up valuable lands elsewhere and at least temporarily solving the problem of Native failure to assimilate. Jefferson, "like so many others of his generation, rejected the idea that Indians and whites could live peacefully together in the same neighborhood and he saw removal as the most humane way to solve this problem."[5] He favored what has been termed voluntary removal. But it was far from being truly voluntary; if necessary removal was to be achieved by creating conditions which would induce and compel the Indians to move, like indebtedness.[6] While especially in the beginning some tribes were able to resist removal, the long-term results of this policy were disastrous, especially when President Andrew Jackson turned it into an official government program in 1830 and thus moved away from treating it as a voluntary step.

The object of the policy was to transfer the Indians to the west of the Mississippi and in that manner to clear the lands east of the river for unhindered white settlement. While for some Americans greed would have been the prevalent motive for supporting this policy, others considered removal and separation to be the best or even the only means to keep the Indians from being annihilated. White influence was viewed as being ultimately destructive, especially since in the eyes of the supporters of this measure Indians only seemed to have adopted white vices instead of virtues, and the need was felt to give the Native nations time to gradually adapt and get ready to finally be assimilated into American society. Government rhetoric in support of removal reflected this reasoning even though doubtlessly less noble incentives also played important roles in the evolution of the policy.

Much of general United States policy revolved around land and its ownership as easily becomes apparent by the broad focus on territorial expansion, which resulted in the Louisiana Purchase, the annexation of Florida, the incorporation of what today are parts of Alabama, Louisiana, and Mississippi, and the repeated attempts to acquire Texas first from Spain and then from Mexico. The acquisition of land was an essential matter for the United States, externally as well as internally and there necessarily with regard to Native American lands. This led Vine Deloria, Jr. to conclude that "land, its ownership and use, has been a major theme in the federal-Indian relationship."[7] This was reflected particularly in various legal cases of the time, starting with *Fletcher v. Peck* in 1810. And in 1823 this central question in Indian-European relations, the question of Native land-ownership was taken on by the Supreme Court and Chief Justice John Marshall in the case *Johnson v. McIntosh*. Even though Native Americans were not party to the case the decision passed by the Marshal court was taken to clarify the issue of Native land ownership within the territorial boundaries of the United States. According to the court's opinion, discovery gave the Europeans title to the entire territory and that Indian title had necessarily been impaired by the Europeans. The United States government, it was held, therefore had the exclusive right to extinguish Indian title which Marshall furthermore took to be one of occupancy only. But the Chief Justice also recognized at least a certain degree of Indian sovereignty. In *Cherokee Nation v. Georgia* (1831) he characterized Natives as 'domestic dependent nations,' and thus declared Indian nations to be subject to the guardianship of the United States, yet as nations still in possession of some sovereignty.[8] "Thus, while the tribes did not fall within the category of 'foreign nations' that possessed full sovereignty, they did constitute legitimate legal and political entities that could manage their own affairs, govern themselves internally, and engage in legal and political relations with the federal government and its subdivisions," as Deloria and Lytle have explained.[9] This unclear and puzzling legal status, probably at least partly the result of political and tactical considerations on the part of John Marshall, remains at the heart of American Indian law even today and has caused many problems in the intervening years.

To deal with the Indians the United States government established the Bureau of Indian Affairs (BIA), often also called Indian Office. It was created in 1824 as part of the War Department and transferred to the Department of the Interior in 1849. The BIA was in charge of the administration of Native American ('Indian') affairs, acting on behalf of the United States of America, the trustee of tribal lands and properties. As it was the main instrument to deal with Indian nations the Bureau often came to be regarded as the bearer of bad news and something to be wary of.

REMOVAL

While for some years the United States government and mainly through the BIA had primarily used persuasion to try and make Native Americans vacate their lands, these efforts had met with only very limited success. This changed when Andrew Jackson took office in 1829. The Indian Removal Act of 1830 provided the legislative basis and the funds to remove Native peoples to the west of the Mississippi River. And while the bill's language still suggested voluntary removal the practice often saw Native tribes removed against their will and under highly questionable circumstances. Yet still the United States found ways to justify such measures. As Ronald Takaki has observed: "As the President of the United States responsible for Indian removal, Jackson developed a philosophical explanation which transformed Indian deaths into moral inevitability."[10] This 'inevitability' became very evident in the Supreme Court decision of *Worcester v. Georgia* (1832). John Marshall ruled that the state of Georgia had no right to extent its power over the lands of the Cherokee nation but President Jackson did not enforce Marshall's decision and consequently sealed the fate of the Cherokees even though they managed to resist removal as late as 1839. Their tragic removal acquired a sad fame under the fitting name 'Trail of Tears' and at least 4000 of 18000 Cherokees died in the course of the trek to their new lands in Indian Territory.

According to the BIA, at the close of Jackson's terms in office only about 9,000 Indians were without removal treaties.[11] These were mostly tribes from the old Northwest. So by 1840 the area east of the Mississippi was largely cleared of Native Americans living as tribes though some had chosen to stay as individuals and to take up United States citizenship. The removal of such a large number of people was partly achieved by means of treaty, but also through war. In the Seminole Wars of the 1830s the United States had had to re-discover that fighting Indians could be a difficult, drawn-out, and costly task with no guarantee for success. To avoid such expensive and time-consuming affairs as far as possible treaties generally took preference over military means. This does not mean, however, that treaties were always legal or even morally justifiable. Bribes to the chiefs or dealings with unauthorized tribal members were a common thing to happen, as for instance the treaty of New Echota (1835) showed which arranged for the removal of the Cherokees to Indian Territory.[12] President Jackson called these bribes 'a few presents' but, far from relying just on such methods, also turned to intimidation and threats, bullying and other not strictly legal methods.[13]

It has been estimated that about eighty to ninety percent of the lands formerly granted to southeastern Indians, roughly 25 million acres, were acquired by speculators once the Natives had been removed from their homes, making it hard to believe in a purely philanthropic nature of removal.[14] As Robert Remini has concluded, "the Indians were invariably cheated, even when the treaties were legitimately obtained."[15]

RESERVATIONS

Between 1845 and 1849 the United States again enlarged their territory, in part through a victorious war with Mexico. In 1848, gold was found in California and soon a gold rush set in, the expansion to the west intensified and a new migratory fever took over. The so-termed 'Manifest Destiny' rationalized this move to the Pacific and the conquest of Native American and Mexican lands.[16] These developments also came to have an impact on Indian policy and saw a modification of the existing removal policy. As Vine Deloria and Clifford Lytle have pointed out, "removal and relocation as policy were doomed from the beginning. Expansionist forces beyond the government's control inevitably destroyed the effort to keep the Indian and white communities apart."[17] Some of those Natives who had already been removed from their Eastern homes once again found themselves in the path of white expansion. The rapidly developing technology and especially the building of railroads helped to speed up new settlements and hence it became impossible to keep up the policy of separation the United States government had initially been trying to achieve by means of Indian removal. Once again, land- and gold-hungry settlers invaded Indian lands. And even though some of the European intruders were only passing through Indian lands, the supposed sanctuary given to the Natives through removal could not be kept intact. Especially with the lands obtained by the United States as a result of the Spanish-American War (1846–1848), the 'Indian question' once again came to be at the center of national attention as settlers wanted to move onto the newly acquired lands immediately and Indians were again considered to be in the way.

As a consequence of these developments this period in United States history saw the birth of what is sometimes called the policy of concentration, which could also be classified as removal, but taken one step further. It was not drastically different from its preceding separation policy since 'whites' and 'reds' were still to be kept apart, Indians were removed to reservations, were concentrated on a smaller amount of land, and Native landholdings thus were yet again reduced, freeing up even more lands for white settlers.[18] That being so, Native American peoples could be more easily supervised with the establishment of strategically placed military forts. The lands like the Great American Desert, formerly only deemed fit to accommodate the undesired Indians, now were viewed in a different light. Suddenly this area was perceived as the nation's heartland and therefore could not be left to Native Americans.

Many tribes signed such removal treaties after the Indian Appropriation Act of 1851 by which Congress allowed $100,000 for this purpose.

Usually there was only one way for Indians to avoid having to leave their old lands: "In the removal treaties tribal members had been given a choice of moving west or accepting land scripts that entitled them to take allotments within the areas they had ceded and to become state citizens."[19] For most this was not a real choice as they were unwilling to surrender their tribal ties and thus had only one option, removal, left. Much of this process took place under the direct influence of various railroad companies trying to acquire land to construct their lines and aided in this endeavor by the United States government. By and by, tribes were thus reduced to reservations in Indian Territory.[20]

This was the situation at the outbreak of the Civil War in 1861. During the war the fighting was not limited to the European part of the population. In Indian Territory, it mostly took place among pro-Northern and pro-Southern groups of the Five Civilized Tribes and 6,000–10,000 were killed. Old conflicts among the Cherokees, stemming from the time of their removal from Georgia continued during the Civil War. About equal numbers of the members of the Five Civilized Tribes served in the Union as in the Confederate Army but still the federal government later used their allegiances as an opportunity to declare the existing treaties with them to be void and forced the tribes into new negotiations and thus more land losses.[21] The government then used the lands surrendered by these tribes to resettle even more tribes onto already established reservations in Indian Territory and thus concentrating Indian land holdings and populations even more.

While the United States troops were still occupied elsewhere during the Civil War only very few could be spared to fight Indians and so clashes were relatively limited. Even so, the Santee Sioux uprising of 1862, caused primarily by hunger, ended in the hanging of 38 of the 'offenders.' And in November 1864, a group of Cheyennes was massacred by the Third Colorado Volunteer Cavalry. The Indians, led by Black Kettle, believed to have made peace arrangements and had also raised a white as well as an American flag. At the time of the nightly attack, there were mostly women, children, and elderly in the camp. They were killed mercilessly and brutally and many were mutilated.

After the end of the war, however, the situation changed drastically. Suddenly experienced troops were available to fight the Natives and public sympathy for non-whites had been largely exhausted in the struggle to free the Southern slaves. The ensuing wars continued well into the Reconstruction period and in September of 1865 William Tecumseh Sherman was appointed as commander of the Division of the Missouri.[22] To solve the Indian question in that area was part of his responsibility. But especially the Plains Indians proved to be very determined in their resistance and the so-called Plains Indian Wars kept the United States military occupied for a long time. Various Plains tribes still controlled large areas of land and had the fighting skills and the resolve to keep it that way, quite successfully resisting United States attempts to resettle them onto reservations. "Only when the army combined conventional tactics with more innovative ones that took advantage of vulnerable aspects of the Plains Indians' way of life—such as General Philip Sheridan's winter campaign with which he defeated the southern Plains tribes in 1868–1869 and again in 1874–1875 during the Red River War, and then crushed the Sioux in 1876–1877 following Custer's Little Bighorn debacle—did the military arm of the government finalize Concentration, effectively enforce the policy, and successfully conclude the Plains Wars."[23] Still, it took until 1886 for Geronimo to surrender, a Chiricahua-Apache who had resisted the reservation policy until the very last and spoilt many governmental attempts to apprehend him and his followers. But the era of Indian military resistance was nearing its end. In December of 1890, in the same year that the Superintendent of United States Census declared the frontier to be closed, a massacre took place at Wounded Knee in South Dakota. About 350 men, women, and children were killed as part of the suppression of the Ghost Dance, a religious ceremony. As Peter Iverson has pointed out, "until recently, for most students of American Indian history, Wounded Knee sounded the death knell of Native life within the United States."[24] And while armed resistance was certainly very scarce after 1890 this did not mean that the Natives had been successfully subjected to United States rule and had ceased all their efforts at resistance. In the 1970s, the American Indian Movement was to once again alert the world to the existence of Wounded Knee and of Native Americans.

Between 1865 and 1877, United States Indian policy pursued two different yet related goals: acculturation and submission of the natives. On the one hand, some tribes were removed to reservations without attracting any attention, like the Delawares; on the other hand, there were the Plains Indian Wars, where the United States was trying to beat the last resurgent tribes into submission. Ultimately, however, both goals intended to achieve the removal of Native Americans, be it the removal of Native resistance, or the removal from sight or from certain lands, and both were eventually supposed to lead to the removal of their distinct 'Indianness.'

In general, it seemed like the Reconstruction-era United States was focussing mainly on 'black-and-white' questions, thereby marginalizing the Indians and others. The Civil Rights Act (1866) prohibited the states from discriminating against any citizen on the grounds of race or color—but it explicitly excluded all Indians not paying taxes, which in actual fact meant most of them and specifically those who continued to live as tribal peoples.

The Fourteenth Amendment (1868), which was also adopted during the Reconstruction, was intended to guarantee equality before the law, to blacks and whites alike. However, just as in the Civil Rights Act, Indians were not included.[25]

AMERICANIZATION

New efforts to solve the 'Indian question' were undertaken under President Grant and were called his 'Peace Policy.' As Donald Fixico has concluded, this mostly meant that "humanitarians allied themselves with practical-minded individuals who believed that fighting Indians was simply too expensive."[26] By 1871, the United States government had reconsidered its treaty-making policy with Native Americans and in a rider to an appropriation bill Congress declared that no Indian nation would henceforth be recognized for the purpose of treaty-making.[27] (Presumably this step was intended at least partly to avoid more legal entanglements.) Still, the government kept negotiating treaty-like agreements with the Indians.[28]

In the 1880s, Indian policy turned to an increased effort to achieve 'Americanization,' attempting to achieve the ultimate blending with mainstream society. The policy of Americanization intended for Indians to be educated in the ways of the white man and to give up their tribal identification. Tribal peoples were supposed to become individuals, looking out only for themselves. This was by many seen as the only way to secure them equal standing with United States citizens and for some it had always been the goal they had ultimately hoped to achieve after removal had afforded the Natives more time to adapt. Indians were to finally become Americans, mainly through education and land reform. In this manner the government attempted to solve two problems at the same time, the Indian problem and the land problem. "First, there no longer would be a need either for the federal government to maintain land reserves for Indians or for it to defend Indians and reservation land from the constant threat of white encroachment. Second, Indians would be productive, self-sufficient members of American society."[29] The most well-known school for Indians was *Carlisle Indian Industrial School,* founded in 1879. Indian education was no longer the sporadic activity it had once been but an official program. At the turn of the century about 50 percent of Indian children were enrolled in a school, most of them boarding schools far from their homes, where they were trained to become Americans, albeit mostly with an emphasis on manual skills. "The system of Indian education was successful in accomplishing half of its intended aim; it destroyed much of the social cohesiveness and the tribal identification of the Indians."[30] Still, the process did not produce the assimilated Indians the government had hoped for.

The Dawes General Allotment Act was passed in 1887 and supposed to help further the goal of Americanization through land reform.[31] It allowed the president to allot Indian lands without Native consent. Parcels of land were to be given to individuals, at first protected through a trust period during which their Native owners were not permitted to sell their plot. What was left over once the reservation lands had been so distributed, the so-called surplus land, was sold.[32] In this manner vast quantities of land once again were made available to non-Indians. "Everyone could agree that the Indians owned too much land and that holding land in tracts of millions of acres unnecessarily impeded the orderly settlement of the western states."[33] Additionally, under the Dawes Act citizenship was linked to private land ownership and Natives were given no choice in this matter. If they held a fee-simple title to a plot of land they had to become American citizens. Allotment was supposedly intended as a protective measure that would preserve adequate holdings for Indians to earn their personal livelihood. Yet in practice, this was again a measure that turned out to be detrimental for the Indians. It is telling that Congress appropriated only about $10 per allotment in 1888, indicating that it thought farming could be done almost without any money. In the end, "Indians received less from their property than other citizens, . . . because Indian lands were isolated from markets and generally non-productive."[34] Many times even the trust period was violated or circumvented and whites acquired the lands in spite of the regulations, leaving the Natives with nothing. And in 1906, the Burke Act legally gave the Secretary of the Interior the right to issue fee patents before the expiration of the trust period.[35] "The act produced rapid alienation of lands when the allottees discovered they could immediately sell their lands. Citizenship thereupon became a function of the patent-in-fee status of land and not an indication that Indians were capable of performing their duties as citizens."[36] While the BIA "preached self-sufficiency for the Indians at the same time it placated non-Indians who wanted access to Native lands."[37] As had been the case with many of the previous Indian policies, Natives were losing out to non-Natives.

The World Wars also had an impact on Native Americans. As Peter Iverson has pointed out, "Native participation in the war had been encouraged by federal officials and assimilationists who believed the war would accelerate assimilation and permit Indians to demonstrate their ability to contribute to American society."[38] To an extent this turned out to be true although the wars also helped to further a growing pan-Indianism as

Natives from different tribes came into increasing contact with one another. In 1919 an act bestowing citizenship on all Indians who had served in the armed forces in WWI was passed, superseding all previous treaty arrangements.[39] Five years later, in 1924, the Indian Citizenship Act conferred citizenship upon all Indians born in the United States without infringing on their rights to tribal or other properties. By this time, about two out of three Indians had already been accorded citizenship. Of course, a mere change in status did not solve the problems the Natives had as "citizenship itself neither magically assimilated Indians nor guaranteed them full rights as Americans."[40] For instance, in many states voting restrictions still applied, which were excluding Natives from one of the main benefits of United States citizenship.

As early as the beginning of the twentieth century, it was obvious that the allotment policy had failed. But Congress was not yet ready to admit this and even at the beginning of the twentieth century the assimilationist efforts continued. Efforts of re-assessment were undertaken only in the 1920s when an exhaustive study, the Meriam Report, was published. It reported very unfavorable economic and educational circumstances among Native Americans, something Congress was not ready to believe until a Senate study initiated the following year, 1929, and taking eight years, confirmed the findings. Consequently, the suggestions from the report were taken up to a large extent, even though it sometimes took decades to do so.[41] A radical reform came with the government lead by Franklin D. Roosevelt, his (Indian) New Deal, and his Commissioner of Indian Affairs, John Collier. Under Collier, the Indian Reorganization Act (IRA), also known as Wheeler-Howard Act, was passed in June 1934 and this legislation finally ended the failed allotment policy. It was supposed to move power away from the 'Indian Office,' the BIA, and to the tribal governments whose inherent powers it recognized. Unfortunately, Collier had had to significantly modify his draft proposal in order to get the legislation passed at all. At least partly as a consequence of these compromises the act did not prove to be as beneficial for Indians as originally anticipated. In general the new tribal constitutions and bylaws created through the IRA were standardized and modeled after the United States constitution and were therefore strongly rejected by many traditional Indians.[42] For this reason as well as for other IRA-related problems Collier, well intentioned as he may have been, became a very controversial figure. He resigned in 1945, believing that his person attracted so much criticism that he did as much bad as good. But, as Deloria and Lytle have judged, "even with his faults and limitations, he had been the first commissioner who understood that Indians would not disappear, that Indian societies could adapt, change, and respond to the challenges presented by the modern age."[43]

THE EARLY TWENTIETH CENTURY

And they indeed were continuously presented with new challenges. During the Second World War Native Americans were United States citizens and thus subject to draft. "As they were in World War I, Indians were still stereotyped as 'natural' scouts, and they frequently drew dangerous assignments that exposed them to even greater danger than they might otherwise have encountered."[44] Still, many of them distinguished themselves, and among them were the famous Code Talkers.

As a consequence of the war, the domestic budget was extremely small and many government agencies were closed or operated on a very restricted budget, the BIA among them. During the war, it moved to Chicago and contented itself with taking care of already existing programs. Yet even after the end of the war money was tight and the government was attempting to reduce federal expenditures in many ways. Consequently, Acting Commissioner of Indian Affairs William Zimmerman in 1947 was made to draw up a list of tribes which could immediately do without federal help, of the ones who would be able to do so within a reasonable amount of time and the ones who would continue to need federal assistance. This list came to be used in the Termination program initiated by a resolution passed in June 1953.

To aid in finding a solution to the largely unresolved Indian land claims, the Indian Claims Commission was established in 1946. "The commission ... had to determine whether Indian groups had appropriately claimed occupation and use of specific territories, whether they had been unjustly dispossessed of these lands, and if they had, how much compensation they should be awarded."[45] It had to deal with 370 petitions but was dissolved in 1978, before it had managed to do so.[46] The payments made did not settle treaty obligations but were instead a mere compensation for real estate. Among the chief causes for discontent with the commission was the fact that it was not authorized to restore land but merely to hand out money. However, many tribes wanted land and not money.

The post-war policy of termination implied that the government no longer upheld treaty agreements to protect Native lands and to provide various services, like health and education. Under the termination program reservation lands were to be taken over by county and state organizations, and the terminated Native communities would no longer carry the status and benefits of a federally recognized Indian tribe.[47] This was yet again a method the government hoped would result in the Indians' assimilation and Americanization. The effects on the terminated tribes were often disastrous. Land ownership changed fundamentally, the trust relationship was ended, state jurisdiction and state judicial authority were imposed, exemption from state taxing power was terminated, federal programs were discontinued, and—most importantly—tribal sovereignty was ended.[48] The benefits the Indians gained in return were very small, usually limited to a single payment. But, as Peter Iverson has stated, "the threat of federal withdrawal helped galvanize the beginnings of the modern Native American movement toward self-determination" and hence in some respects termination could be considered to have backfired.[49] While the program furthered urban migration that did not automatically bring about assimilation. Donald Fixico has pointed out that "urban Indians chose not to assimilate and white society did not encourage acceptance of Indians."[50] Pan-Indianism was encouraged through the common experience of racism and other problems in the cities. Between 1953 and 1958, 109 indigenous nations or parts thereof were terminated under this policy.[51]

The Termination program was brought to a halt as quickly as it had begun. In 1958 it was announced that no Indian tribe would be terminated without its consent. But it took until 1970 and the government of Richard Nixon to officially repudiate the policy of termination. Some communities like the Klamath and Menominee were later restored after petitioning Congress but others are still trying to accomplish this goal today.

Another post-war policy and also yet another attempt to assimilate the Indians into the American mainstream of the 1950s and 60s was relocation. It was based on a public law commonly know as the Relocation Act, which was passed in 1956. Federal funds available for Indian programs were rapidly decreasing, and already poor services suffered even more. The relocation program induced reservation residents to migrate to urban areas to live and work and where they were told they would find a better life than on the reservations. Through this policy, Los Angeles became the city with the largest Native population. While relocation uprooted many Indians and made them lose their tribal ties and identity, it promoted pan-Indianism in a similar way to termination.

The period of the 1960s saw the beginning of the contemporary self-determination policy, even though the termination policy, as mentioned, was not officially repudiated until 1970. The Indian Civil Rights Act (ICRA) of 1968 kept states from assuming jurisdiction over Indian Country under a public law; but it was also intended to further IRA-like governance. Furthermore, as George Grossman has pointed out, "although the Indian Civil Rights Act of 1968 mandates that tribal governments must provide most of the individual rights contained in the United States Constitution, some rights available in state and federal courts . . . are not included in the act, and the Supreme Court has ruled that the included rights can be enforced by appeals to the federal courts only in cases involving incarceration."[52] The ICRA prohibited tribal governments from abridging the basic freedoms of speech, religion, dress, assembly, and petition for redress. It also protected other rights from American constitutional law at the time of passage.[53] In short, "it (re)affirmed the applicability of much of the Bill of Rights to those [tribal] persons, including free speech."[54] But while the act provided some new rights, it also neglected old ones and so the ICRA yet again tried to turn tribal peoples into individual people.

ACTIVISM

The 1960s and 70s were a time of great activism in the United States, saw the civil rights and the anti-Vietnam movement. Natives participated only marginally in the civil rights movement as Native rights were often based on treaties and on tribal sovereignty, rather than on equal rights under the United States Constitution. But when AIM, the American Indian Movement, was founded in 1968 by Dennis Banks, Clyde Bellecourt, and George Mitchell (Anishinabeg/Ojibwe) in Minneapolis, Indians soon came to share the spotlight. American Indian activism, mostly dominated by—although not limited to—AIM, saw a multitude of events, garnering Native Americans media attention, alerting the nation and the world to their continued presence.

The first event to attract massive attention was the 1969 occupation of Alcatraz Island by the 'Indians of All Tribes,' which lasted until 1971. While AIM was not directly involved in this endeavor, some of its members were and it also served as an example and an inspiration for many later events. In a statement issued after they had taken over the abandoned prison facility, the occupiers informed the United States government that, among other things, they wanted to use the island as a Center for Native American studies.[55] They offered to give $24 in glass beads for it, according to a precedent set about 300 years ago but also calculating the increase in value. The occupation raised awareness of and for Indians. Other similar activities followed, mostly organized by AIM and intended to raise awareness for the rights and problems of Native Americans. In particular, AIM wanted the United States to live up to its treaty obligations.[56] The Trail of Broken Treaties, a march on Washington, took place at the eve of the presidential elections in November of 1972 and was followed by a spontaneous and improvised week-long occupation of the Bureau of Indian Affairs headquarters. The Twenty Points document produced by members of the Trail demanded that the United States abide by its treaties with American

Indians and also called for self-determination.⁵⁷ In 1973, a seventy-one-day armed conflict took place at Wounded Knee, a small settlement on the Pine Ridge reservation, where in 1890 Lakota Sioux had been massacred by the 7ᵗʰ Cavalry. The modern events were prompted by a number of reasons, some old and some new, but were sparked by the murder of a Native American man which the local Indian community was afraid would go unpunished. AIM was invited to help in the matter and things soon escalated. The ensuing siege which pitched a few badly armed Natives against a veritable army of FBI agents and United States marshals was turned into a media spectacle but ended with little bloodshed.⁵⁸ Yet the charges against major AIM figures like Russell Means and Dennis Banks which resulted from this occupation tied up the leadership for years and significantly contributed to the decline of AIM in the following years. A 1975 shootout at Pine Ridge left two FBI agents and one Indian dead, and in 1977 Leonard Peltier most likely unjustly convicted; he remains imprisoned to this day. The 'Longest Walk' of 1978 took place from Alcatraz to Washington, DC. And through it once again the federal definition of self-determination was challenged. Other highly publicized demonstrations took place at Mount Rushmore and the Mayflower replica.

In the mid-1970s AIM increasingly turned to treaty issues and serving elders on reservations. It also cooperated with other indigenous groups around the world in bringing rights issues before the United Nations. Thus during this time the federal government came under scrutiny about its Indian affairs more than ever before. But maybe even more importantly, these events changed the way Indians were viewed and most significantly the way they perceived themselves.

THE LATE TWENTIETH CENTURY

In 1975, yet another piece of Indian legislation, the Indian Self-Determination Act was passed by Congress. Like so frequently, the name is misleading because this act did not arrange for Indian self-determination at all even though this had been a frequently voiced goal by AIM and others. Instead, the act called for an increase of Indian staff in government-formulated programs. Furthermore, it yet again placed emphasis on education, the old assimilationist tool. As Russell Means, one of AIM's most prominent figures, termed it, the act was supposed to have Indians administer their own colonization.⁵⁹

But the seventies also brought more positive legislation. In 1978, for instance, the Indian Child Welfare Act was passed, establishing much-needed stricter rules for the adoption of Indian children. The same year, the American Indian Religious Freedom Act was passed. In 1987, a special committee chaired by Hawaii Senator Daniel Inouye was instated to investigate BIA behavior. Two years later, it called for a less paternalistic attitude concerning tribal affairs and an assumption of full responsibility of self-government by the tribes, among other things. Yet at the same time the 1980s also brought new problems. The Reagan administration established sizeable budget cuts while problems like unemployment and other economic and social issues also remained prevalent. Gaming somewhat helped to soothe the financial situation of some tribes but also caused problems for them. R. David Edmunds has judged that "by 1920 most federal officials had abandoned plans to assimilate Indians into the America mainstream in favor of policies that would integrate Indian economic resources while keeping Native American communities from American society."[60]

CONTEMPORARY ISSUES

As has been pointed out repeatedly, land had been a major issue for Indians and whites alike during much of their earlier history. "Throughout Indian America one could not disregard the importance of the land itself."[61] But to the Indians, land always seems to have been more than just soil. And that has changed little to this day. Today, Indian-owned land is usually held 'in trust' by the federal government. It is exempt from state and county taxes and can be sold only in accordance with federal regulations. But many land claims remain unresolved to this day. For instance, the Sioux claim to the Black Hills continues to be a controversial issue even though the Sioux have already been awarded restitution money for the illegal loss of the land in question. However, the tribe has so far refused to accept the payment and insists on the return of the Black Hills themselves.

And there are many other confrontational issues left, like water rights, fishing rights, federal recognition, or sovereignty issues, to name just a few. As Duane Champagne has pointed out, "economic development, retention of culture and ceremonies, education, high unemployment, and health all remain major challenges for U.S. Native reservation communities."[62] But other, more spiritual issues also remain, as for instance the continuing debates about the 1990 Native American Graves Protection and Repatriation Act show.

Matters may also have become more complicated because the political importance of Native Americans has also changed. "A century ago, Indians constituted one of the most important groups in the domestic affairs of the nation, but they have lost status during the intervening decades."[63] Where once the Senate and the House of Representatives dealt with Indian Affairs, since 1976 it has been only a select committee of the Senate. While Congress still retains the constitutional powers the Indian Delegation Act of 1946 gave the Department and Secretary of the Interior the authority to delegate administrative responsibility to lower-ranking federal employees.[64] These days, Native issues are mostly relegated to the courts, possibly reflective of diminished Native sovereignty. American Indians thus have largely been removed from the political realm.

The most surprising thing happened to Native Americans after having experienced all these policies, events and treatments—they survived. Their numbers have increased since the 1930 census and in 1990 about 53% enrolled in a particular tribe.[65] "Although there has been loss of land and loss of language for some groups, there also has been the acquisition and retention of territory and cultural revitalization by others."[66] And there has been a resurgence of American Indian ethnic identity particularly since the 1970s which also caused a more general revitalization of community and culture.[67]

Today, Indian presence has become very obvious—at least to the people looking for it. For example, the National Museum of the American Indian has been built within the National Mall in Washington, DC. But to many others, Indians remain hidden. Yet this may be simply a problem of perception and arrogance. "Somehow non-Indians are inclined to classify Native peoples as 'less Indian' if they incorporate comparable changes in their lives, even though Indian identity has never depended upon isolation."[68] Robert Berkhofer, one of the major contributors to Native American Studies once used a telling example. No Americans today would consider themselves less American than Abraham Lincoln had been even though they are now driving Cadillacs. Yet as far as many contemporaries are concerned Indians are not allowed to make comparable changes in their lifestyle without losing what has been considered their distinct 'Indianness.'

Looking back at the history of United States-Indian relations and policies, it becomes obvious that for the most part and the longest time, only one goal was pursued. Policies may have had different names and may have received different headings from people subsequently studying them. But removal, separation, concentration, self-determination, termination, relocation, etc. mostly attempted to achieve one thing only—to meet 'white' economic aims and to 'do away' with 'the Indians.' There may have been exceptions, people genuinely wanting the best for the Indians and at the same time realizing that 'the best' was not necessarily the 'white' way. In fact, Richard White sees Indian policy as probably dominated by pro-Indian factions, a judgement I would not necessarily agree with.[69] Yet the fact that the policies created and applied were not in all cases born of evil or selfish intentions did not change their generally detrimental outcomes in the least. Most aimed to remove Natives, be that in a geographical, a cultural, a physical, or even a definitional sense of the term, making removal a central theme in United States Indian policy.

Chapter Two
The Longest Removal

The Delawares are an Algonquian tribe, which calls itself Lenape, meaning 'common people' in the sense of 'We, the people.'[1] The English name by which they by now have become known was derived from the river Delaware, which in turn was named after Thomas West, Lord de la Warr, who was appointed governor of Virginia in 1610. Although Lenape numbers at time of contact were probably relatively small, they occupied the large inter-river drainage basins between the lower Hudson and the Delaware Rivers. Some even lived in the middle Chesapeake area, extending Delaware territory over what is today southeastern Pennsylvania, southeastern New York, as well as what by now has become the states of Delaware and New Jersey. They lived in scattered, semi-permanent villages and these communities were independent, each with its own chiefs.[2] Villages in close proximity to one another may have constituted a band. There was no authoritarian chief with power over all Lenape and decisions were made collectively in general council.[3] The Delawares were probably not a unified tribe until after they had moved—or had been moved—to Ohio in the first half of the eighteenth century.[4] Before that time their organization had most likely been rather lose and had emphasized the independence of each village.

Originally there were probably at least three dialects in use among the Delawares: Munsee, Northern and Southern Unami, and Unalachtigo, although these were mutually intelligible.[5] Division lines between individual Lenape as well as between villages were probably drawn on the basis of language. Like some of their neighboring tribes, the Delawares were also subdivided into three clans: Wolf, Turkey, and Turtle.[6] Clan membership as well as kinship was determined through the mother, according to the matrilineal organization of the tribe.[7] The age and importance of the Lenape was emphasized by the fact that other Algonquian tribes of the Northeast called the Delawares their 'grandfathers.'[8] (References to this title can be found as late as 1861, in a letter from the Delaware head chief John Connor and his assistant chiefs to O-Puth-La-Yar-Ho-La, Muscogee Head Warrior; orally it has even been used as late as the 1970s.[9]) Pursuing a mixed economy of hunting and farming, the Lenape moved around seasonally, alternating between summer and winter camps. Their primary weapons were bow and arrow, but they also used snares. They had no system of land ownership in the European sense, but instead used land in common. Still, different families and also different tribes had different hunting grounds and disrespect of the borders often resulted in intermittent feuds.

In addition to being hunters and gatherers, the Lenape were agriculturists. While men did the hunting and fishing, women were in charge of working the land and thus of producing corn, squash, beans, wild potatoes, and tobacco. Clothing items were made of deerskins and decorated with shell beads, porcupine quills, or feathers. Shell beads, called wampum and manufactured by those living within reach of the sea, were also a valuable trade item. Among other things, they were used to make wampum belts, important in both politics and ceremony. They remained a valuable commodity even after the introduction of European glass beads.

PEOPLE OF THE FIRST FRONTIER

Since they were living along the coast the Delawares had early contacts with Europeans, not only early English and French arrivals but also Dutch and Swedish. When exactly the first contact took place has never been unequivocally determined, but apparently in 1524 the Lenape were not surprised by the appearance of Europeans. Because of those early contacts, the Delawares and other Algonquians were later termed 'people of the first frontier' as they were among the first Natives to be pushed back by waves of European invaders. But the earliest contacts were of a more sporadic nature. Dutch traders set up trading posts on the Delaware River in the early seventeenth century, in 1638 the first Swedish settlements were established, and in 1664 the area was granted to the Duke of York, an event that was followed by the first more sustained settlements.

As with other Native tribes the population at time of contact can hardly be ascertained. Estimates by some early European arrivals range from 8,000 to about 12,000 members of the entire tribe.[10] Yet most of these estimates were based on guesses by contemporaries who were generally only interested in warrior strength in a very limited area and thus produced numbers that were not particularly reliable and also most likely to be low.

After the first Europeans settled down permanently in the area, the life of the Delawares became increasingly influenced by the reciprocal trade with them. At first these exchanges of goods could be mutually beneficial. Trading with the newcomers, the Delawares managed to play the different groups of Europeans against each other. Yet soon they became increasingly dependent on European trade goods and services. Especially thereafter trade affected their hunting behavior as they hunted greater numbers of animals than before to obtain pelts for barter.

The negative effects the Lenape suffered from living at close quarters with the settlers soon became even more obvious. Initially, there were many misunderstandings about the European concept of permanently selling land and excluding its previous owners thereafter. The Delawares like so many other Natives had often assumed that they were only granting the Europeans the right to use the land and that they received gifts in appreciation thereof and as a token of friendship. So they quickly lost large areas of what formerly had solely been their territory. Traditional Lenape environment was replaced by what the settlers would have called 'civilization' but what often brought a less than civilized treatment to the Indians. In addition to the results this change of environment brought, the Delawares also suffered from the devastating effects of European diseases as well as from the confrontations with the settlers and others. The Natives living closest to the Europeans first saw the need to vacate what was left of their lands and move away, out of the settlers' path. At that time much of their land had already changed into European ownership, often against their will. Moving also allowed them to leave the direct European sphere of influence and thus preserve their traditional ways. Fragmentation thus began early for the Lenape as this destiny caught up with some of the 'people of the first frontier' before it found others, inducing them to start moving away at different times. These were the first removals the Delawares experienced, albeit in an impromptu and disorganized manner which nevertheless foreshadowed a prevalent trend in the history of Native-white relations, and especially so for the Lenape.

In the 1660s intrusions by the Five Nations began.[11] The Iroquois or Haudenosaunee, as the Five Nations are also called, were then still a force even the colonial powers had to reckon with. And the Lenape had probably lost much of their pre-contact strength mainly through the effects of prolonged contact with Europeans. These intrusions ultimately resulted in the Delawares being declared women by the Iroquois confederacy.[12] While the exact meaning of this has been hotly debated among scholars, it most likely was a degrading experience for the Lenape, reducing them in status. This declaration was followed by their resettlement, which allowed the Five Nations to make use of them as a convenient buffer against Europeans. In the following years, the Five Nations put the Delawares where they deemed fit and convenient for their own purposes. Yet while these removals were technically carried out by other Natives, they were still a consequence of the European presence in the area, cementing a trend previously established.

In 1683, the Delawares entered into land cessions contracts with the English Quaker William Penn. In one of these cessions they were to sell him as much land as one man could cover walking in one and a half days. It turned out to be more than they had expected but it also turned out to be a boon, though only a temporary one. For almost fifty years they lived fairly peacefully with the Quakers. This was probably largely due to the fact that Penn himself tried to make sure that the Indians were treated fairly and honestly, even though he himself spent little time in the New World. For instance, he made sure the Lenape understood the terms of the intended treaty. And from the English point of view Penn would have been under no obligation to purchase the land from the Indians at all since it had already been granted to him by the English king. It has been speculated that it was on Penn's account that the Delawares sided with the French during the French and Indian War, objecting to Penn's imprisonment in England on account of his Quaker beliefs.[13] Yet they were probably less making a decision to side with the French than rather one to oppose the British as their relations with them had been strained for some time.[14] Still, fighting against the English and their Iroquois allies, the Lenape found themselves allied to the losers, an experience that would be repeated in the future and which led to increased territorial losses and thus more removals.

Eventually more and more militant settlers entered Delaware lands, terminating the relatively peaceful coexistence between Lenape and Quakers, which had, however, already begun to deteriorate. So starting around 1709, the Lenape began to move to the Susquehanna River Valley, about 100 to 150 miles away from the Delaware Valley. There they were again under the influence of the Haudenosaunee, more specifically the Cayuga and Oneida. The cruelty many Lenape warriors displayed during the French and Indian War may have been their way of showing the Iroquois that they were not women but warriors.

In 1737, by means of the infamous Walking Purchase, Penn's sons fraudulently deprived the Lenape of much of their land.[15] So by 1751, more Delawares had begun to go further westward and to settle in the Ohio River Valley, thus finally managing to escape from the control of the Six Nations / Iroquois. Later, others followed an invitation of the Hurons which resulted in their cohabitation with that tribe. This was just one among many instances during their many removals that the Lenape came to live with other tribes. Yet this further expatriation split the small group of Delawares into even more subdivisions, each moving and acting independently for the most part.[16] Some of the Delawares joined the Ottawa chief Pontiac, who was greatly influenced by Neolin, the so-called Delaware Prophet, in his struggle against European encroachment between 1763 and 1766.[17] After the collapse of that rebellion, they were punished by having to forfeit their land rights and thus were entirely at the mercy of the Six Nations and the English. At this time, Lenape numbers were estimated to be around 3,000.[18]

Like other Natives, the Delawares did not escape the influence of missionaries. Some started to work among them at a very early date. The most influential missionaries to work among the Lenape were the Moravians, the *Unitas Fratrum*. Not only did they want to convert the Lenape but they also intended to change their lifestyle for the better, which in their minds meant a closer approximation to their own one. One of the first mission towns established by them was Friedenshütten, 25 miles north of Bethlehem, Pennsylvania in 1745. Another one, Gnadenhütten, was built in June 1746. Not all of the Delawares within reach were included in the mission towns and many Lenape stubbornly insisted on maintaining their traditional ways, refusing to convert to Christianity. The missionaries were careful to keep a distance between the missions and the unconverted members of the tribe, to keep their disciples away from temptation and from simply slipping back into their old ways.

ENTER THE UNITED STATES

During the American War of Independence some Delawares eventually allied themselves with the English. At this time the total Delaware population in what is now eastern Ohio numbered about 2,500 to 3,000. Only about three or four hundred of these lived in the missions.[19] The Lenape originally stayed neutral during the war, probably largely owing to the influence of chief White Eyes, himself sympathetic to the American cause. Yet not all Delawares were harboring such positive feelings towards the Americans. Had it not been for White Eyes' support, the allegiance may well have been a different one from the very beginning.

In September of 1778, the United States of America signed what was probably their first formal treaty with an Indian nation, the Delawares, giving a clear signal of mutual recognition and friendship. This Treaty of Fort Pitt provided for an alliance between the United States and the Delawares and its final article stated that Indians friendly to the United States would be permitted to form a state of the Union, with the Delawares at their head. It is not clear whether or not the United States were planning to ever actually go through with this, especially since the Continental Congress still lacked a Constitution and did not have the legal power to create a new state.[20] Yet the treaty was still reflective of the status of the Lenape in spite of the decline of their strength, as well as of the need the United States had for allies. The treaty article in question, number six, was probably very much to the liking of White Eyes,' yet he did not live long after the signing of the treaty and thus never witnessed the failure of putting it into practice and of making the vision a reality. He was murdered in November of the same year, under mysterious circumstances. With him, the United States had lost what was probably their foremost supporter among the Delawares, yet this alone might not have been sufficient to change their allegiance.

In spite of this treaty the Americans repeatedly failed to keep their promises to support their Delaware allies. The British, however, did better by their Native supporters. Consequently, the Lenape also turned to the British, thus abandoning their allegiance with the United States and with it the treaty the United States government had already shown no inclination to fulfill. It was against this backdrop of political and military confusion that the massacre of Delawares at Gnadenhütten occurred. The settlers of the vicinity were intent on taking revenge for attacks on their towns for which they blamed the Delawares. They organized a raiding party, which, however, only succeeded in locating the peaceful Christian converts at Gnadenhütten who were blameless of any military involvement anywhere. Still the white raiders showed no mercy and so on March 8, 1782, twenty-nine men, twenty-seven women, and thirty-four children were slain. However, this occurrence probably only served to enrage the non-Christian Delawares even more, who may or may not have been responsible for the attacks the settlers had first taken issue with. So far from teaching them the intended lesson, the massacre at Gnadenhütten would more likely have increased Delaware militancy.

When it became obvious that the insurgent colonists would win the war, some of the Delawares decided to forsake the United States in favor of Canada while others tried to reach Spanish Territory.[21] In January of 1785, various Indian tribes, among them the Delawares, signed a treaty with the United States, in which they acknowledged to be under United States protection. Furthermore, boundaries for their Ohio lands were established and some of their land holdings there were thus opened to white settlement. Soon this concession became very controversial among the Indian signatories and, as the difficulties mounted and the consequences became more and more apparent, fighting resumed once again. It culminated in the Battle of Fallen Timbers, in which the Indians suffered a decisive defeat. This in turn resulted in the Treaty of Greenville (1795) which brought renewed land losses for the Natives and which placed much of the Ohio Valley in

American hands, opening the lands up to yet more white settlement. Even though few Delawares had taken part in the battle, the tribe suffered punitive land losses as well. This territorial reduction led to yet another removal for the Lenape.

The remaining Delawares thus had to vacate large parts of their Ohio Valley lands and were pushed back to Indiana Territory where—with the permission of the United States Government—they settled among the Miami and Piankashaw. The latter had invited the Lenape to live on a part of their lands on the White River. Once again it was probably a very unorganized movement which took the Lenape to their new destination, with isolated families or very small groups going there individually. And once again removal resulted in cohabitation with other Indians. By 1800 the tribe was well established on the White River, where they continued to live their traditionally semi-sedentary life. They refused to give up hunting completely and to take up farming as their sole means of subsistence but instead practiced both. Around this time, the tribal council took steps to remedy the fragmentation of the tribe which had been mainly caused by removal and invited the Moravian Delawares to rejoin them at their new home. The invitation was accepted and the missionaries accompanied their charges and established a mission town in proximity to the settlement areas of the remainder of the tribe. But instead of turning more Lenape to Christianity, the Moravians soon lost some of their converts to their traditional Indian ways, something they had always feared might happen as a consequence of increased contacts with the remainder of the tribe.

MANY MORE REMOVALS

A divisive influence among the Delawares was the Shawnee prophet Tenskwatawa, brother of the famous Tecumseh, who had also moved to the White River. He preached nativism and caused much friction among the Lenape. Several of them, including chiefs, were accused of witchcraft and killed. One of these chiefs was succeeded by William Anderson, who later came to be one of the great leaders of the Delawares. By then, two events had made the United States government turn its attention to Indian policy. In 1800, Indiana Territory was divided, and in 1803 Louisiana Territory purchased from France. Both were supposed to open new areas to white settlement and thus the problem of how to dispose of the Indians to clear the lands for these settlers once again was brought to the forefront of governmental attention. President Jefferson attempted to solve this issue by exchanging Native lands in Indiana Territory for some of at least equal value west of the Mississippi. Accordingly, many treaties of land cession were subsequently made with Indian nations and with these unrest and discontent stirred once again among the Natives.

Responding to these feelings among the Indians of the area, the Shawnee chief Tecumseh planned to consolidate the Indians into a powerful confederacy to oppose the renewed taking of their lands. He was aided in this endeavor by the preachings of his brother, Tenskwatawa. The latter prematurely and probably without Tecumseh's approval brought together warriors who started to hassle white settlers on the Tippecanoe River. This harassment sparked a US military intervention and Tenskwatawa was defeated by American troops in November of 1811. Only very few Delawares had taken part in this famous battle, probably due to the cautioning influence of chief William Anderson. Consequently, the United States continued to pay the Delawares their annuities, while other tribes had forfeited theirs through their involvement in the Battle of Tippecanoe.

The Lenape remained neutral in the War of 1812. This was probably a great challenge for them as their hosts, the Miamis, had decided to side with the English. For their own protection, the United States moved the Delawares from their White River villages to the Upper Piqua Agency. The majority of the tribe returned to the White River lands by 1814. Yet in spite of having remained neutral during the war, the Delawares again had to move after the fighting had eventually ceased. In accordance with prevailing United States Indian policy, they were moved to the west of the Mississippi River. This removal was again arranged for by means of treaty.[22] Through this document, the treaty of St. Mary of 1818, they were to be compensated for the lands vacated and were also to be provided with new lands free of charge. Two Delaware chiefs, among them Chief Anderson, secretly received private annuities, a practice not uncommon in treaty-making between the United States and Native Americans. Without this additional incentive, it could be speculated, they may not have signed the treaty at all, as they were harboring very negative feelings about having to move yet again.[23] By this time, removal had become a staple of Delaware life, be it removal by means of treaty or by simply being crowded out, and the tribe knew about the negative consequences this move was likely to bring.

The Lenape left their old homes in 1820 and 1821 and, in fulfillment of their treaty, moved westward. The Indian Agent in charge of their crossing of the Mississippi River reported to have paid for the passage of 1,345 Delawares and 1,499 horses.[24] It took weeks to get all Lenape and the belongings they had managed to take with them to the other side. At this time it was still unclear where their journey would end, as the destination had not yet been decided on by the officials of the Indian Agency. The latter was relocating various tribes at the same time and was simply overwhelmed by the scale and demands of the task. It even failed to get adequate amounts of food to the removing Indians. These hardships, along with the general insecurity of where they would end up made this removal especially stressful for the Lenape tribe, even in comparison to those migrations they had previously endured.

So after the crossing, chief Anderson decided to take control of the confused destination and to take up a more permanent camp on the Current River. Too many of his people were in too bad a condition to be able to carry on with their journey into the unknown. They stayed on the Current River until September of 1822, when they moved on to the tract of land that had finally been selected for them. But the new land on the James Fork of the White River in Missouri was in part already occupied by white squatters, and therefore friction between them and the Delawares developed almost immediately. The government worked out a compromise by which the settlers paid the Lenape a small rent in exchange for being permitted to remain in place on the lands in question. Yet the land itself posed another problem as it was not suitable for farming due to severe seasonal flooding. Game was also scarce and in the quest for it Delaware hunters found themselves competing with the Osages. This competition caused them additional problems, contributing to making an already undesirable situation even worse. For these reasons, chief Anderson insisted that a new place be found for his people. Therefore, on September 24, 1829, still before the official passage of the Indian Removal Act of 1830, another treaty was signed. It provided for the United States to supply the Delawares with a new home, this time in Kansas Territory. Chief Anderson clearly had learned from the last treaty and attempted to do better for the tribe this time around. Consequently, a delegation of Delawares inspected the proposed lands in Kansas and chief William Anderson made sure the lands were surveyed to avoid future misunderstandings over ownership issues.[25] The chief also wanted a fee simple title issued to the tribe for the lands they were about to receive and settle down on, presumably an effort to forestall any further removals. Yet this request the government denied since it wanted to retain legal ownership of Indian lands and thus would only allow the Delawares occupancy title. The tribe had merely stayed in Missouri for eight years. But during this time they were reunited with other Lenape, among them a group which had migrated there prior to the arrival of the main body.[26] Apparently the wish for tribal unity still remained strong. While this removal had had some negative consequences for the tribe, the Delawares had also taken some very successful steps to overcoming these.

The Treaty of 1829 removed the tribe from Missouri to Kansas, to lands they supposedly were to enjoy forever. Included in the lands granted to them was the so-called Delaware Outlet, which gave them access to the buffalo hunting grounds of the plains, theoretically enabling them to return to their mixed economy of hunting and agriculture. The Lenape began to leave their Missouri lands in 1829, but only in 1831 had they completed their move to the new reservation.[27] However, once there the Delawares again ran into trouble with other Indians, since the United States had failed to notify the Pawnees, who already occupied lands in the area, of the relocation of the Lenape. The Pawnees thus viewed the Delawares as intruders and treated them accordingly. And even though the United States negotiated a treaty between the two tribes in 1833 the conflicts did not cease and the situation remained tense.

In Kansas, other Lenape again rejoined the main body of the Delawares, boosting their numbers somewhat.[28] While the Outlet and its hunting possibilities were put to use, more and more Lenape also increasingly turned to farming. In Kansas, they adopted various degrees of European lifestyle and even had their own schools established. At the same time, while the traditional subdivisions of Turkey, Wolf, and Turtle clans still existed, other political or ceremonial differences rapidly vanished.[29] White influence among the Delawares was also growing, even making it hard to choose new leaders without the approval of the Indian agency. The Delaware agent interfered various times in the succession of a chief. The first time may have been in 1857, when Captain Ketchum, the old chief, had died. One of the three clan chiefs should have succeeded him as head chief but, due to the agent's intervention, this was not the case. After James Connor had refused the position, his brother John Connor, who had been living among the so-called Absentee Delawares, was made head chief. He had been an unlikely candidate for the office especially due to his prolonged absence from the people he was now supposed to lead but he was favored by the white officials. Similarly, in 1861 Charles Journeycake was appointed chief of the Turkey Clan. Under tribal law based on traditional matrilineality he could not even have been a member of that clan since his mother was not a Delaware. His appointment was again the result of United States intervention and was to cause much discontent especially in the long run and may even have crucially affected their last removal, which was yet to come.

The repeated removals the Delawares had had to experience throughout their history differed in character. Quite often they were unorganized and the tribe or factions thereof were simply crowded out and pushed back by white settlers and squatters. Yet even before the official passage of the Indian Removal Act of 1830 the Lenape signed at least two documents which amounted to removal treaties, one in 1818 and one in 1829.

Similarly, the effects and consequences removal had on the Delawares varied. While they were mostly negative, especially the occurrences of 1829 showed that the tribe was not without resources in this process and did not merely passively accept its fate. Quite to the contrary, the Lenape always strove to make the best of the situation they happened to find themselves in and frequently succeeded in this goal, if only within limits.

Throughout their history of repeated removals, the Delawares several times found themselves cohabiting quite successfully and peacefully with other tribes who often had invited them to join them on their lands. At other times frictions with neighbors occurred, usually caused by the role the United States had played in that particular removal. What always seemed prevalent was the desire of the tribe to be reunited with those groups that had left the main body, as could for instance be seen in the invitation to the Moravian Delawares.

By the time they reached Kansas and settled down there, some Lenape seem to have become savvy negotiators who knew from experience what to expect from removal and therefore what to look out for in their dealings with United States representatives. Consequently, while the move to Kansas was probably still taking its toll on the tribe, they also managed to get positive things out of it. They had, for instance, inspected the lands that were to become their new home and thus had managed to secure an area which suited the needs of their lifestyle by offering lands suitable for hunting as well as for agriculture. Even so, they had failed to achieve the outright possessory title for these lands which would have afforded them better protection against possible future removals.

In many ways the Delawares were quite successful in Kansas, even according to white standards. For instance, they took up varying degrees of 'white' lifestyle and some of them became successful farmers. They posed no problem and caused no significant difficulties to their agency. Yet still they did not get to stay on the lands they supposedly were to enjoy forever for longer than a brief 38 years. Four treaties signed in the 1850s and '60s were to eventually lead the Delawares to their final removal to Indian Territory.

Chapter Three
'Loss of Independence Day'

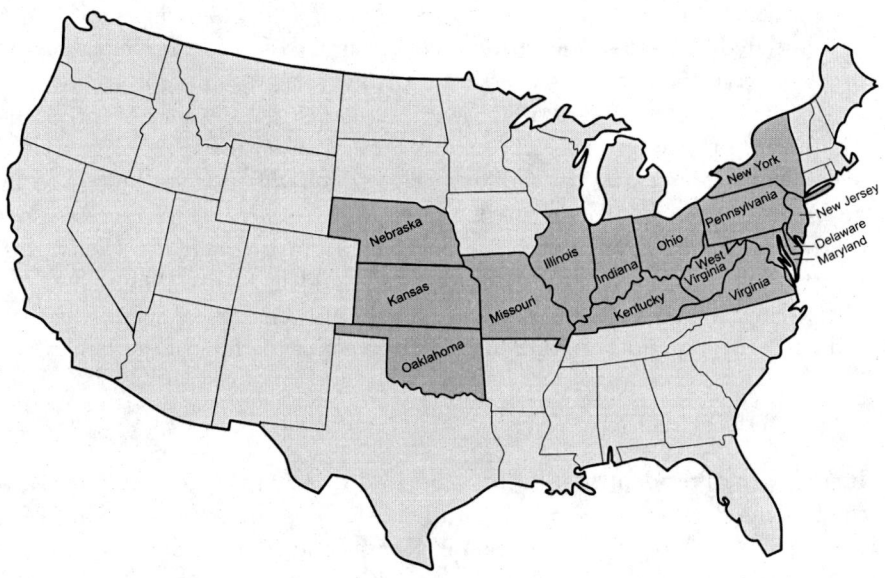

Figure 3-1. Map of the United States (states mentioned in the discussion of Delaware removal are shaded dark grey)

The Treaty of 1829 had removed the Delaware tribe, originally from what is now the Northeastern part of the United States and more specifically the Philadelphia area, to Kansas lands they supposedly were to enjoy forever.[1] In their new home the Delawares adopted various degrees of European lifestyle and some of them became successful farmers in the European style.[2] As Commissioner of Indian Affairs William P. Dole judged in an 1863 letter to the Secretary of the Interior: "They have, to a great extent, adopted the manners and customs of the whites, are fully awakened to the importance of moral and intellectual culture, and in the cultivation of many of their farms."[3] Yet in spite of being successful even by white standards, they did not remain on their Kansas lands for very long. After only 38 years there the United States government saw fit to remove the Lenape yet again, continuing the already long-established removal trend which had seen the tribe go from their homes along the Delaware River to Ohio, Indiana, and Missouri. Four treaties signed in the 1850s and '60s eventually led the Delawares to their final tribal removal, to Indian Territory, to modern-day Oklahoma.

Most of what took place in the years leading up to the fateful final treaty of 1866 was no novelty to the Lenape as a tribe. They had essentially seen it all before, in different places and at different times and may have recognized the signs of what was coming. The California Gold Rush had initiated a massive migration westward, across the continent, leaving the Indians in the path of settlers and fortune seekers. Like the Delawares, the Indian agents were virtually powerless against these waves of intruders. The normal procedure in such intrusion cases consisted of issuing several warnings before asking for military help, which was not very likely to be given. And when finally the plans for building a railroad were advancing, the promoters saw the best route as going right through the Delawares' reservation, over some of the choicest farmland in Kansas. This development also sparked a debate about the northern boundary of what was then Indian Territory, another issue that came to affect the fate of the Lenape.

PRELUDE TO REMOVAL

In 1853, the President had been authorized by Congress to negotiate with the Indians for their removal out of the settlers' path. A year later, in 1854, in the face of a worsening situation in Kansas and simultaneous preludes to a new treaty, the Delaware chief Captain Ketchum addressed a letter to the president, "concerning the condition and welfare of our Delaware Tribe of Indians now residing in the Indian Territory."[4] He invoked the assurances made at the signing of the last treaty, promising the Delawares protection and that the United States "would never desire to push us any further."[5] Yet the reason for him to write that letter was the fact that the United States had obviously started pushing once again. Ketchum further wrote: "Our great father told us when he gave us this land, now my poor Delaware Children I have abused you long enough and too much already, because I have crowded you from the East Atlantic Ocean to this place now Indian Territory and it is a high time for us to quit crowding you and therefore my dear Delaware Children I shall never again request you to remove somewhere else from this place." He also asked that "no other name be given to our Country but Indian Territory," realizing that the loss of the country itself would come with a new name.

In 1854 the Kansas-Nebraska Act was passed, which created the territories of Kansas and Nebraska out of what used to be the northern part of Indian Territory. Subsequently, Kansas became center stage for white politics but the Indians were among the first to feel the effects of the act. It opened the areas in question to white settlement and a new influx of settlers came in addition to the squatters that had already invaded the Indian lands, not respecting what was legally the Natives' property. They cut down their trees, took their horses and cattle, and trespassed on their lands. The squatters also built improvements, which would justify preempting the land. "The government had permitted speculators to make claims in Kansas before legal titles had been acquired from the Indians, and early purchasers were making claims where they supposed towns would spring up and along the line of the anticipated transcontinental railroad."[6] Clearly, Native interests were considered secondary at best.

In addition to this the Indians also came to be affected by the slavery question. Kansas now had to decide if it was to allow slavery. Its resolution was possibly crucial to achieve a majority on the issue in Congress. Opponents and proponents of slavery both came to Kansas to influence the decision, their disputes often resulting in violent confrontations. The result of this conflict came to be known as 'Bleeding Kansas,' and has been called a prelude to Civil War. The Delawares, Wyandots, and Shawnees were also drawn into the confrontation and decided to side with the antislavery forces and they even offered to defend the city of Lawrence.

In the midst of this, the Delawares were unable to withstand white pressures to negotiate another treaty. As old chiefs died they had been replaced by younger men, some of whom were more sympathetic to the 'white' ways. Thus the dissent evidenced in 1853, when their agent reported that "the . . . Delawares . . . refused . . . to sell any portion of their lands . . . although the objections made were of a trivial character" could be overcome already in the following year, when a treaty between them and the United States government was signed.[7] So in 1854, the head chief and the clan chiefs consented to a significant reduction of their land base, including the so-called 'Outlet' which had been used for hunting access.[8] For this, the tribe received $10 000, of which the largest part was to be held in trust for it by the United States government.[9] Article six of the treaty provided for some additional annuities for a few of the chiefs, something that was probably supposed to provide an additional incentive for the chiefs to sign the document.[10] In the rhetoric of the treaty the payments were justified by what was called the Delawares' gratefulness for the services rendered by the chiefs and also by the tribe's wish to provide for them. The remainder of the Delawares were left ignorant of these payments.

Six short years after the conclusion of the first Kansas treaty, in the year 1860, another one reduced this so-called 'diminished reserve' even further.[11] It was, as their agent observed, their only real option in the face of continuous depredations. Already the previous year Agent Thomas Sykes had concluded that "they will sell off the upper half of their Country. This land is doing them no good + [sic] the timber on it is daily being cut and hauled off, by Trespassers."[12] The government wasted no time acting on Sykes' observation and implicit suggestion. At the time of the new treaty, and after a delegation had inspected some lands, the vast majority of the tribe formally voted to favor the Cherokee lands.[13] Agent Sykes reported that the entire tribe had discussed the issue of moving in a number of council meetings and had concluded that "they would remain no longer in this country if they could find elsewhere, a country anything as good as this."[14] This was a decision borne out of perceived necessity rather than a truly voluntary one. White harassment had increased to unbearable levels. As their agent reported at the time of the councils, "the white people around them are continually annoying them with threats, telling them that they cannot nor shall not long own so much land here among them."[15] Unfortunately, the squatters did not leave it at threats, but because they were not United States citizens, the Delawares could only ask the United States for help and to fulfill its treaty obligations by protecting them against the numerous depredations and intrusions. Due to their status as a 'domestic dependent nation,' access to the courts was not as easy to gain as it was for United States citizens, leaving the agent and the government as their only feasible recourse against squatters and outright thieves. Yet most of the time their pleading was to no avail and even the most willing agents proved powerless. As Commissioner of Indian Affairs Mannypenny reported as early as 1855: "The Indian Agents have warned these intruders, again and again, to remove but they have not had the ability to compel obedience, and have had no aid from the military arm of the Government."[16] White depredations continued to increase, with hundreds of whites settling on "the reservation set apart for the Delaware Indians, and in defiance of treaty stipulations," making life next to unbearable for the tribe and making removal appear as the only feasible solution to ensure its survival.[17]

The tribe's only alternative to leaving Kansas was to remain there as United States citizens and thus to surrender all tribal ties. Accordingly, even though the majority of the Lenape families did not want to leave Kansas they saw no other viable option than to do so. The survival of the tribe and the maintenance of their tribal ties even under the dire circumstances for them took precedence over all other matters. The Council consequently discussed moving to the Rocky Mountains or to Texas.[18] As early as 1858, well before the signing of their 1860 treaty, the Delawares reportedly also sent a delegation to the Cherokees in an attempt to determine if they would find a suitable settlement area there.[19] It seems like they attempted to make the best of the situation when facing the inevitable loss of the remainder of their Kansas lands. If they were forced to move they at least wanted control over their destination, especially as they had been sent to poor agricultural lands in the past. Yet someone seems to have indicated to them where they might move, if possibly only by as subtle a method as approving or denying the applications the authorities had to issue to allow the tribe to send delegations to the lands they meant to inspect.[20] Weslager suspects that it "had already been decided in Washington that the Delawares should be persuaded to merge with the Cherokee, who had their own nation of about 14 million acres in Indian Territory."[21] After several delegations had been sent out and reported back the Lenape came to the same conclusion, that the Cherokee lands were the best option available to them. This may have been the result of government rhetoric or, more likely, of government limitations of their choices. But the tribe arrived at this decision only after lengthy debates and after many delegations had reported back.[22] In March of 1860, the agent reported that the tribe had formally voted to favor Cherokee lands, a decision that presumably pleased his superiors.[23] Still, the matter was far from settled even thereafter, as various later requests to be permitted to send out delegations to look at other lands showed.[24] When Ben Simon in 1864 applied for the sum of $800 to "see the Country to the west," the "answer to him was 'That not every men can get, what he wants; Chief nor anybody else.'"[25] The dissenting group of which Ben Simon was part of was later on passed off as "a small portion, a minority" by Delaware Agent Johnson.[26] The decision for the Cherokee lands had been taken, regardless of how the tribe felt about it.

In 1861, the chiefs signed a supplemental treaty and again they received some additional incentive to do so.[27] This time it consisted of money as well as land tracts well exceeding the regular allotment size. And once again the remaining members of the tribe were left in the dark about these additional perks for their chiefs.[28] The two documents of 1860 and 1861 essentially catered to a railroad company, the Leavenworth, Pawnee and Western Railroad. By signing the treaties, the Delawares agreed to have their lands allotted in severalty, 80 acres for each man, woman, or child. And still some of the Delawares seem to have insisted on keeping lands set aside for those Lenape not at the time living with the main body of the tribe. The wish to be reunited with them persisted in spite of the unsettled situation all around them.[29]

The remaining unallocated lands were considered surplus by the United States government and were to be sold off to the Leavenworth, Pawnee and

Western Railroad, which later consolidated with the Union Pacific. The railroad needed these large amounts of land not merely for the tracks but also to cut timber for construction purposes. The surplus lands to them were mainly a real estate investment because the tracks themselves were not actually laid over railroad land but instead over the remaining Delaware plots, in accordance with the right-of-way provisions from the treaties. The railroad bought the land to the low appraisal price and then sold it on for significantly more money. Even the sale of lands to the railroad was in itself somewhat out of the ordinary in treaty practice. As Weslager has pointed out, "by the terms of the old treaties, the Delawares were permitted to sell their lands only to the government, but the treaties of 1860 and 1861 permitted sale to the railroads as well."[30] Given that by law only the United States government could extinguish Native land titles, this was, though maybe not strictly illegal, at least very unusual. It could be argued that this practice was not illegal as it was still the United States that extinguished Delaware land title—though only to pass it on to the railroad right away, within the very same treaty.

Even given that the treaties were very favorable to the railroad company, and that the company therefore should have made a huge profit from these transactions, it still did not manage to meet the scheduled payments to the tribe on time. Yet instead of interceding on the Delawares' behalf, the government decided to make concessions—even though President Lincoln was "not quite satisfied with the plan."[31] When the railroad claimed to be unable to meet its payment obligations, the government in the person of the Secretary of the Interior and the president himself looked at the situation and decided to be lenient with the company.[32] It was then allowed to issue bonds and mortgages on the lands of the 1860 treaty to raise the monies due. In spite of not meeting its treaty obligations, the railroad company was permitted to walk away with the profit, leaving the Indians high and dry. During the treaty negotiations the Lenape had been given the impression that the construction of a railroad would enhance their land's value. This was indeed the case. But it was not the Delaware tribe who came to benefit from this increase. On the contrary, they came to suffer from a number of railroad-related damages, like stock killed. Furthermore, the bonds issued according to the treaty of 1861 did not even cover any improvements the Lenape had made to the land.[33] Once again they only stood to lose from signing treaties with the United States government, who did not seem to care about the fate of the tribe.

Looking at the speed their reservation was reduced through United States intervention it is very surprising to find 170 male Lenape volunteering in 1862 to fight for the Union in the Civil War. This fact is especially outstanding since at the time the entire tribe numbered only 1,085 individuals, and of these just

'Loss of Independence Day'

201 were men between the ages of eighteen and forty-five.[34] Hence the quota of actively fighting Unionists among the Lenape came up to almost 85% of those who could be expected to join. It is extremely doubtful that any other ethnic group sent such a high percentage of its men to fight for the Union cause. Seemingly recognizing this, United States officials explicitly referred to the Delawares as 'friendly.'[35] Historian Laurence Hauptman sees this voluntary enlistment as a survival strategy, trying to incur favor with the 'Great Father' in Washington.[36] Some prominent Delawares were even given commissions and authorized to raise their own companies of Indian volunteers.

One has to esteem this Civil War participation of the tribe even higher when taking into consideration the situation at home. The Delaware warriors left their homes and families unprotected and in a potentially very dangerous situation, having to fend for and defend themselves. They had to weather attacks from both white and Indian secessionists as early as 1862. The situation was aggravated even more by the refugees from Indian Territory, among them Cherokees, some of whom the Delawares fed and supplied with necessary equipment.[37] The precariousness of matters in Kansas and Lenape warrior awareness of this becomes apparent from a letter written by Captain Fall Leaf and addressed to Commissioner of Indian Affairs Dole in September of 1863. In it Fall Leaf explicitly asks for the Delaware men to be sent home "to protect our own women and children and our own property."[38] So their voluntary enlistment clearly was not an easy sacrifice to make. Still the United States did not repay the favor the Delaware volunteers had done them.[39] On the contrary, on July 4, 1866, on Independence Day, one last treaty deprived the Lenape of what remained of their Kansas lands and sent them to live in what used to be the southern part of the old Indian Territory, among the Cherokees.[40]

THE LEGAL SIDE OF REMOVAL

At the end of the war, the United States government resumed its efforts to arrange for a permanent removal of the Delawares from Kansas, more or less imposing a treaty which deprived the Lenape of what still remained of their Kansas lands and urging them to move to the Cherokee Country.[41] This treaty, eventually signed on July 4 1866, provided for a number of things, like the sale of land to the railroad. It also outlined the procedure for the voluntary dissolution of tribal ties and the adoption of United States citizenship for individual Delawares seeking to remain in Kansas.[42] In Article 4 of this document, the United States agreed to sell the Delawares a tract of land "to be selected by the Delawares in one body in as compact a form as practicable." This was to be chosen from the lands already ceded by the

Choctaws, Chickasaws, Creeks, Seminoles, or a tract still to be ceded by the Cherokees. (The latter were the last of the Five Civilized Tribes to sign one of the so-called reconstruction treaties with the United States.)

However, as previously established, the Delawares had already had second thoughts about moving to Cherokee lands; or rather, their original reservations had never been overcome, as the numerous applications for delegations or funding in the intervening years clearly indicated. The chiefs still wanted to send an exploratory party to the Rocky Mountains in search of a new place to settle, but failed to win the approval of the Commissioner of Indian Affairs.[43] From the point of view of the Bureau of Indian Affairs it would probably have been considered essential that the Delawares follow its general policy and move where it wanted them to go. Consequently, Captain Anderson Sarcoxie, an assistant chief of the Delawares, went to the Cherokee Nation in 1864 to look at lands available for settlement and talk about the terms of a possible agreement. By then, the choice of lands presumably indicated to the tribe and their agent previously had been restricted even more. As Agent Pratt reported in a letter to Commissioner of Indian Affairs Dole, "they are informed that the lands of the Osage country are already considered necessary for other purposes, and, therefore, they cannot remove to them."[44] Furthermore, they had come to the conclusion that "the Creek lands are too sickly for them."[45] Judging from Pratt's letter, this effectively left only the Cherokee lands. However, Anderson Sarcoxie found the terms proposed by the Cherokees to be unacceptable and most of the tribe agreed with him. Agent Pratt therefore concluded that "they are unwilling to mingle with the Cherokees."[46]

The Delaware petitions to get delegations authorized by the government did not cease in spite of the repeated denial of their requests.[47] The United States was not prepared to tolerate this resistance, however. After the Cherokee and Delaware failure to reach an agreement in the spring of 1864, it seems to have applied pressure on at least one of the two parties. Like the Delawares, the Cherokees were in no position to effectively resist. In the summer of 1864, at the same time that the discussion over the terms of an agreement with the Delawares went on, the Cherokees were also still in the process of negotiating a treaty with the United States, which was finally concluded on July 19 1866, about two weeks after the signing of the Delaware treaty.[48] This provided, among other things, for the removal of tribes to lands within the boundaries of the Cherokee Nation. Article 15 referred to the settlement of "civilized Indians, friendly with the Cherokees" in two ways.[49] There was a provision under which the tribe in question could abandon its tribal organization and "be incorporated into and ever after remain a part of the Cherokee Nation."[50] The same article, however, provided for tribes wanting "to preserve their tribal organizations, and to maintain their tribal laws, customs, and usages."[51] The latter were to have "a district of country set off for their use," for which they were to pay an amount to be specified into the Cherokee fund.[52] Additionally, they were supposed to pay a proportionate amount in order to "thence afterwards . . . enjoy all the rights of native Cherokees."[53] All of this was subject to the approval of the president of the United States.

After the negotiations between the Delawares and the Cherokees had failed in 1864, the Cherokees modified the terms under which they were willing to accept the Delawares.[54] This was probably in response to the Lenape's explicit "wish to remain Indians, and to preserve our nation, it was a nation from the earliest times," as Captain Fall Leaf put it in a letter to the Commissioner of Indian Affairs.[55] Members of the tribe furthermore impressed upon the United States that "before the Government of the United States was formed, we were a nation, and for time to come, so far as human mind can conceive, we wish to be a nation."[56] Clearly, they were not inclined to compromise on this central issue. The new proposal, which was submitted to Congress by the Cherokees, thus recognized the Delaware tribe as a separate entity.[57] Consequently, in 1866, the Delawares sent a new delegation to survey the Cherokee lands available to them and to discuss once again the terms of the agreement between the two tribes.[58] They decided that the lands west of 96°, which they looked at first, were unsuitable and selected a tract of land on the Little Verdigris, east of 96°, instead. It was also agreed among the Cherokee and Delaware delegates that Delaware tribal organization should be preserved.[59] Accordingly, a new agreement between the two tribes was negotiated.[60] The following year the Delaware delegates, "duly authorized by the whole Delaware people in full council assembled," as was customary, went to Washington to sign these Articles of Agreement.[61] However, in itself this procedure was a departure from Delaware custom, where decisions were traditionally taken by the tribe in council. This had previously been stated by two of the delegates themselves, Charles and Isaac Journeycake, who, in a letter to Commissioner of Indian Affairs Dole declared that "it has ever been our custom, when important matters were to be considered, to have the Council convened, and their views obtained."[62]

THE MODIFIED AGREEMENT

When the Delaware delegates came to sign the agreement, they found that some of its terms had been changed. While most of it remained the same as the version previously agreed to, a number of things had been altered.

It still arranged for payment for the land as well as a pro-rata share into the national fund of the Cherokees. Yet there were to be no lands set aside for the so-called Absentee Delawares, a band the main body hoped would eventually rejoin them, as the original agreement had provided for upon the specific request of the main body of the Delawares.[63] According to the new terms of the agreement, 160 acres per person would be sold to the removing Delawares only. Most problematically from the Delawares' point of view, there was a new article in the agreement, stating that "on the fulfillment by the Delawares of the foregoing stipulations, all the members of the tribe registered as above provided shall become members of the Cherokee Nation, with the same rights and immunities and the same participation (and no other) in the National Funds as Native Cherokees."[64] Furthermore, all "children hereafter born of such Delawares so incorporated into the Cherokee Nation, shall in all respects be regarded as Native Cherokees."[65]

This was not the agreement the Delaware delegates had anticipated signing.[66] The wording in the new document was very ambiguous.[67] It conflated both options contained in Article 15 of the Cherokee treaty, which described ways to surrender as well as to maintain a separate tribal organization. It is not clear how these new terms entered the agreement, or who exactly was responsible for them. On the one hand, it may have been the result of another attempt by the Cherokees to keep as much control as possible. It was only natural for the Cherokees to feel resentful of the Delawares, as the latter were used by the United States government as a way to punish the Cherokees for the role some of them had played in the Civil War. On the other hand, representatives of the federal government might have been responsible. They may have simply been confused or misinformed about the terms and conditions mentioned in the Delaware and Cherokee treaties of 1866. Among several of the officials involved, a genuine confusion about the term does seem to have reigned.[68] An example of this is the 'east-west' question—the common misconception that tribal organization could not be kept east of the 96th meridian. It probably stemmed from the fact that Article 15 of the Cherokee treaty of 1866 provided for ways in which to settle tribes east of the 96th meridian, while Article 16 did so for ways in which to settle them west of this. Among the ones suffering from this confusion were Agent Pratt, Superintendent Murphy and Fall Leaf.[69] Frequent changes of Commissioner of Indian Affairs (July 1865, November 1866, and March 1867) and of the Secretary of the Interior (May 1865 and July 1866) during this period may also have contributed to the confusion of the lower ranking official on the ground and led to his misunderstanding of the prevailing policy's aims.[70]

The officials also may have been reluctant to admit making a mistake with regard to the modified terms and thereby cause themselves additional work remedying that mistake. This also would have delayed the signing process and would thus have caused additional problems for them. It was probably deemed easier to pressure the Delawares into signing than it would have been to renegotiate with the numerically larger Cherokee Nation already on the lands in question. The officials may also have believed that in the future it would be easier to deal with one tribe instead of two (though this is unlikely given that the United States kept up a government-to-government relationship with the Delawares for some years to come). The officials probably regarded this agreement as a necessary evil or a nuisance they had to tolerate. Ordinarily, removal would have been arranged for through treaties with the United States government only. However, since no lands had been ceded by the Cherokees at the time the Delaware treaty of 1866 was concluded, the United States government could not at the time provide for the Lenape's removal to a specific section of the Cherokee lands.[71] Thus, an additional agreement had to be entered into by the two tribes.

Whatever the reasons for the agreement's new terms, it seems likely that the United States officials wanted to have this already drawn-out and unusually complicated matter settled as quickly as possible and the Delawares removed from Kansas to Cherokee lands in Indian Territory. They were not overly concerned about the terms, or about the Lenape, as long as the latter signed the agreement and vacated their lands. So, the ambiguous terms of the agreement most likely stemmed from a mixture of factors, including local misinterpretations of official United States Indian Policy, in particular a genuine confusion about the terms, as well as the clash of interests between the Delawares and the Cherokees.

DELAWARE RESPONSES

The new agreement seems to have come as something of a shock to at least the Delaware delegates, John Connor, Charles Journeycake, Isaac Journeycake, and John Sarcoxie.[72] They were reportedly reluctant to sign. The delegates were surprised at the altered terms of the agreement and immediately expressed their reservations. Agent Pratt, who had supported removal and the agreement, later acknowledged this when questioned in connection with the 1903 Supreme Court case of the Delaware Indians residing in the Cherokee Nation against the Cherokee Nation. Without the presence of representatives of the Department of the Interior, the historian Clinton A. Weslager has argued, the Delaware delegates may not have signed the agreement at all.[73] Charles Journeycake later admitted to the Cherokee Agent that he had made an agreement against the will of the Delaware people.[74] This opposition might have been more pronounced had one of the older and more traditionally oriented Delawares been present. Chief Anderson Sarcoxie, who had previously been involved in the negotiations, had not been invited to Washington to sign the final agreement. This suggests that a United States official must have been aware that some Delawares would oppose the changes and that especially the traditionalist Sarcoxie would have resisted this new agreement and would quite possibly have prevented its signing.

When the delegation returned to Kansas late in the spring of 1867 and reported to their tribe, they found the new terms were indeed contrary to the wishes of most of their people. It was not what the 985 members on the enrollment list had consented to in February 1867, when—based on their knowledge of the previous version of the agreement—they had registered for removal. As Captain Anderson Sarcoxie argued, the delegation had not done what it had been authorized to do but had instead entered into an "arrangement looking towards the incorporation or merging of our tribe as individuals into the Cherokee Nation."[75] I would hold that, while it may only have done what it had been 'duly authorized' to do by white standards, the delegation had violated the trust and expectations invested in it by the Lenape tribe. In contrast to this opinion, Agent Pratt in August of that year claimed that "the Delegation of Delawares who made the arrangement with the Cherokees had full powers to do so, that they exercised those powers wisely, further welfare of their people there cannot be a doubt, and is not questioned by the intelligent members of the Nation."[76] He went on to say that he considered the protests "as the expression of that unlettered class, which seek to perpetuate and keep alive old Indian customs and traditions," belittling them to the best of his abilities.[77]

Yet the Lenape wanted to maintain their tribal organization and were not about to give up easily. This had been their position throughout the negotiations. They made this clear in a letter to Cherokee Chief John Ross in 1866. They reported that Delaware and Cherokee delegates had examined the Cherokee Country west of the 96° and had come to the conclusion that there was not sufficient good land in an unbroken stretch there. So they "therefore—preserving their tribal organization—selected that part of the country on the Little Verdigris . . . beginning at the Kansas line where the 96° Meridian crosses the same."[78] Still, their tribal organization suddenly seemed to be in jeopardy. The majority of the Lenape now immediately protested against 'incorporation' and 'consolidation.' They specifically pointed to their 1866 treaty in which there was no mention of having to give up their tribal organization. And assistant chief Anderson Sarcoxie wanted "to send a delegation to Washington, representing this dissenting party," as a few Delaware councilors told Acting Commissioner of Indian Affairs Mix in a letter later that year.[79]

There was little they could do apart from petitioning and protesting, however. With the signing of the treaty of 1866, the two million acres the Delawares had once owned in Kansas were gone.[80] They now had to leave. The traditionalists among them were especially reluctant to do so under the modified terms of the Cherokee-Delaware Agreement. As General James Blunt, another official involved in the matter, reported in February 1868, three quarters of the Delawares, whom he called 'full bloods,' were "averse to locating among the Cherokees."[81] He realized that their "nationality is dearer to them than all else."[82] Superintendent Thomas Murphy, who was in charge of the Delawares' removal, was probably correct when he mentioned later that fear of the loss of "national organization, name and power" were the principal reasons for the Delawares delaying their removal.[83]

General Blunt claimed that these 'full bloods' were under the influence of Captain Fall Leaf, their war chief. He also argued that it was these 'full bloods' more than the 'half breeds,' led by chiefs Connor and Journeycake, who wanted to "preserve their identity as Delawares."[84] Fall Leaf, along with some other Delawares, wrote to the Commissioner of Indian Affairs, Nathaniel Taylor, declaring that the agreement "was made without their knowledge or consent by a few Delawares claiming to represent the whole tribe."[85] Captain Anderson Sarcoxie, along with other leaders, in June 1867 prepared a letter of protest to the Commissioner of Indian Affairs "to maintain their nationality and separate existence as a tribe."[86] Seven hundred and twelve tribal members, about two-thirds of the Delawares, signed this petition.[87] It stated that, in council and with a majority of the tribe present, "it was agreed unanimously that the Delawares will never give up their nationality and become merged in the Cherokee Nation."[88] Furthermore, the Lenape reminded the Commissioner of the treaty of 1866, which had specified that they were to "go in a body to a distinct reservation," and of the United States' duty as a guardian.[89] Sometime during the second half of 1869, several of the most outspoken of the protesters had sent another letter to the Commissioner of Indian Affairs, insisting that they wanted "to git our money and treet with any other tribe for a home."[90]

Officials like General Blunt in this perceived what they thought were divisions among the Delawares. They conceptualized these in accordance with contemporary racial thinking, referring to 'full bloods' and 'half-breeds.'

These white men were undoubtedly correct in perceiving differences and disagreements amongst the Delawares, which might also be interpreted as conflicts between traditionalists and modernists.

Among the most outspoken of the traditionalists were Chief Anderson Sarcoxie of the Turtle Band, and Fall Leaf, the head brave or war chief of the tribe and also a member of the Turtle band.[91] Both had been important figures within the tribe for a considerable time. Another leader, James Simon(s) of the Wolf Band, rose in importance through his continued protest against the situation in the Cherokee Nation and by leading the exodus of some of the Delawares to lands outside of the Cherokee Nation.[92] He had been second chief of the Wolf Band in 1863 and thus can also be counted among the senior traditionalist figures.[93] In their petitions these traditionalists asked the Government to keep up its protection of the Delawares as a separate tribe rather than as a part of the Cherokee Nation. They reminded the government of its treaty obligation to the Lenape and wanted their common tribal property to be protected.[94] They seem to have believed the only way the tribe would survive was by a continuation of their established ways, and consequently felt betrayed by their chiefs and delegates for signing the agreement.

The modernists among the Delawares seemed to have seen their goal in advancing their people in a different, more individual way. They feared the consequences of the actions of "old men seeking to perpetuate past customs," as they characterized the traditionalists.[95] The way they saw it, these men were willing to "move whenever these long cherished ways" were "invaded," and consequently avoid the advancement the modernists sought.[98] Most notable among the modernists were the current head chief, John Connor, and Charles Journeycake, who later came to be head chief of the Delaware tribe. Yet they, too, cared about tribal unity, since one of their most pronounced fears was the scattering of their people.[97] Nevertheless, the modernists were disposed to accept more of what has been called 'white ways.' They probably viewed the acceptance of the modified terms as the only feasible option in the face of a worsening situation in Kansas and their virtual powerlessness vis-à-vis the federal government.

The Bureau of Indian Affairs officials like Delaware agent Pratt not only observed differences in the Lenape but actually contributed to them. Pratt and others often favored the modernists. In 1861, for instance, the United States government had appointed Charles Journeycake, a Baptist minister, chief of the Turkey Clan, which was in violation of the Delawares' matrilineal model of descent since Journeycake's mother had been white.[98] Consequently, many tribal members resented this appointment and did not accept it as readily as that of John Connor, the grandson of a previous

'Loss of Independence Day' 55

chief in 1857.[99] In Lenape tradition, upon the death of the old chief, one of the three clan chiefs would have ascended to head chief; now, however, it was the intervention of officials that decided the matter. The 'full bloods' resented this.

The officials, however, misrepresented the conflict amongst the Delawares, confusing differences for division. In actual fact, even this internal conflict between traditionalists and modernists, 'full bloods' and 'half breeds,' only serves to illustrate how much all the removing Delawares cared about the preservation of their tribal ties. After all, it was only the Delawares who remained in Kansas as United States citizens who opted to give up their tribal affiliation. Everyone who chose to remove did so specifically in order to maintain the tribal ties. It just happened that different groups among the Lenape had different opinions about what were the best *means* of achieving this goal in the circumstances. Both modernists and traditionalists repeatedly emphasized their interest in the well-being of the nation and came to especially stress tribal ties and their identity as Delawares.[100] Fall Leaf, in a letter to the Commissioner of Indian Affairs as early as 1864, explained that the Lenape wished "to remain Indians, and to preserve our nation."[101] Charles Journeycake likewise expressed concern "for the welfare of our nation."[102] Yet he saw one of the principal dangers for the tribe in "old men seeking to perpetuate past customs."[103] He also thought that the old chiefs were unable to comprehend the treaties and thus likely to be taken advantage of by the government, while Fall Leaf claimed that the Delaware people were left ignorant of the treaty provisions.[104] Both positions at their core were not very dissimilar.

It is likely that the Lenape used blood quantum as a way to express and illustrate their positions in their correspondence with United States officials, but, contrary to the opinion of officials like Blunt, this did not signify that an internal rift existed that was too deep to be overcome, as their post-removal history was to prove.

EXPERIENCING REMOVAL

Under the original agreement, 985 of the Kansas Delawares had opted to go to Indian Territory rather than give up their tribal ties in exchange for United States citizenship. Yet this can under no circumstances be interpreted as voluntary removal, even though there was no need to involve the military and no blood was shed. It was merely the only feasible option for the tribe in the face of white intrusions and prevailing United States Indian policy. Still, as already indicated many among the Delawares stubbornly opposed the terms of the new Cherokee-Delaware agreement. Next to Anderson Sarcoxie, the famous scout Fall Leaf was probably the most outspoken opponent of removal under the specified conditions.[105]

Fall Leaf had opposed the Delaware leadership as early as during the war, while he himself was fighting for the Union. He was very much opposed to the terms of the treaties of 1860 and 1861. An ardent traditionalist, he wanted his people to go back to the old ways. But Fall Leaf was not the only one among the Lenape to resist removal; others shared his views on the matter. Even some of the Lenape who had originally backed the forging of an agreement with the Cherokees were dissatisfied with the outcome of the matter, with the change of the Articles of Agreement. As Weslager states, even "the members of the Delaware delegation were not fully satisfied with the terms of the agreement, and there was considerable discussion, and some argument, between the Delawares and the Cherokee."[106] Representatives of the Department of the Interior, who had arranged the meeting in the first place, seem to have obliged the Delaware delegates to sign it.[107]

Regardless of this discontent and opposition, the movement to Cherokee lands began in 1867 and continued well into the following year. After all, there was not much choice but to leave, in spite of the prevailing feeling of discontent. Much of the Lenape's belongings had to be sold at a loss or left behind but some also traveled back to collect the remainder of their things. The distance to be covered measured about 200 miles and the Delawares themselves had to cover the expenses, without receiving any governmental help.[108] And the costs were considerable as the Lenape had to purchase "quite a number of wagons" as well as horses and ponies.[109]

But, as the protest beforehand had already suggested, not everyone went readily. The ones who had been most bitterly opposing the content and phrasing of the Articles of Agreement now steadfastly resisted actual physical removal as well. Agent Pratt and others dismissed this protest and criticized the petition the tribe put together and signed in 1866 as a forgery since some of the members had attached their signatures to it several times.[110] However, these multiple signatures were most likely just mistakes caused by the impromptu way they were collected. In May 1867, the Lenape unanimously refused to ratify the Articles of Agreement between the two tribes.[111] Captain Fall Leaf and Chief Anderson Sarcoxie continued to be important leaders and spokespersons of the dissenting Delawares.[112] They feared the planned consolidation with the Cherokees so much that they refused to leave Kansas, even though they had already had to leave their old reservation. They stated that they did not want to lose their honor by moving with the Cherokees, that they were "entirely unacquainted with the language and laws of the Cherokee Nation," and that consequently they feared "trouble and disastrous consequences."[113]

In the end, all of this protest and explanation was to no avail. For the dissenting Delawares as well there was no other option than removing since they had been deprived of most things necessary to ensure their mere survival.[114] Their annuities were not to be paid until they agreed to leave although eventually the agent in charge of their removal was ordered to pay "to enable them to go to the Indian Country."[115] They had had to vacate their old reservation and were encamped south of Lawrence but lacked the means to ensure their mere survival.[116] In the face of this, even Fall Leaf's steadfastly resisting group had to measure up to a reality of starvation and destitution and grudgingly consented to rejoin those "four-fifths of the Delaware now at their new homes in the Cherokee Country."[117] However, they did not agree to remove until the Commissioner of Indian Affairs had traveled to Kansas to negotiate with them personally.

Steven Newcomb has called the Delawares' removal a "migration of a dispersed, erratically led, destitute remnant."[118] Unlike other tribes removed previously, the Delawares' needed no military escort to force them to leave their Kansas homes and to go to Indian Territory. Their removal was not as dramatic as the Trail of Tears of the Five Civilized Tribes, the Choctaw, Creek, Chickasaw, Cherokees, and Seminoles as it lacked the military presence that had marked these. Even so, the drawn-out trek to Indian Territory took a toll of about 200 lives and while it was not as such a violent removal, the underlying threat of violence was omnipresent.[119] Resisting their removal and thus the powerful United States government would have been a futile undertaking especially for the numerically weak Delawares. Particularly the elderly or very young Lenape suffered greatly due to the hardships on the way and also, especially after finally arriving on their designated lands, due to climatic changes. The approximately 200 deaths were not a small percentage considering that only 985 Delawares were listed on the removal roll drawn up by Agent Pratt in 1867. Yet ironically, in 1869 Pratt claimed that "mortality has been small."[120] And even though with these deaths considerably fewer of the Lenape than originally expected and thus calculated for came to move in with the Cherokees, the United States in 1869 still paid the full amount of money to the latter, the sum that had originally been intended to pay for all 985 Delawares to set out on the trek to join the Cherokees.[121]

When they finally reached their new homes in Indian Territory, some of the elderly Delawares had moved four times throughout their lives: from Indiana to Missouri to Kansas, and eventually to Indian Territory, which soon was to become the state of Oklahoma. And even there, at their final destination, removal did not end for the Lenape tribe, but a few of them had to move yet again, due to survey errors. Yet even those who were not affected by these mistakes did not necessarily get to enjoy their new homes. The Delawares were supposed to settle on the Little Verdigris River but this area was not set aside exclusively for them. So Cherokees and Osages, old enemies of the Delawares, partly due to previous United States meddling, harassed them in their new homes. Worn out, a group of some 300 Lenape, about a quarter of the tribe, eventually fled to the Neosho River west of 96° to escape this situation.[122] They could eventually be persuaded to return but many of their problems and grievances even thereafter remained unresolved. As will be seen in the following chapter, the post-removal situation at first aggravated internal divisions only to later on aid in mending them.

By moving in with the Cherokees, the Delawares juridically seemed to have given up their tribal identity and become Cherokee citizens.[123] They even had to pay to obtain Cherokee citizenship. Weslager points to the advantages of this by stating that the "Delawares had full citizenship rights, which entitled them to vote and to hold office."[124] And they did both, though the traditionalist Delawares also recognized their own unofficial leaders.[125] Quite obviously, they did not view themselves (merely) as Cherokees.

The Delawares' refusal to ratify the terms of the agreement remained without any impact. In the case of the Lenape, the General Council refused to do so because the agreement the delegates had signed was not what they had been authorized to assent to. It appears that representatives of the Department of the Interior had put pressure on the delegates to sign the modified version in spite of their doubts and reservations. It seems likely that the officials just wanted to have the matter settled and the Delawares removed from Kansas and did not really care about the terms, since there does not seem to be any inherent logic in the conduct. In this case, it was probably easier to talk the Delawares into signing than the numerically larger Cherokee Nation already in place on the lands in question. As so often, the Indians' interests were considered secondary to those of the United States and neglected even by those officials responsible for them. This was the case when it came to the interests of the Delawares as well as those of the Cherokees, also 'wards' to the United States government.

Of course, as the late Barry Goldwater, a former United States senator once so perceptively remarked, moral behavior cannot be legislated.[126] But since the United States had assumed a position similar to one of a guardian to the Delawares, and in each treaty promised to protect the tribe, in 'normal' life it would very probably be facing a negligence suit.[127] The President of the United States, Andrew Johnson, countersigned the agreement between the two tribes. Consequently the entity functioning 'like a guardian,' to speak with Supreme Justice Marshall's words, had a direct input in the making of the agreement and without governmental pressure it would never have been made. If anything, it was the moral obligation of the United States government to make sure that what happened was in the best interest of the Delawares. But the tribe was in too weak a position vis-à-vis the United States to make it comply with the requirements of moral behavior, which the United States government quite obviously was unwilling to fulfill voluntarily.

It is highly ironical that the final treaty to remove the Delawares was signed on July 4, on Independence Day. The nation whose independence had first been acknowledged by the Lenape, in the Treaty of Fort Pitt in which it had offered the Lenape an all-Indian state of the union, took yet another piece of their independence away.

Chapter Four
Identity (in) Crisis?: Delawares in the Cherokee Nation

The treaty of 1866 and the subsequent agreement between the Delawares and the Cherokees have sometimes been interpreted as spelling out the end of the tribe. This was what especially the dissenting Delawares were afraid of and at the same time the reason why almost every tribal member was dissatisfied with the agreement of 1867. And removal did indeed bring about many of the consequences the Lenape had feared it was going to cause, but it also turned out that, true to their history, the resilient Delaware tribal identity survived even this crisis.

The Delawares had once again lost their lands, this time the Kansas ones, by means of treaty and, when they had nothing left, reluctantly agreed to go to the recently reduced Indian Territory. But this was a slow process, initiated by the Kansas-Nebraska Act in 1854 that created the Territory of Kansas and thus brought new legal conditions. This led to negotiations between the Lenape and United States governmental officials about the land and to four treaties between 1854 and 1866, depriving the Delawares of all their land in Kansas and leaving them no choice but to leave for the Indian Territory. The invasion of the land had started earlier by settlers, squatters simply moving in and taking over the Indian's land, stealing their horses and cattle and cutting down their trees to build houses and other so-called improvements on stolen land. As a 'domestic dependent nation' they had few recourses against these intrusions, and the local government representatives would not commit political suicide by helping the non-voting Indians instead of ingratiating themselves with actual voters.

As life in Kansas had become unbearable, the Delawares attempted to make the best of a bad situation and to at least make sure their new home would offer them favorable conditions. They tried to keep in as much control as possible when it came to their removal, much like the

Cherokees did in the negotiation of the agreement between the two tribes which addressed the conditions under which the Lenape were to settle on Cherokee lands. Yet all the Lenape could do was to apply for permission and money to send out delegations to explore possible future settlement areas. As removal seemed to be the only option they had left, it was all they realistically could do. While at one point, Cherokee lands appeared to be the best option for them especially in the light of their limited choices and as far as the majority of the tribe was concerned, they did change their minds about this, at the very latest when the delegates reported on the revised agreement they had signed, though pronounced discontent had been in evidence much earlier.

ARTICLES OF AGREEMENT

The agreement between the two tribes was signed on April 8, 1867. Through it, the Cherokees sold the Lenape 160 acres of land for every man, woman, and child on the enrollment list, thus providing them with plots for their new homes.[1] Yet even though they had not received the unbroken settlement area they had been promised this land was not what the tribe mainly took issue with. What did cause them concern was that—according to the new agreement—all the members of the Delaware tribe settled on the reservation were to "become members of the Cherokee nation, with the same rights and immunities and the same participation (and no other) in the National Funds as Native Cherokees." Furthermore, all children were to "be regarded as Native Cherokees."[2] This language to a number of Delawares was highly suggestive of the loss of their legal identity. In a letter to the Commissioner of Indian Affairs they reported that "the delegation has now returned and report that instead of making such purchase that they have made an arrangement looking towards the incorporation or merging our tribe as individuals into the Cherokee Nation."[3] The discontent and fear among many Lenape was immediate and pronounced. They reported that "the diffusion of this information among our people has produced a deep feeling of excitement and a determination in the minds of a large majority of our people to maintain their nationality."[4] Consequently, they reaffirmed "the earnest desire of a large majority of our people to purchase and occupy a reservation of our own by ourselves."[5]

To these concerned Lenape, it must have seemed like the delegates had signed their tribal identity away without getting anything in return but land. So, "after thorough discussion and consultation it was agreed unanimous ... that the Delawares will never give up their nationality and become merged in the Cherokee Nation."[6] Instead, they insisted on their "nationality and separate existence as a tribe" and asked to "go in a body, to a distinct reservation of their own."[7] Their wish was not granted and they had to remove to the Cherokee lands after the 1867 agreement had been signed by delegates from the two tribes and countersigned by the president of the United States. And the land they received there was not even the unbroken settlement area they had sought.[8] Mainly because they did not get what they wanted in this respect, the land caused even more unforeseen problems to them. Due to errors in surveys and also to harassment from other Indians, many tribal members had to move again, so in a way their trek to the new lands had not even been their last removal.

Yet while almost every removing Delaware was opposed to the revised agreement, different people had different fears and expectations of what the consequences for the tribe might be. The dissenting Delawares clearly feared the worst, and that to them was the loss of their nationality, as they themselves put it. Other Lenape still believed the tribe to be protected by the provisions of their 1866 treaty. As they "interpreted the agreement, they purchased citizenship in the Cherokee Nation for the purpose of enjoying the privileges of Cherokee citizens, but at the same time they also retained their identity as members of the Delaware tribe."[9] They had lived with other tribes before without ever having been legally incorporated into those and so had little reason to expect this to happen now. As everything had been agreed to earlier and especially as they believed to have a treaty on their side, they also might have viewed the new terms the result of a confusion which, while unpleasant, would not necessarily have any repercussions for them and would be clarified later. As early as July of 1867, they thus reminded the Commissioner of Indian Affairs of "the spirit and letter of the treaty made between the United States and the Delaware Tribe of Indians."[10] They also had become quite used to the mysterious ways of the government where more often than not rhetoric and reality remained very far apart.

It is not quite clear how exactly the United States or the Cherokees viewed the agreement. The United States government seems to have purposely inserted the contents of Article 15 into the Cherokee Treaty of 1866 to respond to the situation of the Lenape and maybe others as well.[11] It talked about the settling of civilized Indians in the Cherokee Country. This provision was needed to facilitate Delaware removal to Cherokee lands as the Cherokees had not ceded any lands to the United States by the time the Delaware treaty was signed. Thus the treaty with the Lenape could not arrange for their removal to a specific section of Cherokee Country; this needed to be done later, after both treaties had been finalized and signed. The fact that article 15 of the Cherokee treaty did not rule out that tribes keep their organization but specifically allowed for them to "preserve their tribal organizations, and to maintain their tribal laws customs, and usages" would have made it more likely for the Lenape to enter into negotiations in the first place.[12] However, the same article also provided for tribes wanting to "abandon their tribal organization." The fact that both methods were described in the same treaty article was partly accountable for the ensuing confusion about the Delawares' legal status. Ideally, the United States would probably have wanted the Delawares to move to the Cherokee Nation under the provisions outlined in article 16 of the Cherokee treaty, which minimized Cherokee control while maximizing that of the United States government.[13] But the lands available under this article were not as good as the ones east of the 96th degrees which were covered by article 15 only. Presumably, the Cherokees held on to the best parts of their land when negotiating the treaty with the United States, successfully to an extent in defending it against the federal government but unable to keep complete control over it and thus other Indians off it. The Cherokees would have been in an even weaker position vis-à-vis the United States than the Delawares as the federal government could still hold their role in the Civil War against them and to use it to pressure them into a new treaty as well as into accepting conditions undesirable to them. Still the Cherokees seem to have been able to hold on to some things important to them throughout the negotiations, thus complicating matters for the Delawares.

Thus, while the United States could compel both tribes into negotiating and signing an agreement by eliminating all their other viable options, it still had to go through with the legalistic requirement of the Articles of Agreement of 1867 between them as they had been quicker in negotiating the Delaware treaty in an attempt to clear the tribe off their Kansas lands. However, while it was considered a legally necessary formality, this agreement must also have seemed like an unnecessary nuisance to the white officials involved. Consequently, they would have done their best to get it over with as speedily as possible. Speed was especially important as article 15 of the Delaware treaty of 1866 stated that "nothing in this treaty shall be so construed as to require the Delawares to remove from their present homes, until after they shall have selected and received title to lands for new homes elsewhere."[14] Through this clause, everything hinged on Delaware consent and failure to secure a rapid signing of the Cherokee-Delaware Agreement would have at least temporarily invalidated the United States' efforts to make the Delaware lands in Kansas available to white settlement. So even when the Delawares immediately expressed their discontent and said that they would "send another delegation to the Indian territory to look at the land west of the 96th degree and select a place for our new homes," it was to no avail as it would have delayed the process of removal.[15]

This may have been one of the reasons why the Articles of Agreement came to be signed in spite of legal peculiarities and possible violations of at least one of the two 1866 treaties. The Delaware Treaty indicated nothing about a loss of tribal organization, except for those Lenape who elected to become United States citizens. Quite to the contrary, the language used suggested their removal as a tribe talking about lands "to be selected by the Delawares in one body in as compact a form as practicable."[16] Yet the United States president countersigned the Articles of Agreement in disregard of possible violations of previous treaties and also mindless of the ambiguous language therein. If the United States officials really wanted the Delawares' incorporation or merely did not care about their fate as long as they only rapidly vacated their Kansas lands cannot be determined. Still, the United States had no reason whatsoever to feel any kind of resentment towards the Delawares but should indeed have been grateful for Lenape support during the Civil War.

However, it would be somewhat understandable if the Cherokees were feeling resentful toward the Lenape. The former were forced to accept 'civilized Indians friendly with the Cherokees' among them due to the backing a fraction of them had given to the Confederates during the Civil War. The Delawares in their midst were a living reminder of that injustice. As the Cherokees had no choice but to accept the Lenape due to United States pressures it was only natural for the tribal leaders to attempt to get the best possible deal and to keep in as much control as they somehow could. But, as they were unable to oppose the United States themselves, the origin of the injustice, they turned against the Delawares, the outward reminder thereof. To them, any concessions not given to the Delawares would have been a victory against the United States government. Consequently, the Cherokees had attempted to legally have the Lenape incorporated into their nation during the negotiations of the original agreement. If they were forced to accept them at least then the Delawares would have to answer to Cherokee law—and to pay good money for it. When this initial attempt during the first negotiations had failed, the Cherokees appear to have secretly altered the terms after the negotiations had finally been successfully concluded. At the time the United States were more interested in concluding the entire affair rather than doing right by the Delawares. In spite of being in a disadvantaged position, the Cherokees in charge managed to play all parties involved, maximizing their own advantage. So, in a righteous effort to get even with the United States and to protect themselves, the Cherokees came to disadvantage and even punish the Lenape.

THE EFFECTS OF REMOVAL

The Delaware movement to Oklahoma began in December of 1867 and continued during the spring and summer of 1868, 35 years after the removal of the Choctaws who had been the first to suffer this fate on the basis of the Indian Removal Act of 1830. Each family had to make their own preparations and arrangements and traveled at their own expense. Many joined together but some also went separately. Sometimes the men had to return later to get the remainder of their belongings, causing removal to be even more time-consuming and stressful than it otherwise would have been. They had to travel a distance of 180 to 200 miles until they arrived at their new homes in Indian Territory. The removal of the Delawares was not accompanied and supervised by the military, as had been the case for example with the 'Trail of Tears' of the Cherokees, their future hosts. There was no force needed to remove the Lenape from what had been their home for almost 38 years. They looked back on a long history of attempting to live peacefully with the Europeans and remained true to this tradition even during removal. Furthermore, too few of them were left to even attempt a fight by military means, the futility of which they must have recognized.

There was no immediate cause for the removal of the Delawares. They had lived peacefully on their Kansas lands for nearly 40 years and in 1862 had shown their goodwill for the cause of the Union by sending an extremely large percentage of their male population to fight. They were not a threat to the USA; they were simply considered a nuisance, an obstacle. They were not regarded as being of any real use or value to the country and its citizens of European extraction; instead, they were viewed as a hindrance to them. People wanted their land and so the Delawares, like so many other tribes before and after them, had to leave those lands. This was a continuation of the very first policy used in dealing with Native Americans and also one the Lenape had had to experience with great frequency. Indians were either subordinated and incorporated as a service labor force, or expelled or annihilated. Indian Territory was simply the latest measure to take away their land because by concentrating as many tribes as possible there, lands became available elsewhere, at their former homes. But removal in itself was nothing new to the Delaware tribe. In fact, to them it had become the most marked and prevailing consequence of their contacts with Europeans, something they had never been able to escape from. Yet as traumatic as this renewed removal in itself was for the Delawares, its effects proved to be just as bad or worse. They proceeded to settle on the Little Verdigris River, in accordance with the terms of the agreement of 1867. This area was not set aside exclusively for the Lenape, but they were allowed to settle on plots not already taken by Cherokees. Some Cherokees moved in shortly before the Delawares arrived to make a profit by claiming lots and then selling them to the Lenape, even though the latter technically had already purchased these lands. Many Delawares were also harassed by other Indians, Cherokees as well as Osages.[17] The latter had formerly claimed the land the Lenape were now settling on and thus had reason to consider them to be intruders and to feel resentment towards them. (This was the second time in Lenape history that the tribe was resettled by the United States government onto lands claimed by the Osages.) The United States had sent the tribe to a place where they alienated virtually everyone by merely arriving and then even more so by staying. There was very little the Lenape could do to remedy this situation, so by 1868, John Sarcoxie, himself a non-English speaking signatory of the Articles of Agreement, wrote to Cherokee chief Lewis Downing, unsuccessfully asking him for a cancellation of the agreement.[18] At this time, however, the monies due the Cherokees under the agreement had not yet been paid, making it less likely for Downing to acquiesce to the request as it may have meant forfeiting the payment.

Not surprisingly given these circumstances, discontent among the Delawares soon grew even greater.[19] Already in March of 1869 head chief John Connor informed the Commissioner of Indian Affairs of the "destitute condition of . . . the Tribe."[20] A significant number of the Lenape had been opposed to the agreement in the first place and the situation they found themselves in did not do anything to change their opinion. In February 1870, Chief John Connor, in a letter to Commissioner of Indian Affairs Ely S. Parker reported that "a Bout one Hundred of my people ar not not satisfied."[21] The superintendent had previously informed his superior that these Delawares petitioned for a home among the Quapaws and Peorias, "where they can live in peace."[22] The Quapaws had already stated their willingness to sell the Delawares some land.[23] He explained that according to Chief Sarcoxie "the Delawares have selected a good county in the C.N. They are not dissatisfied with it" but that the reasons for discontent were more complex.[24] Hoag clarified that the Delawares were not dissatisfied with the land but that "they are insecure in the enjoyment of their civil rights" because they received no protection from Cherokee laws.[25] He wrote that "the Cherokee Laws are not executed and the Delawares live in constant fear."[26] Hoag illustrated this fear by explaining that "several murders were committed, and no power to arrest and hold the perpetrators" and he even acknowledged that the "Indians made great sacrifices in the exchange of their valuable lands in Kansas for their new homes south."[27] Hoag feared that all that would leave "the ancient tribe disintegrated" and suggested to remedy the situation in the Cherokee Nation rather to let this disintegration happen by allowing part of the tribe to move away.[28] Hoag's genuine concern was somewhat unusual in a situation where few people cared and many officials would have actively welcomed the disappearance of the tribe. The Delawares themselves, however, were desperately seeking a way out of their misery, over time considering moving with various other tribes to escape the situation they found themselves in among the Cherokees.

A Lenape man who experienced various kinds of harassment was James Simons, one of the 985 Delawares to remove from Kansas to the Indian Territory and who—like so many—had been opposed to the revised Articles of Agreement from the very beginning.[29] He would have been among the last members of the tribe to leave Kansas, one of the group of Captain Fall Leaf who held out there the longest. For the latecomers this also meant having to choose from a smaller selection of lands available to them than to the ones who had arrived earlier. So those opposed to removal from the outset were likely to experience it at its worst. What then happened to James Simons occurred to many of the Lenape trying to pick a piece of land and to settle down, regardless of when they arrived and of how they felt about the revised agreement. Instead of the unoccupied lands they had been promised, they found a quadrangle of timbers laid out on a lot, put there by some Cherokee. This 'construction' counted as an improvement made on the land and put the Cherokee in the position to sell it in accordance with a treaty provision, even though the Delawares had already paid for the land they were to receive. This payment only applied to unoccupied lands but these somewhat improvised improvements changed the status of the lot in question from unoccupied to occupied. So before James Simons could settle down on the land he had picked he had to purchase it once more. One Cherokee sold as many as five or even six lots in this manner.[30] To the individual in question this may have been a welcome opportunity to get back at the intruders as well as a lucrative business venture. From his point of view it was making the best of a bad situation. For the Lenape it aggravated something that had been bad in the first place.

After Simons had finally bought a piece of land, for one hundred dollars, a considerable expense at the time, other parties temporarily drove him off through application of violence.[31] But this was by far not the end of his troubles. Even after he had finally managed to build a house he still never got a chance to enjoy his new home, due to the constant harassment he—along with any others—experienced. This culminated in someone firing shots into the house while Simons was at home due to illness. Luckily for him he remained unharmed.

Sadly, James Simons was not an isolated case. Even the Indian agents admitted that not all was well in the treatment the Delawares received from the Cherokees. Their houses were burned, making them fearful and never allowing them to relax. A number of murders committed on Lenape were also reported. These occurred with sufficient frequency to become a topic in the official correspondence between the Cherokee agent and the Commissioner of Indian Affairs. In the light of all this, in June of 1870 the long-suffering James Simons and others were asking Superintendent Hoag for their share of the Delaware funds because a group of them had already "made an arrangement with the Peorias for the purchase of the land acquired by them of the Quapaw Indians."[32] Maybe mindful of what happened with the Cherokee agreement, this time it seems like the dissenting Delawares drew up one with the Confederate Peoria, Wea, Piankashaw and Kaskaskia Indians without any outside intervention.[33] This time they did not intend to take any chances by surrendering control of the matter and thus their future as a tribe.

DISSENT AND SECESSION

Not waiting for the outcome of this endeavor by the dissenting Delawares, James Simons, along with 21 families, a total of about three hundred people, moved away from the homes they had purchased, to the lands west of 96° longitude that had previously been considered to be too poor.[34] Due to a misunderstanding about their treaty conditions some of them had always believed that this was the only area where they would be permitted to keep their tribal organization. That together with the demands and stresses of renewed removal led to the dissenting Delawares being "in a suffering condition," as the official in charge of that agency stated.[35] Simons later came to be considered one of the headmen of the so-called seceding, wild, or Neosho Delawares, mostly made up of Sarcoxie's band, the source of the earliest dissent voiced about removal.[36] He was very vocal in his criticism, often writing to the Bureau of Indian Affairs, describing the problems of the Neosho Delawares with the Cherokees, asking the Government for help "to treet with any other tribe for a home."[37] The dissenting Delawares wanted the United States to continue protecting the Lenape as a tribe, instead of a part of the Cherokee Nation.[38] They specifically wanted to "remind the Government of the U.S. to our old compacts and promises which she has made from time to time to wards the Delawares."[39] Simons and others also claimed that "there is more Troubles in the Cherokee Nation, there is no Trouble on this side of the Neosho" and gave this as the reason why they wanted to purchase the lands they then occupied.[40] Under no condition whatsoever were they willing to tolerate the loss of their legal identity, which they felt was threatened should they remain in the Cherokee Nation. They even stated they would rather lose the lands they had already paid for and buy new ones among other Indians than to let this happen.[41] Financial loss to them was nothing in comparison to the loss of their national identity. As Simons saw it, the Cherokees "are doing all in their power to keep us under their rule."[42] And it was this rule, among other things, which the dissenting Delawares objected to especially in the face of the unacceptable situation they found themselves in post-removal.

And there was no indication that this situation was about to change for the better. On the contrary, Superintendent Hoag in June of 1871 reported that the number of Lenape on Peoria lands was about to increase to over 500, which spoke a telling tale about the conditions the tribe was exposed to while living on Cherokee lands.[43] The conditions on the stretch of land the Neoshos intended to buy seemed to have been infinitely better than what the Delawares had to deal with inside the boundaries of the Cherokee Nation even though the land itself may have been poorer. Consequently, roughly half of the tribe eventually went to live there, "on the lands of the confederate Peoria."[44] After all, even excellent agricultural lands would do them no good if they did not have the peace to work them.

The Neoshos also claimed to have been deceived by their chiefs about the status they would have after moving to Indian Territory.[45] The exodus of such large numbers speaks a very clear language concerning the situation they found themselves in and particularly about their opinion about the terms of the agreement. They informed the government that "our people are all one in trying to get this land and to never go back to the Cherokee country where we see so much trouble we believe the rule with the white man is if a man in office is not doing his duty honorably he will not be trusted by the people any more this same rule we want follow, we do not want our old rulers to rule us."[46] They believed they had been "deceived by their head men as to what their status would be in the Indian Country."[47] Therefore, their only option seemed to be to leave the troublesome lands in disobedience to the chiefs by whom they felt betrayed.

Even though they had made all the necessary arrangements with their new host tribes and were willing to give up their land and money to the Cherokees without getting virtually anything at all in return, the Neoshos were not allowed to stay on the lands newly settled by them where they felt so much safer and more content. The Secretary of the Interior concluded that the Kaskaskias had no right to sell their land without congressional approval and that no part of the Delawares could be allowed to secede after having signed the agreement with the Cherokees.[48] Secretary of the Interior Columbus Delano claimed that "certainly there is now, no authority by which the Department can permit a portion of the Delawares to withdraw at will beyond the operation of the laws of the Cherokee nation under which through their representatives, they voluntarily placed themselves."[49] I believe the Department of the Interior would not want to allow the Delawares to set a costly precedent other tribes might want to follow. Evidently, Delano particularly feared "the effect such a precedent might exert upon other Indian tribes similarly situated as the Delawares" and even specifically mentioned the Shawnee, who had signed a similar agreement with the Cherokees.[50]

The Neoshos' secession also caused even more internal friction among the Lenape, aggravating older problems and deepening divisions. In November of 1871, head chief John Connor and others wrote to the Secretary of the Interior, complaining about the beneficial treatment the Neoshos had supposedly received by the sympathetic Superintendent Hoag and that by making annuity payments to them at all he had recognized James Simons and others as chiefs and councilors. The traditional chiefs felt threatened by the Neosho chiefs who had attracted over half of the tribe as followers.[51]

UNHAPPY RETURNS

The Neosho Delawares were forced to move back after about two years, but their situation turned out to be even worse than before.[52] They were yet again driven off their new lands in the Cherokee Nation, this time mostly by accident as they were believed "to be intruders on Osage lands."[53] And because they were so very poor it was easy for the traders to take advantage of them.[54] In 1873, some of the Neoshos, and among them James Simons, again reported to live in fear due to harassment and specifically the burning down of their houses, which seems to have been a relatively frequent occurrence once again.[55] They feared a repetition of earlier occurrences:

> "And now we like to know bout these houses in the Nation we little A fraid to move in to them because some our people When they first come just went in the houses and when they was in houses some man come and burn the house and now we are afraid to stay in houses because we think they might do so again."[56]

Moreover, the internal differences which had been aggravated by the secession were not remedied merely by the return of the Neoshos.[57] Superintendent Hoag called the government's attention to this fact in

Aril of 1873, reporting that "the differences existing between that portion of the tribe formerly known as 'Neosha Delawares' and those of the tribe who, under provisions of treaty removed to and remained with the Cherokees" remained unresolved.[58] And due to the geographically mixed settlements of Delawares and Cherokees it was still hard to even attempt to keep up some kind of coherent tribal organization. As Weslager has concluded, "geographically, there was no Lenape Indian community in which an intact social organization could be preserved."[59] The payment of annuities for a while seems to have been the only occasion for the entire tribe to meet.

The mistreatment the Delawares experienced in the Cherokee Nation was not limited to the original dissenting Lenape. Someone who also greatly suffered from it was Isaac Journeycake, whose brother Charles was one of the assistant chiefs and who himself had been a signatory of the Articles of Agreement of 1867 and who had probably been in favor of removal and possibly even the agreement itself. Charles Journeycake, usually sympathetic to the moderate or 'white' cause, tried to intervene on behalf of his brother, warning the government that "Brother Isaac will likely move away from here as he has no place to winter in" as his house had been burned down.[60] Isaac himself was characterized by Superintendent Hoag as a "very enterprising farmer and stock raiser and . . . influential in advancing the Delawares in industry," so the government stood to lose an ally should he feel forced to leave.[61] However, this fact failed to make the desired impression on the government which Charles Journeycake must have probably hoped for since no steps were taken to remedy the situation from that side. In 1878, Isaac Journeycake was murdered, presumably by a Cherokee.[62] Clearly, the harassment experienced by the Delawares was arbitrary when it came to the conduct and attitudes of the victims. Those who had been in favor of removal were not spared. Merely being Lenape could make one a target. Sadly, Isaac Journeycake was by far not the only victim of the conflicts between Cherokees and Delawares.[63]

It may have been the death of his brother, which finally made even Charles Journeycake realize that something needed to be done to improve the Delawares' situation, something the temporary secession had been seemingly unable to achieve. Consequently, soon the entire tribe petitioned Congress to be removed to a reservation of its own, on the grounds that the Cherokees executed their laws unjustly.[64]

> "After an experience of several years your humble petitioners think they have abundant reason to complain that they are treated with great injustice by the Cherokees and that their laws have been executed in a

very partial manner screening and excusing the Cherokees but falling with great severity on the Delaware."[65]

They pointed especially to the occurrence of several murders committed against Lenape, to mention just a few of the grievances from the petition. In it the Delawares called attention to the injustices they were experiencing through fault of the United States.

> "Our people are now and ever have been loyal to the United States Gov't, but our immediate neighbors were in arms during the recent Rebellion and its most ardent supporters and are bitter towards those who remained loyal to the Gov't. Hence an almost daily annoyance to us.—our nights are made fearful from their threatening presence and the pursuit of business is constantly interrupted from the necessity to act on the defense."[66]

The petition stated furthermore that the tribe had previously attempted to solve the matter among themselves and the Cherokees. It therefore had "petitioned the Cherokee Council to cause our district to be set apart, so that we might have offices from our own tribe to execute its laws, but this was refused us and we are discouraged."[67] Such actions would have been in keeping with the original agreement yet not with the revised terms thereof. In the name of the entire tribe, the signatories, among them head chief James Connor, Charles Journeycake, John Sarcoxie, Captain Fall Leaf and others, traditionalists as well as modernists, requested a separate reservation to be set aside within the Cherokee Nation. They demanded "that there be set apart a Reservation for the Delawares within the Cherokee Nation to be governed by themselves but not to conflict with the laws of the Cherokee Nation when honestly and properly administered," something they believed to be their right according to their 1866 treaty and the original Articles of Agreement.[68] They also asked for their share of the monies which the Cherokees had not paid them. (The fact that the Cherokees had refused to include the Delawares in these payments shows that they did not really consider them to be part of the Cherokee Nation.) The petitioners illustrated the hopelessness and desperation of the tribe, explaining that "some of our people are moving away and living with other tribes, willing to sacrifice their own lands and home for an uncertain residence with those more peacefully disposed."[69]

It is not clear if the petition ever made it to Congress but even if it did, it was to no avail. By this time, the United States already were planning on dissolving all the reservations to finally achieve the complete integration of all Indians into mainstream society by means of allotment.

UNITY

Yet while open questions about the legal identity of the Delawares remained, at least in their wish to have their own reservation the Lenape were once again united, as the petition clearly shows. The dire consequences of removal had thus helped to overcome the rifts introduced or at least aggravated by removal. Traditionalists and modernists had come together in their quest for a separate Delaware reservation. Legally, however, they continued in the same ambiguous state as before. The United States government still held monies in trust for the Lenape after the payment to the Cherokees in 1869. And it did so through direct communication with the Lenape chiefs and council, which it also used in overseeing Delaware affairs.[70] And in 1873, Superintendent Enoch Hoag reported that by treaty the Delawares were Cherokees but that "they retain with the government certain interests—exclusively their own—so long as these interests continue separate from the Cherokees, they will require separate organization."[71] These words echo a statement made in 1868, by Acting Commissioner of Indian Affairs Charles Mix: "As the Delawares have not yet dissolved their tribal organization and become members of the Cherokee Nation they must be treated and dealt with as Delawares."[72] While this sounds like in the eyes of these United States officials the dissolution of the tribe was inevitable and only a matter of time, this need not necessarily have been an accurate reflection of the legal situation. As seen before, confusion about the exact terms of the treaties had become evident before and these confusions may still have been prevalent at this later time. The only thing that was beyond doubt was that the Lenape in 1877 certainly had no interest not to continue separately from the Cherokees or to dissolve their tribal organization. This they had made amply clear.

This fact is not only evidenced by the Delawares' correspondence but also by their comportment. After the Neoshos' return, the tribe intensified the attempts to keep up its organization. Although there are no records about the election to head chief after 1872, modernists Charles Journeycake is referred to as head chief from 1877 on and until his death in 1894. Also in 1877, the following settlement chiefs are listed in a government document: For the Cana settlement John Sarcoxie, for the Verdigris Charles Journeycake, and for the Grand River settlement James Ketchum.[73] It is not clear if these settlements are more or less identical with the old clans / phratries of Wolf, Turkey, and Turtle, but the fact alone that Delawares headed

Delaware settlements indicate that they to some extend upheld their tribal organization. Their agent was not in favor of this, however. He wanted to have the number of chiefs reduced, presumably to make his own life easier.[74] After Journeycake's death a body which became known as the Delaware Business Committee was installed upon request of the United States. The traditional duties of the former chiefs were taken over by a ceremonial chief. Nevertheless, important elements of Delaware culture were upheld.

And the chiefs, as well as later on the Business Committee, did well in overseeing matters of interest to the Lenape tribe. "By 1898, the Delaware settlements boasted a council house and two churches, two schools along the Caney River, two schools along the California River, and one on Lightning Creek—all built an paid for by the Delaware Tribe."[75] They had turned the lack of government support into a virtue, a point of strength. The council also employed physicians and raised money for their pay, since the federal government would not allow them any of their own money for that matter.[76] The tribe looked out for itself—was quite literally forced to do so—and managed to do this without letting itself be absorbed into the Cherokee Nation.

Probably the best indicator for the separateness, in which Cherokees and Delawares continued, was the low intermarriage rate. "Of the first 212 Delaware marriages after the removal, only 5 were with blood Cherokee, and only by those Delawares born after 1890."[77] The Lenape also continued to speak their own language, which is decidedly different from the Iroquoian Cherokees' native tongue.[78] The Lenape language was spoken fluently well into the twentieth century.[79] Up to that time English, if spoken at all by Delaware tribal members, was usually only the second language. Clearly, in the aftermath of removal, there was little mixing between Delawares and Cherokees on a day to day basis and even at the administrative level and in interactions with the United States government officials a considerable degree of separateness was kept.

"A NATION FROM THE EARLIEST TIMES"

The years to follow their removal showed that the Delawares did not just vanish from view. They were quite articulate, repeatedly voicing concerns about the tribe and all matters connected to it. Their actions were aimed at the preservation of their tribal organization. And, even though it may seem strange at first glance, so was the consent to removal. Kansas, for close to forty years home to the main body of the Lenape, in the late 1850s did not offer the tribe the conditions it needed to thrive. On the contrary, the prevalent situation at the time severely endangered the Delawares. And matters got worse with the effects the Kansas-Nebraska Act had on the area and its inhabitants. Especially after the Civil War, the Delawares' living conditions once again deteriorated drastically.[80] In Kansas they had no future as a tribe. Removal to Indian Territory was preferable and must have seemed like a logical step in the Lenape's efforts to safeguard the tribe. While they were taking this crucial step, the correspondence between various Lenape and government officials reveals that the preservation of their tribal identity was of prime importance to them. It had been their principal reason to consent to removal. They repeatedly and specifically stated that they wanted "to maintain their nationality," a wording clearly geared towards what they thought they United States would be able to comprehend, but also to express what they really cared about the most.[81]

Even the internal conflict, which arose over the changed terms of the agreement with the Cherokees, only serves to illustrate how much the removing Delawares cared about the preservation of their tribal ties. After all, it was only those very few who chose to remain in Kansas as United States citizens who opted to give up their tribal affiliation. Both modernists and traditionalists specifically wanted to maintain Delaware tribal organization; they simply disagreed on what would be the best way to achieve this. In any case, both groups repeatedly emphasized tribal ties and their identity as Delawares. And while the conduct of the chiefs and delegates sometimes may have been questionable, there is no evidence that, in spite of occasionally seeking their personal favor or letting themselves be pressured by white officials, they did not also have the tribes' interests at heart.

But as it turned out, removal to Indian Territory did not bring the relief the modernists had probably expected but instead all the bad consequences the traditionalists had feared. Accordingly, the internal friction, which had developed—or which maybe had predated the event and thus had only been aggravated—after the signing of the modified agreement got progressively worse.[82] It climaxed with the ongoing exodus of the Neosho Delawares, yet did not mend immediately upon their return. Only when living within the Cherokee Nation finally got unbearable for all its members, the Delaware tribe was once again internally united in their quest for a new reservation, a reservation of their own. A shared goal born out of removal once again united traditionalists and modernists.

In spite of all their troubles while cohabiting with the Cherokees, the Lenape did not lose their sense of tribal identity, even though they were fractionalized over the conditions of removal for a while. They were still Delawares, even to the Cherokee Nation itself, as became only too apparent by the mistreatment the Delawares, the 'others' received from them.[83] The Cherokees' wish to completely incorporate the Delawares was probably more born out of a desire to keep in control and to take their revenge on the United States than by any intent to really merge the two tribes into one. At the same time, the mistreatment of Lenape by Cherokees was most likely primarily intended to hurt the United States rather than the Delawares. After all, it was not like the Cherokees had voluntarily invited the Lenape to join them, but they had been forced by the United States to accept them within their territorial boundaries. To an extent, it is understandable that the Delawares, fiercely refusing to give up their tribal ties and to surrender control to the Cherokee Nation, were considered by the latter as intruders, troublemakers, and undesirable if not for their money.[84]

As the Delawares never did manage to obtain a reservation of their own, their problems with the Cherokees remained unresolved even in the years to follow. Frequently, their issues were taken to the courts where they sometimes were resolved in favor of the Cherokees and sometimes in a manner benefiting the Lenape. Yet it was not until the 1970s that the 1867 agreement was legally interpreted as having terminated the Delawares' existence as a tribe. At that point in time the Cherokee government claimed that the Delawares had legally been incorporated into the Cherokee Nation with the signing of the 1867 Articles of Agreement. The Bureau of Indian Affairs followed suit and in 1979 the Delawares were informed that their tribe had ceased to exist in 1867, leaving the Lenape without federal recognition and its benefits. In this way, federal recognition and the question of tribal sovereignty turned into issues that were—and still are—discussed in United States courts as well as outside of them.

Given that all parties involved have turned to the United States legal system to try and resolve their issues and also because legal documents and ambiguities are at the heart of the very problems, it is not surprising that discussions of Delaware post-removal history have often evolved around the legal issues surrounding the treaties of 1866 and the Articles of Agreement of 1867.

Yet this legal approach is a treacherous one since, as seen, legal requirements were likely considered mere formalities when the events of the 1860s themselves took place. Back then the officials involved went through the motions and paid lip service only to the legal requirements. If this is not openly admitted and taken into account, then legal processes cannot be the solution to Lenape or Cherokee problems today. United States' interests were and are at the center of these problems. This fact has been disguised so effectively that today the legal conflicts are largely limited to the Cherokees and the Delawares, even though they are being carried out within the United States legal system. As a matter of fact, both tribes vie for United States' support in their endeavors against each other, seemingly unaware of the true culprit—or simply hesitant to take on the overwhelmingly powerful United States, their 'guardian,' on its own ground.

In particular the notion of indigenous or tribal sovereignty, so hotly contested between the two tribes today, has been shown by Peter d'Errico to be an instrument of colonialism, and in this particular case has merely served to turn the tribes against one another and has thus hidden the guilt of the United States government.[85]

Through their resilience and perseverance and their continued insistence on their tribal identity and separateness, the Delawares have proved that they have been and still are a tribe or a nation. Arbitrary rules set up by the colonizing outsider and then utilized by others as well can never change this fact, although they will put increased pressures on the tribe that it may not be able to hold out against in the long run.

Chapter Five
History Is Not Over Yet: The Delawares and the Law

Looking at the situations the Yaquis and Delawares found themselves in immediately after removal one cannot help but think that matters looked bleak for the tribe. The Delawares perceived their legal identity to be threatened and so immediately post-removal it did look as if they were likely to succumb to state pressures. But that was not the case. The Delawares did not vanish, even though they were involved in a long struggle concerning the loss of their federal recognition.

As already seen in the previous chapters, a considerable part of the Delaware tribe immediately fought the terms of the modified agreement governing their removal to the Cherokee Nation. Most of the Lenape were unwilling to face what they believed would bring the loss of their nationality and their tribal ties.

Even under the ambiguous terms of the modified agreement and while the tribe, in different ways, had been fighting it, the Lenape had always maintained themselves separate from the Cherokee Nation in whose midst they resided. The Delaware tribe had refused to ratify the modified Articles of Agreement as they perceived them to be a threat to their separate tribal existence and some had refused to leave their Kansas homes under these conditions. Once on Cherokee lands, a number of Delawares had removed to an area outside the Cherokee Nation, to escape the latter's control and harassment. And while they had been temporarily fractionalized by these events, the entire tribe petitioned to be removed to a reservation of their own in 1876. The outside pressures, which had torn them apart, reunited the Delawares in the question of having their own reservation. And they had maintained their own government and tribal organization all the time, supervised by the United States administration.

The question of the ambiguous terms of the agreement with the Cherokee Nation (1867) was not even temporarily resolved until the Comptroller General in 1905 issued an opinion at the request of the U.S. Attorney General and the Secretary of the Interior. This statement clarified that the Delawares were a separate tribal entity from the Cherokees. Furthermore, he specifically determined that under Article 15 of the Treaty of 1866 with the Cherokees, the Delaware Tribe removed to Cherokee country but there maintained its tribal organization as a separate band of the Cherokee Nation. Yet he still recognized the Delawares' right to participate in all Cherokee funds, which the tribe had acquired along with citizenship in the Cherokee Nation. Therefore it was finally reaffirmed that, although the Delawares had purchased full citizenship rights in the Cherokee Nation, the tribe also preserved the right to keep its separate tribal organization, and to continue as inherently sovereign, separate and distinct from the Cherokees.[1] It had taken almost forty years of Lenape residence within the Cherokee Nation to get these ambiguities straightened out. Yet the legal status of the Delaware tribe was resolved only for the time being.

A Business Committee and ceremonial chief were running the tribe for part of the 20th century. The tribal members practiced mixed farming between the Verdigris and Caney Rivers, while Cherokees and whites were primarily cattle rangers. After the dissolution of the Cherokee Nation following the Dawes and Curtis Acts the Delawares were referred to as residing in Oklahoma instead of within the Cherokee Nation. Over the following years the Lenape were directly supervised by the Bureau of Indian Affairs. In the 1950s, presumably to avert a costly claim for treaty violations the United States government argued that the tribe had already been terminated by the 1867 agreement. But the US lost on this claim in various courts and so the BIA supervised the drafting of a constitution and bylaws, which had been initiated upon request of the Department of the Interior in 1958.[2] In 1977, then, even the United States Supreme Court ruled that the Delaware Tribe of Indians had enjoyed continuous federal recognition.[3]

Yet even though these legal decisions seem to indicate that the Delawares' legal identity was no longer under threat, events would soon show that this was not the case. Ironically, it was in a time that more attention than ever since the fighting days was called to Native Americans, the late 1960s and 70s, that the Delawares encountered grave problems once again. In 1975, the Cherokee Nation had received administrative approval for its reorganization after almost 65 years without a tribal government. In 1977, Cherokee chief Ross Swimmer, an attorney and banker, all of a sudden declared that the Delaware Tribe had ceased to exist in 1867, with the signing of the Cherokee-Delaware Agreement. Consequently any monies connected to the Delawares would have to be turned over to the newly reorganized Cherokee Nation. Significantly, the Delawares had just been given a large amount of money when Swimmer decided to take them over in this manner. And by boosting their numbers the Delawares also supplemented the Cherokees' federal monies. At the time the Cherokees had only some 10,000 members, while the Delawares numbered about 7,000. Two years later, in 1979, the Delawares were informed by the BIA that they did not exist, had not existed since 1867, except for claims purposes.

Tragically, at first the Lenape considered this to be just another confusion of the BIA, something the Delawares had already gotten used to due to repeated occurrences throughout their history. And the situation was aggravated by internal confusions due to a change in the Delawares' leadership.[4] By the mid-1980s, however, the Lenape had well realized the full significance of the decision and had decided to fight it. It would have been impossible not to take the termination seriously considering the effects it had on the members of the tribe. With the revoking of their federal recognition the Delawares ceased to be eligible to contract for those services it had been providing to its members since the early 1970s, had become ineligible for any BIA funding, as well as for funding for tribal social and cultural events. The BIA also withheld millions of dollars in programming funds, specifically appropriated by Congress for the Delaware Tribe of Indians. There were also problems with health care, as especially many elderly Lenape were forced to enroll within the Cherokee Nation and to obtain a Certificate Degree of Indian Blood (CDIB) stating that they were Cherokee Indians, in order to receive much-needed health care at all. Yet even while it officially did not exist, the Delaware Tribe provided a number of services for its members and kept running the tribal headquarters, even without the help of governmental funding.

The attempts to regain federal recognition ceased temporarily as they appeared to be futile. And after all, the Lenape did not need outside confirmation to know who they were; they had no crisis of identity. But the significance of formal federal recognition soon became very obvious, since the outside world predominantly measured the tribe by its appearance on the list of federally recognized tribes. Also, it was hard for the leaders to represent the Delawares without being accepted as such by the necessary people.[5] In 1993, upon request of Cherokee chief Wilma Mankiller, the Delawares held a nation-wide vote about whether or not to keep pursuing federal recognition. In response, 88% of the tribe voted in favor of doing so. Then, in September of 1996, the Lenape's efforts were finally crowned by success and the Delawares regained federal recognition. The 1996 decision clarified the government-to-government relationship between the United

States and the Delawares, which was understood to have existed before the 1979 determination. With this ruling, the Delawares once again held the same legal rights and responsibilities as other tribes and were returned to the Department of the Interior's list of federally recognized tribes. The decision was repeatedly challenged by the Cherokee Nation, which claimed that the Cherokees had a treaty right to perpetually govern the Delawares. The case was heard by several courts over the following years, with various outcomes. In 2005 a decision against the Delawares was passed but the Lenape show no signs of surrender even in the face of this and conflict is ongoing.

Before this event, the Delaware Tribe of Indians maintained its tribal offices in Bartlesville, Oklahoma, and counted about 11,000 members. Since their removal, the Delawares have primarily occupied modern-day Washington and Nowata Counties in Oklahoma. They were governed by an elected chief whose term lasted for four years. While they were recognized, the tribe offered its members various services, including a number of childcare services, different types of health assistance, housing and utility assistance, and burial assistance, to name just a few.[6] Educational programs were also offered, ranging from school supply assistance over language classes to scholarship grants. The tribe was also putting out a newspaper.

The Delaware Tribe of Western Oklahoma, with its headquarters at Anadarko is recognized by the United States government. This group consists of the so-called Absentee Delawares and has about 1000 members. After 200 years of separate existence the Absentees arrived at a destination less than 200 miles from the main body.

Even though quite naturally the main energy of the Delaware tribe in recent years has been focused on regaining federal recognition and clarifying misconceptions about their history, life has always gone on outside of the political arena as well. The traditional Big House ceremony continued until well into the twentieth century, until 1924, and there was a short-lived revival after World War II.[7] The annual Delaware Doll Dance and various other dances were also still performed.[8] In addition, there is an annual Powwow.[9]

The post-contact history of the Delawares is one of continuous removal. Almost immediately the 'people of the first frontier' were forced to migrate and to give up their native lands. From then on they have been in motion almost constantly, only occasionally given time to rescue, recover and rebuild before they were forced to move again. Fractions often stayed behind or chose different ways, some only to be later reunited with the main body. Oklahoma was only the last step in their long trek—and even there removal as such was not over for everyone. Those Lenape settling on lands claimed by Cherokees sometimes had to move again and the seceding Neosho Delawares were forced to move repeatedly. Yet after all this, still the tribe was able to present unity while trying to solve the legal ambiguities connected to the 1867 agreement, to survive the termination era, and later to fight the loss of federal recognition—yet another attempt at 'removing' them.

One would have to concur with Robert Grumet, that "the story of their survival is a testimony to the strength of their traditions. It is also a testimony to the human will not just to survive but to preserve a unique sense of identity and purpose in a changing and often hostile world."[10] To this day the Delawares refuse to vanish.

Looking at the often tragic histories of the two peoples, the Lenape and the Yoeme, one cannot help but be amazed that they still exist today and have preserved some unique identity traits. There have been many occurrences in these histories which would have made vanishing a plausible consequence; indeed they would have made not-vanishing implausible. Removal, the main focus of this study, probably came closest to eradicating the tribes as such. Yet they are still there, not unchanged and certainly not without scars, but they have not vanished. The Delawares in Indian Territory/Oklahoma were, after a hard period of adjustment to life among the Cherokees, given the chance to reconstruct and/or rediscover their identity and possibly even grew stronger in the process, especially by fighting their 1979 termination.

Therefore, what had appeared so bleak for the Delawares, bringing immediate fragmentation and other grave consequences like the possible loss of juridical identity, in the end only served to make them stronger by making the Lenape even more aware of what it means to be Delawares and thus more determined in their fight for federal recognition.

What factors exactly may have had the most crucial impact on tribal survival will be explored in the concluding chapters.

Chapter Six
Indian Policy in Mexico: Removal of Indianness?

Whereas US American Indian policy has been fairly well explored, the same cannot be said about the policies towards indigenous nations in Mexico.[1] Thus the chapter at hand can only be understood as a very broad outline of what could be called Mexican Indian Policy. The deficit is due to various factors, among them the fact that after Independence Indians in Mexico legally ceased to be Indians, in the sense of having a special, discernable status as indigenous peoples.[2] The rhetoric of Independence as well as some of that of the Mexican Revolution also has suggested a decisive break with the past. While a number of scholars have shown just how big the gap between such rhetoric and reality really was, they have so far not managed to sufficiently emphasize the extent of the existing continuities, especially of labor and land.

A further, albeit post-revolutionary reason for the lack of scholarship on Mexican Indian Policy may have been José Vasconcelos' idea of the *raza cósmica,* the allegedly uniquely Mexican 'race blend,' which also served to eliminate the category of the 'Indian.'[3] Where there are no Indians there can be no Indian policy. Indeed, most policies affecting Mexican indigenous peoples at least on the face of it were aimed at peasants (*campesinos*) and rural populaces, not specifically at Indians as was the case in the United States of America. Exceptions were the treatments particular Indian communities received and there were regional variants as well.[4] But for the longest time there was just no interest in viewing Indians as distinctly indigenous peoples but instead attempts to Mexicanize them dominated. Another factor may have been that racial mixture has been a much more pronounced phenomenon in Mexico than in the United States, thus making it harder to establish who was and who was not a Native American.

THE COLONIAL LEGACY

From the very beginning of interactions between Spaniards and Natives, labor and land were dominant themes. But, partially due to the rapid depopulation taking place especially in the early colonial period, labor was clearly the more important issue for the time being. The Spanish *conquistadores*, arriving in what today is Mexico in the early 16th century and with a view to find gold and silver, saw the locals as an asset rather than just a nuisance to be subjugated or expelled.[5] After some initial discussion whether or not the Natives were human at all or, at the other end of the spectrum of opinions, possibly even members of the lost tribes of Israel, the Spaniards quickly realized the immense possibilities of putting them to work.[6] At the same time, through their Catholic religion, they felt themselves obligated to Christianize the Indians.[7] The result, Guillermo Flores has determined, was a "tension between Christian doctrine and financial necessity."[8] Initially, the Natives were enslaved but the Spanish Crown put an end to that practice as early as 1500.[9] Eric Wolf points out that it had been the "initial intention of the Crown to deny the incoming conquerors any direct control of land and of Indian hands to work it" because it had "wanted to inhibit the development of an independent class of tributary overlords."[10] It was not always successful in this endeavor though and was frequently forced to compromise. But from then on, even former Indian slaves were considered to be subjects of the Crown, with at least in principle and potentially the same rights and duties as Spaniards. Yet even though Indians were considered human, they were also viewed as child-like and in need of guidance.[11] They were therefore time and again subject to colonial paternalistic laws which were aimed specifically at Natives and thus formed a discernable colonial Indian policy. Indeed, it has been argued that colonial law even in its initial 'period of indecision' about indigenous peoples first created the category of the Indian and imbued it with rights and duties.[12]

David Weber has argued that the Spanish Crown vacillated in the contested question on how to shape Indian policy so that "pragmatism and power usually prevailed over ideas."[13] In part this may have been occasioned by it having to juggle its own interests, those of its Spanish subjects in the Americas, and those of the Indians. A certain pragmatism was one of the hallmarks of Spain's attitudes toward the Indians. The *conquistadores* saw cheap labor much needed to extract the riches they were after. And it has been shown that "at first, especially in mining and agriculture, Indians supplied the labor, generated some of the capital, and provided much of the necessary technology and social organization for the production of goods."[14] But since the Indians were not only viewed as laborers but also to resemble children in need of guidance, it was also considered the Crown's duty to Christianize them and to introduce them to European—more specifically, Spanish-Catholic—ways.[15] Refusal was deemed sufficient reason to wage war on the Natives. A document, the *requerimiento*, 'informing' them about this and other matters, was read to them upon contact, asking them to submit and thus justifying military means should this not be the case.[16] In this way, any objections to Spanish rule(s) could be eradicated quickly. Pragmatism was thus paired with Christianity, gaining the conquerors maximum advantages over Native labor and land without, in their reasoning, jeopardizing their eternal salvation.

For the time being, the Spaniards were preoccupied with titles to labor, mainly the so-called *encomiendas,* more than with formal land titles, as was the case with colonial competitor England. "From the beginning of the colonial period, control of labor was always more important to Spaniards as a means of exploitation than ownership of land," as William Taylor has concluded.[17] Yet they still managed to acquire significant amounts of Indian land. While they, who referred to themselves as *gente de razón,* people of reason, considered themselves obligated to bring the infidels over to Christianity, they were getting Indian land and labor in return for their efforts, something they seem to have considered a fair deal.

The *encomienda* was an integral part of this arrangement and effectively addressed labor shortages which plagued the Spaniards from the very beginning. Initially, subjugated Indians were divided among the *conquistadores* to allow them to exploit the indigenous labor force. This ad-hoc system was legalized in 1503 and developed into the more formal one of the *encomienda,* giving a contingent of Indians varying in size to individual Spaniards.[18] These were entitled to the labor force of the Indians but at the same time were obliged to educate them in the Catholic faith. Since they were not legally owned by the *encomenderos,* the Indians were still considered to be free, thus at least theoretically differentiating this system from outright slavery. The *encomienda,* described in the Laws of Burgos in 1512, was specifically designed for the extraction of wealth from the continent, a pragmatic marriage of exploitation and Christianity, of business and morals.[19]

A similar means to exploit Native labor was the so-called *repartimiento*. It was likewise a measure intended to counteract labor shortages. In one of its many forms, Indian villages had to perform certain duties, usually labor. In this system, a quota of workers was assigned to the colonists and also to cities and these workers were only temporarily extracted from their villages to fulfill their labor duties. The official end of the *repartimiento* came about in 1632 although its last vestiges, like those of the *encomienda,* were not abolished until Independence in 1811.[20]

It was similar considerations of economic pragmatism which saw Indians resettled in the so-called *pueblos de indios,* from the mid-sixteenth century onwards.[21] This allowed for easier collection of tribute as well as for more convenient access to Native labor. In addition to the *repartimiento* and the *encomienda,* free labor and various forms of debt labor existed. As wages often tended to be low, Indians could find themselves drawn into the system of debt labor without being able to find their way out again. Nominally, Christian requirements were met but all these labor-oriented measures were also a result of pragmatism or perceived necessity.

This 'Christian' exploitation of the indigenous population also had some welcome though mostly unintended side-effects concerning another matter of importance—land. Indian labor in the service of the Spanish, through death and resettlement, vacated lands which could then be more easily appropriated by Spaniards. Temporarily, this facilitated land grabbing so much that the Spaniards could focus their main efforts almost exclusively on labor issues. Partially in response to the ruthless exploitation of such opportunities, in 1542/43 the New Laws (*Leyes Nuevas*) forbade further allocation of Indian lands to colonists.[22] They also abolished the inheritance of *encomiendas,* and stipulated for them to revert to the Crown upon the death of the *encomendero.* While these laws had mainly been intended to preserve the interests and the power of the Crown, they also benefited the Indians. Unfortunately, large parts of the legislation soon proved to be impossible to enforce and consequently were revoked as early as 1545. Thus the benefits for the Indians, described as vassals of the Crown though still in need of protection, were extremely short-lived. But these laws nevertheless exemplified Spanish attitudes—attitudes that were to prevail for the entire colonial era.

The Spaniards contrasted themselves, the *república de españoles,* with the Indians, the *república de indios.* This concept fitted their general attitude as it fulfilled Christian requirements as well as practical needs by allowing them to view Indians as potentially—but not yet—equal and thus being able to exploit them in the name of God and supposedly for their own good. Patricia Seed has pointed out that "the idea that defeated peoples resided in their own parallel communities was culturally familiar to Spaniards" due to their experiences with the *reconquista,* the regaining of Spanish lands from the Moors which preceded the *conquista* of the so-called New World.[23] Pragmatically, they adapted this concept to the needs of the novel situation posed by the conquest of the New World.

Another form of extracting indigenous labor in what was to become Mexico was the mission. The missionaries were meant to gradually familiarize their indigenous disciples with Spanish society and its rules. Edward Spicer has pointed out, that "the concept of Indians as, ultimately, full citizens of the Spanish Empire was generally accepted as the basis of missionary work."[24] Thus for a relatively short period, Indian communities benefited from the sheltering that was afforded to them by the missionaries as well as by being temporarily exempt from the payment of certain tributes. Yet in return the Natives had to put their labor force into the service of the missionary societies. However, over time it got increasingly difficult for the orders to protect the Indians and especially their land as the latter was beginning to get scarcer in New Spain and thus became more desirable and sought-after. This led to increasing attempts to get to indigenous lands, sometimes through illegal means. So at the beginning of the seventeenth century, the Crown offered the colonists the chance to acquire legal titles to land they already de facto held by means of payments. This so-called *composición de tierras* effectively reduced Indian landholdings and legally deprived Natives of lands that had initially been taken from them illegally while benefiting colonists as well as the Crown's coffers. Towards the end of the colonial era Spanish *haciendas* thus surrounded many Indian communities, including those that had been under missionary protection. And even without the *encomienda* many Indians found themselves tied into labor arrangements through debt peonage. However, this—I hold—was not a goal of colonial Indian policy but rather the result of a shortcoming thereof. It benefited individual Spaniards more than the Crown which commonly tried to achieve a balance between aiding its subjects (from which it often benefited financially) and keeping them from assuming too much power (which sometimes coincidentally also helped the Indians). Indigenous assimilation and Christianization, it would seem, were secondary rather than primary goals of colonial Indian policy. The primary importance of these measures was the exploitation of Indian labor to benefit Spain. A more stringent and determined protection of the Indians as such could have helped their situation—and fulfilled Christian requirements in more than just the letters of the laws—while still preserving many of the Crown's interest. However, as this protection was not extended to indigenous peoples for, I suggest, mainly pragmatic—and often financial—reasons which took precedence over Christian duties.

As for instance the *composición de tierras* suggests, the matter of land ownership was a difficult one and also an area where indigenous peoples got drawn into Spanish power struggles. Following a papal charter, legally the Spanish Crown considered (vacant) lands as its own.[25] According to the doctrine derived therefrom, only the Crown could distribute lands, to individuals as well as to communities. This principle did, however, to an extent accept indigenous ownership of lands, which by right of discovery only the Crown was entitled to extinguish, usually through the consent of the Indians in question.[26] "But in practice," Charles Gibson has emphasized, "this principle was not adhered to."[27] As María Teresa Vázquez has summed up the situation:

> "Although the Spanish Crown endorsed the right of Indians to their lands, at the same time it decreed itself as the holder of rights to all lands and waters in the colony, and treated unevenly the property rights of the Spanish and those of Indians. Spanish properties could be sold, alienated, transmitted; Indigenous property could not. Furthermore, when the Crown decided that lands in Indigenous towns or cities were *baldíos* meaning 'abandoned' or 'not worked,' it rescinded the Indigenous rights and granted the lands to new owners, generally Spaniards."[28]

And all too often law or principles were not conformed to and so the manners in which the Indians' lands were usurped were multifold.

At first the land question was of only minor importance in colonial Mexico because of the great decrease in population numbers, due mainly to diseases, overwork, and malnutrition, which vacated large stretches of land. Originally, the Spanish colonists were attracted primarily to Central Mexico with its zones of dense settlement and thus readily available labor forces.[29] Nonetheless, the land question existed, as Frans Schryer has shown by determining that much—though not all—of Indian resistance against the colonizers focused on retaining or repossessing land, as well as on opposing forced labor or taxes.[30] Resistance thus specifically opposed these measures that can tentatively be identified as a central element of colonial Spain's Indian policy. In quelling such resulting unrest, officials usually resorted to brute force only if negotiations failed as the destruction of the indigenous communities would have meant the annihilation of a valuable labor force and that was far from desirable to the colonial power, even though it would have contributed to the clearing of lands.

Policies changed towards the end of the colonial period, when Habsburg rule, which, as Weber has concluded, had forced its paternalistic rules unevenly, was replaced by that of the Bourbon's. "After 1700," Weber argues, "Bourbon Spain narrowed, but never closed, the still sizable gap between policy and practice."[31] However, event his new regime never managed to stick to one uniform Indian policy, and labor, trade, diplomacy, war and others continued to coexist, often called upon through primarily practical calculations to the benefit of the conquerors.[32] Colonial Indian policy was to a large extent motivated through reasons other than mere humanitarian ones, as Horst Pietschmann has shown convincingly.[33] Economic and political issues were at the heart of colonial policy, accounting for its central importance. During the colonial era, Spanish policy towards the Indians was ostentatiously aimed at integrating the indigenous peoples into a Spanish-dominated society the colonial power was keen to construct. However, while some Spaniards may genuinely have believed this to be an achievable and beneficial goal, in general these were not genuine attempts to assimilate the Indians as the Spanish idea of the new society rather envisaged two *repúblicas,* with the Spanish one outranking that of the Indians.[34] In practice, it seems to have been more important to integrate the Natives into the colonizers' economic system than to incorporate them into Spanish society or even the Catholic belief system.

Throughout the colonial period, land and labor were important issues shaping the interactions between colonizers and colonized, with labor initially taking precedence. However, with the increasing scarcity of available lands towards the end of the colonial period the focus shifted and this trend continued after Mexican Independence.

INDEPENDENT MEXICO

Independence saw an instrumentalization of the indigenous population for the purpose of justifying the attempts to shake off Spain's control. The wrongs committed against the Indians were one of the arguments used by the leading *criollo* (American-born Spaniards) elites against Spain. In 1813, Independence leader Morelos declared that if the conquest represented negation of Indian values by the Spanish, the Wars for Independence represented the negation of Spanish values by the Indians. He also invoked the names of Moctezuma and Cuauthémoc, former indigenous emperors.[35]

Unfortunately, revolutionary rhetoric often remained just that. The revolutionary *Plan de Iguala* of February 24, 1821 declared that all Mexican nationals were citizens, without further distinctions and called for 'Religión, Independencia y Unión.' With the passing of the post-Independence Constitutions, Indians became citizens and ceased to have the special and discernable status they had held under Spanish colonial law and which had at least afforded them a few, if often ineffective, protections.[36] "Al inicio de le Independencia, los insurgentes trataron de suprimir a la sociedad estratificada y racista de la época novohispana, que separaba a las repúblicas de indios del resto de la comunidad novohispana," as Patricia Galeana has stated in a somewhat naive take on the goals of the Independence movement.[37] With these 'changes attempting to erase the stratification of the colonial society,' Natives were to be treated just like any other citizens. R. David Edmunds has also concluded that "unlike the United States and Canada, Mexico attempted to break from the Indian policy of its colonial past."[38] However, I see the main purpose in overcoming earlier stratifications in lifting the *criollos* up and much less so the Indians. *Criollos* had become disgruntled by the lack of opportunities available to them in the colonial system. They, and not the Indians utilized to justify the break with Spain, were the real focus of the evolving Independence movement.[39] Still, at least according to official creed, Mexico aimed for an accelerated integration of Indians and rejected transitional communities which had been acceptable during the colonial era. Yet even though, as Wolfgang Gabbert has shown for Yucatán, independence and liberal ideology aimed in principle at the formal equality of all citizens, "nevertheless, an estatelike system legally distinguishing between Indians and non-Indians (vecinos) remained in force for almost fifty years."[40] Supposedly, any more assimilation and integration would have been disadvantageous for *criollo* business interests as they may have reduced the cheap labor pool mostly made up of unintegrated Indians. And, as David Weber has argued, "in areas where land had commercial value non-Indians expanded their landholdings . . . and Indians quickly became landless laborers," doubly benefiting the Spaniards.[41] Independence-era rhetoric and reality showed considerable discrepancies right from the start and regional varieties prevailed in spite of supposed national uniformity.

The paternalistic colonial laws, which resembled a discernable if not always uniform Indian policy, were also abolished with Independence.[42] And in a political or legal sense, Indians ceased to exist and became peasants, *campesinos*.[43] The dominant liberalist-positivist attitude saw no place for indigenous peoples as such in the construction of the new national culture.[44] John Kicza tells us that "the new national governments, usually dominated by liberals, thought that Indians should lose both the special protections afforded and the obligations placed upon them during the colonial period and become full and equal citizens."[45] They were eventually to be fully incorporated, under the federal government as well as under their respective state governments. However, sometimes this was found to be a difficult task and therefore the term and the category 'Indian' time and again crept back into laws and legal texts when reality asserted itself upon rhetoric.[46] Furthermore, I assume that, except for a few idealists, most *criollos* did not really want this kind of full integration which would have implied equality but really sought a rather subservient one, reminiscent of the colonial 'two republics.' David Weber makes a similar argument, stating that in the nineteenth century there was "an insurmountable wall between savagery and civilization" and that its existence "implicitly rejected Spain's frequently reiterated goal of gradually acculturating and incorporating Indians."[47]

Patricia Seed has called attention to the fact that "by liberating subject Native communities . . . newly independent Spanish-American nations also eliminated the historic protection of communally owned lands."[48] Such developments were not as novel as they appeared at first sight. Some at least nominally integrative efforts at individual land assignment and taxation had already been made by the colonial authorities, but had never really been carried through.[49] With Independence, individual land tenure came to be seen as a key element of the Indians' development and consequently was pursued with more vigor than ever before.[50] Again, pragmatism reigned supreme as the elimination of such protections, which was supposed to help the Natives integrate into the new society, also made more lands available to non-Indians. And even though they had gained equality on a theoretical level, the Natives still could not enjoy the same political and civil liberties as others, because they lacked the necessary economic basis and furthermore suffered from discrimination.[51] This once again provided others with opportunities to take their land.

Land, as already seen, had been one important factor in Indian-Spanish relations in colonial Mexico, even though it had at first been overshadowed by labor. The importance of the latter had not changed with Independence. But this event meant a new departure in the realm of land. Individual land ownership was deemed to be in the best interest of everyone involved, including the Indians. However, until the mid-1850s and the passage of the so-called Reform Laws, in spite of this belief Indian lands were generally still communally owned, mostly as there was too much political change and upheaval to attempt to enforce a stringent and coherent policy in this respect. The *desamortización* laws that were eventually implemented during the period known as *la Reforma* were targeted mainly at the Church but affected Indians as well.[52] According to laws like the *Ley Lerdo* of 1856, no corporation was to own property. While peasant *ejidos,* in which pre-Hispanic notions of collective land ownership survived, were partially and temporary exempted—as they were from taxes—this did not help much as its protection was soon eliminated and huge parts of Indian communal land could then be confiscated or bought.[53] And it was mostly those people who already had accumulated considerable wealth who could afford to purchase the lands that had become available in this manner. Consequently, the law worked against the rural population in general and Indian *ejidos* in particular.

The Indians, however, did not simply accept the new regulations quietly and passively. "The policies were offered as liberation from oppressive

Spanish policies and as an opportunity to abandon unenlightened primitive custom. They were, however, received as a new form of oppression and a threat to a well-established way of life."⁵⁴ Yet, as Edward Spicer has asserted, "the resistance was seen by the Mexicans not as an indication that the means adopted were badly conceived, but rather as demonstrating the barbarism of the Indians."⁵⁵ Instead of heeding the Natives' warning, the Mexican government resolved to rigorously enforce the new laws. Whenever the Indians resisted the measures, this opposition was met by force. With the putting down of a revolt in Tehuantepec, president Benito Juárez "held that the existence of Indian communities based in the colonial system constituted a threat to the nation," as Spicer has argued.⁵⁶

In 1863, Juárez, himself of Zapotecan Indian ancestry, issued the first federal laws allowing for the sale of 'vacant' lands (*terrenos baldíos*) to raise money to fight the French invaders. The consequences for indigenous peoples, traditional occupants of many of the areas affected, were grave. James Cockroft tells us that "in four years, some 4.5 million acres of prime land, much of it belonging to Indians who could not prove title, passed into the hands of *latifundistas*."⁵⁷ Theoretically this land was open for sale to anyone but in fact the ones who had the money to buy were once again those people who already did own vast amounts. "In theory, federal and state policies were designed to redistribute communally held land and assign small farms to former members of the Indian community, but in actuality much of the redistributed land was purchased by large haciendas which then employed the individual Indians . . . as rural laborers," as Edmunds has explained.⁵⁸ Communities only managed to hold on to parts of their former lands and often ended up working on their lost lands in the service of rich *hacendados*. The ultimate goal—in the liberal view of the time the most beneficial thing that could happen to the Indians—was their vanishing through joining the mainstream Mexican society, and loss of land brought this outcome much closer. Still, both sale and distribution of such public lands "slowed down considerably after the Liberal victory in 1867" had eliminated Emperor Maximilian's competition for the rule of the country and thus the need to raise funds to fight him.⁵⁹ This was in part due to higher prices and more stringent rules governing such sales.

Under Emperor Maximilian and during his short-lived and contested reign which overlapped with the Juárez presidency, many of the liberal reforms were kept up. Maximilian seemingly sincerely intended to improve conditions for the Indians and one of his three agrarian laws was even published in *Nahuatl*.⁶⁰ Yet de facto very little changed for the Indians during his brief rule.⁶¹

During this time—as before and after—it was especially the loss of their land that affected the indigenous communities most gravely, and which brought them closer to the assimilation or integration supposedly desired by the government(s).[62] As Enrique Florescano has argued, by the application of this measure the ruling classes also wanted the Indians to relinquish their traditions, institutions, and identities.[63]

Over the first half of the nineteenth century independent Mexico was very much a rural country and Indians made up over 1/3 of the population, even though there were significant regional variations. They generally lived in small isolated villages. This was to change after the election of Porfirio Díaz to the presidency. Before Díaz, the governments on average had lasted for less than a year, permitting few coherent policies, whereas Díaz one way or another remained in charge of the country for 35 years and was thus able to implement more coherent policies to which the Indians were furthermore exposed for a much longer time than ever before. So in a way, his rule was a new departure, for the country and its indigenous populations, but it also remained entrenched in the same old attitudes and thus land and labor still were vital aspects of what could pass as Porfirian Indian Policy.

During the rule of the Porfiriato, the presidency/dictatorship of Porfirio Diaz between 1876 and 1911, Indian policy was commonly left to the respective state governments. The goal with which the regime was occupied was the modernization of the country, along with state-building.[64] Indians were considered an obstacle to both, and even as an anti-national element. Floris has argued that "it was especially the "Indian's obstinate attachment to communal land [that] was considered contrary to the spirit of the times."[65] To further the aforementioned goals, Díaz encouraged immigration of members of select nations, who, in his opinion, were best suited to help modernize the country. He also invited capital investment from other countries, among them the United States. Indians were largely considered a hindrance to these aims as they occupied lands coveted by the state for its modernization program. Alan Knight has asserted, that the "large-scale Indian wars—integral parts of the Porfirian state-building project—were carried out with all the operational and ideological panoply of U.S. or Argentine frontier expansion."[66] The Porfiriato could be ruthless when Indians were in the way or occupied desirable lands. But in general, "Porfirian Indian policy demanded maximum economic exploitation of Indians for the capitalistic modernization of the nation" and would not resort to war unless the state (or one of the states) felt that it had compelling reasons to do so.[67] Those Indians who insisted on remaining in their villages and on maintaining their traditional way of life were not useful to the state economically. Rapid growth raised new demands for Indian labor, which had to be satisfied but traditional communities often refused to do so. Yet should assimilation fail and thus not bring about the desired effects, like the transfer of land in addition to the exploitation of indigenous labor, the Mexican government was willing to resort to more drastic measures like deportation and extermination. For instance, Mayas from Yucatán were deported to Cuba and Yaquis to the Yucatán peninsula.[68] Gabbert has emphasized that "the extension of commercial agriculture led to mounting competition for tillable land," which often negatively impacted on the rights of the Natives.[69] The Díaz government often enforced the *Ley Lerdo* vigorously, and, as William Taylor has shown, "land survey laws allowed the alienation of more lands for which the peasant occupants could not produce formal titles."[70] An 1883 law about *terrenos baldíos* brought even more land onto the market and especially affected Indian *ejidos*.[71] Native resistance against such measures was usually answered by state violence. The state only displayed generosity when it did not interfere with the pursuit of its primary aims. Taylor has determined, that

> "the assault on peasant lands was one of a variety of incursions against rural villages that intensified in the nineteenth century: peasant labor was the object of an expanding system of debt peonage and captive labor on the plantations; and the value placed on modernization ... led to a view of peasant villages as hard lumps of backwardness that had to be separated from their traditional ways if they were to become Mexican."[72]

Modernization was put before the interests of the Indian populace. "Though the Porfiriato saw stirrings of interest in and concern for the plight of the Indian—anticipations of the full-blown *indigenismo* of the twentieth century—the prevailing view among the political nation, when it went beyond indifference, was at best paternalistic, at worst domineering and racist," as Alan Knight has determined.[73] Indians could not be tolerated as peoples different from Mexicans; instead, they were supposed to become Mexicans. While colonial rule had, it could be argued, in many respects created the (category) Indian, post-Independence governments to an extend strove to eliminate it, along with the benefits and protections it had afforded them especially with regards to land and labor. Friedrich Katz has pointed to the effects of such policies:

> "When Mexico gained its independence from Spain in the early nineteenth century, it is estimated that approximately 40 per cent of all land suited for agriculture in the central and southern parts of the country belonged

//
Indian Policy in Mexico

to communal villages. When Díaz fell in 1911, only 5 per cent remained in their hands."[74]

POST-REVOLUTIONARY MEXICO

The demographic, economic, and social pressures and changes during the presidency of Díaz led to the outbreak of the Mexican Revolution. In November of 1910, Francisco I. Madero called to arms and against re-election of Díaz, who eventually drew the consequences and resigned in May 1911. John Kicza has asserted, that "the struggle to regain communally owned lands that had been alienated from indigenous villages over the previous half century played a major role within this movement."[75] But even though indigenous peoples took part in the revolution it cannot be said to have primarily represented their interests and the situation was thus somewhat reminiscent of Independence. Still, Indian fighters were of utmost importance to virtually all the revolutionary factions, even though few revolutionary leaders honestly and lastingly took up the Indians' cause. The most notable among these leaders and also the staunchest supporter of land reform was Emiliano Zapata, followed by Francisco 'Pancho' Villa.

> "The most important difference between Villa and Zapata regarding agrarian reform was that Villa supported small private ownership of property, while for Zapata, redistribution respected the communal aspect of Indigenous lands, and the identity and interest in their constituencies. Another important difference was that Zapata exclusively redistributed land of *haciendas,* while Villa kept most *haciendas* under his administration."[76]

Yet Zapata's and Villa's endeavors were somewhat isolated among the revolutionaries.

Natives were affected by the Revolution in different ways and suffered from new intrusions of their lands in these chaotic years. According to revolutionary doctrine, Native *campesinos* were supposed to be rescued from poverty and ignorance by integration into Mexican society.[77] This goal was not all that novel but once again rather reminiscent of Independence rhetoric. Yet revolutionary *indigenistas* argued against the older perception of this philosophy, stating that integration had previously only been achieved by means of coercion and at the expense of the Indians. That was supposed to change in the new Mexico. Yet, as Vázquez has pointed out, symptomatically, future president "Carranza's 1913 *Plan de Guadalupe* omitted any reference to land reform, nor did he redistribute or affect in any way the *haciendas.* His only 'radical' measure was to increase taxes for foreign enterprises in the region under his control in order to generate revenues to support his military bases during the Revolution."[78] It was only in the face of waning support, as among many others Vázquez and Ute Schüren have argued, that Carranza modified his policy, at least on the face of it. His *Ley Agraria* of 1915 thus went even beyond the Zapatistas, stipulating a return of those lands that had been taken from the *comunidades,* but also the distribution of lands as *ejidos* to those communities without land.[79] But once Villa and Zapata had been eliminated as political opponents, Carranza took steps to block his own decree. Even during the Constitutional Convention in 1916 did he endeavor to do so, but the majority of the delegates insisted on more far-reaching measures, possibly alienated by the evidence that Carranza already sought to tone down the measures taken to implement agrarian reform. So they voted in favor of Article 27 which declared the nation to be the sole owner of all land within its limits. It reserved the right to give this land to individuals and thus to create private property. But it also entitled the state to expropriate land should this become necessary. Thus the state effectively controlled all land within the territorial limits of Mexico. The article was also intended as "a means to expropriate large land holdings, restore land to Indigenous communities, redistribute land to dispossessed rural communities, and to achieve the goal of *Zapatistas*: to award 'land for those who worked it,'" as Vázquez has summed it up.[80] The *ejidos* created or restored in such a fashion could not be conveyed, leased, mortgaged, or even be used to secure loans. However, it would all too soon become apparent that there were many ways around these legal and constitutional safeguards. Vázquez has speculated that "these exceptions were the legal mechanisms implemented by Carranza and later presidents to return *hacienda* land that had been confiscated during the Revolution, invalidating in this way the redistribution that had taken place during combat."[81]

But even more well-meaning attempts to benefit indigenous and other landless peoples did not necessarily bear fruit. Jean Meyer has explained, that "in the course of the civil war decisive legal measures were taken, in an improvised fashion and under pressure of necessity, against large-scale private land ownership, as illustrated by the decree of January 1915 and Article 27 of the constitution of 1917."[82] In spite of revolutionary creed and revolutionary agrarian laws, the agrarian reform failed to take off in the time immediately following the cessation of most large-scale open and armed hostilities. While some *hacienda* lands were indeed expropriated, land redistribution remained a very slow and uneven process. Even though the presidency of Victoriano Huerta saw what has been called the beginning of 'indigenist' policies, these were only slow and very tentative steps at putting theory into practice. Under Huerta and some of his successors, at least some *ejidos* were returned to the

Indians. Generally, post-revolutionary Mexico now put a greater emphasis on agrarianism and some of the pressures still resulting from the reform laws were lifted.[83] But the principles embodied in the agrarian reform were only really put into effect many years later, after the election of president Lázaro Cárdenas in 1934. "The post-Revolution governments of de la Huerta, Calles and Obregón moved very slowly to expropriate and redistribute haciendas, due in no small part to the tasks they all faced in consolidating power and reconstructing the country following the Revolution," as Marc Alan Sills has explained.[84] Some of these governments, as well as later ones, turned instead to education—mostly focusing on language and vocational skills—in ostensible attempts to integrate the Indians into Mexican society. It was in such a context that José Vasconcelos famously propagated the idea of the *raza cósmica*, which idealized the merging of races to create something new and superior.

In the aftermath of the Revolution, when governments changed frequently, there were also serious setbacks and considerable opposition to the implementation of Article 27. After only a few years of the program being in effect, Plutarco Elías Calles in 1930 pronounced the agrarian reform a failure and stopped all land distributions. Instead, he placed a heavy emphasis on Spanish language teaching to achieve acculturation. However, Emilio Portes Gil, transitional president from 1928 to 1930, resumed land distribution.[85] Between 1929 and 1930, 1,700,000 hectares of land were thus distributed to those who needed it, probably primarily Indians and *mestizos,* people of mixed race ancestry. All in all it came to 7,600,000 hectares between 1915 and 1930. The presidency of Abelardo Rodríguez saw 2,500,000 hectares being distributed. In conjunction with this, about 4,000 *ejidos* were created, though most were confined to certain areas only. And generally, the core of existing *haciendas* was respected and left intact.

In spite of this, the agrarian reform created quite a few conflicts. This, as Meyer has insightfully suggested, was because "the revolutionaries in power never had a true agrarian programme."[86] But, Ute Schüren has asserted, especially the Sonoran presidents also merely considered the *ejido* as a temporary measure and not as an alternative to privately-owned large-scale agriculture.[87] That is one reason why they stopped short of attacking the principle of the *hacienda*. Furthermore, few regional governors were willing to engage in land distributions as this would have made them unpopular with the rich and influential *hacendados*.[88] And the few parcels that were distributed to Natives and others were often of poor quality. Thus the reprised land redistribution program managed to limit the power of large landowners but not to break it—and it never even aspired to do the latter. Once again, the peasants were used as instruments of power only to become victims in the course thereof.

Yet in spite of the reforms falling short of what had been promised by the Revolution, the *hacienda* system was in decline. This process had begun even before the reforms of the 1930s and so landholders were already looking for new opportunities. This may have helped the reforms yet to come under Cárdenas, the most drastic ones of the revolution, even though they were based on a 'revolutionary' law that had existed—but not been implemented and enforced stringently and earnestly—for almost twenty years.

More stability and a more far-reaching restructuring of Mexican land ownership was finally achieved with the election of Lázaro Cárdenas in 1934. He was to be the first president to actually listen to and actively attempt to help the indigenous population. As opposed to his Sonoran predecessors like de la Huerta, Calles and Obregón, Cárdenas saw the *ejido* as more than a transitional device and rather as a countermodel to capitalistic agriculture. Cárdenas distributed 18 million hectares of land to some 800,000 recipients, for the first time including lands that had formerly been used commercially.[89] The *ejidos* now held 47 per cent of all cultivated land, a huge increase compared to the mere 15 per cent in 1930. The *ejidal* population had also more than doubled, from 668,000 to 1.6 million, and the landless population had fallen from 2.5 million to 1.9 million. Still, few people had enough land to make farming profitable, illustrating the problems with and also the once again somewhat improvised nature of these well-intentioned reforms.

Problems and shortcomings were partially caused as Cárdenas' "power to take action on the ground was always limited by his ability to gain the compliance of local officials," as Alexander Dawson has shown.[90] While well-intentioned, the president had to fight considerable opposition. Furthermore, Cárdenas had a simple view of Natives, believing "that the Indian was a backward proletarian, possessed of a number of vices (alcoholism, fanaticism, isolation, etc) and continually exploited by a variety of class enemies, but open to redemption" and he did not want to see them treated as distinct from the national community.[91] Still, he created the *Departamento Autónomo de Asuntos Indígenas* in 1936 which was exclusively dedicated to indigenous issues.[92] Various educational programs were pioneered but even though these were more open to indigenous values than many of the previous or following ones, they still mostly emphasized the Spanish language as key to indigenous advancement.[93] As Dawson has shown, policies under Cárdenas did not empower all Indians but only those who accepted the overarching goal of modernization.[94] He contends that "the Cardenista state promised protection against exploiters and the material benefits of modernity, but in return required some degree of political allegiance."[95] And even though there were certainly qualifications and requirements to be fulfilled, as Dawson states, I believe Wolfgang Gabbert to be correct when he contends that "it was only during the time of Lázaro Cárdenas that the Indian question began to be seen as an independent issue." He therefore classifies this period as the beginning—or, as I would hold, the 'post-colonial' resumption—of a specific Indian policy.[96] "However," Gabbert clarifies that "during Cárdenas's term of office, and even more so under his successors, the intention was not to foster a consciousness of ethnic separateness among Indians but to make them part of the national people."[97] The prevailing policy was still one of assimilation and integration, which Cárdenas himself illustrated by stating that the task was not to make the Indian remain Indian or to Indianize Mexico, but instead to Mexicanize the Indian.[98] Like many of his contemporaries, he considered what he did a way of keeping the Indians from disappearing. In this respect he was not unique. Dawson has argued that, "keenly concerned with remedying Mexico's backwardness, early Indigenistas believed that modernity and nationhood were essentially synonymous" and shaped their policies accordingly.[99]

This relatively fruitful time under Lázaro Cárdenas was followed by the election of Manuel Ávila Camacho in 1940 after Cárdenas term had expired. He initiated a new agrarian policy which, as Schüren has asserted, at its core has remained unchanged to the present day.[100] Ávila himself only distributed about 6 million hectares of land, and, as Vázquez has emphasized, "although the 1942 Agrarian Code bestowed *ejidatarios* with titles and certificates, those documents took years to obtain and in most cases *ejidatarios* just gave up on them."[101] The Agrarian Code included three ways of circumventing the mechanism protecting *ejido* landholdings: expropriation, exchange (*permuta*), and the formation of urban *ejido* zones.[102] Post-Cárdenas agrarian policies, like for instance irrigation development, once again favored the private sector and large-scale landholdings over the *ejidos*. Distribution of *ejidal* land came to an almost complete stop. Several presidents, like Ávila Camacho (1940–46), Alemán Valdés (1946–52) und Ruíz Cortines (1952–58), even sought to dispose of the *ejidos* by breaking them up into parcels.[103] (The reduced interest in the Indians' cause was also reflected by the closing of the *Departamento de Asuntos Indígenas* under Miguel Alemán as well as by the fact that, while the protests this step had caused achieved the creation of the *Inistituto Nacional Indigenista* (INI), this institution remained confined to a very limited budget and also saw its responsibilities reduced.)[104]

Especially since the 1950s the trend has gone towards *neolatifundios*, new large-scale landholdings. This led to increasing protest by peasants and thus forced the following two presidents to make some concessions in order to at least temporarily appease them.[105] Yet while Adolfo López Mateos

(1958–64) returned almost 30 million acres, *ladinos,* not Indians or *mestizos,* received large parts of them. On the whole, the thirty years following the Cárdenas administration probably succeeded only in making Mexican agriculture more capitalist. And in August 1969, President Díaz Ordaz once again declared the end of land redistributions under the pretext that there were no more lands available.

Matters changed mostly for the better with the election of Luis Echeverría Alvarez in 1970, who distributed over 6.5 million hectares of land. He, next to Lázaro Cárdenas, came to be regarded as the Mexican president most concerned with Indian welfare, even though, as Vázquez has pointed out, some of his achievements were "built on spaces provided by expropriated *ejido* lands" and that "those expropriations, although carried out in the name of public interest, displaced and dispossessed *ejido* and other rural communities from their living and working spaces."[106] At the beginning of his term in 1970, anthropologist Gonzalo Aguirre Beltrán came to be the head of INI and the previous official *indigenismo de assimilación* was forced to modify its integrative goal and instead turn towards a concept of *indigenismo de participación*. Echeverría, as Schryer has argued, "resurrected a policy of radical *indigenismo* in an era of renewed social tensions in the countryside caused by great regional disparities and a crisis in agricultural production because of two decades of rapid but lopsided economic development."[107] Finally, Indians were supposed to take part in forming their own political destiny.[108]

The economic crisis under Adolfo López Portillo (1976–1982) and especially the oil crisis forced his successor in office, Miguel de la Madrid (1982–1988) to liberalize Mexico's policies. Thus de la Madrid changed Article 27 in order to open up *ejidos* for investments from the private sector.[109] And he also joined the ranks of those who declared the end of all land redistributions.[110] His successor, Carlos Salinas de Gortari (1988–1994) largely followed de la Madrid's neoliberal policies, but his also fell short off reaching his proclaimed goal of simultaneously contributing to the improvement of the situation of small-scale landholders. On the contrary, measures like the reduction of trade restrictions and the opening of some *ejidos* for private investment contributed to an aggravation of the agrarian crisis and thus to a deterioration of the conditions experienced by most rural populations.[111]

The year 1992 saw drastic reforms of Article 27 of the 1917 Constitution which had at least nominally governed many land issues until then. The resulting legislation for the first time in Mexican post-Revolutionary history permitted the transformation of *ejido* lands into privately owned ones. It also arranged for long-term leases thereof as well as for other such measures. It has thus been held that these reforms "basically erased the premises of the 1917 article 27."[112] This was not a radical break with history, as Schüren has emphasized, but rather, as Vázquez holds, "has formalized the existing informal processes of *ejido* land privatization, but by doing so, has also accelerated privatization in certain *ejidos*."[113] Upon close inspection, this policy and others like it follow very closely in the footsteps of colonial and post-Independence ones, retracting on those few advances previously made.

With the exceptions of Cárdenas, Echeverría, and, to an extent, López Portillo, who sought the expansion and modernization of the *ejidos*, post-Revolutionary Mexican governments have limited themselves essentially to the mere (and very limited) redistribution of generally poor lands to landless peasants and small farmers.[114] As Schüren contends, the *ejido* was thus more a symbol than of much practical value and its problems can be traced to this fact.[115] Dawson has judged that "far from being a truly centralized state, the political system that emerged in the aftermath of the Revolution was more a series of political arrangements that allowed local elites to monopolize power with the consent of federal officials, as long as they supported federal officials on key issues."[116] It may be that the state was not strong enough for a coherent policy towards the indigenous members of the nation, or, more likely, that it was unwilling to face the political consequences this would have brought.[117]

As seen above, 'Indian Policy' post-Revolution seems to have been largely limited to land redistribution. And, as this measure was not solely geared towards indigenous Mexicans but towards the landless poor in general, it can only very tentatively be identified as 'Indian policy' but in the majority these landless poor were and are of indigenous ancestry—a fact that the state is well aware of. However, even this policy was throughout most of Mexican history more myth than reality and was furthermore used as a political or rhetorical/propagandistic, rather than a social or an economic tool. As Alexander Dawson has observed: "The revolutionary state was given to highly symbolic acts (often in the absence of systematic programs)."[118] This did not change once the revolution was considered to have been concluded (or institutionalized) but rather proves to be symptomatic for what I have called Indian policy.

Guillermo Floris Margadant has determined that "official Mexican policy toward Indians has passed through three distinguishable stages. The colonial period was an era of official guardianship imbued with the Christian ideal of brotherhood."[119] However, I would emphasize that this time was also one of exploitation mainly of the Natives' labor, which the Spaniards may have considered as a fair exchange for saving indigenous souls by introducing them to Christianity. The same dual attitude evidenced in labor relations became apparent in a number of colonial laws which protected the Indians but also benefited the Crown. So although theoretically colonial policies at least to an extend aimed for the gradual integration of indigenous peoples, like post-Independence and post-Revolutionary Mexico, this mixture of Christianity and pragmatism also created the category of the Indian. Yet even though this introduced some uniformity, it never managed to overcome regionally defined identities which usually focused on the village and the land even though in recent years there have been more and more strategic incentives for Indians to identify themselves as indigenous, something that previously had been much less the case.

As land was readily available especially during the early colonial period, the focus of colonial Indian policy was clearly on labor even though land gained in importance towards the end of the period. This changed especially after Independence, when land had become scarcer and there was thus much more of a competition for it. Floris identifies the post-Independence era as the second stage of Indian Policy and states that "from 1821 to 1910, after Independence but before the Mexican Revolution, the Indian was officially considered a citizen equal to all others in the eyes of the law."[120] However, as seen, there was often a considerable gap between theory and practice and ideas about citizenship furthermore did not necessarily conform to the modern notion of equal rights. I thus hold that overall—strictly speaking and in contrast to colonial rule—there has been no Indian Policy as such in post-Independence Mexico, at least not until the presidency of Lázaro Cárdenas after the Mexican Revolution. Until then policies were mainly directed at peasants and more often than not pretended that Indians did not exist as a discernable population, rather as if hoping that the 'problem' would disappear if ignored. To all practical effects, however, this amounted to an Indian Policy in disguise.

Under colonial rule matters had been different as indigenous peoples still held a discernable legal status, which they proceeded to lose with Independence (even though there was some backtracking on the issue now and then in the face of reality). In the colonial period it was thus comparatively easy to discern policies directly aimed at the indigenous population. This was not the case in independent Mexico anymore which had eliminated the category of the Indian, supposedly in an attempt to integrate them into Mexican society (something that had also been proclaimed as a long-term goal of colonial Indian Policy). However, this does not mean that post-Independence Mexico had no policies which were primarily geared towards the indigenous part of the population but rather that these were framed differently. Most of these measures were aiming to integrate regional Indian populaces (and their lands) into Mexican society, albeit probably as a subservient labor force, and thus to eliminate Indians practically as had already been done legally. These measures are much harder to identify, mainly due to the absence of a legal definition of what it meant to be 'Indian.' Along with indigenous peoples themselves, Indian policy remained hidden yet omnipresent at the same time, and amounted almost to a people disowned and a policy disguised.

Floris claims that in the third period, namely "since 1917, a new form of guardianship has evolved. This new policy, conceived as temporary, is based on increasing anthropological knowledge and is relatively free of Western feelings of superiority toward the Indians."[121] This policy has been accompanied by the inclusion of multiculturalism in the Mexican Constitution in 1992.[122] However, as seen even the post-Revolutionary period has been far from uniform, with Cárdenas' Indian policy being the exception more than the rule. And even his ultimate goal was the Mexicanization of the Indians.

This Mexicanization, I hold, post-Independence and especially post-Revolution was very much part of one of the two central themes of Mexican Indian Policy. It has come in different guises and the meaning of terms like integration, assimilation, and later 'Mexicanization' has changed over time. Yet the remnants of the colonial vision of two separate republics has never been completely abandoned and at times the integration and assimilation of the Indians would probably have envisaged them as a subservient labor force rather than as full citizens, in spite of all rhetoric to the contrary. So in a sense, 'Mexicanization' (as well as integration and assimilation) was and is just a new label for the intended exploitation of Native labor and thus not all that dissimilar from colonial and post-Independence tactics. This phenomenon post-Revolution was less pronounced under Cárdenas but became more apparent under most of his successors, as it had been prevalent under his predecessors. Yet while this trend has remained a constantly dominant one, the means used to achieve it have varied over time, ranged from coercion over violence to education attempts mainly focusing on language and vocational training.

Yet while colonial attitudes envisioned a complete surrender of indigenous identities and lifestyles, later times and especially the twentieth century came to be more tolerant of these. It would be fair to assume that a number of earlier proponents of measures like the laws about *terrenos baldíos,* the various educational programs, or of the reforms of Article 27 may have been genuinely interested in the Indians' well-being and may have felt that these and other measures were in the best interest of the Natives, but others would have been under no such delusions and would only have seen their own potential profit. At no time so far have Indians been allowed to remain Indians. And while the colonial regimes had been willing to permit the Natives time to adapt to the new Spanish way of life this was much less the case later on. At all times, however, were non-indigenous ways of life considered to be superior, no matter how much Native ways were romanticized or even to an extent supposedly embraced. Especially post-Independence, Native legal status or rather the absence thereof gave a clear signal of what was expected of indigenous peoples. And even in the instances that definitions were created, Native opinions and self-identification were usually ignored. Just like the special status they had held in colonial times, Indians were supposed to disappear post-Independence, to let themselves be integrated into mainstream society and preferably as lowly *campesinos*. As a consequence thereof, 'Indian Policy' in Mexico has often been aimed at peasants, probably the most 'indigenous' group in the country. (However, government policies also to an extend work(ed) on defeating their own goal, as Gabbert has shown when looking at reasons to self-identify as *indígena*.)[123]

In each of the stages identified by Guillermo Floris Margadant the regimes failed to live up to their own rhetoric, claims, and ideologies regarding the Natives, signaling through many different Indian policies that there was no place for Indians in Mexico. Still, the various rhetorics used over time to this day have managed to distort and obstruct the real and unchanged centrality of issues of land and labor within Mexican Indian Policy.

Chapter Seven
The Will to Endure

If the history of the Delawares was one of movement and accommodation, the history of the Yaquis is one of adaptation, standing firm, and determined resistance to external tension. While this does sound like the Yoeme, as they refer to themselves, were decidedly more likely to succeed in their struggle for land and tribal autonomy, they, too, came to the verge of being overcome in their attempt to remain Yaquis.[1]

CONTACTS WITH EUROPEANS

The Yaquis belong to the so-called *ranchería* people and were originally loosely organized into scattered semi-permanent settlements, numbering approximately 80 different *rancherías*.[2] The area they occupied was about 60 miles long and 15 miles wide on both sides of the Yaqui River, which flows from the mountains of Northwest Mexico to the Pacific. This traditional Yaqui homeland was known to the tribe as *Yaquimi* and was structured into three sections of settlements, each with different lifestyles due to the requirements of their subsistence. The villages on the arid mouth of the river depended heavily on fishing; those in the middle section, in the lush and fertile valley of the Yaqui river, relied primarily on agriculture; and the settlements up north, in the mountains of the Sierra de Bacatete, existed mostly by hunting and gathering, as do many semi-nomadic peoples. The primary weapons of the Yoeme were bows and arrows and they seem to have engaged in limited trade.[3] Like the neighboring Mayos, they spoke a form of Cahita, an Uto-Aztecan language. In peacetime, the *rancherías* of the Yaquis were politically autonomous while in times of war the Yoeme united and were led by both a council and military leaders.

The first contacts between Yaquis and Spaniards on the Pacific coast of what today is Mexico occurred around the year 1533. At the time, the

Yaquis probably numbered about 30,000 people.[4] Location was a factor that must have influenced Yaqui reaction to the European presence on their lands as the Yoeme had probably heard of the arrival of Europeans before they actually came in direct contact with them as Spaniards arrived earlier in other parts of Mexico (which was then still New Spain) and the news would have traveled faster than the intruders themselves. They therefore had time to listen to reports about the newcomers and to adjust—an advantage many other indigenous communities never had. These early contacts between Yoeme and Spaniards alternated between hostility and friendship, depending on the conduct of the colonists and also on very practical assessments by the Yaquis. For example, a slave trader, Diego de Guzmán, was repulsed by the tribe while Francisco de Ibarra spent several months living peacefully among the Yoeme.[5] Early on they profited from the Hapsburg's general neglect of New Spain's northwest frontier which seemed unattractive to most Europeans due to the absence of mineral wealth. So between 1533 and 1617, the Yaquis managed to survive the rather sporadic encounters with the Europeans without substantial changes in the way their life was shaped.[6]

In 1617 the Yoeme were joined by Jesuits, and the missionaries henceforth remodeled Yaqui society and gave it a new rigid and cohesive structure. Under Jesuit tutelage, the eighty or so formerly independent *ranchería* hamlets were transformed into eight tightly structured towns, each eventually supervised by a priest. These changes included the entire tribe and the mission of the Yaquis became the cornerstone of the Jesuits' missions of the area, especially due to their economic productivity. This reorganization by the *padres* was important for two reasons: first it improved local production and made the Yoeme economically self-sufficient, and secondly it gave them a heightened sense of political and cultural, of tribal identity that came to be of vital importance in the future.

The Jesuits assigned the Yaquis plots of their own land for their subsistence to be worked on three days a week. On the remaining three days, they were to labor on communal plots. The mission's surplus, produced on these communal lands, was appropriated entirely by the missionaries. The padres used it for the purpose of trade and the earnings enabled them to found new missions, and, occasionally, to help out the Yaquis themselves during food shortages. Besides these work schedules the Jesuits also introduced new tools, new crops, and new animals.

For over a hundred years these arrangements seem to have worked comparatively well, apparently leaving both Jesuits and Yaquis content enough not to question the relationship as such. Still, Jesuit control was not necessarily always harmonious. In 1740 there was a significant uprising against some of the *padres*. Yet the revolt was not directed against the Jesuits' sporadic presence in general, as a petition by the rebellious Yoeme proved, but against some individual friars who the Yaquis felt were mistreating them. The uprising was sparked by a long-lasting food shortage, which the missionaries had failed to alleviate by handing out the surplus obtained from the Yoeme and stored for trade and emergencies. Even though the Indians knew the food to be there and also that it was a product of their very own labor, the padres adamantly refused to use the agricultural products they controlled to help the tribe out. The situation was aggravated by a broader conflict on the frontier, which pitched the differing interests of Jesuits and Spanish colonists about the secularization of the missions against each other. The *vecinos*, the Spanish colonists, wanted the missions to be integrated into colonial society mainly to be able to exploit the Indians more easily, while the Jesuits argued against this proposition and did not want to surrender their paternalistic control over their disciples. Since the Yaqui missions for them were also a flourishing economic venture, this fact may well have influenced the Jesuits' position, in addition to possible religious motivations. But the 1740 uprising was also a signal that the Yoeme were unwilling to accept just any given treatment by the missionaries. The now prospering frontier economy with its mines and *haciendas* offered the Yaquis multiple opportunities to work outside of their traditional territory on the Río Yaqui and they did not intend to let them pass them by.

Among the grievances the Yoeme' representatives uttered as early as 1736 was that they wanted to be allowed to carry their traditional weapons, bows and arrows. In the petition they also argued against the taking of their land by the missionaries and especially to their converting them to uses other than the ones the Yaquis themselves had intended. They wanted to elect their traditional authorities themselves and not be forced to accept the friars' choices in this respect. Among the many grievances stated, these were the ones that were to be heard again and again over the course of three centuries.

The uprising of 1740 did not last very long and neither did it bring about many changes. It seems like the Yaquis were very clear about what they wanted and what were disposed to accept from the Jesuits and also about what they rejected—and they did not oppose Jesuit presence as such but merely some aspects thereof. The Yoeme did seem to value benefits like the exemption from tribute they reaped simply by living in a mission community and also the general protection they received through the Jesuits. However, the uprising was a first indication of the decline of Jesuit hegemony and their Yaqui missions along with it. During this rebellion the Yoeme established a military leadership while preserving the principles of their otherwise almost egalitarian society. This military leadership in later years proved to be essential for the numerous military conflicts the Yoeme would have with various governments.

The 1740 conflict ended with the Yaquis' surrender, yet not all of them returned to the mission and their fields. The mines of the Northwest were one alternative sought out by a number of Yoeme, while others opted to work on haciendas as they had done before even against the will of the friars. This rebellion was the only major one under what remained of colonial rule. Instead of staging more uprisings, the Yaquis "ensured their own survival by becoming the key and indispensable source of labor for the mining industry," as Evelyn Hu-DeHart has concluded.[7] This was a strategy they would turn to repeatedly throughout their later history, usually with great success until it would eventually come to work against them.

After the Jesuits were expelled from Spanish America in 1767, the Yaqui communities—unlike most other missions—did not simply fall apart. Yet they did change after the departure of the *padres*. The most prominent of these changes was probably that the tribe no longer produced the former surplus, something that may have been a decisive factor in the preservation of their more or less egalitarian society. But they intensified the work on *haciendas* and in mines outside of their territory which they had begun under Jesuit rule, thereby becoming an indispensable source of labor especially for the flourishing mines. Although there may have been disagreements among the Yoeme they always shared one core belief when it came to questions of tribal autonomy. They insisted that in their territory there would be only Yaquis, no outsiders, and they always distinguished between their own government and the colonial one as well later on the Mexican authorities.[8] Through their steadfast and unwavering insistence on that attitude they managed to an extent to keep *yoris,* non-Yaquis, from settling among them and within the territorial limits of *Yaquimi*. While, after the change from Hapsburg to Bourbon rule, the authorities attempted to extract tribute from the Yaquis, through the Yoeme's opposition they were eventually forced to settle for the surplus labor of the tribe instead, something the Indians gave rather willingly. Thus a fragile balance was achieved between the demands of the state and the *vecinos* on one side, and the aims and goals of the Yoeme on the other one.

THE YAQUIS POST-INDEPENDENCE

This uneasy equilibrium lasted for a long time, even though to the dismay of the government. It held through Independence and the change of status this brought to all Indians, making them citizens of the newly created state. This the Yoeme did not acknowledge at all but carried on exactly as before.[9] What they still claimed for themselves was the sole ownership of the Yaqui territory in one piece and without any settlements of outsiders. They would not be coerced into paying taxes or serving in the Mexican military.[10] Quite to the contrary, if need arose, the Yoeme took up arms against the Mexicans. And especially since many Yaquis had returned to their pueblos after the post-Independence decline of the mines they were indeed a force to be reckoned with. This was especially so as they had at their disposal an advanced tribal and military organization. While each village elected its own "*gobernadores* in the tradition of local village autonomy, they retained the position of captain general as an overall military leader and as spokesman with the outside world."[11] The Apaches coincidentally proved to be a great help for the Yaquis in such situations, by time and again distracting the state's military forces from them and by keeping the army occupied. Repeatedly, this distraction was crucial for Yaqui resistance. Yet the central factor working in favor of the Yoeme was their great reputation as workers, something that was to be of the utmost importance to them for the longest time but which would eventually come to work against them.

Shortly after Independence, in 1826, the Yaquis drew attention because of their fighting abilities. The reasons for these troubles were the tax matter as well as the attempted drafting of Yoeme fighters for an expedition against Apaches. As the Yaquis were opposed to both, a conflict developed between them and the state government. At the time of this uprising, the main force of the Sonoran military, along with its overall commander, was still after the Apaches and therefore not available to fight against the Yaquis. Two punitive expeditions by the limited available forces remained fruitless so that eventually the Yaqui rebels were granted an amnesty for lack of a better solution. The governor's terms for this amnesty included the return of stolen property and the reinstatement of the original Yaqui *capitán general*, among other things. But the Yaquis had terms as well and insisted on the retreat of all troops from the Yaqui River, as well as to be recognized as sole and undisputed owners of their land. They insisted that the *yori*-families, the name the Yoeme used for non-Yaquis, having fled the river as a consequence of the rebellion would not return. Even after the Yoeme rebels had been appeased and the fighting had ceased the situation remained tense as the issues at the heart of it had not been resolves satisfactorily for either side. Therefore some Yoeme continued the rebellion. While contemporary Mexican interpretations saw the conflict rooted in race issues or as relating to citizenship and democracy, the Indians' demands clearly show that it was primarily land and autonomy they wanted.[12]

Among the Yaquis who had refused to surrender in this conflict was Juan Ignacio Jusacamea, more commonly known as Juan de la Cruz Banderas or just Juan Banderas. His war name, Banderas, means 'flags' or 'banners' and he acquired it by carrying a banner of the Vírgen de Guadalupe with him. Banderas claimed to have been sent by the Virgin to restore the sovereignty of Emperor Moctezuma.[13] At one time his plan seems to have been to achieve the unification of all the Indians of the Northwest.[14] Unfortunately, Banderas' attempt to draw other Indian nations into the rebellion he was so keen on continuing failed. Still, he and his men kept up their fight even though he dropped the messianic appeals later on.

Banderas and his supporters never stopped raiding nearby *haciendas* and soon gained a large following among the Yoeme as well as among the neighboring Mayos. For a number of reasons the commanding general of the state forces found it immensely difficult and challenging to fight the Yaquis. Many of his men deserted, mainly due to the hardships of the campaign, he lacked arms and money, and the terrain was almost as hard to deal with as the troublesome Indians themselves. In addition, while he was fighting the Yaquis he was forced to neglect the Apache campaign as he lacked sufficient forces to tackle both problems at the same time. By the time some of the Yaquis surrendered after a series of defeats the general had learned not to easily trust appearances. Though some individuals Indians gave up their arms, mostly bows and arrows, they could not be considered truly pacified while their leaders were still at large and carrying on with the struggle.

All through the summer of 1826 the commanding general failed to gain any important advantages over the Yoeme. The wet season proved to be an added difficulty to the problems already mentioned. The Indians dealt with the difficult conditions with considerably more ease than the government's soldiers, giving the Yoeme an advantage over the military forces. Still, in October of that year yet another punitive expedition was undertaken. Frustrated by their own inability to win, the treatment of the Yaquis taken prisoner by the Mexican troops became more and more ruthless. Many were executed on the spot, while others were sent to Mexico City. Supposedly these men were to be tried in court for their crimes but were actually drafted into the marines of Veracruz.[15] Evelyn Hu-DeHart has argued that "this was the first documented case of deportation, a punishment which was meted out sporadically during the next few decades but which became a major policy at the end of the century."[16]

Yet none of the methods employed by the Mexicans really bore fruit and therefore the state government returned to a measure that had previously proved itself successful, to the granting of an amnesty. Thus a period of six months was given to the Yaquis to hand over their arms and to swear allegiance to the government. Within half a year, many rebels had taken up this opportunity to cease fighting. Now it became clear that the rebellion had taken their toll on the Indians as well as on the Mexican troops. The Yaquis had been largely unable to pursue their seasonal planting and therefore to grow sufficient crops to ensure their own subsistence and had thus been unable to practice the autonomy and to work the land they were fighting for. Faced with this situation, the amnesty to many Yoeme must have seemed like the best option available. Some of them were now recruited to follow the rebels still at large who remained unwilling to surrender. A passport-system, something that had been used with limited success before, was reintroduced in an attempt to separate the rebels from the peaceful Yaquis. Passports were issued to the peaceful members of the tribe and anyone being caught without a passport and within certain part of the territory would be considered to be and thus treated as a rebel. (This system was used again later on although again with only limited success.)

Juan Banderas himself remained at large and continued his attacks, always threatening though never really attacking several big population centers of the region. Contemporary observers judged that he could have easily done so had he only wanted to. The reasons for his restraint remain in the dark. Maybe it was because he did not consider this option quite worth the risk. All through this continued fighting and raiding, the government authorities were trying to fix blame for the outbreak of the rebellion on someone, usually resorting to holding unspecified Spaniards accountable. The grievances the Indians had and which contributed considerably to the outbreak of the uprising were continuously neglected and therefore remained unaddressed. And as long as some of the Yaquis remained discontent they were unlikely to completely abandon their fight.

The government forces were equally unsuccessful in judging the enemy's strength in numbers as they were in fighting the Yoeme rebels. It was probably next to impossible to determine how many fighters there actually were because of the way Yaqui rebels sometimes turned into Yaqui laborers and vice versa. This method made their resistance all the more effective. This was also to continuously puzzle many successive governments and may have been one of the decisive factors leading to the deportation of the Yoeme in the late nineteenth century. In spite of this effective and hard to overcome strategy it proved to be impossible for the Yaquis to keep up the fight for much longer. So on April 13, 1827, Juan Banderas surrendered formally. Hu-DeHart suspects the surrender to have been a tactical step at a time when matters were not going all that well for Banderas and his supporters. Indeed, the submission did not mark the end of the government's troubles with Juan Banderas.[17]

Following this formal surrender, in 1828 steps were taken by the local government to finally pacify the area for good and to take the opportunity and develop it at the same time. Accordingly, decrees were passed regulating land administration and other matters. *Vecinos* settling in the Yaqui territory were to be exempt from certain taxes in order to encourage them to expose themselves to a potentially dangerous situation by moving to the *Yaquimi*. White migration to the Yaqui River was thereby actively promoted and, in addition to that, the political and economic supervision of the area was also to fall into *yori* hands. As part of this move, the Yoeme were supposed to receive individual titles for plots of land instead of holding it in common. But the government had considerable trouble putting these laws into practice. The land titles for the Yaquis went unclaimed and no divisions were made in spite of the high-flying plans for pacification. While a small number of Yaquis returned to their fields, others still held out in the sierra, refusing to accept and surrender to these new conditions.

It took until 1831 for the governor to attempt to enforce the 1828 decrees more rigidly, as they had so far failed to meet their objective. Additionally, he abolished the Yaqui position of *capitán general* and established various regulations for Indian towns. Far from finally achieving the desired results, these measures only made the rebellion flare up anew, once again led by Banderas. Even though Banderas and his followers now almost continuously threatened Mexican towns he never actually attempted to take one. Banderas also never discouraged the Yoeme from working on the *haciendas*. Instead, he actively used these workers as spies and thus in the service of the Yaquis' cause. Yet he still encouraged the cultivation of their own land and thus the production of their own food, presumably in an effort to keep up the traditional autonomy.

The renewed rebellion came at the time that the state of Occidente was being divided into Sonora and Sinaloa, thus making a mobilization of the military in strength harder than had previously been the case. However, this time it was some of the Yaquis themselves who offered a political solution, demanding self-government in exchange for a cessation of hostilities. The government reluctantly accepted the conditions yet this did not actually signify the end of the rebellion or of the threat posed by Banderas and other Yoeme who still appeared to be discontent with the situation. However, the pacification campaign mainly directed towards Banderas proved to be as costly as inefficient even though it did come to take a serious toll on the Yaquis. The rebellion could only be suppressed when government forces finally managed to arrest Juan Banderas in December of 1832. This hastened the capitulation of other Yaqui groupings still in rebellion and which had already been at the verge of surrender. The following January,

Banderas and his second in command were condemned to death and subsequently executed. Other leaders were sentenced to hard labor in a Chihuahua presidio and thus removed from the area where they might have incited more uprisings.

THE WILL TO ENDURE

Even the loss of the charismatic figure of Banderas did not spell out the end of what was on the contrary going to be a very long-lasting rebellion. Still, rebel activities temporarily subsided afterwards. But even while the Yoeme remained relatively calm, they did carry out the occasional raid on *haciendas* as well as on travelers. In addition, interior disputes were often sparked by conflicts between so-called *ladino yaquis,* the acculturated ones who were leaning more toward Mexican ways, and traditionalists. So throughout the nineteenth century, the Yaquis were in a state of almost incessant revolt, with only brief respites from time to time. As a result the Yoeme came to be very militaristic in their organization and their way of life. Their goals then as much as now were control over their own land and also autonomy, something that had become very obvious already during the Banderas revolt, if not before. These shared central goals and the Yaquis' ancestral rights to the territory they so adamantly claimed only for themselves were what separated them from common bandits.

Various Sonoran governments between the 1830s and 1850s repeatedly attempted to revive and enforce the 1828 decrees about the division of Yaqui lands and the colonization of *Yaquimi.* Yet the Yoeme never resigned themselves to Mexican encroachment upon their land and continued to contest it again and again. The Yaquis most common course of action in such cases was to appeal to the state government and, if that measure failed, to take up arms against the invaders. While they did so with a considerable degree of success, by the middle of the nineteenth century Mexicans were still more and more closing in on Yaqui territory. At this time, the Yoeme were also divided into those living inside and out of the traditional territory. Those living outside, mostly because they were employed in mines and *haciendas,* usually encountered the problem of debt acquisition. This was common to many Indians (and non-Indians), but the Yaquis solved it with characteristic uniqueness, by simply returning home, where it was next to impossible to find and apprehend them to recover what they owed.

The problem of pacifying the Yaquis remained unsolved at the time Porfirio Díaz came to power in Mexico in 1876. What was more, the Yaqui resistance had already acquired a new leader, a Yaqui known as Cajeme (He who does not drink). Cajeme's real name was José María Leyva and he was born in Hermosillo / Sonora in 1837, the son of two full-blood Yaquis. He spent his adolescence mostly outside of *Yaquimi*. Cajeme joined the Mexican military and repeatedly fought for the government, proving himself a reliable soldier and thus rising to the rank of captain and commanding a company of 100 men. Once he even took up arms against his own people, the Yoeme. It seemed like the Mexican government had no reason to suspect that Cajeme might be loyal to the Yaqui but instead every indication to expect him to keep his allegiance to the government. So the government sent him back to Yaqui territory in yet another attempt to appease the tribe. As it turned out, he was to do quite the contrary.

Cajeme was elected to the position of *capitán general* and started yet another rebellion in 1875. During this time, significant changes were introduced into Yaqui society. "Using a combination of Yaqui traditions and what he had learned from the Mexicans, Cajeme disciplined his people to rely on their own resources, initiative and leadership, rather than to work for, pillage from, or ally with, outsiders."[18] Accordingly, for what was probably the first time since the Jesuits had been dispelled, the Yaquis produced a significant surplus due to the re-introduction of the community plots they had worked under Jesuit rule. Part of this surplus was stored while some was traded, probably primarily in order to obtain weapons. Cajeme also introduced a tax system which probably helped to fund the rebellion. An additional source of revenue stemmed from the ransoms the Yaquis demanded for cattle stolen and for people or goods stopped on the river and other places within their territory.

While he structured the *Yaquimi* and its inhabitants tightly, Cajeme rarely ventured outside of Yaqui or neighboring Mayo territory. Essentially, this rebellion was a defensive one, its object merely to keep the traditional territory and to preserve and strengthen Yaqui autonomy. The goals were very clear and in a way also very traditional. And while Cajeme was really the man behind the rebellion, he also reintroduced another traditional measure of the Yaqui tribe which had fallen into disuse, the popular council. In these meetings every male and female Yaqui had equal participation and Cajeme professed to abide by the traditional consensus decisions.

The new rebellion came at a time when Sonora was already torn over political issues and thus when the state government was weak and vulnerable. "Threatening to rebel if his message was not heeded, Cajeme announced he would not recognize the government unless the Yoeme were granted total freedom to govern themselves, because they were the 'natural owners' of the Yaqui River."[19] It was during the ensuing revolt that the Yaquis were the closest to complete isolation they had ever been throughout their history. They hardly accepted work outside their own territory and they did not take any allies. Still, the Yoeme never did shut themselves off entirely since they needed the contacts to the outside, especially in order to be able to obtain the weapons so crucial to maintain the rebellion.

The "Yaqui tradition of not isolating themselves entirely from the outside world, while claiming the right to autonomy,"[20] as Hu-DeHart has correctly pointed out, created something like a state within a state, a nation within, that was unacceptable to the Porfiristas who ruled Mexico at the time. Hence, they attempted both to crush the Yoeme using military means and at the same time to colonize and develop their lands, to truly integrate these lands into the Mexican state. In the 1880s, the Apache problem was solved partly through United States help or intervention and therefore additional military forces were free to be employed against the Yaquis. Overall the government was in a stronger position than ever before. In the 1880s it therefore once again attempted to gain control over Yaqui lands and thus "Yaqui and Mayo lands were declared terrenos baldíos and, because the Indians were unable to produce recorded titles to their property, their lands were surveyed and sold."[21] Naturally, the Yoeme did not simply accept this. They were still set on autonomy, self-reliance, and self-sufficiency and to achieve these goals they needed control over their lands. Unfortunately, this was now much harder to defend than ever before. "As Cajeme took control, the state and nation which he confronted also became more organized, more powerful than ever before. For the first time since independence, Mexico attained political unity and stability under President Porfirio Díaz, whose strong, centralized rule destroyed the power of regional caudillos."[22] And no strong central government could accept another state within its own boundaries, thus eventually causing the federal government to act itself instead of merely leaving the matter to the state government.

The resulting Yaqui wars lasted twelve years in spite of the serious governmental interest and the involvement of federal forces. It was particularly difficult to defeat the Yaquis under Cajeme, who was eventually apprehended and executed by a firing squad on 21 April, 1887, mainly because the territory, the Sierra de Bacatete where the Yoeme went to hide, was very difficult to negotiate. Furthermore, the climatic conditions were very hard on anyone unused to them and even on the animals utilized in the campaigns. Vast superior strength on the part of the military was needed to finally defeat the Yaquis and the government came out of this conflict badly embarrassed in military matters though theoretically still victorious.

At this point probably only the veto of President Díaz himself saved the Yaquis from outright deportation, a method that had occasionally been used with great success before.[23] It is possible that Díaz did not want to risk an all-out war against the Yaquis, who were believed to prefer death to exile and who might have fought to death rather than to surrender. But their main advantage was probably that the Yoeme were too important as a crucial source of labor to simply eradicate the tribe or to lose their valuable labor through deporting them all. Indeed, the growing economy of Sonora with its booming mines and railroad construction and the resulting need for cheap labor seemed to have been the crucial advantage working in favor of the Yaquis.

Even after the defeat and the death of Cajeme in 1887 the resistance of the Yaqui tribe remained solid in spite of the government's hopes of having finally broken and pacified them. Now the Indians carried on with the battle by means of guerrilla warfare, relying on hit-and-run tactics that had previously been successful for them. According to the government's plans the Yoeme were to keep as much of their land as they could cultivate themselves and the remainder was to be put to other uses by non-Yaquis. Few Yoeme were willing to accept the option of working their traditional land as mere colonists. "The mass exodus of Yaquis that followed Cajeme's defeat amounted to a self-imposed exile that would have been acceptable to the government as a final solution to the Yaqui problem had it entailed no other consequences," Hu-DeHart has determined.[24] But, unsurprisingly, the Yaquis did not simply choose permanent exile over their traditional lands. Rather, in once again opting for wage labor they adapted their resistance to meet the needs of yet another change in the prevailing circumstances. The by then accustomed raiding and hit-and-run attacks which had been used under Cajeme were kept up, but at this time the Yaqui rebels resorted exclusively to guerrilla warfare, at first under the leadership of a Yaqui known as Tetabiate. The Yoeme who worked outside of *Yaquimi* once again functioned as a base for the active resistance of the so-called *broncos,* the hard core of the rebels.

Though many of the features (re-)introduced by Cajeme disappeared once again after his death, the Yaquis still kept alive the ideal of an autonomous Yaqui community in the *Yaquimi,* something that had preceded Cajeme and was at the very core of Yoeme live and culture.[25] And it once more proved to be next to impossible to dry-up the social base supporting and replenishing the rebels so that the Sonoran and the federal government were forced to experiment with every means imaginable. In the end, they arrived at deportation as the only promising option left to them to achieve results where all else had failed. (This will be explored in the following chapter.)

Against continuously changing threats from the outside, the Yaquis for over three centuries used varying tactics to survive, and so managed to surprise their opponents time and again. In addition to military prowess the need for their labor was a major trump card for them. As Evelyn Hu-DeHart

The Will to Endure

has determined: "Armed resistance against invaders and developers inside the Yaqui valley, while participating in the economy outside the valley without concurrent integration into the yori social structure—this twin strategy ensured their survival as the Yaqui people into the twentieth century."[26] Yet in spite of their many successes their goals were not always met entirely. In the end, some of their strategies may even have worked against them. While other tribes were subjugated through the application of social and military means the Yaquis were removed from their homeland, deported to Yucatán and Oaxaca, precisely because all other means had failed to 'pacify' them, because their will to endure had been so great and had seen them through so much. The better the opponent, the harsher the methods applied against him. "Beginning as only a local problem, the Yaquis had finally generated national concern, as a potential embarrassment to President Díaz's program of national social integration and a troublesome obstacle to his vision of national economic development."[27] Through their tenacious resistance and considerable successes the Yoeme had sealed their own fate.

Chapter Eight
Removal of the Yaquis: Out of *Yaquimi*

The Yaquis' greatest advantage throughout most of their history was perhaps the need for their labor, along with the slow pace of state-building in Mexico. Consequently, the almost complete isolation during the rebellion led by Cajeme was in itself a powerful weapon as it reduced the availability of Yaqui labor during the uprising which had started in 1875. Only limited trade connected them to the outside world. At this time they concentrated mostly on keeping people out of *Yaquimi,* the territory they claimed for themselves, and this goal remained unchanged throughout their struggles.

    This essentially defensive method of the Yoeme had proved itself quite successful until the Porfiristas, the government of president Porfirio Díaz, came to power in Mexico in 1876. Until then they had at least to an extent been able to keep their core territory free from European intruders but they had not been successful when attempting to prevent a dangerous encroachment thereof. The strong central government under Díaz was ill disposed to accept a Yaqui state within Mexico's territorial boundaries, especially not as Indians, in the opinion of the government, stood in the way of progress. And modernization and progress were among the most important aims for Díaz, thus contributing to intensity of the governmental responses to the Yoeme and their objectives. "The explicit aims of the Díaz regime in Sonora were to eliminate its antiprogressive elements and develop the potentially rich state, ending the internecine wars."[1] The Yaquis had to face a stronger and more determined enemy than ever before and along with it a severe test of their determination and will to endure. In this struggle, the growing economy of Sonora seemed to have been the biggest advantage of the Yaquis as they were required as a cheap source of labor to sustain it. Yet eventually this advantage would turn into a disadvantage and work against the Yoeme instead of for them.

GUERILLA

Even after Cajeme's execution in 1887, the resistance of the Yaqui tribe did not crumble and their goal to keep their territory free of outsiders remained the same. A few hundred of the Yaquis still refused to surrender and so when the government in April of 1887 announced peace, about four hundred Yaquis and their families went to the Sierra de Bacatete. The Yoeme switched to guerrilla warfare, a method that had already been used occasionally under Cajeme. And once again, the government found itself unable to control them and to put an end to the fighting. The seemingly peaceful remainder of the Yaqui population supported the *broncos*, the active rebels. It was specifically this exchange between the *pacíficos* and the rebels that made it so hard to overcome the Yoeme, who, in spite of their reputation as excellent workers now became known as "enemigos de la civilización y el trabajo," as enemies of civilization and work.[2]

The first rebel chief was a man named Tetabiate, otherwise known as Juan Maldonado. The fugitive rebels under his leadership repeatedly refused to surrender and kept up raiding to sustain themselves. Quite often these raids were rather insignificant especially in comparison with the activities under Cajeme or Banderas. Sometimes the parties in question just stole a head of cattle or gutted the animal on the spot, taking the meat they needed.[3] Fortunately for them, the men in charge of the current Yaqui campaign did not seem to have taken these remnants of the earlier rebellion overly serious. They seemed to consider it a non-urgent mopping-up effort which would only hasten the end of an insurgency already in decline. Apparently, the government was much more preoccupied with conducting a survey of *Yaquimi,* a step that was hoped would precede colonization. But due to constant harassment by the rebels, the engineers required military protection in order to be able to conduct their work at all. The object of this survey was to measure and sub-divide the land to prepare it for the settlement of colonists and thus the undertaking had a high priority. Yet a census in 1889 showed that colonization of the Yaqui River area made only very slow progress. Few white colonists were brave enough to settle on the Yaqui River and hardly any Yaquis accepted the lots offered to them. Instead, they took work outside of their traditional territory. So in 1890 the new military commander, Marcos Carrillo, concluded that the attempt to attract colonists to the region had failed along with the pacification of the rebels. And especially the latter was a prerequisite for the successful development of the area. Accordingly, the campaign against the Yaquis was resumed with renewed vigor and with the hope of achieving this dual goal.

As part of this campaign, general Carrillo made a clear distinction between the rebels in the sierra and the peaceful Yaquis, also known as *mansos*. On the surface the latter were peaceful laborers on *haciendas* and in mines. As such and because their labor was highly valued these workers would have been instrumental in fending off drastic measures like deportation for the longest time as they had successfully turned themselves into a labor force Sonora could not do without.[4] Many employers would not even tell on Yaquis with questionable behavior for fear of losing valuable laborers. However, it was soon to become apparent that a distinction as attempted by Carrillo was impossible since the groupings in reality were not that clear-cut. Although only a minority of Yoeme was actually involved actively in the fighting, almost every Yaqui had a part in this struggle. The *pacíficos* or *mansos*, the supposedly non-fighting workers, played a crucial role in the conflict as they supported the *broncos*, the active rebels, and so made it hard, if not impossible, for the Mexican forces to overcome the armed resistance fueled by the 'peaceful' members of the tribe. Additionally, the rebels sometimes went to the *haciendas* to rest and recharge while the Yaquis who had worked there took their part in the ongoing fight.[5] As a contemporary observer recorded about this practice: "Yaquis que dicen son manzos que son los mas malos de todos los que hay en esta region.... Los Yaquis andan en ésta siempre buscando trabajo, pero en vez de trabajar andan tomando noticias de lo que pasa ... y en la noche van y dan aviso á los que estan en la sierra. Disiendoles donde pueden robar y matar si es necesario."[6] So it seems like in addition to occasionally swapping places with active rebels the *pacíficos* also served as spies, singling out possible future targets for the rebels. This constant exchange prevented the military from effectively isolating the rebels from the other Yoeme.[7] It was impossible to overcome the rebellion by merely targeting the active rebels as seemingly innocent workers could be turned into fearsome fighters and vice versa. The workers were crucial as well because they could be turned into fighters but also because the money they made went into supplies and especially weapons—usually into high-calls American manufactured ones.[8] In a way, almost every Yaqui was a rebel.

Over the years, it seemed like rebel strength augmented, yet to even more or less accurately reflect the number of Yaqui fighters in the sierra was impossible. The rebels never ventured out in a body but instead practiced hit-and-run attacks in small groups, making it impossible to gauge their real strength which furthermore fluctuated. Therefore estimates range from about 100 to 400 hardcore rebels.[9] To combat them, and especially in consideration of earlier failed attempts to do so, spies and a secret police system were introduced but at first to little avail. This was to change only later, when a new measure, mass deportation, had set in full force and was complemented by these measures. Additionally, the military leadership had maps made of the Yaqui River Valley and the sierra in an attempt to overcome the advantage the Yaquis had through their unparalleled knowledge of the territory. Yet even these maps did not nearly give the military the intimate knowledge the Yaquis had of the area.[10] And it still left the soldiers with the problem of the harsh climatic conditions and especially in the rainy season when hot sunshine and heavy rains alternated. The papers reported that at times not even animals could stand the climate and this prompted a newspaper to refer to the Yoeme as a type of human salamanders, an "especie de salamandras humanas," as they were the only ones able to withstand the conditions.[11] All non-Indians were affected, sometimes severely so. Rafael Izábal, one of Sonora's leading men, in a letter from May 1902 recounted how in these conditions a very popular member of the troop suddenly went crazy, started shooting to all sides and was shot by his friends in self-defense.[12]

At some time during this campaign deportation of captured rebels was introduced as a measure.[13] This practice had been applied before if only in very few cases. This time male Yaquis were taken to the south of Mexico and drafted into the army while some women and children allegedly were sent into labor gangs.[14] In addition to these increasingly drastic and desperate measures taken against the Yaquis another practice revived at this time was the mission. Some secular priests had from time to time served in the *Yaquimi* but now members of a regular order were sent to the Yaquis in yet another attempt to 'pacify' them. Fortunately, most of these measures and the relentless campaign itself—while hard on the rebels and those Yoeme living within *Yaquimi*—left those Yoeme working outside of their territory relatively unaffected, enabling them to continue to covertly support the resistance.

In spite of the apparent inability of the military to overcome the successful guerilla tactics of the Yoeme, rebel chief Tetabiate gave signs of interest in a peaceful solution to the conflict. However, he stated the removal of all troops from the *Yaquimi* as a prerequisite for peace negotiations. Still, this condition was not met when eventually an unconditional peace agreement was signed on May 15, 1897 at Ortiz. The document did not include any compromise with the Yaquis and even at the time the peace was concluded the troops had not withdrawn. It is impossible to guess at what moved Tetabiate to sign this document as it did not meet many of the Yoeme's demands. It may be that he and his men did not understand the content of the agreement or maybe that they had believed their demands would be met regardless. As the Yaquis in 1904 asked the government for a similar arrangement it seems like they must have thought the solution to be a desirable one for the tribe.[15] Tetabiate and his men stayed impassive during the ceremony, making it impossible to gage their feelings. However, as Juan Maldonado—Tetabiate—was referred to in the document as Chief of the Yaqui Tribe, something he was not and had never claimed to be, there was some indication that not all was as it should have been. All of these factors may have eventually had a part in the end of the fragile peace only two years later.

INTERLUDE

Until the outbreak of renewed hostilities, the peace of Ortiz of 1897 sent over 6,000 Yaquis back to the river within the following two years.[16] They mostly settled the abandoned pueblos of Bácum and Vícam, both traditional Yaqui settlements. As Hu-DeHart explained, "this mass migration back to the Yaqui ... poignantly illustrated the desire of Yaquis to return home after a long sojourn outside."[17] But this return took place on a set of unwritten premises like the aforementioned withdrawal of troops. And when the expectations of the Yoeme were not met and instead more and more white colonists settled within their territory, the Yaquis again took up arms in July 1899, a mere two years after the signing of the peace agreement. The reason for the renewed fighting was clearly stated in a letter sent in the name of the traditional Eight Pueblos to General Torres in which the Indians expressed their discontent, and stated that they wanted for the non-Yaquis, including soldiers, to leave.[18]

Though Tetabiate may not have been part of this new rebellion from the outset he soon joined in. But, due to a slight change in tactics, things did not go well for the Yoeme fighters who at first suffered huge losses even though they benefited from the rainy season and of having caught the government forces unawares. By the end of the year they had thus reverted to the guerilla tactics already used previously and with much success and these presented the government with the same problems as before.[19] But by January 1900 the Secretary of War, Bernardo Reyes, had sent military reinforcements so that General Lorenzo Torres was in a position to attack the rebel stronghold of Mazocoba. This encounter was later on often termed the Massacre of Mazocoba as of the estimated 3,000 Yaquis inside the natural fort in the morning at nightfall 400 could be found dead on the battlefield. Over 1,000 Yoeme were taken prisoner, among them many women and children. And of these only 834 survived the long march to the military headquarters. The government forces lost 54 men and another 124 were wounded. Typically but still extraordinary under the circumstances, only forty firearms were recovered from the Yaquis.

After Mazocoba Tetabiate once again assumed the rebel leadership. At his disposal were, according to contemporary estimates, about 900 to 1,000 active rebels.[20] But to cope with the renewed Yaqui problem the government also launched yet another attempt to finally subjugate and pacify the Yaquis in order to colonize the river. Counting the federal reinforcements, the number of those forces came up to almost 5,000 men. Additional measures were reintroduced or more strictly enforced than before.[21] For instance, the *hacendados* were by law required to keep a register of their Yaqui workers and to detain all suspects of being rebels. Yaquis were only to live in designated areas and every Yoeme was supposed to carry a passport with him, a so-called 'salvo conducto.'[22] "Indios sospechosos," suspect Indians, were kept under surveillance.[23] And, to the dismay of travelers and businessmen, the strictest measures were adopted in gun control and many Yaqui living quarters were searched for guns and ammunition, often with disappointing results.[24] In addition to this the formerly rather sporadic deportations were stepped up.

While none of these measures managed to effect the Yaquis' surrender they did reduce the number of active rebels to about 300. In one encounter Tetabiate was killed, ironically by a group led by a former Yaqui follower turned government scout.[25] And even though this by no means meant a complete victory of the government forces the campaign was once again called off on August 31, 1901. The officials in charge hoped to be able to control the Yaquis by exhorting pressure on them and their employers as well as by the severe gun control measures. Again what was considered to merely be a limited clean-up program aimed at 150 to 300 rebels was left to the state government of Sonora. The latter put together a surveillance program and established compulsory Yaqui registers.[26] But once more things were not quite as easy and did not go as smoothly as expected. The gun control measures turned out to be so strict that they had to be relaxed again in order to appease the commercial houses suffering from loss of trade.[27] And the passport system proved ineffective since the rebels often borrowed papers from other Yoeme or even obtained work without them. The Sonoran *hacendados* were desperate for workers and therefore even willing to break the law to get them, as for instance the behavior of the Maytorena clan proved. These *hacendados* were generally unwilling to cooperate but, more drastically, also attempted to smuggle some of their Yaqui workers to safety by train.[28]

When these measures did not work out for the government even after two years, it saw its only remaining chance in drying up the social base of the rebels, concluding that without it the fighting would necessarily cease.

As Hu-DeHart has explained, "it was far easier to deal with the visible, relatively stable working population than with the ghost-like rebels in the sierra."[29] Consequently, between 1902 and 1904, several hundred Yoeme, men, women, children, were rounded up and jailed. At this time it was still official policy to deport only hardcore rebels though this was not followed strictly. Some women and children were also deported and some men were hanged or sentenced to other punishments.

Another factor that contributed to the increase in deportations was the growing interest of outsiders, Mexicans and Americans, in the fertile lands of the Yaqui Valley in particular and in Sonora in general. Ironically, it was partly the commercial interest from the United States, especially from Arizona, that inspired the Mexican government to finally rid itself of the 'Yaqui nuisance' for good and open the way for commercial agricultural development of the area. This was so ironical because without the Yaquis and their labor the very same development would in all likelihood have been much slower in taking off. For instance, the Yaquis suffered from technical innovations, especially from the advance of railroads. At first, they had been convenient for this development, supplying mines, railroads, industries, but most of all the expanding agriculture, with cheap labor.[30] But then the need for Yaqui labor in Sonora was counteracted by the demand for labor on the henequen plantations in Yucatán. The Northern *hacendados* had usually been willing to balance the need for the Yaqui labor force against the fear of attacks and until that point the government had agreed because otherwise the Yaqui labor would have been lost. But now it could have both; it could deport the Yoeme from Sonora and at the same time satisfy Mexican labor needs albeit Yucatecan instead of Sonoran ones. The government may also have hoped to finally be able to colonize the Yaqui River Valley once it was rendered devoid of Yoeme. While Sonora was going to suffer from this bargain, Yucatán and its rich and influential plantation owners were going to profit. And so the fate of the Yaquis was sealed. Once this decision had been taken, there was nothing they could do to avoid the deportations which now looked like the best and most profitable option all around for the national government.

The drastic measures did show some result and seriously affected the Yaquis, as a letter from 1904 shows in which they complained to Rafael Izábal that troops killed them even though they were born in Sonora, "aunque Seamos nacidos aqui En Sonora."[31] They stated that they were not in Sonora to fight but because that was where they were from, "porque Somos de aqui," thus signaling their strong attachment to their land.[32] The Yoeme obviously felt that being native to the area gave them rights which were violated by the behavior of the government. They specifically objected to the killing of persons who did not even carry weapons, "sinque Tenga arma."³³ In the letter the Yoeme also complained about hangings and said that they did not know why and for what they were to blame, "no Sabemos que culpa tenemos."³⁴ They also specifically denied an assault on a train for which they seem to have been blamed.

Yet the rebels still held out and kept up their steadfast resistance. In another letter to the government they warned or even threatened the officials in question not to come to the river (Yaqui).³⁵ In their attempts to evade capture they roamed an even wider area than before. Raids and plunder sustained them along with what the *mansos*—by then severely restricted through government measures—could muster. Still, these disadvantageous conditions eventually took their toll on the rebellion.

Therefore, in 1904, peace negotiations with a group of Yaqui rebels were again taking place. The 'Nueve Capitanes,' nine Yaqui captains, in a letter from April 25 to the Sonoran State Governor Rafael Izábal stated that the rebellion was taking place only at the river and not in the countryside, presumably to convince the military to spare the *mansos* as they were so crucial to the rebellion.³⁶ They generally expressed concern for the Yoeme working outside the *Yaquimi*. Apparently, many of them feared the relentless persecution by governmental forces and hanging in particular. The men who referred to themselves as the Nine Captains also expressed their fear for the Sonoran harvest, which they claimed was going to be lost without Yaqui labor. This argument was also used in a letter to the *vecinos* on the same day, probably echoing and feeding fears the *hacendados* had anyway while at the same time proving the Yaquis' awareness of their main advantage.³⁷ In this letter the Yoeme insisted they did not know what they had done wrong and that they had always kept their word.³⁸ They showed themselves desirous of a "Santa Paz," a holy peace, and hence they implored the recipients of the letter to 'do them the favor' with "El Señor Presidente."³⁹

In spite of their efforts, their pleas and threats, the efforts to subjugate the Yaquis were redoubled as a consequence of the failure of the earlier peace negotiations. Vice-President Ramón Corral, himself a Sonoran, had actively encouraged this step and so by then had President Díaz himself. Now the deportation of the Yaquis would not threaten but instead doubly support his proclaimed goal of Mexican modernization as Yaqui labor was needed and was made available outside of Sonora through the deportations while at the same time making the Yoeme's territory available for colonization.

DESPERATE MEASURES

Now all Yaquis were suspected of being rebels and consequently in danger of being removed from Sonora. Almost everywhere the Yoeme came under close scrutiny, to the great dismay especially of the severely labor-deprived *hacendados*. But hardly ever were their complaints heeded and many applications to have servants or workers returned were turned down.[40] Troops were reinforced to meet the increased demands of the campaign. Contrary to previous ones, this time there was a lack of volunteers and the number of deserters seems to have been considerable.[41] Crucial to the campaign were the so-called *rurales,* a professional federal force which in Sonora was commanded by Luis Medina Barrón.

The persecutions of the Yaquis were stepped up and the results very visible as large groups of Yoeme were apprehended. Whole areas were at times cleared of Yaquis, of *mansos* as well as of *broncos*. No distinctions were made since labor was needed in Yucatán and it thus did not make sense for the government to distinguish between peaceful and actively fighting members anymore as both could and would be turned into plantation workers once they had been deported to Yucatán or Oaxaca. Later on entire districts were declared to be free of Yoeme.[42] Whole *haciendas* and mines were cleared of Yaquis of all ages. The prisoners were taken first to Hermosillo and then to Guaymas to be shipped to their future destinations.[43] Most were jailed repeatedly or put into guarded camps where they awaited their fate and quite possibly their deportation from Sonora. Judging from the frequent deaths, the conditions inside the prisons must have been very harsh. At one time an investigation was launched to find out why so many children were dying while imprisoned.[44] A doctor concluded that the deaths were due to diseases, which in turn were caused by the lack of space and of medical attention. Considering what was undertaken to rid the state of the Yaquis it is surprising to find such concern for the welfare of the jailed Yaquis. It would seem like someone was attempting to protect a valuable commodity.[45]

The government also again attempted to use Yaquis against Yaquis—and in more than just one way. Some Yoeme had already been part of special Yaqui-peacekeeping forces and thus at times been considered traitors by their own people.[46] Others had been drafted into the regular army. Both may at times have served as strategies to escape the drastic measures the government had resorted to in combating the Yoeme. Still, very few of them switched sides in this manner.

The apprehended Yaquis were intensely interrogated, even tortured, in order to get to information about the rebels and their whereabouts. Through this the Yoeme came to be known for their resilience under torture.[47] But when threatened with deportation some did talk, hinting at the terror this possibility carried for them. To these Yoeme the thought of being removed from their homeland was unbearable, yet the minutes only dryly state that the Yaquis in question were "offering to help."[48] But the very same minutes often also recorded only very vague answers, for instance admitting to helping others in very minor ways and a long time ago.[49] Many Yaquis even under duress claimed not to know where their *parientes,* their fellow Yaquis, had gone. They had 'lost' weapons just before they had been arrested or they had been 'stolen.' They told on Yaquis long dead, thus rendering the denunciation ineffective. Furthermore, they gave incomplete names or claimed not to know them at all, dead-ending the government efforts in yet another way. Some admitted to having fed the rebels, claiming to have done it out of fear or saying that everybody did so. But others also denounced neighbors, friends, or even family members. Only very few of the Yoeme admitted freely to their own direct and intentional involvement in the rebellion while yet others refused to say anything at all. Indeed, after interrogating the Yaqui Miguel León, his captors stated: "No quizo decir nada, que mejor quiere morir."[50] This Yoeme would have chosen to die rather than talk. Yet even those who did talk—quite possibly in a bid to avoid the very fate those they denounced would have to suffer as a consequence of this betrayal—did not necessarily escape deportation.[51] Furthermore, those Yoeme who assisted the government even in minor ways, like working as messengers, were often considered traitors by their own people and treated accordingly.[52]

Apparently removal to the Yoeme was an incredibly harsh measure, suggesting that earlier on Díaz had been correct in assuming them to prefer death to exile. And by 1904 the deportations had increased so much that they had come to be an obvious threat to the tribe. In 1904 alone the surviving official correspondence in Sonora mentions 822 Yaquis to be scheduled for deportation or to have been deported already, mostly in small groups.[53] Four years later, in 1908, the number came up to 1198.[54] Both Yucatán and Oaxaca were mentioned as destinations for the shipments of Yoeme but the former decidedly more than the latter.[55] It therefore seems likely that the main destination was Yucatán and only a fraction of the deportees were sent to Oaxaca. This may have been the result of Yucatecan demand for labor or possibly of the influence of the Yucatecan plantation owners. Yet not everything worked according to such logical principles.

In the venture that was removal, the decision of who had to leave and who got to stay was not always a logical one. Some Yoeme who admitted to be involved in the rebellion were let go while others, including children, were deported. And even those Yaquis who had fought for the government were not necessarily safe from deportation.[56] A few of the captured men were always hanged though it is impossible to tell from the source material why some were selected for this punishment and others went free. Hanging might have been used by the government forces as an intimidation tactic as repeatedly the corpses of Yaquis were left dangling in the trees, serving as a warning to others more than their mere disappearance by means of removal could have done. As the emphasis on this form of punishment in the letter from the Nine Captains made clear, hanging was considered a horrible fate.[57] Many *pacíficos* fled the *haciendas* for fear of either being hanged or being deported. One such group of workers who left a *hacienda* in September of 1904 had actually voiced their fear of hanging right before they took flight. Among these Yaquis had been a blind man, someone who at least in theory would not have needed to be afraid of being suspect of implication with the rebellion and who most likely would not have been deported because his disability made him undesirable for plantation work.[58] But he, too, left out of sheer terror of the terrible fate and the threat of his dead body being left behind to rot in a tree or being forced to leave his homeland.

Right around this time the government ceased its efforts at disguising the deportations, and instead tried to pass them off as benevolent acts as they permitted the Yaquis to live. Yet to the Yoeme, deportation was the harshest punishment they ever had to face since they were deeply rooted in the Yaqui River Valley, the *Yaquimi*. In view of all this Alan Knight has termed the fight against the Yaquis a 'crusade.'[59]

Considering the drastic measures taken against the Yoeme, the *hacendados* and sometimes even the local authorities were reluctant to file precise and exact reports when requested to do so, let alone to volunteer any information about the Yaquis. After all, by doing that they more or less sent away their irreplaceable workers, causing themselves great financial damages. So the reports on entire districts being free of Yaquis may have been optimistic. And as the Yaquis had always been very mobile there could never be sufficient troops to hinder their movements completely, something that for instance the weapon runs over the United States border proved. When auxiliary troops or groups of *vecinos* pursued rebels one could at times detect what appears to be a certain reluctance to actually catch up with them. It almost seemed like they went through the motions without actually wanting to apprehend the fugitives or to engage in a fight with them. This most probably did not merely happen out of concern for the scarcity of labor but also out of sheer fear. And even the *rurales* and other official troops were often unable to apprehend the plundering rebel groups. So even though they were under serious pressure and clearly suffered from the drastic measures employed against them the Yoeme had not yet exhausted their recourses and may at times even have benefited from white sympathy and/or timidity.

In their raids, the Yaquis took everything that could be of use to them; they even stripped the corpses of the opponents they had killed.[60] Still, there is no way of telling how many of the attacks taking place during the rebellion were actually undertaken by the Yoeme as they were also a convenient scapegoat to blame any kind of crime on. Only in very few cases were the real villains found out, like the time when some *vaqueros,* cowboys, had disguised themselves as Yaquis when carrying out a raid.[61] Still, most raids and attacks were blamed on the Yoeme. By 1907, the Indians who had formerly been praised as untiring workers were passed off as a "tribu cobarde villana y asesina," as a cowardly and villainous tribe of assassins.[62]

SEMI-PRIVATE VENTURE

In view of the rebels' success in still somehow at times eluding apprehension and castigation or deportation, by 1907 the government's step to adopt deportation as the official policy becomes almost logical and even understandable from the official point of view.[63] It was a measure in part born out of desperation but also a cunning business decision. It is not evident from the sources available who was behind this decision or even the idea behind the program. Hu-DeHart speaks of the "ruling elites of Sonora and Yucatán" and Raquel Padilla Ramos corroborates this.[64] Yet this does not explain why a few Yaquis were sent to Oaxaca rather than to Yucatán. However, the information that can be found in the archives in Sonora and Yucatán is also rather sketchy. The apprehension and the rounding up of Yaquis clearly seems to have fallen among the responsibilities assigned to various Sonoran government officials like the prefects. Troops were used to guard the captives and the latter were often kept in prisons, buildings owned by the government. The official correspondence also points to at least a degree of governmental involvement in the organization of the shipment of Yaquis at least to their first stopover on their way to Yucatán.[65] What is startling is that some areas of the project are so well documented through official governmental and military correspondence while others remain almost entirely in the dark. This may be due to the fact that certain government officials, (ab)used their positions for some kind of semi-private business enterprise.

To the federal government the officials could justify the deportations as a necessary cleanup-program in response to the Yaqui rebellion while at the same time they themselves stood to benefit financially from sending the Yaquis to a Yucatán as starved for labor as Sonora. These men may have received money for their efforts and might also at times have benefited from the sales of the Indians' belongings. Money changing hands like this would have contributed to the talk of the Yaquis being outrightly sold into slavery.[66] And the Sonorans in charge of the deportations would not have suffered from them the way others from the same area did. They would not have deprived themselves of Yaqui labor the way they did others as there is evidence that as late as 1905 there was no shortage of Yaqui labor on the hacienda of Rafael Izábal, one of the key figures of the deportation venture, and that he maybe even received new contingents of Yaquis.[67] The henequen industry on Yucatán was booming and considered to be of higher importance than the Sonoran economy. Yet it is doubtful if this program had ever been undertaken if the men in charge had only been government officials and not also private businessmen with a knack for advancing their own fortunes.[68] Individuals involved could profit handsomely through the deportations and also through the sale of the Indians' belongings.[69] Greed and private profit seem to have been crucial in the venture that was deportation.

Yet while individuals may have profited from the venture this was not necessarily so for the Mexican state, at least not in purely financial terms. However, for the government this may have been an acceptable price to pay to clear the so-called Yaqui nuisance from Sonora and supplying Yucatán with much-needed labor. About the costs of 'project deportation,' the Sonoran sources reveal next to nothing. But costs were incurred all along the way, for instance when it came to guarding the Yoeme. The Secretary of State authorized funds for this purpose, "a efecto de vigilar á los indios yaquis prisioneros de guerra," for the guarding of the Yaquis held as so-called prisoners of war.[70] Various ships were supposed to take the Yaquis a part of the way to Yucatán, their final destination. At least one of the vessels mentioned was a warship which might have made this part of the transport free as far as the Sonoran government was concerned.[71] In 1907, Luis Torres who then served as governor of the Yaqui town Tórin, asked the Secretary of War for a "buque de guerra," a warship so that 200 Yaquis of both sexes could be deported.[72] However, this form of transportation would have caused further expenses to the military and the federal government. But since this was only a part of the trip to Yucatán at some point in time further costs must have arisen through the enforcement of removal, even though it seems like shipments of Yoeme were only sent out once a sufficient number of them had become available for deportation, "suficientes para completar el viaje de un buque."[73] This is even more probable since there is no evidence that the second leg of the shipment was also conducted by warships. However, it remains unclear who covered the costs for this part of the journey. When after the Mexican Revolution the deportations were resumed under a new government some cotton growers asked for a contingent of Yaquis and offered to arrange for part of the transport.[74]

(This application was turned down as the Yaquis in question were already spoken for.) It is possible that this suggestion was made with knowledge of the arrangements that had been customary the first time around.

Some captives were also hired out to work on *haciendas* in Sonora.[75] Presumably the money they earned went at least partly to the state. The passages of the Yaquis to their Sonoran employers were paid for by the latter, presumably as they stood to benefit the most from this arrangement. The practice in these instances was for the state government to pay up front only to be later reimbursed.[76] Again the procedure may have been similar when it came to the deportees to Yucatán. As contemporary spectators spoke of an outright sale of Yaquis to Yucatán, the money to cover the expenses for the transports may have come from the Yaquis' recipients.[77] The money that did exchange hands, no matter if as a fee or a real sales price, may have been used to cover such costs. Or maybe the Yucatecan employers specifically paid for at least part of the passage. And to the government footing the bill for the first part of the Yoeme's voyage may have seemed like an investment, like an acceptable price to pay for the elimination of the Yaquis from Sonora.

The peak of the deportations was probably around the year 1908. Exact numbers are not known but it seems to be certain that thousands of Yaquis—and not only Yaquis but also other Indians—were removed from their homes this way. Raquel Padilla, as a preliminary estimate, has calculated a number of over 6,000 Yaqui deportees to Yucatán alone.[78] Other estimates for the period between 1902 and 1908 run as high as 15,000 to Yucatán and Oaxaca together.[79] Even assuming a population of 30,000 Yoeme on the eve of the deportations, which is probably too high a figure, that would still mean that the tribe lost between one-fourth and one-half of the entire Sonoran Yaqui population. And these numbers do not even include the Yoeme who escaped over the border to the United States or those who died as a consequence of the fighting.

The apprehension of the Yoeme generally seems to have been followed by their transfer into special camps or by imprisonment. They were then shipped by boat from Guyamas down the coast, marched across the width of Mexico in order to be shipped again, to Yucatán, their final destination. At least parts of the deportations were thoroughly organized in some of their aspects. The main problem seems to have been the apprehension of the Yaquis in Sonora. On this first step all the following hinged. From that moment on, the captives were watched closely and therefore the chances to escape were minimal.[80] However, even this effective undertaking had its occasional slips. In one case, a captive Yaqui was accidentally sent to join the government troops as a replacement for a regular soldier. As it turned out, the Yaqui had been supposed to be deported and as a result of this stroke of luck was at least temporarily saved from this fate.[81] But apart from some glitches the deportation venture and especially the shipments of Yaquis seem to have been well organized, particularly on the Sonoran side. After the problem of Yellow Fever had become an issue of importance among the Yaquis deported to Yucatán, it was arranged to have them vaccinated even before they ever left Sonora when previously they had only received the necessary vaccinations upon their arrival on Yucatán, if at all.[82] Once the Yoeme deportees reached the Yucatán peninsula a thought-out structure was in place as well, but the voyage in-between seems to have been more improvised and ad-hoc.

THE TOLL OF DEPORTATION

The deportations were aggravated for the Sonoran Yaquis by the closing of the borders to the United States. Previously, they had been able to escape to Arizona, but due to a recession in the United States the borders were now more efficiently closed than ever before—though still not hermetically enough to keep some Yaquis from successfully crossing them, usually to obtain weapons.

As the Yoeme ran more and more out of options it became harder and harder for them to keep up the fight. So by 1908, the deportations had taken their final toll on the rebellion, they had removed the base that had supported the venture for so long. The same year, a delegation of Yaquis approached the officials for peace—under the traditional conditions of keeping their arms while keeping intruders out of their territory. It is telling that the Yaquis seeking peace were *pacíficos* and not rebels.[83] Not surprisingly the government refused these demands as it had the upper hand in the conflict and thus probably felt it could dictate the conditions. But once negotiations had been initiated both sides seemed interested in further exploring this option. So in May of 1908, government representatives met with the rebel chieftain Luis Bule to explain to him their conditions.[84] They required complete submission to the government and also disarmament.[85] In return they promised necessities like food and clothing, among other things, and for the Yoeme to be allowed to keep a few hunting weapons. Bule was also supposed to convince the other rebel leaders to surrender. In turn, Bule asked for the return of the Yaquis who had been deported to Yucatán.[86] Furthermore, he refused to accept any of the proposed conditions and asked for time to gather the *parientes,* the other members of the tribe, so that the matter could be properly discussed among them.[87] While Bule had asked for an extension for just this purpose this had not been granted as negotiator Luis Torres, who probably can be counted among the major beneficiaries of the deportations, was doubtful and distrustful about the underlying motives.[88] Unfortunately, as Bule did not represent all the Yaquis and was not given the time to consult with all of them, he could not convince the other Yoeme to surrender and so the deadline to turn over the weapons could not be met. Infuriated, the government enforced the deportations with renewed vigor, just as it had threatened to do in early June of 1908 when it had talked specifically about a return of the war and the continuation of deportations to Yucatán.[89]

The largest shipments probably took place in June and July of 1908, when, following orders from Luis Torres and the Secretary of War, all Yaquis were to be deported without any distinction between *broncos* and *pacíficos*.[90] The only exceptions made were for small Yaqui orphans, brought up in non-Yaqui families, not speaking any Yaqui.[91] Even spouses of non-Yaquis and offspring from mixed unions living outside of *Yaquimi* were often included in the shipments though at other times spouses or adopted children were spared.[92] Yoeme children were also distributed to non-Yaquis, presumably as servants.[93] Almost all Yaquis were pursued relentlessly as the Vice-President and the Secretary of War had decreed that all Yaquis, "sin excepción," were to be removed from Sonora, something officials also called a "deportación absoluta."[94] And even those who had come to the aid of the government were not necessarily spared from this fate so terrible to them.[95] On the other hand, those who had offended the government by their conduct were likely to be deported in retaliation, if not hanged.[96] Temporary exceptions were made for those who were sick, possibly because a contagious disease might have endangered the quality or even the survival of the entire shipment.[97]

Since the borders to Arizona were watched more closely, the Yoeme had literally nowhere to go. In July the Secretary of War made it known to the Yaquis that for every attack 500 of them would be deported to Yucatán.[98] This was to be communicated to the *mansos* so that they in turn would relate the news to the rebels. The massive embarkations of Yaquis stopped abruptly and somewhat mysteriously at the end of July of 1908 but smaller numbers continued to be deported.[99] There were also still prices on the heads of Yaquis but by the end of this month the so-called concentration of *pacíficos* was thought to be completed.[100] Maybe the slowdown in the deportations was due to the mounting protests which had been ignored for so long. Sonoran employers were especially outraged since the lack of labor was dragging their economy down. But the consequences for the economy of the state probably would have been without effect as they had been ignored earlier, had not the demand for labor in Yucatán decreased.

The henequen market depended largely on export and thus also suffered from the depression in the United States, possibly having a beneficial effect for the Yaquis. Or maybe the government once again considered the war won and thus may have intended for the easing of the deportations to serve as an incentive to surrender to the government.

In late August of 1908, Bule and his second-in-command, Luis Matus, agreed to the peace conditions from May. This time, he spoke in the name of the eight pueblos, or at least this was assumed by the government.[101] But, as it turned out, once again not all the Yaquis backed Bule. The problems again began with the inability to gather all Yoeme in one place to discuss the options.[102] And even though the initial talks seem to have gone well for the government the Yaquis later insisted on keeping their arms and also their religious ceremonies and practices. They also specifically asked for guarantees for their lives and also for the return of the deported *parientes*.[103] To an extent the government was even willing to compromise. Life guarantees were to be given under the condition of the complete submission of the Yaquis and a few of them were to be allowed to keep their weapons. They were also told that the return of the deportees depended entirely on the conduct of the Sonoran Yaquis.[104] However, the government refused to make any further concessions.

In January of 1909, Luis Bule and some 180 rebels met with government officials to enter into a formal agreement about the original peace conditions and were disarmed. The deportees to Yucatán remained unmentioned in this agreement. But even before the conclusion of the meeting the government representatives present had doubts about the validity of the peace for the Yaquis as a tribe, since not all the rebels had come together for the occasion, hinting at disconformity in the ranks. They were soon to find out that they had been correct in this assumption. For the time being, however, Luis Bule and some of his men were incorporated into the government troops as a special auxiliary force to be used against the remaining rebels. Bule seems to have honestly tried to fulfill his promises and repeatedly sent letters to the rebels still in the sierra, attempting to entice them to surrender. However, only occasionally did a few men come down from the mountains. Luis Espinosa, one of Bule's old comrades, eventually commanded the last faction holding out there. But since the remaining rebels were few in number and did not constitute much of a problem in the eyes of the government, the troops only went after the small groups venturing out of the sierra instead of risking a pursuit in the difficult mountainous terrain. Not much changed the following year, 1910, but compared to previous years the area did indeed appear tranquil with no one but the Espinosa faction occasionally causing trouble. The other Yoeme stayed quiet, finally worn out through the prolonged fighting and the drastic measure of deportation.

Apparently, the government's efforts were finally paying off. "Had it not been for the Mexican Revolution which terminated the Díaz regime in 1911," as Evelyn Hu-DeHart has argued, "it might have succeeded in isolating the Espinosa faction from the rest of the Yaqui people, ultimately destroying it."[105] In the end, the Yaqui tribe was saved from complete disintegration by the outbreak of the Mexican Revolution, because it enabled some of them to go back to their original homes from their Yucatecan (and also their Oaxacan) exile.[106]

Although on the eve of the Mexican Revolution the struggle of the Yaquis still continued on a very small scale, and even though they had been able to hold out against the powerful dictatorship of the Porfiriato, the Yaquis had gained very little in this heroic fight which had furthermore brought them to the verge of destruction. By death and by removal their numbers were severely decimated. They did not manage to avoid intrusions into their land, and these even resumed soon after the Revolution. They suffered from dispersion and fragmentation, as can be seen in the complicated negotiations with the Mexican government where repeatedly different groups were of opposing opinions when it came to accepting or rejecting the government's conditions for peace. Only the one faction under the leadership of Luis Espinosa held up the traditional Yaqui strategy of resistance in an attempt to defend their land and their autonomy. And this faction, the last to keep up the Yaquis' traditional fight and consequently an important factor in keeping their sense of identity, profited from the outbreak of the Mexican Revolution and the Porfiriato's fall from power in 1911. But even the Revolution turned out to be only a break for the Yaquis, only a short suspension in their long struggle for autonomy, as will be seen in the following chapter.

Chapter Nine
Silences from Yucatán

Figure 9-1. Map of Mexico at around the time of the deportations of the Yaquis (places mentioned in the discussion of the Yaquis' removal are shaded in dark grey)

As seen in the previous chapters, over centuries the Sonoran Yaquis' behavior can best be described as non-conformist. This had been the case since their first contacts with Europeans in the early sixteenth century. When they felt the situation called for it, the Yaquis always seemed willing to rise up for their demands. In their conflicts with non-Yaquis, the

Yoeme had proved that they considered themselves to be outside of the social hierarchy envisioned by the government. It became evident by their steadfast attempts to resist incorporation and the annexation of their lands. The latter did not meet with complete success and there were some territorial losses and encroachment. However, the Yaquis retained something like an autonomous space, both in a metaphorical way—their separateness and autonomy—and also in a very tangible, practical way—the territory they referred to as *Yaquimi*. And they managed to do so even in the face of the massive military intervention during the Porfiriato. Still, the repeated failure of the negotiations, the problems of representation and decision-making, as well as the evident fragmentation illustrate just how much strain the campaign and the deportations had put on the Sonoran Yaquis. Yet while Yoeme resistance may have been in decline from around 1908 onward, it was nonetheless kept up until saved by the Mexican Revolution. However, the success with which the Yaquis had kept up their fight and defended their land and autonomy before the Díaz regime took over eventually contributed to the deportation and forced exile of a significant number of Yaquis to Yucatán, where their will to continue their resistance would be sorely tested.

The life of the exiled Yoeme was characterized by an uncharacteristical and thus eerie quietness as well as by an almost complete absence of any attempts to resist.[1] This surrender, unimaginable for Sonora, is puzzling especially in view of the Yoeme's long history of resistance but can be explained by the situation they encountered in their forced exile, by the hardships they were exposed to and especially through the few occasions when Yaquis voices, however indirect, broke the silence on Yucatán.

DESTINATION YUCATÁN

While the continued resistance in Sonora ensured that the Yoeme never vanished from the official correspondence, the same cannot be said about Yucatán, the place where the vast majority of the deportees ended up. This already indicates the drastic change in the Yaquis' behavior that was to take place after their displacement. The deportations took place without leaving many traces in the official paperwork, and even less in Yucatán than in Sonora.[2] This might suggest that they were a private or semi-private business enterprise as much as a federal and a state policy to remove the Yaquis from Sonora, even though the deportees were sometimes referred to as 'Prisoners of War.' Edward Spicer even speaks of quota having to be met on the Sonoran end of the enterprise, also hinting at a business rationale behind the events.[3] As seen from the chapter on Yaqui removal, some

Silences from Yucatán

official involvement is doubtless especially on the Sonoran side, as well as judging from a contract covering the Yucatecan side of the venture.

By the time the deported Yoeme eventually reached the Yucatán peninsula, it seems that most of them were already slated to go to a fixed destination, a plantation. At least in some cases future destinations and the owners of the respective *haciendas* were mentioned in connection with Yaquis waiting in the harbor of Progreso.[4] How, where, and exactly by whom this was arranged remains in the dark but it seems clear that some Sonoran and Yucatecan élites collaborated effectively.[5] Thus, two birds were killed with one stone: Sonora was rid of the 'Yaqui menace' and Yucatán at the same time helped out with much needed labor. What the exact conditions were to which the Yaquis were sent—and maybe even sold—to the henequen plantations also remains in the dark.[6] Money exchanging hands does not necessarily imply an outright sale, not even in the context at hand but could also have been a fee for organizational tasks and paperwork, or might have paid for transport. Still, the conditions the Yaquis found on the plantations probably approximated slavery in most practical aspects.[7] Some of the language used in the official correspondence especially on Yucatán also more or less implies this, talking of Yaquis "pertenecientes á," belonging to, somebody.[8]

A surviving contract from the year 1900 specified the conditions under which the Yaquis were supposed to work though these may have been changed later on or may have varied throughout. This contract was signed by the Secretaría del Estado (de Yucatán) and Manuel Arrigunaga, the representative of a female plantation owner.[9] It specifically referred to "familias pertenecientes a los indios rebeldes del río Yaqui que han sido hecho prisioneros," to families of Indian rebels from the Yaqui River who had been taken prisoners.[10] It talked about adequate work and pay and even a share of the profits of the work the Indians were to do on the plantation. The *hacendado* was supposed to supply houses, firewood, and to pay for medical services including medication. Children were to go to especially established schools at night. All of this was to be checked upon by a governmental inspector. However, all the protective functions could easily have been rendered useless by advancing the Yaquis a sum of money and thus keeping them in debt until the sum was paid back, as another provision of the contract provided for. It also remains unclear how the contract could be terminated and no specific time of duration is mentioned therein. A clause specified that it would be declared void after multiple non-compliances on the part of the *hacendado*, but he would only be fined for initial transgressions.[11]

No evidence for the existence of the government inspector mentioned in the document, nor for any fines or voided contracts has been recorded.

But since this is the only contract of this kind on file, the conclusions that can be drawn from it are limited. It does show, however, that the Yucatecan state government was indeed in some way actively involved in the removal of the Yoeme. Similar to what took place on the Sonoran end of the enterprise, it is probable that the Yucatecan forces behind the venture were high state officials using and abusing their positions and that this was probably condoned or even encouraged by the federal government.

FEVER BREAKS

In Sonora, as has become evident, the Yaquis could not be silenced by the deportations. Official correspondence was filled with all kinds of reports and remarks concerning them up until the outbreak of the Revolution and even later.[12] This proved that the resistance survived and that the Yoeme's demands remained essentially unchanged. "No aceptarán la paz si no á condición de que se retiren todos los blancos y les dejen el Rio completamente libre" is how a report to the Sonoran governor described the Yaquis' demands in 1911.[13] They would not accept any offer of peace unless all whites would leave the river. In 1913 Luis Espinosa and others reiterated that they were not hostile to anyone without a reason, "nosotros no somos hostiles á nadie sin que para ello haya razón."[14] They declared that their fight was only to recover their rights and their lands which had been taken from them with brute force, "nuestra lucha se reduce únicamente a reconquistar nuestros derechos y nuestras tierras arrebatadas por la fuerza bruta," though they also acknowledged that they had to eat.[15] They seem to specifically have objected to non-Yaquis sowing on Yaqui lands.[16] Thus they insisted on land and autonomy and were willing to fight in their defense.

Yet once in Yucatán the situation changed drastically. "Deportation created a new, much more severe kind of diaspora, which saw not only individual Yaquis flung farther afield than ever but communities and families torn apart as well, that caused the legendary Yaqui stamina finally to a near breaking point," as Evelyn Hu-DeHart has observed.[17] It was aggravated by the breaking up of families, of husbands and wives as well as of others and their children which at least sometimes took place.[18] And this extreme diaspora was one of the prime causes for Yaqui resistance to disappear once the deportees had reached Yucatán.

Consequently, hardly a trace can be found about the Yaquis once they had reached the peninsula and the largest part of the information available is due to the fact that a sizeable number of them at one time or other suffered from Yellow Fever.[19] Yucatecan officials were desperately

Silences from Yucatán

trying to curb outbreaks of the much-feared disease. They called it "el gran problema sanitario de nuestro Estado"[20] and saw in it "una barrera en nuestra conveniencia para la inmigración," a barrier that would impede the much-desired immigration which in turn was supposed to further modernization.[21] The Black Vomit, as the disease was also called, is spread by a mosquito and therefore can infect many people over a short period of time. Fighting the mosquitoes in the dense jungles of the peninsula proved to be all but impossible, so all precautions had to be taken to keep the fever, which existed in other parts of the country as well, from entering the area in the first place. For a while the officials were especially concerned with passengers who had passed through or come directly from Veracruz, since the fever had been spreading rapidly there. During peak times of the recurring epidemic, the Yaquis disembarked in Progreso only to find themselves in camps yet again, this time being vaccinated against *la Fiebre Amarilla*, if that had not already been done during one of the stops along the way.[22] By 1908 they had often already been vaccinated in Sonora, before they even set out for their long journey to Yucatán.[23]

In the matter of the Black Vomit the officials were very strict and diligent, producing so-called *Boletines Sanitarios*, documentations about people suffering from the often fatal disease, in an effort to curb it by increasing their knowledge about the way it spread.[24] On the whole, the quality of the information that can be drawn from these papers varies considerably. And in all likelihood, only a fraction of the sick Yoeme was actually among those who were recorded in the *Boletines Sanitarios* as others may have remained on the *haciendas*, in spite of rules and regulations saying they should be reported and taken to a hospital.[25] Still, these documents make up the brunt of the surviving official correspondence about the Yoeme on Yucatán. And as such they shed a little additional light on the character of the semi-private deportation enterprise, for instance by supplying information on the route into Yucatecan captivity.

In 1901, fourteen-year old Josefa Lehan was a suspect of Yellow Fever and thus recorded in a *Boletín Sanitario* from July 30, which clearly identified her as Yaqui, something that only seldomly happened.[26] Josefa, who was twelve or thirteen years old when she was deported, reported to have passed through 'Vera-Cruz' on her way to Yucatán, and maybe that is where she had first been exposed to the virus.[27] As the girl was already in a bad condition and vomiting blood when she was sent to town to get medical attention it is highly probable that she did not survive. Similarly, the following year a woman who was originally from Tórin stated to have passed through Tampico.[28] From the time of her arrival on the Yucatán peninsula she stayed on a *finca*, until her sickness made it necessary to send her to Mérida.

In 1907, 74 Yaquis were mentioned in the *boletines* as suspects of Yellow Fever.[29] Often it was not clear if the diseased Yaquis recovered or died, but several times a detailed travel route into captivity was mentioned for the respective individual who had been "desterrado por el Gobierno Federal," removed from their land by the Federal Government. One male individual spent four months in Maitorena (Sonora), then four days in Veracruz and then arrived in Mérida, presumably via the harbor of Progreso.[30] A Yaqui woman mentioned in the same document reportedly spent four months in Guyamas (Sonora), and then traveled via San Blas, Tepic, Guadalajara, Mexico City and Veracruz to Yucatán. She was hospitalized the very day she arrived, making it evident that she had picked up the disease somewhere along the way. On May 13 the Yoeme José Valencia, who said he had been away from 'su tierra' for five months also said that he had stayed for four months in Guaymas, four days in San Blas, five days in Mexico City and one in Veracruz, to eventually arrive in Progreso.[31] He reported to have been ill for six days.[32] In an undated *boletín* of that year nine Yaquis, five men and four women, were mentioned as suspects of the feared disease. They had left 'su tierra,' Sonora, fifteen days previously and had arrived in Mérida three days before, having traveled 'directly.'[33] They all ended up on the same *hacienda*, owned by Olegario Molina, one of the key figures in the deportation undertaking. The next diseased Yoeme to appear in the *boletines* was a male Yaqui who had left his 'tierra' two years before, coming through Veracruz where he spent two days. Then there were two men who left together to come directly to Yucatán, passing through the port of San Blas where they stayed three months, and through Veracruz where they spent one day, to arrive two days previously on the finca Kuché, property of José I. Espinosa. The same year, three other individuals spent two days in the port of Veracruz, while one stayed there for just a day.[34]

In August of 1911 a soldier named Juan Valenzuela, originally from Ures (Sonora) displayed signs of Yellow Fever.[35] He had been in Puebla, Veracrúz, and Progreso (on his way to Valladolid, also on Yucatán). Two days after he had been admitted to the hospital it turned out that he is merely suffering from the flu, making him one of the luckier ones. Another Yaqui suspected of having contracted the Black Vomit stated to have passed through Tampico.[36]

Taking into account all the travel-related information collected from the *boletines*, one can deduct a general route that confirms Evelyn Hu-DeHart's findings. After having been captured and rounded up in various camps or prisons in Sonora, where the Yoeme sometimes remained for great lengths of time, the route seems to have generally been more or less the same. Starting out in Guyamas / Sonora, where the deportees were 'collected' for shipment, they were taken to San Blas and Tepic on the western coast of Mexico. They were then marched to Veracruz, passing through or by Guadalajara, Mexico City and Puebla. From there they were again by ship taken to Progreso and then sent to their future destinations on Yucatán.[37] But, as seen by the repeated mention of Tampico, alternative routes may have existed.[38]

This evidence suggests that the middle part of the Yaquis' journey was the most improvised, with routes that sometimes varied. Presumably whoever organized this part of the trip would have looked out for the best and cheapest opportunities to get the Yaquis to Yucatán. Accordingly, the size of the shipments arriving on Yucatán also varied considerably, suggesting that this part of the journey, which was conducted by commercial vessels, was undertaken on a space-available basis. This is supported by those *boletines* that supply information about the number of incoming persons not immune to the Yellow Fever. These *boletines* usually gave the name of the ship on which these people arrived but only rarely the origin of the passengers. Still, in some instances 'yaquis' or 'jornaleros yaquis,' Yaqui workers, were referred to. Sometimes as few as twelve were on board of such a commercial ship, while at other times the number came to well over four hundred. In some instances, the Yaquis were listed after the regular passengers, as if they were a commodity rather than human beings, making it seem likely they would have traveled in the cargo hold of the ships.

It is difficult to estimate the time the trip may have taken because the surviving sources are not very specific. For many Yaquis the entire journey seems to have lasted between two weeks and about a month, not including the time they had to wait in Sonora.[39] The longer time spans mentioned for the voyage were probably due to the fact that no space was available on any vessel at the time the Yaquis arrived at the port in question and hence the deportees had to wait there for the next ship willing to take them. Thus the journey into captivity could take on different faces for different Yoeme yet it would always have been a hard transition.

FEVER STRATEGIES

Although there is next to no evidence for Yaqui resistance on Yucatán that does not imply that the Yoeme just docilely settled into their new lives of quasi-slavery. Some of them appeared in court records, albeit usually for only very minor and individual transgressions. (These will be examined later on in this chapter.) And many of them attempted to make the best of a bad situation, making the most of the little freedoms allowed them. While life on the *haciendas* would always have been hard and sometimes dangerous, on some plantations the Yaquis to an extent found themselves in a position to pursue their traditions and customs.[40] And even after the outbreak of the Mexican Revolution, when many Yoeme left the plantations and often went to Mérida, they were not left without resources.[41]

There is for instance the case of María Yoqihua, who in all probability checked herself into the quarantine hospital several times, possibly as a survival strategy.[42] A woman of that name was hospitalized in 1912 on three different occasions, all within the month of July.[43] The entries were always identified as María Yoqihua from Sonora, yet with varying places of origin, Tórin ("Tori"), Cócorit ("Cori"), and Guaymas ("Uaymas"). The woman was in her late 40s or early 50s, lived in Mérida, and did 'female work,' "labores de su sexo." She was also married and had been 'out of Sonora' for six to eleven years. On July 15, she checked into the hospital O'Horán for the first time, to be released the following day, having been diagnosed with the flu. Four days later, on July 20, one María Yoqihua was again admitted to the hospital, once more under the suspicion of having contracted Yellow Fever. This time she remained hospitalized for two days, to be released once again with the diagnosis of influenza. She came back the same day, to remain for only one night. Again, the medical personnel's first guess was the flu but María was released on July 23, this time having been diagnosed with 'paludismo' (malaria).

It seems not unlikely that María Yoqihua had left a *hacienda* after the imminent arrival of the revolution in Yucatán had enabled her to do so and was thus forced to fend for herself. Living in Mérida, she indeed found herself to be sick, though not actually suffering from the dreaded *Fiebre Amarilla*. But while being hospitalized for the first time, she probably discovered the benefits of having at least a sheltered place to sleep. Consequently, she may have felt inclined to come back instead of dealing with her disease and weakness all by herself.

María Yoquihua was not an isolated case and, and while none of the evidence is absolutely clear and convincing, there are several identical factors that speak for the possibility of a few Yaquis checking themselves into the hospital as a survival strategy, to find shelter and maybe even food. In all likelihood, the city did not offer enough work and income for all the refugees.[44] Accordingly, they had to think of different ways to make a living and to ensure their survival. Checking themselves into the hospital, one of the few places where at least a few things were for free may have been one of the strategies.[45] Men often seem to have enlisted in the armed forces, but the options available to women at this point in time were more limited, leaving them to sell food or to find a companion to provide for them and their children.[46]

Silences from Yucatán

While it cost countless Yoeme their lives, the Black Vomit helped to give some insights into their history in exile, hinting at the hardships of their existence in quasi-slavery but also at strategies for survival and at attempts to conserve their culture and to return home.

RESISTANCE ON TRIAL

Yet while the Yellow Fever disclosed many small details about the Yaquis' existence on Yucatán it is the instances of Yoeme appearing in court cases that tell most about the life of the deportees. They tell the Yucatecan story most clearly and may help to explain the lack of resistance there.[47]

In the court proceedings against Octaviano Bacasena, a hacienda worker of eighteen years of age, the court's investigation uncovered a fight between him and his coworkers, compañeros de trabajo, also presumably Yoeme. Bacasena, a native of Alamos (Sonora) worked on the hacienda Cancachén; Augustín Matos, the victim, was a servant "del Señor Ingeniero David Casáres."[48] On October 17, 1907, at around eight o'clock at night, Bacasena and three of his compañeros were at the Estación de Cholul, and all of them were drinking together. As the victim, Augustín Matos, recalled, they had been drinking and talking to a man called Antonio Valencia when something Matos said caused Bacasena to get mad at him and to lash out with a bottle. Of what character exactly Matos' wounds were cannot be ascertained, but a physician declared them to be of the kind that "ordinariamente sanan en un término no mayor de quince días sin poner en peligro la vida," the type that heals in under two weeks and does not endanger the life.[49] (As it turned out, the healing process took slightly longer than fifteen days.) None of the witnesses recalled what Matos had said to cause Bacasena to make the latter so mad at him. Octaviano Bacasena himself claimed that he thought Matos wanted to fight with yet another man, Villanueva, and Bacasena intended to intervene.[50] Bacasena also stated Matos to have been drunk. The witnesses, Ignacio Molina and Antonio Valencia, did not throw any more light on the matter and just claimed to ignore the reason for the falling-out. In the end, since Matos' wounds were not particularly grave, Octaviano Bacasena was sentenced to 24 days of arrest and was to cover the costs of the trial.

In June of 1908, Francisca Loor Ségua received a sentence of 69 days of arrest. A native of Hermosillo (Sonora), she lived on the hacienda Tanil where she did 'female work.'[51] Francisca was married and in her early forties.[52] The evidence compiled states that Francisca, the 'mujer,' the wife or woman of José Salazar, was accused for bodily harming the 'mujer' of a man named José María Mendoza.[53] The incident happened on the same *hacienda*, Fanil

[Tanil], where all of them lived. Not untypically there was some confusion about the names of one of the persons involved, probably because the typical Yaqui names sounded more than strange to Yucatecan ears. First, the defendant was referred to as Francisca Flores until she explicitly stated her name to be Francisca Loor Ségua.[54] During the length of the court proceedings a veritable drama of love, hate, and jealousy between exiled Yoeme unfolded. The victim, Luz Yoqihua, reported that Francisca came to her house at ten o'clock in the morning and attacked her with a chisel. Luz cried out for help and a female neighbor came to her aid. Francisca herself readily admitted to the attack and explained that it happened in revenge for a beating she herself had received from her husband a week before. As it turned out, her husband had been having an affair with Luz Yoqihua, which angered Francisca greatly. So she took the opportunity when she knew Luz to be home alone, "to give her what she deserved."[55] Luz' wounds were not very grave; something that always was of prime importance to the courts. But what really must have spoken for Francisca was that Luz was suffering from a venereal disease which Francisca's husband had contracted through her and passed on to his wife. Luz herself had been in such a bad condition on account of this disease that in May of that year she had had to be hospitalized. Because of good conduct, part of Francisca's sentence was lifted.

While the court cases involving Yaquis were more than scarce with only two criminal offenses by *Yoeme* in 1908—and one of them even with the crime having already taken place in 1907—two more can be found in 1912.[56] These two cases confirm the tendency of Yaquis to isolate themselves from non-Yaquis which has already become obvious in the preceding ones. In both, the offense was bodily harm, in one instance committed by a man, in the other by a woman.

At the bottom of the occurrences in the month of May was the "jornalero yaqui" Miguel Buitimea, who had been attacked by his compatriot Fidencio Alvarado Fodo.[57] Buitimea was 40 years old, married, and from Magdalena (Sonora). In 1912 he worked and lived on the finca San Ignacio. Alvarado, his attacker, was 26, unmarried, originally from Tórin (Sonora) and residing on the same *hacienda*. Both men were drunk. Alvarado was reported to have said "voy a chingar al yaqüi, voy a matarlo," threatening to 'screw' and kill 'the Yaqui.'[58] The two fought and Miguel Buitimea was knocked down. He claimed to have had no chance because he was intoxicated while Alvarado was sober. Apparently there were some bystanders but none known to Miguel Buitimea. The latter added that he believed Alvarado to have been fed up with the work for a while, "disgustado por trabajo."[59] In contrast to what Buitimea had claimed, Alvarado also admitted to having been drunk. Thus both Buitimea and Alvarado seem to have been under the influence. The resulting fight culminated in Buitimea having the tip of his nose bitten off by Alvarado. The defendant claimed to remember nothing of the fight itself but knew some things since his wife, Luz Giosa, had later told him about it. The court made an attempt at obtaining her for a statement but she seemed to have left the *finca*. (Indeed, she may have been among those who left the *haciendas* in 1912, making their way to Mérida and presumably also to Progreso.[60]) Apparently, other Yaquis were also missing from the same *finca*.[61] Alvarado was punished by imprisonment.[62]

In the court proceedings against María de la Luz Flores, taking place in January of 1912, we have not only a case of Yaquis fighting among themselves but also of a couple quarrelling. The whole affair puzzled the court so much that it was investigated repeatedly. It was assumed that Luz had wounded her spouse with a knife but since she was also injured the investigators were unclear about what had actually taken place. The defendant, Luz, was a widow, originally from Sonora, and thirty years old. As it turned out in the course of the hearings, she had been living with the victim, Juan Fierros, for seven years, presumably always on the same hacienda, Tixnuc. Upon questioning, she stated that they had never legalized their relationship, which in the following was therefore referred to by the court as a 'concubinato.' Juan was 26, unmarried, and also from Sonora. Upon him, four large wounds had been inflicted and, when questioned, he blamed his spouse Luz for causing them. He claimed the weapon to have been an axe, not a knife, and the woman to have been drunk. He also said that there had been no falling-out with her and that he could not explain her behavior to himself. Luz, however, reported to be ignorant of who had attacked and wounded Juan since she had been very intoxicated and hence could not remember anything. Luz and a friend, Flora Velazco, had been drinking *aguardiente* ("anis") in Flora's house. When asked if anyone else had been present, Luz named a woman called Josefa whose last name she did not know. However, she did declare this woman to be a "Yaqui de origen."[63]

The first witness to testify was Marcelo Manuelino, a neighbor.[64] He was a worker, 26 years old, and originally from Ures (Sonora) but now making a living as a worker on the *hacienda* Tixnuc. His statement has been lost but it seems like he supported Fierros' story. Yet the court also wanted Josefa, Luz' female friend, to bear witness but no documentation of this can be found among the records.[65] Flora Velazco, the woman Luz had reportedly been drinking with, was questioned in order to find out how much Luz had been having. Apparently, she spoke of "largas y continuas copas de aguardiente," of drinking a lot.[66]

Yet even though several witnesses, neighbors and friends, had been questioned, all of them Yaquis, no one could or would shed any light on the matter. Consequently, Luz was interrogated once again and that time around stated that Juan had hurt her a few days previously, in an attempt to kill her with a knife. So the mysterious knife wounds on Luz were accounted for. Later on, both Juan and Luz seemed to have agreed that he had only wanted to scare and not to hurt or kill her. But, in an attempt to take the knife away from him, she had been injured anyway. Once talking, she also reported that Juan had been speaking about leaving her and about going back home "á su tierra," to his country or land, by himself. He had told her he did not want to be with her anymore. Finally, she also admitted that she did believe she had hurt him with the axe referred to earlier. She explained that when drunk she always got very sad, cried, and remembered the children she had been forced to leave behind in Hermosillo and the one child who had died. This along with the physical and emotional hurt Juan had caused her had finally brought her to the brink and, together with her intoxication, was the cause for attacking him.

Luz was released from prison in March of 1912.

Especially the latter two cases are very revealing about the situation the Yoeme faced on Yucatán. The work must have been very hard and the life probably equally unappealing. Insufficient diet may even have led to cases of mental disturbance.[67] The deportees also had hardly any contacts with other workers on the haciendas.[68] Unfortunately, this also saw them hurting each other instead of venting their anger on others or engaging in their customary resistance. This isolationism may have been due to the language barrier—as some of the Yoeme hardly spoke any Spanish, let alone Maya–, or to *hacendado* policies, or it could have been by choice.[69] Maybe by isolating themselves they somehow tried to keep up their sense of identity.

The most typical and telling one is probably the case of María de la Luz Flores. Through it we gain insights into the situation many *Yoreme* faced and learn how they might have felt. Luz is far removed from her home in Sonora. She was widowed, maybe through the ongoing guerilla fight in Sonora or even the very deportations. Her children were presumably still in Hermosillo and, quite naturally, she missed them unbearably, even though, or maybe because, she had been away from them for at least seven years. Another child of hers had apparently died and she still had not got over the loss. It seems like she had coped with her sadness for the longest time but it resurfaced and overwhelmed her when her situation in enforced captivity changed drastically once again. She had found some consolation and maybe even love through the company of Juan. With the revolution, changes were also brought to Yucatán and consequently many, maybe most, Yaquis left the *haciendas,* as becomes evident from the *boletines* of that time as well as from the case of Buitimea and Alvarado.[70] And Luz' spouse, Juan, also did talk about leaving—leaving the state and leaving her. He wanted to return to his native Sonora and threatened her with not taking her along. Luz may or may not have loved Juan, but he had given her some security over the past years, a sense of belonging. All of a sudden she was faced with being abandoned and being alone once again, with losing what little she had retained without gaining anything in return. She may have feared that by herself she would never make it home and therefore never to see her surviving children and her home again. All of this completely overwhelmed her when her defenses were lowered by alcoholic intoxication. And in this situation she did lose control and both she and Juan got hurt in the process. Yet for us this was a most fortunate occurrence since it prompted a court action and her to testify in the course of it. Thus Luz was one of the few voices breaking the silence from Yucatán.

Other evidence from the court records tentatively supports the theory that Yoeme were trying to hold on to at least some of their traditions.[71] This may not have been a conscious choice but nevertheless shows how important their culture and identity as Yaqui still was to the deportees.

In 1905, Angel Bacamea and Luz Yoquiva were accused of breaking the burial regulations. Luz, the wife of Hilario Buitamea, had given birth to a baby on December 2, 1904. Sadly, the child had died within two days of its birth and the grieving parents had asked another Yaqui, Angel Bacamea, to bury the baby for them.[72] He did so according to the traditions of the Yoeme and thus accidentally broke Yucatecan regulations by leaving the child without a 'proper' internment. Upon discovery of the dead infant's body, a culprit had been sought. Bacamea, probably entirely unaware of having committed a legal infringement, readily confessed. It seems like he had only meant to help out Luz and Hilario; presumably Hilario, who died soon after his child, had been unable to perform the task of laying his dead son to rest himself, and Luz may still have been too weak to do it. Even though the court recognized that the Yaqui had only complied with his people's customs, seventy-two year old Angel was sentenced to one month and fifteen days imprisonment. The child was subsequently interred in the hacienda's graveyard.

This case was an example of Yoeme upholding their own customs and helping each other out. Again there is evidence of Yaquis sticking together—this time without harming each other. The case also illustrates the high mortality on the haciendas.

In addition to the number of Yaqui orphans for whom the courts looked for legal representation, this mortality rate is also evidenced by a number of cases recorded by the court in 1911. In August of that year, the court undertook to determine the cause of the death of Joaquin Flores.[73] Flores, originally from Hermosillo (Sonora), a widower and worker on the finca rústica 'Xecuya,' identified to be of to be of "la raza yaqui" was only 35 years old when he died. The body was identified by Matias González, thirty years old and originally also from Hermosillo. Matias presumed Joaquin to have died from alcohol abuse, stating that he had been found on the street in a state of severe pain and that he had been in the habit of getting drunk and falling asleep on the road. José Duarte, a sixty-year old Yaqui from Sonora, also suspected alcohol to have been the cause of Flores' death. He had known Joaquin since he had been a child and said that he had been the legitimate son of José Flores and Lola Yoquihua and that his wife, Josefa Yuli, had preceded him in death. Duarte was the one to officially identify the body for the required documentation. Other inhabitants of the hacienda, Yoeme and others, had also been present during Joaquin Flores' last hours but had little to add to what González and Duarte had already stated. Their statements merely reinforced that Joaquin's death must have been extremely painful. It is unclear whether the non-Yaquis had even known Flores by name or had only found out about him through his Yaqui companions after he had been discovered in agony.[74]

The court determined that this death did not require any criminal proceedings since it had probably been alcohol that had been responsible for the demise of Flores.[75] Given the number of alcohol-related incidents on file it seems unlikely that this death was an isolated occurrence.[76]

While alcohol also played a part in the killing of Mariano Valencia, the main culprit in this case on record was a non-Yaqui named Augustín Canto.[77] The murder case against him poses the only case found in which some kind of significant interaction between Yaquis and non-Yaquis could at least be suspected. Valencia and his wife, (María) Andrea Machilea, had somehow aroused the ire of Canto who had proceeded to shoot (at) them. It remains unclear whether or not he had meant to harm either of them or if he had just literally taken a shot in the dark. It is difficult to determine exactly what took place since the stories of Valencia, Machilea, and Canto do not add up at all. Valencia furthermore could only be questioned once and in extreme pain before he died from his gunshot wound. He claimed that Canto had been drunk and that he had taken a shot at him without warning. Andrea first stated not to know her assailant but later admitted to have known him before the incident. It seems like she herself was injured either in an attempt to help her wounded husband or maybe during a fight between the two men over her. Another Yaqui, Agapito Septimea, was presumably hurt in an attempt to help Andrea and Mariano against Canto and his brother who had been called to the scene by the commotion.

Much about this case remained unclear, as for instance who had caused Andrea's wounds or how exactly Septimea and Canto's brother had been involved. Canto was sentenced to 15 years but it is unknown what happened to Andrea and her three little children, Fernando, Ygnacio and Micaela, who had suddenly become fatherless.

This is the only case with Yoeme involvement which witnessed a degree of non-Yaqui participation. However, due to the number of unanswered questions, the exact kind of this involvement remains unclear. Judging from Andrea's statement, her contacts with the non-Yaqui Augustín Canto were minimal and that it had been merely the alcohol which had provoked him to kill Mariano Valencia. However, her statement as well as Canto's and others displayed some irregularities. In Andrea's case these could very well have been due to language problems; however, it is equally possible that she was attempting to hide something, as for instance an affair with Canto.[78] Canto may well have intended to portray himself in a better light to avoid a harsher judgment. And especially Agapito Septimea's involvement remains very nebulous.

What is still fairly obvious is the fact that most of the cases which saw Yaqui involvement and made it to the courts seem to have been largely limited to the exiled Yoeme, and that there was hardly any involvement of workers of other ethnicities or even the hacendados or their representatives.[79] Even in the case last discussed it seems likely that the aggression originated with Canto, the non-Yaqui, and not with the Yoeme. The spirit of resistance, which made the Yaquis stand up for themselves, seemed to have been left behind in Sonora.

The reasons for this virtual isolation against non-Yaquis could have been due to language problems or they could well have been much more complex. Since there are virtually no documents from the deportees themselves, it will not be possible to ascertain what really went on. The court documents examined here are the only voice given to the Yaquis on Yucatán.[80] However, many cases would not even have made it to the official courts but instead 'justice' would have been seen to by the hacendados as "by law, the latter were in charge of maintaining 'peace and order,' and of sanctioning minor offenses with, for instance, arrest and corporal punishment. Thus, landowners and administrators became prosecutors, judges, and inflicters of punishment at one and the same time."[81] What the existing documents do tell us is that the Yaquis seemed to have given up their resistance against the authorities once they had been removed from their native Sonora, or more accurately from their traditional territory, and that they largely stuck to themselves even when it came to quarrelling and fighting. Only this explains the almost complete absence of other cases like riots or uprisings by Yaquis—as were typical for Sonora.[82] The way the Yaquis had been distributed to the haciendas may also have been a factor.

Instead of adhering to their customary resistance, many of the deportees seem to have sought refuge in alcohol, as the cases at hand as well as others prove. Still, they kept their sense of (ethnic) identity by limiting their contacts with others and holding on to some of their customs, as evidenced for instance in the traditional burial.[83] Since alcohol seems to have been part of the rations the workers received, the plantation owners must have followed some objective by distributing it, most likely to keep the workers docile. While this worked to an extent, even frequent intoxication could not take the longing away the Yaquis felt for their homeland. The case of Luz and Juan illustrates that the exiled Yoeme never ceased to consider Sonora and more specifically *Yaquimi* to be their home. They refer to their 'tierra' as the place they wanted to go back to yet seemed unable to put up a coordinated fight for it, possibly partly due to the detrimental circumstances they encountered in exile. As laborers were forbidden to leave the haciendas without permission it would have been hard to build up the networks necessary.[84] So even though active rebels had been among those deported to Yucatán their resistance did not survive the move. They had always been outsiders in Yucatán and the hacendados' policies did everything to keep it that way. Therefore, the exiled Yoeme only regained some hope, their return to Sonora, and some of their fighting spirit when the possibility to return home suddenly appeared with the ripples of the revolution reaching Yucatán.

THE ROOTS OF RESISTANCE

There is no clear and conclusive explanation why the Yaquis ceased their resistance upon arrival to Yucatán. As Evelyn Hu-DeHart has concluded: "Deportation created a new, much more severe kind of diaspora, which saw not only individual Yaquis flung farther afield than ever but communities and families torn apart as well, that caused the legendary Yaqui stamina finally to a near breaking point."[85] In Sonora, their resistance drew on a number of elements, like community, land, customs and religion, as Alejandro Figueroa has pointed out.[86] Land probably gained additional importance by being tied closely to religion, customs, and even community so that being removed from the land would have affected the Yoeme in the gravest of ways.[87] Thus I would conclude that land was the link between all these elements. In the documents analyzed here, this became especially obvious when Juan Fierros voiced his desire to return 'a su tierra,' to his land/country. When they were forced away from their homeland the Yucatecan Yaquis had lost a map which had enabled them to navigate through their problems and to structure their lives. So the base for effective resistance lacked in Yucatán, along with feasible perspectives for the deportees and therefore the resistance could not be kept up in exile. This was so even though active fighters had been among the deportees. Isolated from other rebels due to the distribution to different plantations, severed from their communities, and removed from the lands they knew and loved, they lacked the spirit to keep fighting. They also may have known that they stood to gain very little by rebelling so far away from their homeland and without a support network. And the trauma of the often lengthy and gruesome voyage into exile may have showed them the futility of attempting an escape and a return home on their own.

The will to resist came back with the possibility to go home to Sonora, when, after the outbreak of the Revolution, the Yaquis were enabled to leave the haciendas, hoping to return to their native land, trying to regain their base of power along with their home.[88] The move away from the *haciendas* also enabled them to revive traditional ceremonies they most likely had not been able to practice on the plantations. They also eagerly took the opportunity to practice their traditional fiestas.[89] Yet even then, there were no uprisings as such, even though the Yaquis did take up arms. However, they did this under the command of Yucatecans who were using the Yoeme as tools in their own quest for power. The Yaquis, as Padilla has argued, probably joined up in order to secure passage home to Sonora as well as to earn money or for reasons of status.[90] As the massive flux of Yaquis to Mérida and Progreso showed, the Yoeme were still eager to go home and seemed to have believed in the myth of a war ship which would come to take them back home.[91]

In Sonora, on the other hand, the deportations may even have given the Yaquis an additional incentive to fight—the demand that the deportees be returned—along with the traditional demand for autonomy.[92] And even though the massive presence by governmental troops would have had a disruptive influence on community, religion, and traditions there as well, it would certainly have been less detrimental than the uprooting which was the deportation to Yucatán. Still, the impact of the deportations and the continued fighting on those who managed to remain in Sonora should not be underestimated. Traditionally, they relied on consensus decisions but, as the peace negotiations of Luis Bule showed, this was increasingly hard to achieve, and so did the growing factionalism.[93] In Sonora, Yoeme still had the land to help them keep up traditions and community spirit. Proximity and access to those still maintaining the resistance would also have been a factor contributing to the successful continuation of the resistance in Sonora. The Yucatecan Yaquis were deprived of both land and community, two crucial factors in maintaining the resistance, as well as of a realistical chance to regain either by rebelling against the *hacendados*. So all they could do under the circumstances was to bide their time and to wait for their chance. In the meantime, as seen, they stuck with each other instead of mingling much with other workers, attempted to keep up some of their traditions, and longed to go back to Sonora, to their land and to their people.

Ultimately, it was the extreme diaspora caused by the deportations which accounted for these two very different stories of Yaqui resistance in Sonora and Yucatán. Community was an important factor, as the insistence of the Sonoran Yaquis on the return of the deportees shows. Yet given that some aspects of community survived in Yucatán it seems like land must have been a—if not indeed the—crucial factor next to practical considerations of feasibility. Land, as especially seen in the rhetoric of Luz and Juan, was also of prime importance. It is difficult to evaluate exactly how crucial these factors were, given the scarcity of sources. But, as the cases examined here have shown, some of the solidarity and community spirit prevalent in Sonora did survive in Yucatán. Therefore, it seems likely that land—especially through its ties with religion, tradition, community and other factors—must have been a very important factor in maintaining the resistance. And the fact that Yucatecan Yaquis were completely deprived of one of these elements, land, and partly of the other, community, may have been crucial in the demise of resistance among them while their Sonoran counterparts managed to hold on to it by a thread. While in Sonora resistance did stand the trials of time and military pressure, in Yucatán it was only the trials examined which give some insights into the failure of resistance there and only very few Yaqui voices broke the great Yucatecan silence.

Chapter Ten
History is Not Over Yet: The Yaquis and the Land

Looking at the situations the Yaquis and especially the deportees found themselves in immediately after removal one cannot help but think that matters looked bleak. And the Sonoran Yaquis had barely been saved by the outbreak of the Mexican Revolution. So immediately after removal it did look like both groups had already succumbed to state pressures or were likely to do so in the foreseeable future. However, the Yoeme refused to vanish. Even though part of the rebels had surrendered in 1909 this did not mean that all the Yaquis were 'pacified,' as the government liked to term it. The few remaining rebels under Luis Espinosa held out the longest and thus upheld the Yaqui fighting spirit and their quest for autonomy until the outbreak of the Mexican Revolution which saved them from further deportations.

Some Yaquis actively took part in the Mexican Revolution and it would have been hard to find men with more fighting practice than the Yoeme. Luis Bule, Lino Morales, and Francisco Urbalejo became important military leaders and probably set the example for a number of Yoeme who also joined the forces.[1]

At the outbreak of the revolution many Mexicans did live in what used to be exclusively Yaqui territory and three of the traditional eight towns had been abandoned. Yet the way of life of the Yoeme had not disappeared and "Yaqui patterns persisted, but everywhere in direct competition with the Mexican" ones.[2]

Francisco Madero, the first president after Díaz, in his book about the presidential succession devoted ten pages to the Yaqui Wars. And, just before assuming office, Madero received a delegation of Yaquis. Sibalaume, one of the most famous rebel leaders, had come down from the sierra to support Madero's forces earlier in 1910.[3] In return for Yaqui support, among other things Madero promised them the restoration of their land, temporary tax exemption.[4] Later on, he also "declared himself in favor of the return of deportees from the south east."[5] Yet while with the onset of the revolutionary movement Yoeme slowly returned to *Yaquimi* this would not necessarily have been the result of government policy.[6]

"The Revolution gave Yaquis the opportunity to participate in the life of Mexico on the national level, no longer at the lowest grade as deported or deportable peons, but on par with other citizens," as Spicer has pointed out.[7] Still, this did not mean that suddenly all the Yoeme's problems had been solved. In the course of the revolution they had to experience time and time again that promises could be broken. It was not a new lesson to them. These promises were also among the reasons why Yaquis were fighting on different sides in the revolution and sometimes even against each other.[8] While Spicer claims the only thing these factions had in common was "a lack . . . of interest in maintaining the traditional Yaqui institutions," Hu-DeHart maintains that it was promises that were responsible for the Yoeme taking different sides.[9] They were probably trying to do the best for their community, each in their own way. The unwavering loyalty they displayed for various revolutionary leaders over time could have been an attempt to gain their loyalty in return and benefits for the Yoeme along with it. Others gave temporary support without ever enlisting, possibly also hoping to reap benefits for their people.

Late in 1915, General Alvaro Obregón, a native of Sonora and a dominant figure in President Venustiano Carranza's military, felt compelled to consider the Yaqui question again. There had been a number of killings of Mexican colonists in the traditional Yaqui territory, probably as many Yoeme had returned to their old homesteads only to find their land taken by Mexicans. By December of 1915 the situation had become so bad as to arouse Obregón's attention. The Yaquis had once again become a force which could not be disregarded.[10] Obregón initiated talks with the Yoeme who, as it turned out, voiced the same old demands concerning land and autonomy all over again. They wanted all Mexicans to leave their territory and particularly the soldiers stationed there, and they insisted on the return of their land. The talks failed and the military campaign against the Yaquis was taken up by a new government. And again Yaquis fought against other Yaquis, since Lino Morales and his men were still among Obregón's forces. This time the entire area was placed under martial law. Part of the former Yaqui lands now belonged to Mexicans and Obregón would not have them dispossessed. He insisted the Yoeme act like Mexican citizens and thus refused to allow them special privileges. Obregón, like so many before him, viewed the Yaquis as citizens of the Mexican nation. That is where the Yaquis differed with him fundamentally.

Luckily for the Yoeme this campaign did not last very long as in May 1916 Adolfo de la Huerta was appointed interim governor of Sonora. He stopped the fighting and initiated talks. De la Huerta, himself one quarter Yaqui, decided to transfer land back to the Yaquis as in his opinion it had been taken unjustly during and after the deportation. But the process of return was slow, due to the opposition by the Mexicans who believed themselves the rightful owners of the lands in question. In January of 1917, the Yaqui Espinosa finally signed a peace agreement, although probably with little hopes for its duration.[11]

It was soon to become apparent that Espinosa's doubts had not been without reason. Later that year the agreement was violated by Mexican forces and the Yaquis responded with defensive hostility. The troops retaliated and the conflict soon was in full force once again. In August of 1917 de la Huerta left Sonora for Mexico City, having been appointed by Carranza to his cabinet and thus a figure that had been sympathetic to the Yoeme was removed from a position that would have enabled him to positively influence the tribe's fate. General Plutarco Elías Calles had become governor of Sonora. Obregón, dissatisfied with the situation, and the renewed violence sent troops to Sonora for the pacification of the Yaquis. Soon, the methods already in place under Díaz were put to use once more as the fighting escalated and shipments of Yaquis to the south of the republic were resumed. Still remembering the horrors and effects of the last deportations, the Yaquis reportedly attempted to stop the first shipment by attacking a Mexican town.[12] This time the campaign was to last for two years while the revolution still continued all around.

In September 1919, Adolfo de la Huerta returned to Sonora as governor and promptly resumed his earlier conciliatory policy towards the Yaquis. Unfortunately, while this was popular with the Yaquis, that was not the case with the federal government and president Carranza. The controversy grew and resulted in the Plan of Agua Prieta in April 1920 in which de la Huerta and others, among them Morales, Espinosa, Mori and Matus of the Yaquis, proclaimed themselves against the Carranza government. Possibly in a bid to secure their support the Yaquis also had been promised repatriation and resettlement by de la Huerta.[13] In 1923, de la Huerta was unsuccessful in his bid for power against Obregón (who by the time had ascended to the presidency) and so Obregón's return to Yaqui territory in 1926 was yet another dark hour for the Yoeme. The Yaquis wanted to talk to him about promises not kept, and specifically about the return of their lands and so stopped his train. What took place then remains hazy but in the end there was shooting and battle, in which many Yoeme—men, women, and children—were killed. This event is usually portrayed as the last Yaqui revolt and the available evidence suggests that it was intentionally provoked by Obregón himself.[14]

The immediate result of this confrontation was the Yaquis' rush to the mountains to avoid fighting. Twenty thousand troops were sent after them, along with airplanes that dropped bombs on waterholes in an attempt to flush the Yaquis out of the sierra. After a year, most Yoeme had thus been driven out of hiding and about 400 Yaquis were sent by train to Mexico, D.F., officially for discussions or questioning. Instead, they were drafted into the army or sent to Mérida, Veracruz, and Tlaxcala.[15] As Spicer has determined, "Generals Mori and Espinosa were among those deported and impressed into the army. Both died in Veracruz without ever getting back to the Yaqui country."[16] Especially for Espinosa, who had upheld the resistance against the Porfiriato for such a long time, this must have been a cruel fate. Inside the Yaqui territory, a systematic occupation followed.

When Lázaro Cárdenas was elected president in 1934, the Yaquis repeatedly petitioned him for redress of various grievances. In 1937, Cárdenas responded by creating a 'zona indígena,' which encompassed much of the original Yaqui territory. He also urged all Yaquis to return and to rebuild the towns. Additionally, he promised them water from a dam, which was to be built upstream. For about a decade, the Yoeme therefore concentrated on farming. Water and land were free, and, as Hu-DeHart has found out, "conforming to the past, Yaquis paid no taxes to the Mexican government, state or federal."[17]

But Cárdenas' successors pushed agrarian development without much concern for the Yaquis. The newly-built dams along with major advances in agricultural development initiated what has often been called the 'green revolution.' The new agriculture was not labor intensive anymore and thus Yaqui labor became dispensable. In addition the federal government assumed control over the water and it ended the natural flooding the Yaquis' traditional agriculture depended on. "The government that had given the Yaqui people their own reserve of land, later took away the water that made the land productive," as Hu-DeHart has described the paradoxical situation.[18] And the banks advancing them money forced the Yaquis to cultivate cash crops. In view of these changes, Hu-DeHart speaks of a resulting declining commitment to traditions and a decline of identity.[19]

Yet even in recent years, the causes of conflict between Yaquis and Mexicans seem to be unchanged. They still mainly evolve around land and water issues and about Yaqui autonomy. For instance, the Yaquis once again clearly voiced their demands in the context of the campaigns for the elections of 2000. They stated that they wanted the territorial problem solved, their water rights and their autonomy respected, wanted to preserve the union among the Yaqui communities, and that the political and economical interests of the state were not to be confused with those of the Yaquis. They made it clear that while they wanted help they did not look for any paternalistic attitudes. They only wanted their young people to be able to work the land, a work they say they are meant for.

Chapter Eleven
Removal in Comparative Perspective

Looking at the often tragic histories of the two peoples, the Lenape and the Yoeme, one cannot help but be amazed that they still exist today and have preserved their separate identity. There have been many occurrences in these histories which would have made vanishing a plausible consequence; indeed they would have made not-vanishing implausible. Removal, the main focus of this study, probably came closest to eradicating the tribes as such. Yet they are still there, not unchanged and certainly not without scars, but they have not vanished.

If one follows the course of the Yaqui tribes' post-deportation history one discovers that it was modern agriculture's destruction of their home, their territorial base, which affected the Yaquis and their sense of community most gravely, along with their redundancy in this process. The Delawares, on the other hand, in Indian Territory / Oklahoma were, after a hard period of adjustment to life among the Cherokees, given the chance to reconstruct and / or rediscover their identity and possibly even grew stronger in the process, especially by fighting their 1979 termination.

While the post-removal situation looked almost promising for the Yaquis when the Revolution broke out, it completely changed when modern agriculture took over. What centuries of fighting had been unable to accomplish, modern land machines suddenly brought within reach even though the Yoeme essentially stuck to their traditional demands throughout. And what had appeared so bleak for the Delawares, bringing immediate fragmentation and other grave consequences like the possible loss of juridical identity, in the end only served to make them stronger by making the Lenape even more aware of what it means to be Delawares.

163

PRE-REMOVAL

The tribes of the Yaquis and the Delawares, starting out from very similar situations at the time of first contacts with Europeans, eventually moved in different directions, only to both get precariously close to being overcome in the end. Both began as societies subsisting by farming, hunting, and gathering. Both were semi-sedentary and consisted of several partially independent villages. The Yaquis initially had the advantage of location and also the more cohesive intra-tribal organization, at least in times of war. This organization, or rather the lack thereof, very soon proved to be one crucial factor in the fate of the two tribes.

Both societies had early contacts with Europeans, in the early sixteenth century, though the ones between Lenape and Europeans at first were of a more sporadic nature. As was the case with other tribes in the US and Mexico, these contacts could be, and indeed were, of peaceful as well as of aggressive nature. Quite often, the decisive factor in the character of such encounters was the behavior of the Europeans. As Gary B. Nash has suggested, "in areas where Indian land, political autonomy, or way of life was at stake or where an Indian slave trade was desired, widespread conflict occurred irrespective of the national origins of the Europeans involved."[1] And at the basis of these conflicts were usually differences in attitude between the indigenous societies and the newcomers. "For the Europeans the essential components of colonization were land, trade, and physical security. For Indians, land, trade, and physical security also were primary goals, but to these must be added the preservation of political and cultural sovereignty."[2] And, as has become apparent in this study of the removal of Yaquis and Delawares, the preservation of identity was also of prime concern to the Natives. Yet even though there were great similarities between the two tribes at time of contact as well as throughout their later history, there also were dissimilarities, and the latter soon grew, partly in response to the nature of the state policies the tribes encountered.

The Yaquis, residing in the northwest of what today is Mexico, had the advantage of location and a more cohesive social organization. The Delawares on the other hand were literally 'people of the first frontier,' living in the East and by the sea. These communities involuntarily rendered valuable services to others while suffering from the first waves of European intruders, as "their prolonged resistance gave the interior societies time to adapt to the European presence and to devise strategies of survival as the westward-moving frontier approached them."[3] Indeed, the Delawares, one of these coastal societies did not have time to prepare themselves for the inevitable dealings with the newcomers. They could not profit from experiences others had had with the Europeans; instead, they were the ones to make such experiences. They were not given the time to adapt to the new situation but instead came to be removed almost immediately—albeit in a disorganized and impromptu way at first—and also more than just once. As Patricia Nelson Limerick has stated, "tribes were . . . undergoing what was essentially a refugee experience."[4] This is exactly what happened to the Lenape.

And while the Jesuits, missionaries among the Yaquis, managed to help the tribe to keep their settlement area largely clear of intruders and also gave them a more rigid and effective social structure, the Moravian missionaries among the Delawares did not prove to be as useful to them. Thus while both societies were missionized at around the same time, this experience turned out to be very different for Delawares and Yaquis.

Location looms large in the history of both Delawares and Yaquis. The common factor of the removal of the Delawares and the Yaquis is the question of land and also that of diversity, their perceived difference from mainstream society. The former is especially obvious with the Delawares, who started to lose their land almost immediately upon their first contacts with Europeans. Many of these newcomers bought it cheaply by their own standards, and often, especially in the very beginning, the Indians did not understand the concept of the sale of land. They thought they just let other people share the area in question but that no one would in turn actually exclude them from using it as well. Yet over time they did get used to the notion of permanent land sales. Still, they did not manage to hold on to their lands and lost them even more rapidly as the power balance shifted in their disfavor. So over the years they lost their lands time and time again, made treaty after treaty, often trying to compromise instead of resorting to war. On one occasion a Delaware chief even proposed a separate state of the Union for all Native Americans. (A similar attempt was undertaken by the Yaqui known as Juan Banderas, who tried to unify the indigenous societies of the Mexican Northwest.) But the conditions of the treaties were violated many times by the European parties, or reasons were found to make the documents invalid in the eyes of the Americans. The Delawares always ended up as the losing party, no matter what means they resorted to.

In this manner they were rapidly running out of options to avoid losing their lands and having to migrate. They were first removed from their original homelands along the Delaware River to Ohio, then to Indiana, Missouri, and Kansas. Some of these removals were impromptu ones and saw the Delawares crowded out, while others were achieved by means of treaty and thus of a more organized character even before the official passage of the Indian Removal Act of 1830. A brief respite of not even forty years was given to the Lenape tribe in Kansas, their last stop before their final removal to what was to become Oklahoma. This migration, based on the 1830 act, was the most regulated in Delaware history even though in many respects the Indians were still left to their own devices and had to fend for themselves while trying to make their way to their new homes. While in Kansas, at least some tribal members were given the chance to construct flourishing farms and make a comfortable living. And even though this time was far from uneventful, especially once again to growing white intrusions and a demand for Lenape land, this period of time could be termed relatively peaceful in comparison with what was still in store for the tribe. As they had even supported the Union during the Civil War they had certainly not given the United States government a reasons to punish them by means of forced migration. Yet the decision for the removal most likely had been taken before the Civil War and nothing the Delawares could do would have been able to change it.

The Yaquis were left alone on their lands for a relatively long time. First of all they were known to be 'troublesome' and in addition to that, they lived in a very remote area. They were simply not deemed worthy of the effort it would have taken to remove the fierce tribe from its traditional lands. And even the land itself was deemed undesirable because it did not hold any resources considered valuable at that time, like precious metals. Only when this perception changed due to a growing interest in agricultural pursuits did Europeans become interested in the lands of the Yoeme. But by then the Yaquis benefited from the presence of the Jesuit missionaries who effectively kept the Spanish *vecinos* out of the Yaqui territory and sheltered them—perhaps at times more than the Yoeme wanted to be sheltered. The Jesuits often have been criticized of abusing 'their' Indians and this has, in a way, been the case here, since the Yaquis' labor financed other Jesuit missions. However, the *padres* probably considered this an appropriate form of compensation for their efforts as well as the Christian duty of their disciples.[5] But the Yaquis on the whole seemed to have been quite content under Jesuit rule. While there was an uprising in 1740, it was more a manifestation of the discontent the Yaquis felt for individual Jesuits. Even during that uprising they did not seem to have wanted to rid themselves of the brothers altogether. They seemed to have known that the arrangement was to their own advantage since they kept the Spanish *vecinos* out of their territory. And not only did the Yaquis profit from the protection by the Jesuits, they also did so from the reorganization of their own society. The Delawares as a tribe never showed themselves all that welcoming towards the Moravian missionaries. On the contrary, many members of the tribe were opposed to their presence, and so the *Unitas Fratrum* missionized only few tribal members without ever reorganizing the Lenape tribe as such. In that respect their influence on the tribe was much more limited than that of the Jesuits on the Yoeme.

In the 1890s and shortly before their deportation, the Yaquis were engaged in guerrilla warfare against the Mexican government. And although only a minority was actively involved in the fighting, almost every Yaqui had a part in this struggle. The *pacíficos,* the non-fighting members of the tribe, supported the *broncos,* the fighters, and so made it next to impossible for the Mexican forces to overcome the armed resistance fueled by the 'peaceful' members of the tribe. This time period also saw the removal of large numbers of Yaquis from their homelands. The causes of the deportations were to be found in their continuous and generally successful resistance against the Mexican state as well as in two other factors. First, there was a great interest in their rich and fertile lands and, secondly, their former advantage of being good laborers changed into a disadvantage with the rise of the henequen plantations in Yucatán. The Mexican government then was finally in a position to dispose of the Yaquis as they had lost their trump cards in the game of independence.

Thus the circumstances post-contact changed rapidly for both the Delawares and the Yaquis. 'Pre-removal,' both tried peaceful as well as aggressive policies against the European intruders.[6] Both accepted missionaries among them, though the Lenape showed more reluctance than the Yoeme, who, on the other hand, had no qualms about disobeying the missionaries' orders. Yet the Yaquis, due to some advantages of locale and organization, pre-removal were more successful than the Delawares in maintaining a collective identity. They stayed in the Yaqui River Valley while the Delawares had to migrate repeatedly, whether they used peaceful or aggressive approaches. By the time the Delawares' final removal started, several independent groups had already formed and left the main body of the tribe, temporarily or for good, whereas while some Yaquis left the Yaqui River Valley to work, they usually returned there. Partly as a consequence of these differing post-contact developments, and partly due to the divergent ways the two encapsulating nation states conducted removal, the measure turned out differently for both communities, even though its outcome also showed some striking similarities. For the Delawares, removal was merely a continuation of the already established trend of being pushed away by advancing white settlements. Yet for the Yoeme it was a novelty.

REMOVAL OF THE DELAWARES

The relatively peaceful time the Lenape experienced in Kansas turned out to be only the calm before the storm; it led to their to-date ultimate (physical) removal. Yet theirs never reached the same sad fame as the Trail of Tears of the Five Civilized Nations in the 1830s. The Delawares' removal was less spectacular. Once again they lost their lands by means of treaty and, when they had nothing left and found all other options barred, agreed to go to the Indian Territory. But this was a slow process, initiated by the Kansas–Nebraska Act in 1854 that created the Territory of Kansas and brought new legal conditions with it. This led to new negotiations about the land and to four treaties between 1854 and 1866 which eventually deprived the Delawares of all their land and leaving them no choice but to leave, to once more vacate what had been their home. The invasion of the land had started earlier by settlers, by squatters simply moving in and taking over the Indians' land, stealing their horses and cattle and cutting down their trees to build houses or other so-called improvements on Indian-owned ground.[7] The Delawares were not American citizens and thus had only very limited options when it came to keeping settlers and squatters out.[8] Nor did the government help them to do so in spite of agreements fixed in the treaties to leave this land exclusively to the Delawares and in spite of having promised to protect the Natives. Worse still, the US government was also very accommodating towards the railroads, which coveted Indian lands to construct and help finance their lines in addition to having been given the right of way over Native lands. Therefore, two of the Delaware removal treaties were essentially about the sale of lands to railroads. And while the tribe had been promised that such a construction would result in an increase of the value of their lands, they were not the ones to benefit from it.

All they could do about the continuous depredations was ask the government for compensation. For instance, many Delaware treaties arranged for payments to reimburse the tribe for losses induced by of whites. And still the trespassing continued as the local government representatives would not commit political suicide by helping the non-voting Indians. The Indian agents, should they be at all willing to take steps to aid the Indians against such intrusions, were often helpless and had to rely on military help which was seldomly granted. So in 1860, the same year that the Treaty of May 30 introduced the allotment of the diminished reserve, the Delawares sent a delegation to Oklahoma to decide whether to move there, or someplace else in Indian Territory, or to stay where they were only as United States citizens. But no decision was reached at that point in time. The allotment following the treaty left them with 80 acres per person and the rest, the so-called surplus, went to railroad companies. The treaty of 1861 once again favored the railroads.[9] And still the tribe was sympathetic to the American government, or maybe just trying to make it sympathetic to them, when in 1862 170 out of 201 Delaware men between 18 and 45 years of age volunteered to fight for the Union and against the South.

On July 4th, 1866, the final treaty to remove the Delawares to Oklahoma was signed. The Lenape looked at lands available to them and eventually decided to relocate within the boundaries of the Cherokee reservation. A treaty between the Cherokee Nation and the USA, signed shortly after the Delaware treaty, allowed the US to settle "civilized Indians friendly with the Cherokees" on their territory.[10] But in order to be able to settle there, the Delawares had to make another compact, this time with the Cherokees. Therefore, after much discussion between the Cherokees and the Lenape, on April 8, 1867 the two tribes entered into an agreement. According to this document the Cherokees sold the Delawares 160 acres of land for every man, woman, and child on the enrollment list. Yet when the time came to sign the final version of the agreement, the Delawares discovered that a few terms had been changed from the version the two parties had previously agreed on. For instance, the new wording spoke of incorporation of the Lenape into the Cherokee Nation, possibly suggesting the dissolution of Delaware tribal ties. This and other legal ambiguities of the Articles of Agreement were to have the gravest impact on the legal identity of the Lenape and thus also come to endanger their identity as a tribe.

The Delaware delegates sent to sign the agreement did so in spite of it having been modified from the agreed-upon version and probably at least partly due to pressure from the government officials present. They had been authorized to sign the Articles of Agreement and, presumably, also to accept or refuse any changes thereof, as was customary. Yet that written authorization was based on a bona fide agreement between the delegates and their tribe, on an unwritten agreement that the former would act in the best interest of the tribe and not to consent to any changes that would be unacceptable to the community. The authorization document itself was probably considered just one of the many strange 'white' things the government officials insisted on and were customarily accommodated to by the tribe. And even though technically it was Delawares who brought this fate upon fellow Delawares, that does not make what took place right and it certainly does not absolve the Cherokees or especially the US government from blame. After all, the President of the US cannot single-handedly determine the fate of the entire Nation. There is a system of checks and balances to prevent such abuse. Yet when the Delawares subsequently refused to ratify the Agreement, it was to no avail. Their protests were futile, their system of checks and balances simply ignored.

The movement to Oklahoma began in December of 1867 and continued during the spring and summer of 1868, thirty-five years after the removal of the Choctaws who had been the first to suffer removal on the basis of the 1830 Indian Removal Act. Each family had to make its own preparations and arrangements, though sometimes several families traveled together. They had to cover a distance of 180 to 200 miles until they arrived in Indian Territory. They were not accompanied and supervised by the military. Unlike it had been the case with several of the Five Civilized Tribes, there was no force necessary to remove the Delawares from what had been their home for close to 38 years. There was obviously no need for that. After all, probably only a little over a thousand Lenape were left, and they had for a long time attempted to live peacefully with the Europeans. But there was no immediate cause for removal, either. On the contrary, they had lived peacefully on their Kansas lands for almost forty years, and had even fought for the Union during the Civil War. Clearly, they posed no threat to the USA; they were simply viewed as a nuisance and an obstacle. Unlike the Yaquis, they were not considered to be of any real use or value to the country and its citizens of European extraction; instead, the Lenape were seen as a hindrance to them. People coveted their land and so the Lenape once again had to leave. Other tribes before and after them found themselves in similar situations and it certainly was no novelty for the Lenape themselves. This was a continuation of the very first (informal) policy used in dealing with Native Americans.[11] Indian Territory was simply the latest measure to take away their land. But removal in itself was nothing new to the Delaware tribe.

REMOVAL OF THE YAQUIS

Physical removal, however, was new to the Yaquis. Before the mass deportations started in 1902, there had been occasional relocations but only on an individual basis and for active rebels. The dislocation of 1902 was directed at the entire tribe, at men, women, and children. In that respect it was a new policy. The Porfiriato tried to drain the Yaqui rebellion by taking away the peaceful people clandestinely supporting it, especially since the line between *broncos* and *pacíficos* had become increasingly hazy, making it difficult if not impossible to deport only active rebels as sooner or later most male Yoeme could be counted among that group. The excuse for the full-on adoption of this measure was the guerrilla warfare the Yoeme quite successfully employed against the Mexicans. Drying up the social base seemed to be the only means to bring an end to the guerrilla movement. After all, earlier measures such as drawing up registers and designating special camps to the *pacífico*-population had not had the desired effects. The government had not been able to prevent the active interchange between *broncos* and *pacíficos*. But this was not the whole truth. There was also the growing interest of outsiders, Mexicans and Americans, in the fertile lands of the Yaqui Valley and in Sonora in general, partly caused by its proximity to Arizona. It was to an extent the commercial interest from the United States that inspired the Mexican government to finally rid itself of the 'Yaqui nuisance' and to open the way for the commercial agricultural development of the area, while at the same time helping the Yucatecan henequeneros out who were desirous to obtain cheap labor for their plantations.

Just like the Delawares, the Yoeme suffered from technological innovations, and especially from the advance of railroads. At first, they were convenient for this development, supplying mines, railroads, industries, but most of all the expanding agriculture, with cheap labor. But, coincidentally, at about the same time there arose an almost insatiable market for workers on the henequen plantations in Yucatán, counteracting the need for Yaqui labor in Sonora. The Northern hacendados had been willing to balance the need for the Yaqui labor force against the fear of attacks and until that point in time the government had largely agreed to tolerate Yaqui behavior so as not to lose Yoeme labor. But now the government could have both; they were able to deport the Yaquis and could at the same time satisfy labor needs. Yet the demand for workers would only be met on Yucatán. Of course, Sonora was going to suffer from this bargain but Yucatán with its rich and influential plantation owners was going to profit tipping the scales in favor of the removal of the Yoeme. And so the fate of the Yaquis was sealed. At this point, there was nothing they could do to avoid the deportations. Even the option of joining the Mexican mainstream society by then was closed to them.

After 1902, the government forces increasingly put Yoeme, men, women, and children, in jail, where they had to await their fate. Sometimes the children were taken to prominent families to work since the theory was that early contacts with Mexican people would 'civilize' them, but the less fortunate ones were simply left in jail. Although the official policy in the beginning was only to deport hard-core rebels, this premise was not always followed. Instead, removal was rather arbitrary. Consequently, most of the captured men, as well as some women and children were removed by this means, although some were punished otherwise, for instance by hanging. Yet in 1904, after two years of deportations and in spite of the draconian measures generally employed against the Yoeme, the government had to acknowledge that some Yaquis still somehow managed to carry on with their resistance. This made President Díaz encourage the state government to renew its efforts and as a result sealed the fate of the entire Yaqui population. He also sent some federal troops to help the Sonoran government out, a somewhat unusual measure since ordinarily these matters were left to the state governments. From then on many times no distinction at all between *pacíficos* and rebels was made. All Yoeme were required to live in three Sonoran districts. All other areas, and especially the border districts, were supposed to round up the Yaquis and to send them to Hermosillo. By 1907 all areas, even haciendas, mines, and railroads were instructed not to employ Yaquis anymore. At that time the government also stopped its efforts at disguising the war against the tribe, and openly tried to clear all Yoeme from Sonora. It attempted to pass off and justify the deportations as benevolent acts because they permitted the Yaquis to live instead of resorting to killing them outright to solve the problem they posed. So they were rounded up, thrown in jail, deported to Yucatán (and Oaxaca), and had their belongings confiscated. To the Yaquis, removal was the harshest punishment they ever had to face.

By 1908, the deportations had taken their toll on the rebellion as they had largely removed the base that had supported the entire venture. Therefore, a delegation of Yaquis approached the officials for peace in that year. They adhered to the traditional conditions of keeping their arms while keeping intruders out of their territory. Not surprisingly, the government refused these terms, but the negotiations were continued nonetheless. Unfortunately, Luis Bule, the rebel leader who had initiated negotiations, did not represent all the Yaquis and failed to convince all of them to make peace by the time the government-imposed deadline to turn over all their weapons came around. As the deadline was not met the Díaz government continued the deportations. The largest shipments of Yoeme took place in June and July of 1908. The only exceptions made at this point in time were probably for small orphans, brought up in non-Yaqui families, not speaking any Yaqui. All the other Yoeme were pursued relentlessly. And as at the same time the borders to Arizona were watched more closely than ever the Yaquis had literally nowhere to go to avoid this fate.

The massive embarkations of Yaquis stopped abruptly at the end of July of 1908 but smaller numbers continued to be deported. The government still had prices on the heads of Yaquis and, to avoid more attacks by the few remaining rebels, threats were made that each would be avenged by more deportations. Maybe the slowdown in the removal was due to the mounting protests of the Northern hacendados. Sonoran employers were especially outraged since the lack of labor was dragging their economy down. But, as they had been ignored earlier, the consequences for the Sonoran economy probably would have been without effect on the removal policy if the demand for labor in Yucatán had not decreased. The henequen market depended largely on export and thus had suffered from the depression in the United States. While the Yucatecan demand for labor had been instrumental in bringing about the mass deportations of the Yoeme it was also crucial in their final slowdown.

The exact numbers of Yaquis deported remain unknown, but estimates for the period between 1902 and 1908 run as high as fifteen thousand. Raquel Padilla, as a preliminary estimate, states a number of over 6,000 Yaqui deportees to Yucatán alone.[12] Even assuming a population of 30,000 Yaquis on the eve of the deportations, which is probably too high, that would still mean that the tribe lost between one-fourth and one-half of its entire Sonoran population. And these calculations do not even include the Yoeme who escaped over the border into the United States or the ones who were killed in fights or by means of hanging so the total population loss of Yaquis in Sonora may even have been significantly higher.

In August 1908, after the deportations had stopped, some of the Yaquis, represented by one of the leaders of the rebellion, Luis Bule accepted the original peace conditions of the government. Three other rebel factions refused to make peace under these terms and hence continued their attacks. They insisted on having the Yaqui River Valley cleared of all non-Yaquis. Some of them later on agreed to peace, but a few Yoeme still carried on with their struggle. Bule and a few of his followers volunteered to go after the remaining rebels and were allowed to keep their arms for this purpose. On the part of all the Yaquis, whether they agreed to the peace or not, there generally appeared to have reigned a deep mistrust against the government. For instance, the Indians wanted to have a guarantee for the safety of their lives, obviously not believing in the validity of the promises of the officials dealing with them. Another demand they made again and again was the return of all the deported Yoeme, something they had asked for from the very earliest phase of the peace negotiations. This, according to the governor, depended entirely on the behavior of the Yaquis still hiding in the Sierra de Bacatete. If they surrendered, he stated, the pleas for the return of the deportees would at least be considered.

When most of the Yaquis had finally agreed to make peace with the Mexican government, it was under a number of conditions. The government would attend to and sustain all those who surrendered and all but sixty would be disarmed. The Yaquis were permitted to occupy vacant lands on the Yaqui River but were not to resettle the original eight pueblos but instead were to spread out. They would be provided with work in other parts of the state and transportation to their new location would be provided. In spite of the many requests of the Yoeme, the deportees to Yucatán remained unmentioned.

So although the struggle of the Yaquis still continued on a very small scale and even though they had long been able to hold out against the powerful dictatorship of the Porfiriato, the Yoeme had gained very little in this heroic fight that had furthermore brought them on the verge of destruction. By death and by removal, their numbers were severely decimated. They did not manage to avoid intrusions into their land and most of them lost the right to carry weapons. They suffered from dispersion and fragmentation, as became especially apparent in the peace negotiations with the Mexican government, where repeatedly leadership matters caused friction and the abortion of the discussions. (However, this aspect was aggravated by the government's inability or unwillingness to engage with the tribe's traditional manner of consensus decisions.) And even though the peace they entered into eventually allowed the Sonoran Yaquis to somewhat recover from the ordeals they had been through it did not achieve anything at all for the deportees. The traditional Yaqui policy of resistance at the eve of the Mexican Revolution was held up by only one faction under the leadership of Luis Espinosa. And this faction profited from the outbreak of the revolution and the Porfiriato's fall from power in 1910/11. But even the Mexican Revolution turned out to be only a break for the Yaquis; only a short suspension of their long struggle for autonomy.

REMOVAL IN COMPARATIVE PERSPECTIVE

The comparison of Delaware and Yaqui experiences raises some interesting questions about resistance and accommodation to change. Starting out from a very similar pre-contact situation, their history, while still sharing some key elements, developed in different directions. Yet with the onset of removal, both tribes found themselves in a very similar situation once again.

The efficiency, or 'fitness,' with which each group could respond to European intrusion and the development of nation states depended on more than a single factor and the crucial determinants sometimes changed over time. Initially, it was the combination of timing, locality, and prevailing circumstances that was crucial for these groups. Both Lenape and Yoeme faced fundamental challenges by the relocation of European intruders into their original spheres of influence. Their collective approaches to this new situation were not all that dissimilar in the two cases. Both attempted their best to survive an extremely difficult situation in which they were clearly at a disadvantage especially as time progressed. They used a combination of methods against the intruders which included sacrifices, petitions, negotiations, entreaties, treaties, and occasionally even resorted to open warfare. The degree to which the Native communities found maneuverability initially depended on time, place, and circumstances, later on mainly on the attitude of the nation-state they resided in. And these attitudes, as will be seen in the following chapters, were not all that dissimilar. Yet even if the initial circumstances mentioned above were unfavorable for them, perhaps even more so in the case of the Delawares than in that of the Yaquis, that did not mean the doom of their identity in the confrontation with the nation state.

Looking at the consequences removal had on the two tribes, one is inclined to think that, while there might be hope for the Yaquis, the Delawares as a tribe were doomed or maybe already dead. With the signing of the Articles of Agreement, at a glance it seemed like the legal identity of the tribe had effectively been erased, and that, as a tribe, they had ceased to exist. The Yaquis, on the other hand, could benefit from the outbreak of the Mexican Revolution which temporarily eased the pressures on them. Some of the deportees were enabled to come back to their native Sonora and so the worst consequences for the tribe could be avoided for the time being. So purely judging from the situation a few years post-removal, it seemed like the Yaquis would have a chance to recover while the Delawares were sure to vanish as a tribe.

Yet when investigating the history that followed these two removals one discovers an entirely different situation. The Delawares did not lose their sense of identity, even though they were fractionalized for a while over matters of tribal identity. And these internal conflicts arose specifically over different plans and ideas of how best to preserve tribal unity and separateness, thereby confirming a continued sense of tribal identity in spite of internal disagreements. There were also many indications that the outside world and especially the United States officials and the Cherokees still considered the Lenape a distinct group. The frequent clashes with Cherokees certainly proved that that tribe was not inclined to really have the Delawares merge with them. So what at least some of the officials in charge of the Lenape's removal may have been hoping for—a disappearance of the tribe by merging it with the Cherokees—never did occur.

Two of the four Delaware delegates still signed the Articles of Agreement of 1867 using x-marks, obviously dependent on assistance in dealing with the document and making it easier to take advantage of them. To many of the tribal members, it probably also was not a contradiction to be Delawares while being incorporated into the Cherokee Nation. They were used to dealing with different worlds while remaining Delawares and they had lived with and among other tribes as well as in close proximity to whites before. Obviously, never before had such cohabitation resulted in the loss of their legal identity or even the threat of such an occurrence. It could also be that some of the delegates just did not see any other option in the face of losing their land to white settlers and railroads. Maybe to these delegates it seemed preferable to follow the wishes of the US officials rather than to put up a fight they felt would prove to be in vain and might even turn out to be to the detriment of their tribe. In the face of such considerations they may not have felt able to resist the urging and possible intimidations by the officials. While it may never be determined without doubt what exactly took place at the signing of the Articles of Agreement there can be no doubt about how the majority of the tribe felt about the terms thus imposed upon them as tribal members protested immediately and almost incessantly against what they perceived to be the end of their tribal existence as Delawares.

This determination shown early on did not simply ebb away later on and so the years to follow their removal showed that the Lenape did not just vanish from view as might have been expected. Quite to the contrary, they continued to fight the Articles of Agreement and what they feared might be the consequences thereof. They were quite articulate, especially the dissenting ones known as the Neosho Delawares who were the ones most ardently opposed to the terms included in the document. Over time and especially when the negative consequences of this forced removal and resulting cohabitation with the Cherokees became apparent even to those who had originally been disposed to accepting the terms of the agreement, the tribe came to jointly oppose the conditions they found themselves in. In fact, it seems like the Delawares got more articulate over time, learning to use what d'Arcy McNickle has called the white man's weapons, taking their claims to the officials and to the courts.[13] And partly through their fight against the prevalent conditions the tribe found together again.

For the Yaquis, on the other hand, a more optimistic situation presented itself at the outbreak of the Mexican Revolution. The deportees were given the chance to leave the plantations and to make their way back to their native Sonora, where the merciless campaign against the tribe was discontinued. But there were many parties involved in this revolution, so that the Yaquis, listening to promises made by several of these groups, sometimes even found themselves fighting on opposite sides. And keeping the Yoeme occupied in such a way had the added benefit that they would be less likely to revolt while a large number of their fighters was occupied elsewhere.[14] Yet even though many Yaquis had supposedly joined the revolution to achieve benefits for the tribes they found that hardly ever were these promises kept once the Yaquis, after all the 'Mexicans' with the most fighting experience, were not needed anymore after most of the fighting had at least temporarily ceased. Thus the participation in the revolution may mainly have served to introduce friction. Ironically, the same seems to have been true for the Yoeme returning from Yucatan—after all something the Sonoran Yaquis had repeatedly asked for pre-Revolution. Yet this return after long years of enforced exile and without any contact to the Sonoran homeland was not unproblematic for the deportees or the ones who had managed to remain in Sonora during the period of the deportations.[15]

Therefore, the immediate post-removal period may have been similarly disruptive and challenging for the tribe as removal itself had been. Still, the Yaquis were one of the few groups to participate in the Revolution on the basis of their ethnic identity, hoping to achieve something for the tribe of the Yoeme by joining the fights.[16] Yet somehow both tribes had survived the event of removal, neither unharmed nor unchanged, but still alive. The savior of the Yaquis was the Mexican Revolution though it soon turned out to cause them more difficulties. The Delawares as a tribe survived removal damaged but with the goal of tribal unity unchanged.

If one further follows the course of the history of the two tribes one discovers that it was modern agriculture's destruction of their home, their territorial base, that affected the Yaquis and their sense of community most gravely. With the advent of modern technology even in this sector the Yaquis were not needed as laborers anymore and the intricacies of financing such agricultural enterprises along with the conditions imposed upon them by the banks saw the tribe increasingly surrender control over their lands. The Delawares, on the other hand, in Indian Territory/Oklahoma were, after a hard period of adjustment to life among the Cherokees, given the chance to rediscover and also to reconstruct their identity and grew stronger in the process. Maybe living in a quasi doubly hostile environment, with both mainstream and Cherokee society largely against them, made the Lenape realize even more how precious their tribal identity was to them. This later enabled them to fight the revoking of their federal recognition. In that respect, the increased outside oppression created through removal and cohabitation with the Cherokees may actually have served to ultimately help ensure the survival of Delaware tribal identity.

While the situation looked almost promising for the Yaquis when the Revolution broke out, it completely changed when modern agriculture took over in the 1970s. Modern land machines suddenly brought within reach what centuries of fighting had been unable to accomplish but over time the Yoeme nonetheless insisted on their traditional demands. And the situation that had appeared so bleak for the Delawares, with removal bringing immediate fragmentation and other grave consequences, in the end turned out to have strengthened tribal unity and determination.

In the end, both tribes had to find a way to adapt themselves and their resistance to the changing societies and situations around them and it is these societal and governmental attitudes that will be explored in the following chapters.

Chapter Twelve
Survival of the Fittest?

As the previous chapters have shown, both Lenape and Yoeme survived the trauma of removal against all odds as in both cases they were faced with a much more powerful encapsulating nation state. While neither the United States nor Mexico were technically new states at the crucial time of the Natives' removals, they both were involved in a phase of nation (re)building. Mexico under Díaz attempted to achieve its proclaimed goal of modernization and the United States of the Reconstruction had to cope with the legacy of the Civil War. Their attitudes and policies determined how much room to maneuver the Natives had in shaping their responses to removal and thus ultimately affected the form the Indians' fight for their tribal identity could take.

REMOVAL AND THE NATION STATE

Yet survival was not easy and especially removal at times brought the two tribes close to destruction, almost costing them their identity as a tribe. The maneuverability of both groups depended to a large extent on the nation-state they resided in. During removal, the Delawares and the Yaquis had to deal with evolving nation states, which especially in their initial phases did not feel they could accommodate diversity. As Richard Adams as noted: "In their dealings with nondominant ethnicities, states usually favor one of three rather different strategies of control: encapsulation, assimilation, or extermination."[1] Both the United States and Mexico over time explored all three choices, although with varying degrees of single-mindedness and not always openly. And, in my opinion, removal was present in all of them. Encapsulation could be viewed as removal (or restriction) to confinable areas, assimilation as removal of 'Indianness,' and extermination as a more drastic version thereof, as permanently removing the peoples themselves by killing them.

Furthermore, I would hold that most—if not all—policies towards the Lenape and the Yoeme can be subsumed under the heading of removal, at times in the literary sense of the word and at other times in a more metaphorical one. In this respect, I believe, the two tribes were not all that dissimilar from many—if not most—others, thus making removal a—if not the—central theme of Native-white relations.

While encapsulation in the hope of the ultimate assimilation or disappearance of the tribes was sometimes used in the states' dealings with Delawares and Yaquis, more or less nominal assimilation attempts and forms of extermination were much more the norm. In the United States even many philanthropists, among the only ones who truly cared about the fate awaiting the Indians, seem to have considered assimilation to be the only viable option for the survival of the Natives.[2] Others would have backed the policy for more self-serving reasons. The central question for all involved was how to achieve such assimilation and integration of the Indians into the mainstream society. In this context, removal to reservations—encapsulation—probably served a dual purpose. It at least temporarily removed the Indians from sight and thus as a concern or consideration, and it supposedly gave them time to get used to the 'white ways' gradually.

However, while the removal to reservations put great stress on tribal integrity, as can be seen for instance in the cases of the Delawares and also the Cherokees, removal affected entire tribes. Consequently, their tribal ties and structures at least in theory were removed as well.[3] Hence removal could be considered as something of a departure from the previous hopes for the assimilation of the Indians. Indeed, the measure was sometimes justified by the supposed failure of the assimilation policy although it did not mean a complete abandoning thereof as the rhetoric still called for a gradual assimilation of the Natives. As Bernard Sheehan has argued, "removal merely testified to the failure to dissolve the tribal ties and create autonomous, individual Indians ready for incorporation."[4] However, at least in some cases it can be maintained that the Indians had assimilated too successfully. This was for instance the case (some of) with the Cherokees who had become so civilized that the states they resided in considered them a threat to their own endeavors at land acquisition. They had to remove not only in spite of their civilized lifestyle but because of it. And other Native societies had to follow on in the same pattern. As Reginald Horsman has concluded from his examination of the origins of Indian removal, "whether they liked it or not, or whether they had become civilized or not, the Indians were to be removed."[5] Removal had thus become a tool of territorial expansion more than an element of United States federal Indian policy.

In contrast to the experience of the Delawares, which saw the entire tribe transplanted, the Yoeme, in the course of the deportations to Yucatán, often found themselves broken up and were thus faced with various degrees of isolation. The deportees were sent over more or less as they had been rounded up and incarcerated or were intentionally separated. Families were broken up, and even mothers and children were sometimes separated. And of course others remained behind in Sonora or fled to the United States, increasing the fragmentation of the tribe. Therefore the removal of significant numbers of Yaquis, and not merely of active rebels, was an important step towards fractionalizing the Yoeme and to drying up the base from which the rebels drew much of their strength. How successful at least part of this strategy was can be seen in the lack of fighting spirit among the Yaqui deportees. However, this loss of spirit was not only due to the loss of family members and friends, but also to the very practical lack of support, of reinforcements and supplies, of knowledge of the territory, of fairly safe places to rest in and tend to wounds. And since deportation was such a dreaded measure for the Yoeme many turned informants in hopes of avoiding it. This introduced an added element of fear and distrust into the tribe, something that had probably never been present on such a scale before.

As becomes quite plain from the cases examined in this study, the goal both states at the time of removal strove to achieve was the elimination of the Indians as Indians.[6] One way of doing that was through assimilation and integration; and if that was not possible, extermination was considered preferable to letting the Natives be. For certain people, outright extermination was probably even preferable to assimilation. As Gary Nash has insightfully pointed out, "so far as the assimilation of Indians was concerned, nothing could have been less desirable to European settlers, who coveted Indian land but not land with Indians on it."[7] The Indians had to vacate their lands and to disappear—one way or another. Naturally, in both countries there were individuals with opinions differing to both sides of the attitudes sketched above. Yet even the benevolent ones usually considered 'white ways' superior to Indian ones and therefore disagreed mainly about the time scale in which incorporation and thus the elimination of Indianness was to be achieved. But it is especially the more drastic and aggressive voices show a striking resemblance in both countries.[8] For instance, in 1869, during the Plains Indian Wars, General Philip Sheridan reportedly uttered the following famous remark: "The only good Indians I ever saw were dead." Similarly, when, well into the twentieth century, Alvaro Obregón resumed the fight against the Yaquis, the general commissioned with that task is reputed to have said: "El mejor yaqui es el yaqui muerto."[9]

While the United States and Mexico differed little in what they were hoping to achieve by removal of the Indians, the way they conducted these removals varied sometimes considerably. As Shelley Bowen Hatfield has concluded: "Removal ... was practiced in both nations, but only Mexico formulated a deportation policy designed to exploit Indian labor."[10] This was not only typical for the deportation policy practiced by the Mexicans against the Yaquis, but also for the general treatment of that tribe. After all, their labor was a trump card which had kept them safe for the longest time because Mexico was so intent on exploiting it. So to incorporate this into removal was only logical from the state's perspective. However, Indian labor was not exploited in the United States.[11] As Thomas Berger has stated, "unlike Black slaves, Indians were not perceived to be linked to the future economic development of the nation."[12] Instead, "they were seen as obstacles to civilization, progress and westward expansion."[13] Consequently, the United States government attempted to keep the costs of removal low but did not try to exploit the Indians' labor, settling instead for Indian lands.

Removal, in its essence one of the earliest ways of dealing with Native Americans, also set the tone for later attitudes and policies especially in the United States but also in Mexico. Similarly to removal, allotment, its follow-up policy in the United States, also made Indian lands available to non-Natives. It was supposed to pick up where removal had left off. Allotment and individual land ownership were supposed to turn tribal peoples into individuals, to make them abide by white man's laws, and to free up more Indian lands. In that respect it was not dissimilar to allotment attempts in Mexico and on the Yaqui river which also would have seen some lands go to white settlers. In a sense, allotment was primarily the removal of Indian lands and its assimilationist angle aimed once again at removing the Indianness of the Natives.

Education was to additionally further that particular goal. Especially in the United States it also took the form of removal as the children were taken away from their parents, siblings, kin, and tribe, and sent to far away boarding schools. The famous before-and-after photos were boasting of the success the educators had with turning the Native children into fake white people, of removing or 'killing' the Indian though 'saving' the person. However, as the turn to removal as a policy had previously shown, assimilation had at best been a theoretical or half-hearted attempt at integrating the Natives. I doubt that this had changed very much in the intervening years and would therefore hold that a significant part of these newer assimilationist polices were motivated by ulterior motives instead of a real desire to integrate Natives into mainstream America. Allotment made more Indian lands available to Americans and education, like termination and relocation later on, would ultimately help to make Native Americans self-sufficient and thereby reduce the financial burden on the state. In the case of the Lenape, the inhospitality of white society can best be illustrated by the fact that the Kansas Delawares still seem to have considered themselves separate from mainstream society until well into the twentieth century.[14]

In Mexico, education was at first more or less limited to the teaching of Spanish. Instead of trying to civilize the Yaquis, the Mexican government would have been very content with merely pacifying them and other tribes, like the Apaches. These pacification attempts attracted the most money. The Apache campaign was considered more important and was therefore allocated more funds than the Yaqui war. At this stage, the government would have been content had the Indians ceased to disrupt its modernization programs. Ultimately, however, assimilation and integration were Mexican goals as well. As Hatfield has noted, under Díaz "the federal government wanted to incorporate the Indians, or at least their lands, into the nation."[15] Thus in Mexico, like in the United States, land was of ultimate importance, not the Indians living on and off it or even their continued Indianness.

Not unlike the ruling opinion in the United States, during the reign of Díaz Indians as such and especially the Yaquis were considered obstacles to peace, progress, and prosperity, to his goal of modernizing the nation. Therefore, when pacification and along with it the chance for rapid assimilation failed, Mexico turned to more drastic measures and started deporting members of the tribe. If they ceased to be quarrelsome, the Yoeme were permitted to live—yet only outside of Sonora. The program was supposed to address labor needs and significantly it did so by attempting to turn Indians into laborers who would have to surrender their Indianness in forced exile.

Traditional native values thus collided with the ones desired by the two nation states. As Enrique Florescano has ascertained for the Mexican case, the state tried to implement these values using nationalism as its tool.[16] Cultural diversity, especially, was seen as an anathema to the ideals of the state and therefore culturally different communities had to be relocated or eliminated—one way or another. This for the two states also had the positive effect that it gave them control over the formerly indigenous-owned lands. In their dichotomous world of 'civilization' and 'barbarism' the acceptance of cohesive indigenous communities within the state indicated the persistence of barbarism. This could only be tolerated if the indigenous peoples had something valuable to offer in return, like cheap labor—something the Yaquis could and the Delawares could not do—and only while the Natives did not control any resources coveted by whites, like land. In the application of this pernicious and useful idea of barbarism the two new nation states had the marked advantage of physical force.

Hence in both cases, in the United States as well as in Mexico, the Indians were not allowed to remain Indians, since the states around them would not tolerate them as such and as tribal peoples. As Alejandro Figueroa asserts, Mexico was "una sociedad nacional que tampoco ha tolerado las diferencias," a society that would not tolerate difference.[17] And most importantly, Native share or control of precious resources like land would not be tolerated unless they had something to offer in return. The Yaquis' labor force fulfilled this function for a while before the former advantage turned into a disadvantage. The Delawares never really had anything to offer after the decline of the fur trade. In the absence of such a balancing element difference was not something the two nations were prepared to accept. Díaz's goal was the construction of a Mexican nation, something he felt had not been achieved since Independence. The obstinate Yaquis did not fit into that picture. In that respect the situation there was similar to the one in the United States, where, following the Civil War, Reconstruction was in full progress when the Delawares were removed to Indian Territory. A tribal people, averse to the white way of life could not be tolerated in this situation and the policy already initiated well before the Civil War was continued before the next step, allotment, was taken. At the time of their confrontations with the indigenous communities neither Mexico nor the United States were tolerant of diversity that did not conform to their concept of society, community and culture. In both countries, the 'nations within' had to be eliminated in order to get to their resources as well as to eliminate difference.

In both countries, the treatment of indigenous societies at the time of the removals previously discussed was more a matter of social and certainly of economical origin than of racial one. The nation-state determined who belonged and what had to be done in order to belong, as well as who would control the resources within its borders. Anything outside that mold could generally not be tolerated, especially not since both Mexico and the United States during the time periods in question found themselves in difficult political situations that required all their strength. And even those individuals who were willing to conform had no guarantees of acceptance, especially not if they held valuable resources desired by other members of the nation state. Particularly in such cases, no energy or tolerance could be spared to work out alternative ways to incorporate Native societies, unless they had something valuable to offer in return and thus making it worth the effort. The Delawares never really could make such an offer and the Yaquis were only in a position to do so for a while. At times people would temporarily and to a certain extent let the indigenous communities be and left them alone. This was the case when or while the Indians had been pushed away far enough not to 'disturb' the people's aims for the moment and generally only if the Natives did not control any resources considered valuable by the dominant mainstream society and the government. But should some unfortunate ones find themselves quite literally in the way, they soon saw the end of all tolerance.

Thus the histories of the Delawares and the Yaquis, which had started out similarly but then developed in different directions, post-removal left the two societies in not markedly different positions where tribal identity and the tolerance thereof were concerned. And in both cases the reasons for this development were rooted in a great similarity of the attitudes of the respective nation-states which, while they may have at least temporarily been able to tolerate Indians, at this stage they would certainly not condone valuable property being in Native hands.[18]

REMOVAL AND TRADITION

In the face of state pressures, different tribes often turned to divergent strategies. For instance, many Plains Indians, the Seminoles, and the Yaquis chose to oppose attempts to subjugate and remove them by military means; the Cherokees became civilized by white standards and turned to the courts for help against removal, and the Delawares generally tried to make the best of a bad situation. Yet, while the above seems to suggest unified tribal responses, a closer examination of all of these cases reveals that having to respond to nation-state policies like removal also caused a considerable degree of friction within tribes. In United States Native history these conflicts have often been viewed and explored as ones between so-called halfbreeds and full bloods. I would contend that they can be more meaningfully interpreted as differences of opinion between traditionalist and modernists.

The officials at the time who created these labels may have generalized based on certain trends discernable within the thinking and attitudes of the people they classified as 'full bloods' and 'half breeds.' The so-called half breeds were very likely often raised in a non-traditional way as one of their parents or grandparents was at least partly of European ancestry and consequently had been exposed to corresponding 'white' influences. The 'full bloods,' again, were almost certainly raised and educated in a more traditional way, making them more likely to stay true to that attitude in adult age as well. And, while especially contemporary commentators have often regarded the basic conflict as a choice between civilization and the white way of life as opposed to the 'savage barbarism' of tribal life, more often than not that would have been a gross generalization and a misreading of Native intentions (not to speak of a misjudgment of tribal life), especially of the 'half-breed modernists.' The case of the Delawares illustrates this perfectly as both the traditionalists and the modernists insisted on tribal unity above all else.[19] They simply had different ideas on how best to preserve this goal in the face of massive state pressures and about the effect removal would have.

Pre-removal, the traditionalists at times advocated removal as they hoped that it would enable them to continue in or resume their traditional ways which had become impossible to pursue in Kansas. The modernists were disdainful of this, maintaining that it was impossible to move every time the old ways were threatened and that that was not the way to advance the tribe. Yet over time, these attitudes shifted and the modernists came to support removal and particularly removal to the Cherokee Nation. What exactly changed their view is not clear but it may have been the realization that removal as such was an inevitability. And based on that premise they may have thought that it would be better to move with the civilized Cherokees than to go to a part of the country that would allow the traditionalists to keep up the old ways. (Such considerations may or may not have impacted on the delegates' decision to sign the revised Articles of Agreement.) However, for probably the same reasons the traditionalists had by then become opposed to removal to the Cherokee country.

Consequently, the traditionalists were especially reluctant to leave Kansas under the modified terms of the agreement with the Cherokees. As General James Blunt, an official involved in the matter, reported in February 1868, three quarters of the Delawares, whom he called 'full bloods,' were "averse to locating among the Cherokees."[20] He realized that their "nationality is dearer to them than all else."[21]

General Blunt claimed that these 'full bloods' were under the influence of Captain Fall Leaf, their war chief. He also argued that it was these 'full bloods' more than the 'half breeds,' led by chiefs Connor and Journeycake, who wanted to "preserve their identity as Delawares."[22] Fall Leaf, along with some other Delawares, wrote to the Commissioner of Indian Affairs, Nathaniel Taylor, declaring that the agreement 'was made without their knowledge or consent by a few Delawares claiming to represent the whole tribe."[23] Captain Anderson Sarcoxie, along with other leaders, in June 1867 prepared a letter of protest to the Commissioner of Indian Affairs to maintain their "nationality and separate existence as a tribe."[24] Seven hundred and twelve tribal members, about two-thirds of the Delawares, signed this petition.[25] It stated that, in council and with a majority of the tribe present, "it was agreed unanimously that the Delawares will never give up their nationality and become merged in the Cherokee Nation."[26] Furthermore, the Lenape reminded the Commissioner of the treaty of 1866, which had specified that they were to "go in a body to a distinct reservation," and the United States' duty as a guardian.[27] Sometime during the second half of 1869, several of the most outspoken of the protesters had sent another letter to the Commissioner of Indian Affairs, insisting that they wanted "to git our money and treet with any other tribe for a home."[28]

Officials like General Blunt perceived what they thought were divisions among the Delawares. They conceptualized these in accordance with contemporary racial thinking, referring to 'full bloods' and 'half-breeds.' Yet while these white men were undoubtedly correct in perceiving differences amongst the Delawares these can more accurately be interpreted as conflicts between traditionalists and modernists.

The modernist chiefs of the Delawares seemed to have seen their goal in advancing their people in a different, more individual way. They feared the consequences of the actions of "old men seeking to perpetuate past customs," as they characterized the traditionalists.[29] Yet they, too, cared about tribal unity, since one of their most pronounced fears was the scattering of their people.[30] Nevertheless, the modernists were disposed to accept more of what has been called 'white ways.' They probably viewed the acceptance of the modified terms as the only feasible option in the face of a worsening situation in Kansas and their virtual powerlessness vis-à-vis the federal government.

The Bureau of Indian Affairs officials like Delaware agent Pratt not only observed differences in the Delawares but actually contributed to them. Pratt and others often favored the modernists. In 1861, for instance, the United States government had appointed Charles Journeycake, a Baptist minister, chief of the Turkey Clan, which was in violation of the Delawares' matrilineal model of descent since Journeycake's mother had been white.[31] Consequently, many tribal members resented this appointment.[32] In Delaware tradition, upon the death of the old chief, one of the three clan chiefs would have ascended to head chief; now, however, it was the intervention of officials that decided the matter. The 'full bloods' resented this.

The officials, however, misrepresented the conflict amongst the Delawares, confusing differences for division. In actual fact, even this internal conflict between traditionalists and modernists, 'full bloods' and 'half breeds,' only serves to illustrate how much all the removing Delawares cared about the preservation of their tribal ties. After all, it was only the Delawares who remained in Kansas as United States citizens who opted to give up their tribal affiliation. Everyone who chose to remove did so in order to maintain the tribal ties. It just happened that different groups among the Lenape had different opinions about what were the best means of achieving this goal in the circumstances. Both modernists and traditionalists repeatedly emphasized their interest in the well-being of the nation and came to especially stress tribal ties and their identity as Delawares.[33] Traditionalist Fall Leaf, in a letter to the Commissioner of Indian Affairs as early as 1864, explained that the Lenape wished "to remain Indians, and to preserve our nation."[34] Modernist Charles Journeycake likewise expressed concern "for the welfare of our nation."[35] It is likely that the Lenape used blood quantum as a way to express and illustrate their positions in their correspondence with United States officials, but, contrary to the opinion of officials like Blunt, this did not signify that an internal rift existed that was too deep to be overcome. It also did not mean that the goals of the two groups were radically divergent.

As it turned out, removal to Indian Territory did not bring the relief the modernists had hoped for but instead all the deleterious consequences the traditionalists had feared. The Lenape were seriously threatened by forced cohabitation, a lack of a separate settlement area, and constant harassment. This harassment, the treatment they received as 'others,' is a good indicator that the Lenape had not been accepted as Cherokees.

The internal friction, which had been aggravated by the signing of the modified agreement, had got progressively worse especially after the tribe had relocated to the Cherokee country and begun to experience the negative affects thereof. Consequently about 300 people moved away from the homes already purchased within the Cherokee Nation.[36] At the height of this exodus, about half the tribe could be counted among these wild, seceding, or Neosho Delawares.[37] The Neosho, however, were forced to move back, and upon their return they found that the situation of the other Delawares had not improved. With the exodus of the Neosho Delawares, the internal conflicts among the Delawares had climaxed. These rifts did not mend immediately upon the Neoshos' return. Subsequently, though, as living within the Cherokee Nation finally got unbearable for all its members, the tribe was once again internally united in their quest for a new, separate reservation. Consequently, some time in the fall of 1876, the entire tribe petitioned Congress to be removed to its own reservation.[38] Modernists and traditionalists had come together again in their fight for tribal unity and integrity and in an attempt to maintain a separate tribal identity in the face of adverse circumstances.[39]

This phenomenon of intra-tribal differences in opinion was also present among the Yaquis, even though there it was much less pronounced and lacked the same usage of the blood quantum labels. The men leading the fighting factions of the tribe were, naturally, not always of the same opinion, but as they operated independently for the most part this would under normal circumstances have been less obvious than in the case of the Delawares. And just like the Lenape chiefs, the Yaquis were at times blaming each other for what was happening to the tribe. But with them, a basic position at least initially seems to have been shared by all the men in charge. They wanted their territory to themselves and not to have to share it with any outsiders, as they stated repeatedly in their dealings with the government. In particular they resented the military presence on the Yaqui river. To all of them, autonomy and control over what remained of their traditional territory was of prime importance. They claimed those rights primarily by virtue of being Native to the area, "porque Somos de aqui."[40] This attachment to the land can also be considered a unifying element which may have helped to stave off conflicts especially in the face of government adversity.

However, during the peace negotiations which attempted to end the guerrilla war it became painfully obvious that also among the Yoeme existed chasms in matters of leadership. Therefore, the negotiations, with Luis Bule claiming to be—or maybe rather being forced to assume the position of head chief—failed repeatedly to get all of the rebels to lay down their arms and all of the *pacíficos* to cease to support them. Like it had been the case with the Delawares, governmental intervention can be identified as a factor crucially aggravating existing conflicts as the problems began in earnest with Bule's inability to gather all Yoeme in one place to discuss their options. Governmental pressure and time restrictions had made this impossible and thus forced Bule to act independently in an area that would have required a consensus decision. And later on, in an effort to honor his word to the government, Bule was forced to turn against some of his own people when trying to apprehend the rebels who still managed to hold out.

As far as I could determine, blood quantum criteria and the resulting labels did not figure at all among the Yoeme, or only in a very minor way. There was probably comparatively little intermarriage with outsiders and the offspring of such unions would most likely not have been easily discernable but otherwise the officials who might have introduced such labels, just as their counterparts in the United States had done. This made similar misconceptions and misinterpretation by outsiders less likely and conflicts hence were not couched in terms of blood quantum. But, as even through the period of removal the consensus on land and autonomy seems to have been high, governmental meddling would have had little success in introducing friction into the tribe by aggravating existing conflicts. Friction did develop in response to the negotiations with Luis Bule during which the government held him to assume a role he did not rightly occupy. And as Bule was a man of is word the agreement he had entered into later on forced him to persecute his former comrades. Yet these rifts or even the Yaquis who turned informers in order to avoid their own deportation did not illustrate grossly divergent notions on what was best for the tribe, but rather the results of governmental intervention.[41] Different tribal notions for and of the future most likely did not develop until after the outbreak of the Mexican Revolution when different revolutionary factions made offers to the Yaquis which forced them to take sides in return for what they hoped would be gains for the tribe as such. And these decisions sometimes resulted in Yoeme fighting on opposite sides. Yet even then the internal frictions would not have taken the shape of the conflicts between traditionalists and modernists among the Lenape. Such rifts were late to arrive among the Yoeme who still agreed on what made a Yaqui—on what constituted the shared Yaqui identity—and also on common goals during the period of removal and the years thereafter. Significantly though, in both cases internal conflicts were aggravated by external intervention and thus probably aided the respective government.

REMOVAL AND IDENTITY

As the discussion of competing responses to removal has shown, both tribes have changed in response to the situation and the world around them. Yet their reactions to government policies, as well as their aims and goals for the tribe also made it clear that both retained a certain spirit of tribal identity, have insisted on a collective existence instead of assenting to join mainstream society. Thus I would judge their fight successful in that respect. Had they tried to maintain their communities and their identity unchanged they surely would have perished in the attempt. However, many times it has been viewed as something of a loss, a surrender, and consequently as a negative thing to adapt and to change and even scholars have sometimes decided that Natives are 'less Indian' today. It has been pointed out that a society, after 400 years of white contact, would invariably have changed so much that they are not 'true' Indians anymore. Yet somehow these purity requirements do not seem to apply to the changes in 'white' society, where these supposedly constitute a positive and a natural development.

Throughout their history the Delawares insisted on their own, unique identity, which no one else could share. They rejected all the other choices presented to them and insisted on tribal unity and separateness. They may well have realized that most of these were nominal choices at best as the Cherokees were not inclined to accept them and neither was the United States mainstream. The Lenape, like many other Indians, "rejected both the pressure and the opportunity, struggling to preserve distinct, indigenous communities that for a long time promised little more than poverty and powerlessness."[42] Such steadfast determination and resistance can only partly be explained by political and economic circumstances. It seems like their tribal ties and thus their identity as Delawares offered them something the outside word could not. The same was probably true for the Yaquis who furthermore were deprived of alternate avenues with the onset of the deportations when the rigorous pursuit of that practice even precluded them from joining the mainstream. Yet even while alternatives had still been open to them they—like the Lenape—favored their own (ethnic) identity.

To come back to the example used in the introduction, removal may have damaged parts of the house that is identity and it may have caused others to be partly reconstructed, torn down, or fortified, but it left the house as such still habitable, even though probably not to the taste of everyone.

Thomas H. Eriksen has concluded that, in order for "ethnic membership to have a personal importance, it must provide the individual with something he or she considers valuable."[43] Yet, as both the case of the Delawares and that of the Yaquis has made evident, this importance is not necessarily of an economic or political nature. As George De Vos and Ida Romanucci-Ross have pointed out, "a relative priority must be given to the emotional, even irrational, psychological features underlying one's social identity."[44] Their tribal ties gave the Indians something they could not get anywhere else, a sense of belonging, a sense of self which they could not in quite the same way obtain from national society.

Benedict Anderson, in his *Imagined Communities,* has held that every community larger than one based on face-to-face contact is an imagined one. The Delawares were still part of such a genuine face-to-face community. They thus did not have to imagine a community, which, as Richard Adams has clarified, "implies much more than merely an organized aggregate of co-residents. It involves daily interactions and familiar patterned behavior, internal factions and alliances, love and hatred, but with all, it also involved a recognition of common good and, if necessary, common defense against outsiders."[45] Among the Lenape everyone knew everyone, probably even during the time period the Neosho Delawares spent away from the main tribal settlement area. And even while there was some discontent with the elected tribal leaders, the institution of the tribe as such still offered its members something the abstract, the imagined, nation state could not give them. After all, in spite of all discontent tribal unity and tribal separateness were shared goals for both traditionalists and modernists.

Still, had the exodus of the Neosho Delawares lasted much longer, it may very likely have had repercussions on the tribe as such. But since they were forced back, ironically by the government, which, at least according to its own rhetoric, was really trying to break them up and assimilate them into mainstream society, a decisive step was taken towards maintaining the cohesive nature of the tribe. (This is somewhat ironic as the white officials had taken this step mostly out of convenience, to stop the Delaware chiefs' protests and to facilitate the payment of annuities.) And soon the entire tribe took steps for a 'common defense against outsiders,' thereby uniting once again.

Due to the outbreak of the Mexican Revolution the Yaquis' face-to-face community was able to take steps toward restoration. The deportees were allowed to return from their forced exile, the traditional pueblos were settled once again, and the rebels could come down from the sierra.[46] Yet a number of these rebels were then recruited for the revolutionary armies and therefore were isolated from the other Yoeme for a prolonged time. But even with these absences, the community as such found itself in a decidedly more beneficial situation than during the deportations. Like the Delawares the Yaquis opted for the traditional tribal unity and identity rather than for the nation-state, even though some Yoeme fought for, with, and against various revolutionary leaders. Yet they most likely only did so to bring about gains and advantages for the tribe rather than out of a shared ideology with the revolutionaries. For them "the nation-state was, at best, a source of fiscal and other demands; they owed it no loyalty," as Alan Knight has pointed out in connection to traditionally living Indians.[47] Their loyalty still was to their tribe.

With the two communities not exactly restored but on their way to recovery of their internal unity, both indigenous groups post-removal once again acquired a certain measure of control over matters of identity. As John Kicza has pointed out: "To the extent possible, Indian peoples have been selective about what aspects of the outside world they incorporate into their cultures. . . . They have used their internal unity . . . to incorporate the changes forced upon them on the best terms that they could muster."[48] While in the course of this process described so aptly by Kicza, land, and specifically their ancestral homeland, seems to have been a factor of the utmost importance to the Yaquis. That was not quite so for the Delawares. After their first removals, the Lenape just wanted some land, almost of any kind, as long as it would give them the chance to maintain their tribal ties and provide for their subsistence. They did not necessarily view their tribal identity as tied to a particular piece of land. Even so, while in the further course of their history they abandoned or modified some of their old rituals and also to an extent gave up their language, to this day the Lenape insist on a tribal identity, a collective existence, and an identification as Delawares. The Yaquis have managed to keep at least part of their ancestral homeland, and, like the Delawares, also have preserved a collective, a tribal identity.

And while their fights certainly are far from over yet, the two groups can look back at decisive battles won and the ones they had to fight in response to removal can be counted among them. In fact, the onslaught from the outside that was removal served to strengthen those ethnic ties and aspects of their identity that did survive.

Still, these and other successes have often gone unnoticed or have even been intentionally overlooked. The notion of the 'vanishing American' persists and changed identities are still often held to testify to this. And though it could hardly be expected to find an unchanged tribal identity even had there been no contacts with Europeans at all, the mere existence of change has often been used as evidence against indigenous societies. This is maintained even in the face of compelling evidence and academic findings to the contrary. As Stuart Hall has so eloquently phrased it: "Though they seem to invoke an origin in a historical past with which they continue to correspond, actually identities are about questions of using the resources of history, language, and culture in the process of becoming rather than being: not 'who we are' or 'who we came from,' so much as what we might become, how we have been represented and how that bears on how we might represent ourselves."[49] In a similar vein Vine Deloria, Jr. has insightfully explained that "the flexibility of the tribal viewpoint enables Indians to meet devastating situations and survive. But this flexibility is often seen by non-Indians as incompetence."[50] Yet, as scholarship on identity suggests, identity needs to be flexible as "ethnic identities are constructed, but they are never finished."[51] This is usually acknowledged in other areas of history and life. There the absence of change would most likely be considered a sign of backwardness. It is not only change that is instrumentalized by non-Natives in ways which make it appear to speak against American Indians, it is also the absence of change. According to this attitude Native Americans can only lose. If they adapt and change they are said to have surrendered their (ethnic) identities, yet should they not change at all they would be considered backwards and 'unfit.' Sadly, this repressive view is not limited to mainstream societies and government agencies but can be found among academics as well.

I would hold that tribal or ethnic identity is not merely about meeting a certain number of criteria on some scientist's checklist. Instead, I agree with Richard Adams, who has concluded that "the loss or retention of a particular formal trait . . . does not necessarily indicate a change or lack of change in identity. Thus, a group identity can be reproduced through changing formal traits as well as through a resolute adherence to, or observation of, those traits."[52] Vine Deloria has aptly illustrated this by stating that "the best characterization of tribes is that they stubbornly hold on to what they feel is important to them and discard what they feel is irrelevant to their current needs. Traditions die hard and innovation comes hard."[53] Or, as Duane Champagne has put it: "Societies are not stagnant . . . they have an inherent tendency toward change, although core cultural features may endure for centuries."[54] I see adherence to tribalism as such a core feature which furthermore was a crucial one as it aided in preserving others. As Donald Fixico has stated: "Although Indians are, of course, individuals, they fundamentally view themselves as members of a group."[55] For Natives it was probably their collective identity as members of tribes that enabled them to meet the many challenges by the surrounding societies. The very tribal ties and identity that the outside world was so set on taking away from them was what helped Natives survive and retain agency rather than merely being victimized, possibly indicating some white awareness of how crucial these ties were. John Kicza has written that "to the extent possible, Indian peoples have been selective about what aspects of the outside world they incorporate into their cultures. The indigenous communities have not been without resources. They have used their internal unity . . . to incorporate the changes forced upon them on the best terms that they could muster."[56] While they were most certainly victims they were not limited to that status.

Still, restrictive views and attitudes persist both in and outside of governmental agencies. I believe that one of the central reasons for this is the continued desire to make Indians a thing of the past, to remove them. Restricting access to Native identities is just another way to achieve this goal. In that respect and especially in the United States, the idea of aboriginal purity with regard to identity seems to be tied to the idea of racial purity. One need only look at the federal government's restrictive identification policies which, it has been alleged, may yet define Native Americans out of existence.[57] Jack Forbes has discussed this as a variation of the infamous 'one drop rule': one drop of Black blood suffices to make one Black while Indians need only one drop of other blood to cease to be Indians.[58] Significantly, depriving Natives of their Indianness even today has 'side-effects' highly desirable from the point of view of many Americans. While in the nineteenth century removal opened up Indian lands and was thus attractive for economic reasons, nowadays it would ensure the loss of the inconvenient special legal status still inherent to all federally recognized tribes and their members. Removing Indianness would still quite literally pay off today but the 'vanishing Americans' continue to refuse to acquiesce.

Thus attempts to hold Indians to impossible and outdated standards of aboriginal identity and racial purity can be meaningfully interpreted as modern ways of removal and as a continuation of the very same colonialism Natives have been exposed to for so long.

REMOVAL—A SUCCESS STORY?

If one believes the rhetoric of the United States government that removal as a policy was intended to give Native Americans more time to gradually assimilate into mainstream society then removal did not succeed and would have to be considered a failure as a policy. Removal did not erase Native tribal and ethnic identity, did not turn Indians into (mainstream) Americans. It transplanted entire tribes instead, thus maintaining many of the attributes rhetoric claimed needed to be destroyed. In the case of the Delawares, removal—while doubtlessly a stressful and traumatic event for the tribe—in the end helped to overcome the internal differences it had previously aggravated. Thus, instead of destroying tribal ties and tribal identities in accordance with what supposedly was its agenda, removal ended up strengthening these very ties and identities. Therefore, it may be said to have achieved exactly the opposite of what it proclaimed to have set out to do. As Donald L. Fixico has observed: "Federal and state policy has undoubtedly changed Indian lives and histories. Rarely, however, have those changes reflected the desires of policymakers. Removal did not lead to assimilation."[59] Instead, after a hard period of adjustment, removal strengthened the Lenape as a tribe, thus enabling them to successfully meet most of the challenges posed by future policies and by life among the Cherokees. (However, as I will argue in the following chapter, removal in the United States was a partial success when it came to its 'covert' agenda of economical gains for the nation state and its non-Native citizens.)

Cornell and Hartmann have come to a similar conclusion about the failure of removal as a policy. They state that "the process of land expropriation and reservation confinement, the racial antagonism of many Whites, and the desire to teach Indians the ways of Euro-American civilization before integrating them into American society inadvertently produced a situation in which Indian groups could survive as groups, although typically under stress and in execrable conditions."[60] They went on to point out that "this process of expulsion through violence and treaty-making had an ironic result: It often altered but ultimately preserved tribal boundaries."[61] So in the United States, removal as an assimilationist policy could indeed be considered to have backfired.

United States Indian policy in general also built up an administrative apparatus to organize Indians, usually as tribes, and therefore to an extent again reinforced tribal boundaries. "In other words, and with some important exceptions, it left the group boundaries that organized much of Indian life to some degree intact, even reinforcing them through a kind of grudging political recognition and the formalization of links between Indian groups and their remnant reservation lands."[62] The Delawares, among the last to suffer through removal before the policy got replaced by that of allotment, serve as an almost perfect example for the failure of this policy. While they were resettled in the Cherokee Nation the government kept dealing with them as a tribe. Even had the Lenape assimilated post-removal they would have done so to Cherokee ways, not to white America's. But the Delawares insisted on their separateness as a tribe above all else.

For the Yaquis in Mexico, matters presented themselves somewhat differently. With regard to the Yoeme, removal may have indeed reached its intended goal had it not been for the outbreak of the Mexican Revolution. The Díaz government had wanted to clear Yaqui lands without losing Yaqui labor and it was well on the way of achieving this aim when the revolution put a stop to the program. It had sought assimilation only in as much as it wanted the Yoeme deportees to become subservient workers on Yucatán but removal as such was not intended to turn them into Mexicans nor did it claim that to be its goal. Rather, governmental rhetoric passed the deportations off as a benevolent measure as it permitted the Yaquis to live, implying that they would deserve death. Nothing could be further away from being assimilationist even in name. As far as the government was concerned it seems like the Yoeme had missed their chance to become Mexicans.

This also implies that the measure itself had been born out of something like desperation, a means the government turned to because all other attempts to deal with the so-called Yaqui menace had failed. Much less reflection, both philosophical and legal, had been invested in the planning of the deportations of the Yaqui tribe than had been invested in removal in the United States. Unlike in the United States, removal of the Yaquis was geared to achieve maximum economic exploitation. It was probably the way the tribe was broken up through the deportations, as well as the forced exile that made removal such a destructive force for the Yoeme. It was not the tribe, the community, that was transplanted, but individual workers. What 'needed' to be done was done, without any considerations of philosophical or legal nature. As such justifications were deemed unnecessary and the government was free to pursue its goals in a very direct fashion and without having to worry about maintaining a certain proximity between rhetoric and reality. Mexico reacted with greater flexibility to meet these demands, custom-made a removal policy exclusively for the Yoeme, and so its efforts were crowned by a greater degree of success than was the case in the United States, at least on the face of it.

Linda Gordon has correctly stated that "whether histories have a happy ending or not depends on when the chronicler ends the tale."[63] Had I ended this tale immediately after the removals, things would have looked bleak for the Delawares and little better for the Yaquis. Yet while removal certainly had a grave impact on both societies it was the years to follow that really put them to the test by not giving them a respite to overcome removal, which by itself had not been able to fully achieve its goals in either country. It still seems almost like a miracle that the tribes' managed to preserve an intact identity at all. Richard Adams concurs with this when he writes that "given the overwhelming advantages that states enjoy over unfavored ethnicities, it is surprising not only that the latter have continued to exercise a decisive role historically, but that they have been emerging into ever greater prominence in recent decades."[64] Yet the survival of the Delawares and the Yaquis was no miracle. The Lenape and Yoeme worked hard for it. They proved themselves fit in the fight against what could be called the most deadly predator on earth, to borrow Ward Churchill's allegory, their fellow human beings. (The allegory of prey and predator, though generally fitting, has one important weakness. Non-human predators kill mainly or only to satisfy their needs; greed seems to be the distinguishing feature of human predators.) In this (un)natural selection process the two tribes had ample occasion to prove their fitness by weathering all well or bad intentioned policies applied towards them. This fitness, which enabled them and their identity to survive, was one that for the longest time went unseen or unrecognized by the Euroamerican societies around them. They believed fitness only to exist in scale, in physical strength, in strength in numbers, and the likes. But the Native societies of the Lenape and the Yoeme have shown that a quiet toughness and the sheer will to endure range just as high or even higher. In the end, the predator's attacks may have served to make the prey stronger, 'fitter.'[65]

Chapter Thirteen
Histories of Change and Survival

Colin G. Calloway once observed about the 'reappearance' of New England Indians that "if we ignore the eighteenth and nineteenth centuries, we can make little sense of what is happening in New England in the twentieth century: if Indians disappeared after King Philip's War, how can the people asserting their rights today be 'real' Indians?"[1] He finds the answer to be hidden in stories of change and survival. Two such stories have been the subjects of this study, those of the Delawares (Lenape) and of the Yaquis (Yoeme). And they were found to indeed be 'real' Indians, with living identities and continuing tribal ties. Some of the changes to their identities have been brought about through removal which both tribes were exposed to in the late nineteenth or early twentieth century. Yet, as seen in the previous chapter, removal did not bring about the desired results in either one of the countries. In the United States it failed to reach the outcome of eventual assimilation which the governmental rhetoric proclaimed to have been the overarching goal of the nationwide policy. The Delawares were transplanted as a tribe and steadfastly refused to surrender their separateness and to merge with the Cherokees or with mainstream America. They clung to their own tribal identity in spite and because of all pressures to surrender it. In Mexico, the deportations of a significant part of the Yaqui tribe came close to breaking their will to resist and to incorporating the deportees as docile workers in another part of the country. Yet the tribe was saved by the outbreak of the Mexican Revolution which caused the campaign against them to be discontinued. Throughout their ordeal they had held stubbornly to their demands for control over their traditional lands and for the return of those tribal members who had been deported. Within this fight, land and community were of prime concern and importance for both Lenape and Yoeme.

REMOVAL AND COVERT AGENDAS

Land and community were also important for the encapsulating nation states, for the United States and Mexico. Yet while in the United States the destruction of Native tribal communities was viewed as a benevolent measure and thus openly admitted to in the rhetoric of removal, the matter of land acquisition through removal was a somewhat different matter. While it was no secret that Indians would lose lands through the application of the policy this fact was at best portrayed as a side-effect but not as the driving force I believe it to have been in truth. Land acquisition for the state and its citizens of European extraction was the covert—though dominant—agenda of removal in the United States and this covert agenda, I hold, contributed considerably to the failure of the surface goals of the policy.

Matters were both easier and more complicated in Mexico. As removal was not a nation-wide program that was supposed to apply to all Indians, but instead a measure that was just applied to the Yaquis (though it had been used before), the state did not perceive a need for the sweeping rhetoric that was used in the United States. Only part way through the campaign were the deportations passed off as a benevolent treatment of the tribe as they permitted the Yoeme to live. Thus Mexico's covert agenda was much less covert than was the case in the United States. The government wanted control over the Yaquis' lands and to open them up to non-Native settlers. It also aimed to destroy the Yoeme's community which was held to be responsible for the continued resistance the tribe kept up in the face of attempts to take their lands. (It has been claimed that land was not a crucial issue in former Spanish America and I would agree that this was the case at least for much of the colonial period. Patricia Seed has described colonial attitudes and intentions: "Coming from a region in which land was a central concern, English colonists assumed that the objective of colonization could only be to own the natives' land. In contrast, Spanish and Portuguese settlers equally took it for granted that control of people (and their labor) was the only goal that mattered."[2] Yet this changed once land started to run out and from then on it came to be as important as labor. Still, vestiges of such colonial attitudes are still visible in the removal of the Yaquis with its emphasis on land and labor.)

Hence land and community were as much crucial factors in Mexico as they were in the United States. Yet while for a time the Yaquis were encouraged—albeit in a not very pronounced way—to become Mexicans, the option of joining the mainstream society was closed to them as soon as the deportations started, suggesting that land ranked higher on the government's agenda than assimilation did. However, in contrast to the situation in the United States, in Mexico another factor entered the equation and that was the exploitation of Native labor which was especially significant in the case of the Yaquis who were valued very highly as laborers. While this for the longest time had been a factor staving off removal (and thus helping the Yaquis to hold on to their land) as the Yoeme's labor was crucial in Sonora, it eventually turned into a disadvantage when it could be better exploited on Yucatán which also meant that the Yaquis' lands would become available. I believe that the fact that the exploitation of Native labor ranked high on the government's agenda next to land acquisition is largely accountable for how close Mexico came to also achieving the lesser of the three goals, the breaking up of the tribal community. Instead of transplanting the entire tribe, as had been the case with the Delawares and others in the United States, the Sonoran state government with federal help exported groups of workers who ended up in isolated communities in forced exile, thereby seriously affecting the ties that had made them so successful in matters of survival pre-removal. Because Mexico was not (sub)consciously torn over the pursuit of an official and a covert agenda of removal it was more successful in achieving the goals it openly pursued through removal.

The United States openly proclaimed its intent to destroy tribal communities and to assimilate Indians into American society as individuals. Removal, it claimed, would give Natives more time to assimilate, something that was considered beneficial for them. Yet, as Reginald Horsman has so convincingly shown as early as 1969, removal as a policy failed to truly pursue its stated objectives and to meet its own moral standards. He states that "the object of transforming the Indians into Americans was not reprehensible in the eyes of the early nineteenth century and to attack the policy on these grounds would be to ask that nineteenth century Americans should have had twentieth century values. The failure of American Indian policy in the early nineteenth century came when its own moral objects were repudiated and when those Indians who could have been assimilated were swept aside."[3] At that stage, I hold, the covert (or sometimes subconscious) agenda came to dominate the official one.

However, this is not to say that removal was merely a great scheme to take land away from the Natives and that everyone involved acted only out of selfishness and pursued ulterior motives while only paying lip-service only to the official rhetoric. While I do not necessarily agree with Richard White's opinion that federal Indian policy was probably dominated by well-meaning people, I do believe that at least some well-intentioned human beings contributed to policies which ultimately turned out to be detrimental to the Natives.[4] And wherever in the hierarchy of Indian policy these people may have been there would still have been plenty of room for abuse as the chain of command was so long and policies could look quite different on the ground than they may have been envisaged on the drawing board. Yet even at the legislative level these policies may have been somewhat half-hearted attempts where covert agendas consciously or subconsciously came into play. As Stephen Cornell has concluded, policy responded to interest and circumstance yet, I would hold, even well-meaning individuals could on some level fool themselves into believing that land gains were just welcome side-effects of removal and neither the driving force behind the policy nor detrimental to Native Americans.[5] As Patricia Seed has argued, "self-centeredness was and is not necessarily malicious"—yet it can have detrimental effects nevertheless.[6] Others, however, would have schemed knowingly and consciously, seeking only to further their own advantage or that of their people and at times not even deeming it necessary to adopt the guise of benevolence. As Tim Garrison has pointed out, "prominent Americans such as Jackson and Calhoun began to bemoan the fact that the federal government's policy of recognizing tribal rights stood in the way of that of expansion."[7] Such individuals acted accordingly and pursued the covert agenda more openly than others.[8]

In the United States, this mix of intentions and morals permitted the 'covert' agenda of land acquisition to dominate the official one of assimilation and was probably the main cause for the only half-hearted attempts to assimilate the Indians. Thus, while the covert agenda was very successful (though not completely so), it still enabled tribal survival and thus ultimately greed foiled its own goals as the survival of tribal structures to this day stands in the way of completely accomplishing the covert agenda—which continued/s in different guises after the removal policy had been discontinued.

THE EVOLUTION OF REMOVAL

Although, as I would maintain, removal was one of the very first policies used by Europeans towards Native Americans, it took until 1830 to formulate it as a United States law. Before that, it was practiced on an ad hoc basis and in an often disorganized manner by the state, and it was also brought about by the population pressures exerted by non-Native settlers and squatters. As such, it "was no sudden plan, decisively formulated by Monroe, Calhoun, or Jackson, but a course of action pragmatically arrived at after considerable executive, legislative, and popular discord."[9] It evolved slowly and was casually practiced before it ever officially existed as an actual law. Removal thus was responsible for considerable territorial gains made by the United States even before it became a policy. Yet, as Patricia Seed has pointed out: "Like most successful colonizers, Europeans wanted to create a morality from the facts of success."[10] Dorothy Jones has described this moral and legal dilemma for the post-Independence United States this way: "Unless the Indians could be brought to agree on expansion—which was, in contemporary thought, a prerequisite for prosperity—there would be no peace. If the Indians did not agree and expansion took place anyway, there would be no justice. American postwar policy was a series of attempts to find a way out of this basic dilemma."[11] Hence they needed to justify what had already taken place and what was still going strong. Reginald Horsman concurs that "in this endeavor to give expansion a moral basis the Americans were not, of course, unique. Western Europeans have always tended to justify their advance over large areas of the world in terms of spreading civilization."[12] Yet such a justification was a hard task to accomplish as it needed to incorporate what could be regarded as polar opposites, the continuing expansion of the United States and at the same time the establishment of the morality and legitimacy of the recently created nation. According to Horsman, "in these post-Revolutionary years the young United States faced a typical nineteenth-century dilemma and attempted to solve it in a way which would benefit both the national interest and the national honor."[13] But he also concluded that "by 1820 the full failure of the federal government's efforts to reconcile expansion and morality was becoming apparent."[14] To my mind, the national interest came to take precedence over the national honor even though some proponents of removal may not have realized this or may not have wanted to do so.

"Although some of the friends of the Indians supported removal in the hope that what happened east of the Mississippi would not be repeated, the practical politicians who supported it saw it as the way out of a pressing dilemma. The federal government ... had attempted to pursue an Indian policy which it thought would have some advantage to the Indians as well as achieving the primary objective of American expansion."[15] Already that early on, Native interests took a backseat to the covert agenda, the primary objective of United States expansion. Yet even what was done in terms of attempting to civilize the Indians met with much opposition as it ran contrary to the aims of many Americans of European extraction who openly coveted Indian lands. They were probably disinclined to accept assimilated Natives in general but especially saw their goals threatened by Natives who held land—be they civilized or not. This became obvious in the southern states in general but particularly in Tennessee and Georgia, as Reginald Horsman, Michael D. Green and Tim Alan Garrison, among others, have shown so convincingly.

Still, the official rhetoric that stated that the attempts to civilize the Indians had not born fruit served a purpose. "To say that removal had become essential because of the absolute failure of the civilization policy might well have eased consciences, but it did not fairly represent the situation in the South in 1824."[16] In fact, those tribes who were the most civilized were the first to suffer from the introduction of the new policy. Ironically, it was their high degree of civilization which made them dangerous in the eyes of those around them who saw their own agendas threatened by their success. For these tribes, their advances in the white ways turned out to have been rather counterproductive. Yet the claim about the failure of the civilization program still served to justify the implementation of removal and thus aided the goal of national expansion and helped to satisfy white land hunger at least temporarily. The rhetoric of removal also portrayed white influence as being detrimental for the Natives but, instead of only removing those who truly suffered from bad white influence, it took a more sweeping approach, thus boycotting the advances the civilization program had made. These had turned out to be inconvenient for Euro-Americans and had also become a major bone of contention between the federal government and the southern states in particular. (However, other considerations also entered into this matter. The debate of state rights v. federal rights coincided with and impacted on the evolution of Indian removal as a policy and also held relevance in the context of slavery, thus aggravating matters for Native Americans by highly charging the issues of removal and Native political and legal status.[17]) Some proponents of removal seem to have convinced themselves of the righteousness of their cause (even tough subconsciously they may have realized that there were problems with the policy) and thus may have been all the more convincing themselves.

REMOVAL AND LAND

The history of the Delawares illustrates how much the focus in Indian-white relations had been on land, pre-removal, during the policy, as well as thereafter. At times it seemed like a tragic story made for Hollywood. And this was obvious to contemporaries as well. As early as 1851, in his introduction to the revised edition of 'The Last of the Mohicans,' James Fenimore Cooper observed that the Delawares were the first tribe to be dispossessed, and the "seemingly inevitable fate of all these people, who disappear before the advances, or it might be termed the inroads of civilization, as the verdure of their native forests fall before the nipping frost, is represented as having already befallen them."[18] While Cooper's death sentence for the Delaware tribe was certainly premature, another part of his observation was chillingly accurate as, significantly, Cooper saw a link between the dispossession and the disappearance of the tribe. The emphasis on land was clear, the agenda not as covert or hidden as the official rhetoric seemed to suggest.

Other authors, among them many historians and anthropologists, concur with Cooper that "possession of land is crucial to the survival of aboriginal people as a nation."[19] That was partly due to very practical reasons. As Anya Royce has determined "the most important material resource for gaining a livelihood is a land base—either to work oneself or to rent to others—the income from which provides the means of subsistence ... when livelihood is provided by outsiders, the group's allegiance and goals become those of the providers."[20] For Mexico, Marc Alan Sills views matters similarly: "Language, Education, and Culture are not enough to guarantee cultural survival, mostly because they do not put food on the table or permit people to control the elements of their cultures which they themselves view as vital."[21] Therefore most of the outside 'help' like that of the BIA and similar institutions elsewhere (like the *Instituto Nacional Indigenista* or its successor, the *Comisión Nacional para el Desarrollo de los Pueblos Indígenas* in Mexico) may have in the long run had the reverse effect to what they claimed they wanted to achieve and especially when the (not so) covert agenda of land acquisition dominated policies such as removal. Some authors even go as far as claiming that elusive assimilationist goals might have been achieved had the policymakers left Indians alone. As Paula Mitchell Marks asserts: "Indians were adapting all along, adapting so well that many of the problems in Indian-white relations today might not exist if the Indians had been allowed to continue to evolve at their own pace and according to their own standards."[22] But they were not left alone; they were 'aided' in their adaptation process, often by policies relating to land tenure, as illustrated by the cases of the Delawares and Yaquis.

However, material resources like land avail to little without the presence of the ideological component. "In order for an ideology of resistance to incorporation to develop, a people have to be bound by strong ties of history reinforced by shared values and goals," as Royce as concluded.[23] And one's own identity has to compare favorably to that of outsiders. As seen, all of this was the case for the Delawares and the Yaquis. Few of them could be tempted to join the respective mainstream societies. And in this respect land was again of prime importance.

This was so because there was—and is—another dimension to land tenure, a more spiritual one. As Richard Adams has asserted, "territory may play a number of roles for an ethnicity, but that crucially concerned with identity need not play an economic role. The identification with a lost or future homeland, for example, may have had, and might in the future have, some economic significance, but for the moment it is purely a feature of identity."²⁴ This became obvious in the Yaquis' struggle for their homeland as well as in the intimate way they talked about it. The phenomenon was also evident in the Delawares' quest for an unbroken settlement area to which the tribe could go in a body to preserve tribal unity. The quality of the land—though of high importance to them—thus became a secondary issue. Fleras and Elliott explain that "for aboriginal peoples, land possesses a sacred quality, rooted in an attachment to history, a sense of identity, and a perception of duty towards future generations."²⁵

Looking at the two cases of this study, this attachment became very visible when the Yaquis were taken to Yucatán. All of a sudden, quiet reigned. Quiet, but not peace. It was the quiet of despair, a despair at least in part born out of the loss of, the separation from their land. While removed from their homeland, the Yaqui deportees also seem to have been separated from their fighting spirit. Land to the Yoeme must have been more than just the soil. Land to them quite literally was home, the place where their roots were. Once uprooted, something in them seems to have died. Yet even in this state of despair they seem to have kept other attributes of 'Yaquiness' and kept viewing and identifying themselves as Yaquis. Matters were somewhat different with the Delawares, who survived repeated removals and the loss of land that came with them. While they did not lose their tribal identity, they probably left parts of it behind and had to reconstruct and reinvent. Yet in both cases, Native lives as well as white policies in many ways evolved around land.

And, as seen, especially when it came to policies it was the land more than the culture that matters evolved around. When the US government talked about wanting to assimilate the Indians, this was certainly a means to get to their land—as the eagerness for the sale of so-called surplus lands proved. The Yaquis were more or less left alone while everyone thought their land to be worthless. Once it came to be in demand, the fight for it was on. Only then were pre-existing policies enforced and new measures introduced. White need to possess and not share the land caused this for the Indians, regardless of which nation state they happened to reside in.

Yet the loss of land, as seen, affected Native societies in different ways. The Lenape survived it repeatedly and made do with substitute land, while the deported Yoeme were affected in possibly the gravest way imaginable by the (temporary) loss of their homeland. Unfortunately, the sources available do not allow for even an attempt at judgment about what affected them more—the loss of *their* land or merely the loss of land and the complex community experience that was tied to it.

No matter which of the two, Indians often tried and still try for land instead of monetary compensation. The Indian Claims Commission in the

United States came to that conclusion when repeatedly tribes wanted to refuse money and insisted on land—something the commission was not authorized to grant them. For many Natives this priority remains unchanged to this day, as for instance shown by the refusal of the Sioux to accept reimbursement for the loss of the Black Hills or the Western Shoshones' rejection of monetary compensation for their lands. As Russell Means illustrates the matter: "Would anyone dare suggest that Muslims might take *money* in exchange for Mecca? Who is foolish enough to offer to buy Jerusalem from Israel? Which real estate developer would offer the pope a great deal for the Vatican?"[26]

THE OTHER DIMENSION OF REMOVAL

Thus it can be concluded that the removal rhetoric in the United States did not necessarily conform to all of the removal policy's aims. And more often than not the covert agenda of removal dominated the proceedings and thus rendered the official rhetoric as well as the official objectives of the policy moot.

But apart from the covert agenda of land acquisition, removal as a policy and especially its rhetoric had another function to fulfill in and for the United States. As historian Rhys Isaac has pointed out, the United States is a "nation born in a revolutionary struggle for freedom and equality; it as had a recurrent impulse to measure its history in terms of universal principles, and to recommit itself periodically to its founding ideals."[27] The rhetoric of removal justified the policy and allowed the more scrupulous of the policy makers as well as the general public to believe in the morality and legitimacy of the program while at the same time working on legalizing United States' territorial claims. Some proponents of removal may have genuinely—though shortsightedly—put their faith in the program while others would always have had lingering and maybe subconscious doubts about it. And yet others would have pursued the 'covert' agenda foremost and above all and would only have resorted to the rhetoric of benevolence to rally others to the cause, if they used it at all. In that sense, removal was not really an Indian policy but rather a white one, or at least a policy that had more of a function for non-Natives than for American Indians as it gave the whites land as well as (questionable) morality and legality.

The situation was not all that dissimilar in Mexico where the main goal of removal was also land acquisition but where this agenda item was much less covert than was the case in the United States. There, too, assimilation of Native Americans into the mainstream took a backseat once it might have endangered the primary aim of the policy. However, in Mexico the perceived need for morality and legality was not felt in the same way as in the United States and thus the rhetoric of removal remained much closer to the actual policy than had been the case in the US.[28] As Ward Churchill has pointed out, "recognition of the legal and moral rights by which it occupies whatever landbase it calls its own is one of the most fundamental issues confronting any nation."[29] Or, as Ann Curthoys described the problem in the Australian context, "the legacy of the colonial past is a continuing fear of illegitimacy, and therefore an inability to develop the kind of pluralist inclusive account of the past that might form the basis for a coherent national community."[30] In the United States a certain insecurity over these legal and moral rights has been tangible and discernable in its Indian policy.

THE LEGACY OF REMOVAL

The covert agenda of removal in the United States, the acquisition of Native lands into the nation, was at least in the short run partially successful. It did indeed free-up Native lands and was thus successful in that respect but that also meant that it largely failed to reach the goals stated in its own official rhetoric, namely the ultimate assimilation of Native Americans. In Mexico with its not so covert agenda, the policy of deportation came much closer to achieving the additional goal of turning Yaquis into (landless) workers. Neither country had much interest in truly integrating the Indians as that would have jeopardized the economic benefits so important to the non-Natives in the two nations. Instead, both the United States and Mexico wanted to remove Indians in more than one way. Merely shifting them geographically was insufficient for either nation, so they strove to remove the distinctive Indianness of the peoples in question. This could take the form of eliminating Indianness through (partial) assimilation but could also turn out to be more extreme and involve the physical extinction of the Natives. Here the two countries differed little; Indians had to vanish, one way or another, and to leave their lands for others. Their collective existence legitimated their claims to the land and so any challenge to this collective existence would ultimately serve to challenge their claims to the land.

This general attitude has not disappeared. Many people in both nations as well as elsewhere would still like to see the disappearance of Natives on the American continent and in other parts of the world. And while the more drastic option of physical extermination is slowly disappearing there are many other ways to deny Natives their Indianness. I hold that removal in a metaphorical sense remained important even after the official removals had ended and is still a prevalent theme in the treatment of Native Americans today. Think for instance about the boarding schools in the United States and similar attempts at assimilation through education in Mexico. In the United States, the unilateral extension of citizenship as well as federal identification policy or the criteria for federal recognition can be put in the same tradition and so can policies like termination and relocation, or federal identification, among others. Assimilation in a sense is just another removal albeit a more cultural or spiritual one.

Yet many communities in the United States, Mexico and elsewhere still maintain a strong sense of ethnic identity, a sense that has nothing to do with the racial or cultural purity that has come to be expected from the outside and to which many outsiders would like to hold indigenous peoples. Attempts are made to forcibly press them into a mold. And these go beyond policy-making but permeate everyday life which makes them all the more dangerous. Demanding a certain primordiality of Natives can be just another way of hastening their disappearance. If they do not conform to the criteria others measure them by they are not considered to be 'real' and are thus considered to have been vanished. Alice Kehoe has warned about one aspect of this phenomenon and has counseled on how to overcome it: "If we can drop the myth of the vanishing red child of nature, we can recognize that Indians, like other humans, adapt their cultural patterns of behavior to circumstances, retaining as much as feasible of what still seems precious, dropping and adding to accommodate both outside demands and their own new ideas."[31] The stereotype of being in tune with nature in addition to racial purity is among the most predominant and damaging myths Natives are being held to. Richard White has aptly illustrated the inherent danger in that particular stereotype. "Popular understandings make Native Americans ahistorical by reflexively granting Native Americans a certain 'spiritual' or 'traditional' knowledge. This knowledge is timeless; it seemingly appeared whole at some point far in the past and now can only erode. It cannot be added to. In this formulation Native Americans do not learn; they only forget and disappear."[32] According to that perception, Native Americans are nearly identical with nature itself. Thus they stand outside history. Or, as Patricia Seed has phrased it, "demanding that present-day conduct conform to preconquest (or what are considered to be preconquest) characteristics denies native peoples the opportunity to progress or to participate in history."[33] As in the case of racial purity Natives can only lose as these criteria cannot be met by a living people.

In Mexico, this is reflected by a curiously split picture with the proud traditions of the Aztecs and the Maya on the one hand, and the poor and uneducated *indio* of today on the other hand. This is not so dissimilar to the situation in the United States which at times displays a 'new-agey' ride of Plains warriors on horseback but shuns the supposedly typical drunken Indian, rejecting any responsibility for such a state. Richard White thinks we are "explicitly tying the truth of the narrative to the present worthiness of the groups embracing the narration."[34] And he is not alone with this conclusion. "Anthropologists have taught us that 'knowledge of other cultures and eras' invariably 'depends on the cultures and eras doing the knowing,'" as Jack Green has termed it, which ultimately means that it is non-Natives who bestow 'worthiness.'[35] And so far, as 'worthiness' is determined by outsiders who are 'doing the knowing' and the checklists they bring, the process is victimizing Indians yet again—in a cool, detached, scientific way. "Non-indigenous people insist on their right to define, borrow and usurp Aboriginality and imprint it with trappings of primitivism, while not necessarily addressing ongoing poverty, ill-health, racist denigration and other problems which still underlie the slick presentation of the successful, multicultural nation."[36] Or, as Jan Kociumbas has stated for the Australian case, 'expert' knowledge silenced Aboriginals.[37] The 'vanishing American' is a chilling reality when one looks at non-Native perceptions and attitudes, including academic ones.

But the tribes' history is not over yet. As Patricia Limerick has pointed out: "The legacy of slavery and the legacy of conquest endure, shaping events in our own time."[38] And Thomas Berger has warned us of "the persistence of attitudes that have too often triumphed in the past: that superiority in arms entitles one nation to subdue another; that land can be taken from a people if we deem them or their use of land to be deficient; that all cultures should be judged by our own; that injustice, if it is of sufficiently long standing, need not be redressed."[39] Both Yaquis and Delawares still suffer from the legacy of conquest and the continuing assumptions of cultural superiority which the rhetoric of removal has helped to cement—and both still fight it. Indeed, Vine Deloria could have been thinking specifically about the Delawares' situation when he was speaking of a "legalistic limbo from which there is apparently no escape."[40]

Still, the general public in the US almost seems to have gotten used to Native American lawsuits yet the history underneath these court cases at times seems to have vanished. Limerick calls this phenomenon 'selective amnesia,' eliminating past events from public memory as well as from academic history. And Michel Rolph Truillot has convincingly warned us about the dangers of silences in the writing of history and has identified the phases of the production of these silences. "Silences enter the process of historical production at four crucial moments: the moment of fact creation (the making of *sources*); the moment of fact assembly (the making of *archives*); the moment of fact retrieval (the making of *narratives*); and the moment of retrospective significance (the making of *history* in the final instance)."[41] It is easily obvious that in all four instances of the possible production of silences,

Native Americans had little or no input in the matter. As a result their history is still preeminently written from a 'white' outsider's perspective. It will not be easy to remedy this and along with it the stereotypical assumptions encouraged by national histories. Tellingly, as David William Cohen has pointed out in *The Combing of History*, "Historians ... will in future years have to confront more directly the ways of popular and official constructions of the past, as well as political suppressions of historical knowledge production and the general knowledge of the past in the world."[42]

But it is impossible to come to an exact understanding of the past due to a certain "debatability of the past," as Arjun Appadurai has termed it. And Richard White has adeptly described the problem with an allegory: "Historians make maps of vanished countries. There are only the maps; the past is gone and cannot be recreated."[43] Let me also point to the multitude of 'white' spots on these maps and to all the areas where we incorrectly penciled something in, knowingly or not. Non-Native perceptions of American Indians all too often fall within these categories, partly because the rhetoric of policies like removal is all too often being taken at face value even though as early as 1969 Reginald Horsman did show that "the moral failure is not merely a product of twentieth century hindsight, it also represented a conscious choice."[44] Dipesh Chakrabarty has told us that "all our pasts are ... future in orientation. They help us make the unavoidable journey into the future."[45] Yet if we make faulty maps—to again use White's allegory—because we accept claims like those made in the rhetoric of removal at face value we operate on incorrect assumptions and are not only restricting our paths to the future but also increase the danger of getting ourselves lost along the way. The rhetoric of removal especially in the United States has distracted from and masked the covert agenda of land acquisition and passed the morally more acceptable goal of assimilation off as the central theme of the policy. And such processes of masking or forgetting are still going on, as for instance David Wilkins has shown in his study of the Supreme Court which traces this issue from *Johnson v. M'Intosh* to modern cases like *Department of Human Resources v. Smith*.[46] Like the rhetoric of removal back then they fulfill a function in the here and now. As David Lowenthal has pointed out: "Nations are unique not only in what they choose to remember but in what they feel forced to forget. The heritage of tragedy may well be more effective than that of triumph."[47] This masking and selective remembering still aggravates other legacies of removal like land loss, legal entanglements, and fragmentation.

Ironically, in both nations this masking process is often paired with what Renato Rosaldo has called 'imperialist nostalgia'—something that "uses a pose of 'innocent yearning' both to capture people's imaginations and to conceal its complicity with often brutal domination."[48] Consequently, a possibly subconscious strategy of double-masking and selective amnesia protects the dominant society's interests in the present as well as in the foreseeable future, while supplying a clean conscience with regard to Native pasts.

REMOVAL AND THE FUTURE

The fight for sovereignty, for survival of a collective identity, for land, as well as for and over other issues is still going on. But it has hopefully become apparent in the study of the removal of Yaquis and Delawares that Natives in many cases have shown a resilience which would be hard to best. They proved an almost unparalleled endurance in spite of anything which happened to or was done to them. But mere physical survival is not enough, as has also become quite clear in the Yaquis' and Delawares' fight for their identity. Both needed more, fought for more, and continue to do so. (And the fact that they endured does not absolve Mexico and the USA of a certain responsibility towards these two communities, as well as to others.) They survived events like removal only to find that the changes they had to make in order to do so are now being held against them and that the pressures they were exposed to during the event have only changed on the surface.

Notes

NOTES TO THE INTRODUCTION

1. Richard White: "Using the Past. History and Native American Studies"; in: Russell Thornton (ed.): *Studying Native America. Problems and Prospects*, Madison: University of Wisconsin Press, 1998, p. 227.
2. Language may be a factor in this as sufficient skills are a prerequisite for research.
3. Vine Deloria Jr.: *Custer Died for Your Sins. An Indian Manifesto*, 3rd edition, Norman and London: University of Oklahoma Press, 1989, p. 108.
4. See Christian Feest: "Die Indianerpolitik Mexikos und der USA, 1830–1930"; in: Edelmayer, Friedrich et al. (eds.): *Die vielen Amerikas. Die neue Welt zwischen 1800 und 1930*, Frankfurt: Brandes und Apsel, 2000, p. 104.
5. See White: Using the Past, p. 235. He views this to be the case at least until the twentieth century.
6. Here, the language problem is one of many other factors.
7. This treaty was signed in 1778.
8. I am well aware that the term 'tribe' usually implies the primitive. When I use the term tribe, I generally refer to a political unit, which also has certain ties to communal identity. I think the various meanings and connotations of the word 'tribe' have best been explored by Morton H. Fried in *The Notion of Tribe*. Whereas the term once referred to common ties of culture, language, and origins, in the United States and in recent times, it is used for communities which are federally recognized by the government. Therefore it comes with both positive and negative implications, which will have to be kept in mind. (The term 'indigenous' seems to me to suffer from similar problems as tribe. However, there does not seem to be a more useful expression.)
9. Aside from the similarities mentioned, the communities even initially differed in some important aspects. The Yaquis, in peacetime made up of various semi-autonomous settlements, did unite in times of war. The Delawares failed to do so. I will later on, in the corresponding chapters, elaborate on the implications of these facts.

10. Juan Banderas of the Yaquis and White Eyes of the Delawares both attempted to create an autonomous native State; Banderas in the 1830s and White Eyes at the time of United States Independence.
11. The thirty-five years in-between the two removals should not hamper the comparison since the circumstances were still similar and the time period in question was not overly long.
12. Like many colonized peoples, both Delawares and Yaquis today are known by a name given to them by their colonizers. To break this habit somewhat, I have used both the 'colonized' names as well as the ones the tribes themselves use. Therefore I will, for the Yaquis, also use the name 'Yoeme,' for the Delawares 'Lenape,' the names they also use for themselves.
13. When talking about removal, I will use a wide definition. Basically, the term will be used in its literal sense, roughly meaning migration, displacement, deportation. This usage has already been established in US Indian history. There, the idea of removal was introduced by Thomas Jefferson, favored by James Madison, adopted by James Monroe, and decisively pursued by Andrew Jackson and Martin Van Buren. Many tribes have been 'removed.' Some of them went 'voluntarily' in the sense of without any violent opposition, like the last removal of the Delawares. In other cases, force had to be used in varying degrees.
14. I am sure that, in addition to this, when looking at the years to follow the removal to Indian Territory, one could find other incidents to fit the definition and thus expand the time frame even more.
15. 'People of the first frontier' is a term sometimes used in the literature to describe that it was the coastal tribes who first had to deal with European ventures into their land. The expression was used by T. J. C. Brasser in "The Coastal Algonkians: People of the First Frontiers," in: Eleanor Burke Leacock and Nancy Oestreich Lurie (eds.): *North American Indians in Historical Perspective*, New York: Knopf, 1971.
16. The name the Yaquis use for themselves, *Yoreme,* can be found in a variety of spellings. In addition to the one used throughout the book, there is *Yoeme,* which has been used increasingly in the last years, and also *Yohem,* which according to my impression is used mainly in the Guaymas area.
17. By now, the Pascua Yaquis have obtained federal recognition.
18. It was only possible to undertake this project by limiting the frame of investigation without jeopardizing the validity of the search due to the still highly disorganized state of the archives. The aim of this search was to establish if Yaquis continued to be 'troublemakers' even in their imposed exile. Therefore, I concentrated on penal records within the general section of various court records (which I still had to look at to determine their nature) and limited my search to the years 1905 to 1912. I began my examination in 1905, a year before the deportations were stepped up and continued until 1912, when the progressing revolution had secured the Yaquis' release from the plantations. However, they still remained in the area, attempting to find ways to get home. Within the

general category of penal records, I once again narrowed down the search to those documents where I realistically could expect to find Yaquis. So I eliminated offenses like falsification, abuse of confidence, adultery (presuming that no one would have cared about this in Yaqui workers), sodomy, fraud, divorce, bigamy, etc. I also only looked at robbery and theft (among others of the remaining crimes) in order to determine if Yaquis were among the offenders, presuming that they would not have had any possessions worth stealing and going to court for.

The documents which displayed Yaqui presence in Yucatán most often turned out to be 'lesiones' (bodily harm) and sometimes they also showed up in the event of their death (accident and murder). And they only appeared very rarely; on average I found one document a year but none at all in 1907, 1909, and 1910, indicating that any Yaqui discontent manifested itself very differently from how it did at the same time in Sonora. On Yucatán the Yaquis ceased to be unified troublemakers and instead became unhappy individuals.

The discussion of the Delawares is mainly based on primary sources found in the National Archives of the United States in Washington DC, which encompass correspondence of and with the Bureau of Indian Affairs and other materials produced by that body. These are supplemented by legal documents as well as by some primary sources from the Western History Collection at Oklahoma University.

19. Richard Handler: "Is 'Identity' a Useful Cross-Cultural Concept?," in John R. Gillis (ed.): *Commemorations: The Politics of National Identity*, Princeton: Princeton University Press, 1994, p. 30f.
20. Ibid, p. 30.
21. Craig Calhoun: "Social Theory and the Politics of Identity," in Craig Calhoun (ed.): *Social Theory and the Politics of Identity*, Oxford: Blackwell, 1994, p. 20.
22. John R. Gillis: "Introduction," in John R. Gillis (ed.): *Commemorations: The Politics of National Identity*, Princeton: Princeton University Press, 1994
23. See Stephen Cornell and Douglas Hartmann: *Ethnicity and Race: Making Identities in a Changing World*, London: Pine Forge Press, 1998, p. 15 and 19f, as well as p. 120. See also Max Weber: *Wirtschaft und Gesellschaft. Grundriss der verstehenden Soziologie*, 5th edition, Tübingen: J.C.B. Mohr, 1972, particularly p. 234–240.
24. See Stuart Hall: *Cultural Studies. Ein politisches Theorieprojekt. Ausgewählte Schriften 3*, Hamburg: Argument Verlag, 2000, p. 32.
25. On the importance of territoriality, see George De Vos: "Ethnic Pluralism: Conflict and Accommodation"; in: George De Vos and Ida Romanucci-Ross (eds.): *Ethnic Identity. Cultural Continuities and Change*, 2nd edition, Chicago and London: University of Chicago Press, 1982, p. 11f.
26. To some extent, one has to take the phenotype or 'race' into account as well.
27. Probably, there are legends and tales about the origin of the house, quite possibly, none of which have been confirmed.

28. These changes may have been stemming from their own ideas, owing to outside influences or even pressures.
29. An interesting question, which will only briefly be touched upon in the context of this study, is if and how easily the inhabitants of the house could and can move out and return, as well as how hard it is to move into a different home.
30. Tzvetan Todorov: *The Conquest of America. The Question of the Other,* Norman: Oklahoma University Press, 1999, p. 254.
31. See Claudia Haake: "Identity, Sovereignty and Power: the Cherokee-Delaware Agreement of 1867, Past and Present," *American Indian Quarterly,* vol. 26, no. 3, 2002, p. 418–35.

NOTES TO CHAPTER ONE

1. See Jeffrey D. Schultz, Kerry L. Haynie, Anne M. McCulloch, Andrew L. Aoki (eds.): *Encyclopedia of Minorities in American Politics. Volume 2— Hispanic Americans and Native Americans,* Phoenix: Oryx, 2000, p. 571.
2. The Delaware Treaty of 1778 offered the tribe the creation of an Indian state as part of the union.
3. Robert Remini: *The Revolutionary Age of Andrew Jackson,* New York: Perennial, 1976, p. 106.
4. Arlene Hirschfelder and Martha Kreipe de Montaño: *The Native American Almanac. A Portrait of Native America Today,* New York: Macmillan, 1996, p. 14.
5. Vine Deloria, Jr. and Clifford Lytle: *American Indians, American Justice,* 8th edition, Austin: University of Texas Press, 1997, p. 6.
   In the long run, though, it was his dream that white and red America would unite, would melt into each other.
6. See Ronald Takaki: *A Different Mirror. A History of Multicultural America,* Boston: Brown, Little and Company, 1993, p. 48.
7. Vine Deloria, Jr.: "Congress in its Wisdom: The Course of Indian Legislation," in: Sandra L. Cadwalader and Vine Deloria, Jr. (eds.): *The Aggressions of Civilization. Federal Indian Policy Since the 1880s,* Philadelphia: Temple University Press, 1984, p. 119.
8. In *Cherokee vs. Georgia,* the Cherokees asked for a restraining order against Georgia to stop the removal attempts. It was handed down through Chief Justice John Marshall on March 18, 1831. He saw the Indians as no sovereign nations but as no subject to state law either. He called them "domestic dependent nations in a state of pupilage," formulating the idea of federal wardship. This description, stated as a metaphor, soon became a dogmatic axiom. The principle remains ambiguous and is used both to defend and to attack Indian self-government. See Schultz et al.: *Minorities,* p. 597.
9. Deloria and Lytle: *Justice,* p. 4.
10. Ronald Takaki: *Iron Cages: Race and Culture in Nineteenth-Century America,* London: Athlone Press, 1980, p. 84.

11. See Robert V. Remini: *Andrew Jackson, 3: The Course of American Democracy, 1833–1845*, Baltimore: Johns Hopkins University Press, 1984.
12. "Although 'treaty' seems to imply an equal bargaining position, the Indians were often at a clear disadvantage when negotiating such arrangements. The actual document was always written in English and was generally interpreted by people who had a stake in a successful outcome of the proceedings, so the Indians were not always told the truth during these sessions." (Deloria and Lytle: *Justice*, p. 5.) Toward the end of the treaty process, the original documents were often completely changed by amendments. These amendments were then ratified by any tribal member willing to do so. "More than one Indian war began because the wrong group of Indians agreed to alter treaty provisions." (Deloria and Lytle: *Justice*, p. 5.) Furthermore, so-called 'confidential agents' were used to bribe the chiefs and influential men. (See Takaki: *Iron Cages*, p. 98.) On other policies, like the systematic discreditation or alcoholization of chiefs and others, see Rebecca L Robbins.: "Self-Determination and Subordination. The Past, Present, and Future of American Indian Governance"; in: M. Annette Jaimes (ed.): *The State of Native America. Genocide, Colonization, and Resistance*, Boston: South End Press, 1992, p. 87–121, p. 90.

    In a way, bribes could be viewed as a continuation of the tradition of gift-giving—with a greedy European twist. But because they built on an Indian tradition they were probably very effective.
13. See Robert Remini: *The Legacy of Andrew Jackson*, Baton Rouge: Louisiana State University Press, 1988, p. 52.
14. See Takaki: *Iron Cages*, p. 98.
15. Remini: *Legacy*, p. 45.
16. The Manifest Destiny held that United States territorial expansion was not only inevitable but also divinely ordained.
17. Deloria and Lytle: *Justice*, p. 7.
18. These reservations were different from what was called Indian Territory in the early nineteenth century. These were generally smaller, with specific boundaries, and were frequently established for one tribe. Indian reservations were not subject to state law except by permission of the federal government.
19. Deloria and Lytle: *Justice*, p. 8.
20. The boundaries of Indian Territory were redefined several times, starting in 1834. The original area included most of Oklahoma, parts of Kansas and Nebraska. Homestead and allotment acts opened up parts of the area. The northern section was lost in 1854, when Kansas and Nebraska became territories. There were only the governments of resident tribes. It was legally defined only as late as 1834, as the portion of the United States that was not part of any state or territory. There were three waves of removal to Indian Territory: 1830s, 1854, 1866–1885. In 1890, it was divided into Oklahoma Territory and Indian Territory. In 1907 the remains were joined with Oklahoma Territory to become Oklahoma.

21. For instance, the Cherokee Stand Watie (1806–1871), fighting for the Confederates, was promoted to brigadier general. Stand Watie was the last of the southern generals to surrender, on June 23, 1865.
22. The term 'Reconstruction' refers to the period after the Civil War, when the South was recovering from economic and physical devastation. Southern legislators were trying to avoid the spirit of the 13th amendment by passing so-called black codes, thus restricting black rights. As becomes amply clear above, it also had effects on other areas of society. For instance, the Civil Rights Act of 1866 intended to fight the black codes, excluded Indians not taxed.
23. Weeks, Philip: *Farewell, My Nation. The American Indian and the United States, 1820–1890* (The American History Series), Wheeling, IL: Harlan Davidson, 1990, p. 121. In the Battle of Little Bighorn, also known as Custer's Last Stand, on June 25, 1876, General George Armstrong Custer and approximately 210 soldiers were killed by Cheyenne and Sioux, after attacking an Indian village.
24. Peter Iverson: *"We Are Still Here." American Indians in the Twentieth Century* (The American History Series), Wheeling, IL: Harlan Davidson, 1994, p. 1.
25. Since they were also not specifically excluded from the Fourteenth Amendment, a clarification was issued in 1870, stating that, as tribal peoples, Indians had not been born under the *complete* jurisdiction of the United States. It was not until 1968 and the passage of the Indian Civil Rights Act, that the rights and privileges of the Fourteenth Amendment were applied to tribal Indians. See Schultz, et al.: *Minorities,* p. 621. See also Deloria and Lytle: *Justice,* p. 219.
26. Donald L. Fixico: "Federal and State Policies and American Indians"; in: Philip J. Deloria and Neal Salisbury (eds.): *A Companion to American Indian History,* Oxford: Blackwell, 2002, p. 382.
27. It also declared that all existing treaties would be honored.
28. Federal district courts later acknowledged these agreements to stand on par with treaties as legal documents. See Deloria: *Congress,* p. 107.
29. Weeks: *Farewell,* p. 205.
30. Weeks: *Farewell,* p. 226. For more on American Indian education, see also the corresponding section of Vine Deloria, Jr.: *Spirit and Reason. The Vine Deloria, Jr. Reader,* Golden, Colorado: Fulcrum, 1999.
31. Often, annuities paid under this act were given out in forms of seeds and agricultural tools, to further agriculture, assimilation, and Americanization. See Schultz, et al.: *Minorities,* p. 589.
32. The Dawes Act (General Allotment Act of 1887) gave 160 acres to each family. All others over the age of 18 were to receive 80 acres each. Selection was possible. It was effective until 1934 (when the Indian Reorganization Act was passed). Some tribes, like the Five Civilized Tribes, were exempt. The Dawes Act linked citizenship to private land ownership. Indians were subject to state law only if they lived on allotted lands and were born within the limits of the United States. Allotment was originally intended as a protective measure that would preserve adequate holdings for Indians to earn a livelihood and, by the trust provision, to keep them from selling their land at low

prices. The trust period was supposed to last 25 years. A provision arranged for an annual survey and allotment of lands. The surplus was offered to non-Native settlers. Generally, mixed bloods received fee simple titles, whereas full bloods got trust patents. See Robbins: Self-Determination, p. 93.
33. Deloria and Lytle: *Justice*, p. 9.
34. Deloria: Congress, p. 119.
35. The Burke Act modified the General Allotment Act by providing that even those Indians with allotted land would not become United States citizens until they were deemed legally competent to manage their own affairs. The trust period could also be extended beyond the original 25 years.
36. Deloria and Lytle: *Justice*, p. 10. The Five Civilized Tribes Citizenship Act (1901) made every Native American in the Indian Territory a United States citizen.
37. Iverson: *Still Here*, p. 40.
38. Iverson: *Still Here*, p. 50.
39. In the Constitution, Indians 'not taxed' are mentioned, indicating that some individuals had been successfully assimilated and were taxed as other Americans. Additionally, citizenship had been conferred by treaty as early as 1817. See Theodore W. Taylor: *The Bureau of Indian Affairs*, Boulder, CO: Westview Press, 1984, p. 19.
40. Iverson: *Still Here*, p. 64.
41. Among other things, the report cited cases of malnutrition, high rates of diseases and infant mortality, as well as inadequate education. It urged the allotment of more funds and called for more autonomy for Native Americans. See Schultz, et al.: *Minorities*, p.655f.
42. For one example of a negative position, see Robbins: Self-Determination, p. 95ff. For a more positive judgement see Deloria: Congress, p. 110f; or Taylor: *BIA*, p. 20–22.
Deloria also called the Collier time a "bright spot," and Collier himself "probably the greatest of all Indian commissioners." See Deloria: *Custer Died for Your Sins*, p. 48.
43. Vine Deloria, Jr. and Clifford M. Lytle: *The Nations Within. Past and Future of American Indian Sovereignty*, Austin: University of Texas Press, 1984, p. 102.
44. Iverson: *Still Here*, p. 108.
45. Iverson: *Still Here*, p. 116. The scope of the Claims Commission was very narrow, not taking up many of the issues important to Native Americans, such as treaty issues. It limited itself to land issues and tribal funds held by the United States. Many claims also were not accepted because they were viewed to be individual ones by the Commission.
46. Matters were further complicated when these 370 claims were broken down into subcategories, eventually creating a total of 605 cases. The cases also dragged on infinitely, due to many counterclaims by the government. Furthermore, any part of a decision could be appealed.
47. Some people insisted that the preservation of the federal property trust made Indians second class citizens and therefore put their weight behind the termination program. See Deloria: Congress, p. 117f.

48. See Deloria and Lytle: *Justice*, p. 20.
49. Iverson: *Still Here*, p. 121.
50. Donald L. Fixico: *Termination and Relocation. Federal Indian Policy, 1945—1960*, Albuquerque: University of New Mexico Press, 1986, p. 188.
51. See Robbins: Self-Determination, p. 99.
52. George S. Grossman: "Indians and the Law"; in: Colin G. Calloway (ed.): *New Directions in American Indian History*, Norman and London: University of Oklahoma Press, 1987, p. 115.
53. See Deloria: Congress, p. 118f.
54. Iverson: *Still Here*, p. 169.
55. The occupants believed to have a right to the island as federal surplus property. However, the treaty provision was only a myth, though one they probably honestly believed in. See Deloria and Lytle: *The Nations Within*, p. 236–237.
56. See Russell Means with Marvin J. Wolf: *Where White Man Fear to Tread. The Autobiography of Russell Means*, New York: St. Martin's Press, 1995, p. 421.
57. See Deloria, Jr. and Lytle: *Nations Within*, p. 238ff.
58. The local officials displayed a reluctance to pursue the murderer of an Indian man, by attempts to impeach the government-backed tribal chairman Richard Wilson, and by an old conflict about the gunnery range, a part of the reservation. The gunnery range had been impounded by the War Department in 1942, to be used for the duration of World War II.
59. See Robbins: Self-Determination, p. 104.
60. R. David Edmunds: "Native Americans and the United States, Canada, and Mexico"; in: Philip J. Deloria and Neal Salisbury (eds.): *A Companion to American Indian History*, Oxford: Blackwell, 2002, p. 401.
61. Iverson: *Still Here*, p. 181.
62. Duane Champagne: *Chronology of Native North American History. From Pre-Columbian Times to the Present*, Detroit / Washington, D.C. / London: Gale Research Inc., 1994, p. li.
63. Deloria: Congress, p. 126f.
64. See Deloria: Congress, p. 127.
65. See Iverson: *Still Here*, p. 177.
66. Ibid, p. 3.
67. See Joane Nagel: *American Indian Ethnic Renewal. Red Power and the Resurgence of Identity and Culture*, New York and Oxford: Oxford University Press, 1996, and Cornell, Stephen and Douglas Hartmann: *Ethnicity and Race: Making Identities in a Changing World*, London: Pine Forge Press, 1998.
68. Iverson: *Still Here*, p. 3.
69. See White: Using the Past, p. 235. He views this to be the case at least until the twentieth century.

NOTES TO CHAPTER TWO

1. Algonquian is a family of indigenous languages in the Northeast of the USA. The syllable 'len' stands for common; 'âpé' means people. See Clinton

Alfred Weslager: *The Delaware Indians,* New Brunswick: Rutgers University Press, 1972, p. 32.

I use the terms 'Delawares' and 'Lenape' interchangeably and for variation. Traditionally, the Delawares referred to themselves as Lenape but have long been known by the outside world as Delawares. The latter is the name under which they were federally recognized. They carry both names in their seal.

2. See Weslager: *Delaware Indians,* p. 33.
3. Weslager has called the system "more democratic than the political systems in most European nations." Clinton Alfred Weslager: *The Delaware Indian Westward Migration: With Texts of two Manuscripts, 1821–22, Responding to General Lewis Cass's Inquiries about Lanape Culture and Language,* Wallingford: Middle Atlantic Press, 1978, p. 8. When a singular voice was needed, the most respected chief would act as head chief. Also, war chiefs would be elected based on their ability. See Robert S. Grumet: *The Lenapes,* New York and Philadelphia: Chelsea House Publishers, 1989, p. 23 and Weslager: *Delaware Indians,* p. 62.
4. See Grumet: *Lenapes,* p. 61. He even speaks of a "sense of nationhood." For an in-depth discussion of the term 'tribe,' see Morton H. Fried: *The Notion of Tribe,* Menlo Par, CA: Cummings, 1975.
5. For further information on the Delaware languages, especially on the character of Unalachtigo, see Ives Goddard: "The Delaware Language, Past and Present"; in: Herbert Kraft (ed.): *A Delaware Indian Symposium,* Harrisburg: The Pennsylvania Historical and Museum Commission, 1974.
6. The translation of these clan names follows the standards found in the great majority of books on the subject. For more details see Weslager: *Delaware Indians* or Frederick E. Hoxie: *Encyclopedia of North American Indians,* Boston: Houghton Mifflin Company, 1996, and also Anthony F.C. Wallace: *Teedyuscung. King of the Delawares, 1700–1763,* Philadelphia: University of Pennsylvania Press, 1949. Weslager casts some doubt on the origins of these clans, see Weslager: *Migration,* p. 27.

The head chief, with a few exceptions, always came from the Turtle clan. The position of chief was partly hereditary but needed to be confirmed by election. War chiefs were chosen on the basis of ability. See Weslager: *Migration,* p. 43. For a theory about the interconnection of clans and language groups, see Grumet: *Lenapes,* p. 15f.
7. How important the position of the female was or why kinship was traced matrilineally is a matter of much discussion among experts.

Weslager claims that the position of the woman was a respected one but that she did not partake in political decisions and only in a limited manner in religious ceremonies. See Weslager: *Delaware Indians,* chapter 3. On the other hand, Jay Miller, in an article on the Delawares emphasizes again and again the "female-based society of the Lenape" and the importance of women in most aspects of this society. See the entry under Delaware in Alvin Josephy (ed.): *America in 1492. The World of the Indian Peoples Before the Arrival of Columbus,* New York: Knopf, 1992. Grumet claims that the lines may have blurred after the child-bearing age of women was over. See Grumet: *Lenapes,* p. 21. Most other authors, like Wallace for example, tend to hold a position in-between those two extremes or avoid the subject altogether. On the 'intermediate' position see also Kathleen M. Brown: "The Anglo-Algonquian Gender Frontier"; in: Nancy Shoemaker (ed.): *Negotiators of Change,* New York: Rutledge, 1995. For a more detailed discussion see Regula Trenkwalder Schoenenberger: *Lenape Women, Matriliny and the Colonial Encounter, Resistance and Erosion of Power (c. 1600–1876): An Excursus in Feminist Anthropology,* Bern and New York: P. Lang, 1991. See also Margaret M. Caffrey: "Complimentary Power: Men and Women of the Lenni Lenape"; in: *American Indian Quarterly,* Volume 24, Number 1, 2000, p. 44–63.

8. See Richard C. Adams: *A Delaware Indian Legend and the Story of Their Troubles,* Washington D.C.: n.p., 1899, p. 20. For further information on kinship and family affiliation, see Kraft: *Lenape,* p. 244.
9. See Letter from John Connor to Muscogees, January 3, 1861; National Archives, M234, roll 276. The last oral usage I was made aware of was in the 1970s, by a Kickapoo elder to Mrs. Nora Thompson Dean.
10. See Kraft: *Lenape,* p. 212, and Grumet: *Lenapes,* p. 13.
11. The confederacy of the Five Nations, also known as Iroquois, consisted of the Mohawk, Oneida, Onondaga, Cayuga, and Seneca, who were joined in 1722 by the Tuscarora and from then on were known as the Six Nations. They were neighbors of the Delawares but spoke languages of a different language family, Iroquoian. The joining of another tribe as an equal member of the Iroquois confederacy probably made the Lenape even more aware of their subservient position.
12. The Five Nations declared the Delawares to be women after having won a war against them and thus deprived them of their right to take up arms and to make autonomous decisions. The Iroquois may have inherited some influence over the *Lenape* from the Susquehannocks, whom they had beaten in war.

    A different theory views the status of women as a positive, a peacekeeping one, in line with Iroquois' matrilinearity.
13. See Weslager: *Delaware Indians,* chapter 8. Another explanation could be that they were fighting against the Iroquois. The French and Indian War, also known as Seven Years War, lasted from 1756 until 1763.
14. Grumet suspects they were angered by the fraudulent second Walking Purchase and thus angry at the British. See Grumet: *Lenapes,* p. 44.
15. Penn's sons were selling land really owned by the Lenape. In order to obtain it 'legally' they told the tribe its ancestors had signed a contract for selling it. On the basis of that 'contract' and under highly suspect circumstances, the Delawares lost an area the size of Rhode Island. When the Delawares protested, the Iroquois asserted their power over them to silence them.
16. Even before that, there had been no such thing as one leader over all Delawares, even though the Europeans often assumed the existence or even tried to establish such a thing while dealing with the Delawares. But at least they had all been living close to one another. Now, the groups broke up, probably according to language groups, and continued separately for the most

part. Especially the so-called Moravian Delawares, those accompanied by Moravian missionaries, separated themselves from the others.
17. The Delaware Prophet began preaching in the 1760s after having—or claiming to have—a religious experience. His preaching was in a revivalist style, renouncing all white things.
18. See Weslager: *Delaware Indians,* p. 255.
19. See Weslager: *Migration,* p. 32.
20. Ibid, p. 40.
21. Most of the ones who went to Canada stayed there; only a few rejoined the main body, while the Canadian Delawares were later joined by various other splinter groups. In 1789, the Delawares gone to Spanish territory were officially granted permission to settle there and so they moved with some Shawnees first to Missouri and then to Arkansas. They were thought to be useful as a buffer between Spanish and American settlements and also to offer some protection from the Osages. In 1793 they even received a formal land grant at Cape Girardeau. These Absentee Delawares later left for Texas, where they were welcomed as a protection against Comanches. See H. Allen Anderson: "The Delaware and Shawnee Indians and the Republic of Texas, 1820–1845"; in: *Southwestern Historical Quarterly* 94, October 1990, p. 231–60, and Jean Luis Berlandier: *The Indians of Texas in 1830,* Washington: Smithsonian Institution Press, 1969, p. 223–225. With Napoleon's acquisition of lands from Spain and the Louisiana Purchase (1803) they were once again on United States territory.
22. In the treaty of St. Mary, Ohio (August 1818), the Delawares gave all occupancy rights to their Indiana lands over to the United States. They were given three years to vacate their lands on the White River and were supplied with various things, among them horses and farm implements. The Miamis ceded their lands at the same time.
23. See Weslager: *Migration,* p. 73. The white interpreters probably were also crucial in the signing and did receive land in return.
24. See Kraft: *Lenape,* p. 236. A number of the best horses had been stolen before the tribe even got to the river. More were taken while they were waiting to be ferried over. See Weslager: *Migration,* p. 211.
25. As it turned out, there still were disputes about the boundaries of the Delawares' lands in Kansas. But they were probably mostly due to the government's representatives' loss of the original maps.
26. These were the above mentioned ones, who had settled at Cape Girardeau, Missouri. The recently independent Mexico also was content to have the Delawares settling within its borders. See Grumet: *Lenapes,* p. 77.
27. According to estimates, the reservation consisted of 924,160 acres plus a ten-mile strip called the Outlet, encompassing an additional 960,000 acres. See Weslager: *Migration,* p. 217.
28. By 1855, the Indian Agency saw even fit to dedicate one agency solely to the supervision of the Delawares.
29. See Weslager: *Migration,* p. 220f. Various documents dating from 1863 and 1864 mention the phratries. See National Archives, M234.

NOTES TO CHAPTER THREE

1. Parts of the argument from this chapter follow a previously published article. See Haake: Identity, Sovereignty, and Power, p. 418–435.
2. See Letter dated November 9, 1853, from Commissioner of Indian Affairs George W. Mannypenny to Secretary of the Interior Robert McClelland. National Archives, M348 roll 7.
3. Letter dated October 31, from Commissioner of Indian Affairs William P. Dole to Secretary of the Interior John P. Usher. National Archives, M348, roll 13.
4. Letter (April 10, 1854) from Captain Ketchum to the President of the United States. National Archives, M234, roll 364.
5. Ibid.
6. John M. Blum (ed.): *The National Experience. A History of the United States*, 3rd edition, New York: Harcourt, Brace, Jovanovich Inc., 1973, p. 308. Among those guilty of committing depredations against Delaware property was the Delaware Timber Company. See letter dated January 11, 1866, from Commissioner of Indian Affairs Dennis N. Cooley to Secretary of the Interior James Harlan. National Archives, M348, roll 15.
7. Letter dated November 9, 1853, from Commissioner of Indian Affairs George W. Mannypenny to Secretary of the Interior Robert McClelland.
8. The ceded tract covered more than one million acres. The lands were to be sold at a public auction. The treaty was concluded in Washington.
9. See article 3 of the Delaware Treaty of 1854.
10. See article 6, Delaware Treaty of 1854.

    While it would be easy to condemn the chiefs for taking bribes, they followed a number of white customs they did not understand. An undated letter (probably from 1860) to Commissioner of Indian Affairs Dole and signed by various Delawares, explicitly talks about the chiefs signing papers "the meaning of which, they did not comprehend." (See National Archives, M234, roll 275)
11. Treaty of Sarcoxieville (May 30, 1860).
12. Letter from Special Agent Thomas Sykes to Superintendent B.F. Robinson, dated November 11, 1859. National Archives, M234, roll 275.
13. See Letter from Indian Agent Thomas Sykes to Commissioner of Indian Affairs Alfred B. Greenwood, March 12 1860, National Archives, M234, roll 275. These lands seemed to have suited the Delawares best out of those they did consider. Sykes mentioned that ten or fifteen disagreed. See also Weslager: *Delaware Indians*, p. 407
14. Ibid. Sykes deemed this to be a 'happy result of the council." References to these councils can be found in a number of documents on this roll. They appear to have been going at least since February. The exact dates are hard to determine as the tribe seems to have attempted to keep their agent in the dark about these meetings.
15. Letter from Agent Thomas Sykes to Superintendent B.F. Robinson, dated February 10, 1860. National Archives, M234, roll 275.
16. Letter dated September 22, 1855, from Commissioner of Indian Affairs George W. Mannypenny to Secretary of the Interior Robert McClelland.

National Archives, M348, roll 12. Intrusions were numerous and are mentioned in a range of documents. See for instance M21, roll 60, M234, rolls 274 and 275.
17. Letter dated October 10, 1857, from Acting Commissioner of Indian Affairs Charles Mix to Secretary of the Interior Jacob Thompson.
18. See William W. Newcomb, Jr.: *The Culture and Acculturation of the Delaware Indians,* Ann Arbor: University of Michigan Press, 1956, p. 101.
19. See Weslager: *Delaware Indians,* p. 407.
20. There are numerous applications on file for delegations to expect lands. A letter from Commissioner of Indian Affairs Dennis N. Cooley to Thomas Murphy, dated September 1, 1866, states the selection available to the tribe to be the lands of the Seminoles, the Creeks, the Cherokees, the Choctaw as well as the Quapaw lands. The choice would still have to be approved by the government. See National Archives, M21, roll 82.
21. Weslager: *Westward Migration,* p. 224f. See also Adams: *Legend,* p. 47f.
22. See Weslager: *Delaware Indians,* p. 408. Indian Territory seems to have been the place favored by most.
23. See a letter from Indian Agent Thomas Sykes to unknown recipient (March 3, 1860). National Archives, M234, roll 275.
24. See various correspondences, primarily in M234, rolls 276, 277, and 278.
25. Letter from Captain Fall Leaf and J. W. Armstrong to the (unnamed) Commissioner of Indian Affairs, dated May 10, 1864. National Archives, M234, roll 276.
26. Letter dated March 10, 1864, from Agent Johnson to Commissioner of Indian Affairs William P. Dole. Johnson states that Simon and others wanted to go to Idaho or Washington Territory. National Archives, M234, roll 276.
27. See Treaty of July 2, 1861, at Fort Leavenworth.
28. See Weslager: *Delaware Indians,* p. 405. Weslager also states that the chiefs were intoxicated when signing the 1860 treaty. See Weslager: *Delaware Indians,* p. 414. For ensuing problems see National Archives, M243, roll 277. The chiefs had picked lands already taken up by other tribal members.
29. In 1860, an invitation had been sent to the absentees to rejoin the main body. It had gone unheeded.
30. Weslager: *Delaware Indians,* p. 413.
31. Letter from Abraham Lincoln, May 13, 1861. As reproduced in appendix 7 of Weslager: *Delaware Indians,* p. 508.
32. See letter from Caleb B. Smith, Secretary of the Interior, April 30, 1861. National Archives, M234, roll 276. For more on the payment and its conditions, see National Archives, M348, rolls 12 and 16.
33. See letter dated February 29, 1872, from Commissioner of Indian Affairs Francis Walker to Secretary of the Interior Columbus Delano. National Archives, M348, roll 21.
34. See Laurence Hauptmann: *Between Two Fires: American Indians in the Civil War,* New York: Free Press, 1995, p. 22, Weslager: *Migration,* p. 224. See also a Memorial compiled by Richard C. Adams for a Hearing of the

Committee of Public Lands, House of Representatives, 'To Compensate the Delaware Indians for Services Rendered by them to the United States in Various Wars,' 1909, p. 2 (United States National Archives).

35. See letter dated September 25, 1866, from Commissioner of Indian Affairs Dennis N. Cooley to Superintendent Thomas Murphy. National Archives, M21, roll 81.
36. See Hauptman: *Fires*, p. 23.
37. See letter dated April 2, 1862, written by Agent Fielding Johnson to Commissioner of Indian Affairs William P. Dole. National Archives, M234, roll 276.
38. Letter by Captain Fall Leaf to Commissioner of Indian Affairs W. P. Dole, September 15, 1863. United States National Archives, M234, roll 276. I have found no indication that this wish was granted. However, after Fall Leaf was sent home due to an illness, his men, obeying their traditions, soon followed.
39. In a letter from September 25, 1866, Commissioner of Indian Affairs Cooley to Thomas Murphy, the former described the Delawares as 'friendly Indians.' See National Archives, M21, roll 81.
40. The treaty was ratified on August 10, 1866. A day later, a treaty between the Cherokees and the United States was signed, providing for the removal of friendly Indians to their lands.
41. The treaty was ratified on August 10 1866.
42. This was outlined in Articles 3 and 9 of the treaty of 1866.
43. See National Archives, M234, roll 276, letter dated May 23, 1863. See also Weslager: *Migration*, 224f; see also Adams: *Legends*, 47f.
44. Letter dated January 1, 1865, from Agent John Pratt to Commissioner of Indian Affairs William P. Dole. National Archives, M234, roll 277.
45. Ibid.
46. Agent John Pratt to Commissioner of Indian Affairs William P. Dole, February 1865, National Archives, M234, roll 277.
47. See various documents from 1866, mainly on roll 277 of M234, National Archives, for instance in the months of May and August.
48. This treaty negotiation process was as drawn-out as that of the Cherokee—Delaware agreement. Especially at this time, the Cherokees probably did not dare to alienate the United States further by putting up too much resistance about the agreement and its terms. This may have changed once their 1866 treaty had been safely concluded.
49. According to various correspondences, it was this article under which the Delaware had been removed to the Cherokee Nation. See for instance, S. 2695 / 49th Congress, 1st Session / In the Senate of the United States / June 18, 1886. National Archives, M574, roll 81.
50. Article 15, Cherokee Treaty of 1866.
51. Ibid.
52. Ibid.
53. Ibid.
54. See Gina Carrigan and Clayton Chambers: *A Lesson in Administrative Termination: An Analysis of the Legal Status of the Delaware Tribe of Indians*, ms, 1994, p. 10.

55. Letter from Captain Fall Leaf and J. W. Armstrong to the Commissioner of Indian Affairs, dated February 3, 1864. National Archives, M234, roll 276.
56. Letter dated February 3,1864, addressed to the Department of the Interior, and signed by various Delawares (though not all Chiefs). National Archives, M234, roll 276.
57. See Carrigan and Chambers: *Administrative Termination,* p. 10.
58. See letter dated August 21, 1866, from Agent John Pratt to Superintendent Thomas Murphy. National Archives, M234, roll 277.
59. See Carrigan and Chambers: *Administrative Termination,* p. 10.
60. Ibid.
61. Ratified Treaty No. 267: Documents Relating to the Negotiation of the Treaty of May 6, 1854, With the Delaware Indians. National Archives, M494, roll 5.
62. Letter from Charles and Isaac Journeycake, as well as others, to the Commissioner of Indian Affairs William P. Dole, undated but probably from 1860. National Archives, M234, roll 275.
63. This becomes evident in a number of documents, but particularly in their petition dated June 13, 1867. See National Archives, M234, roll 278.
64. See Cherokee-Delaware Agreement, April 8 1867, in Adams: *Legends,* p. 55.
65. Ibid.
66. See Weslager: *The Delaware Indians,* p. 424–25. Charles Journeycake may have been the exception.
67. The agreement is very short and does not contain numbered clauses or articles.
68. See various letters, primarily M234, roll 279.
69. See for instance Fall Leaf and others to General James Blunt [fall 1869], and Superintendent Thomas Murphy to Commissioner of Indian Affairs Ely S. Parker, November 11 1869, National Archives, M234, roll 280. See also Superintendent Thomas Murphy to Acting Commissioner of Indian Affairs Charles Mix, June 6 1868, and Fall Leaf and others to the Commissioner of Indian Affairs, National Archives, M234, roll 279. See Commissioner of Indian Affairs Nathaniel G. Taylor to Superintendent Thomas Murphy, May 4 1867, National Archives, M21, roll 68.
70. This problems of frequently changing office holders was hinted at in a letter from James Secondine from the Lenape to Commissioner of Indian Affairs James W. Denver (dated August 15, 1857), where Secondine says he had been informed "that the commissioner had just come into office and consequently knew nothing about our business affairs." National Archives, M234, roll 274. The situation even worsened thereafter.

    These changes may also be the reason why several letters from the Delawares to the Commissioner of Indian affairs were sent without including the name of the addressee.
71. For a possible explanation of the haste with which the negotiations were conducted, see Carrigan and Chambers: *Administrative Termination,* p. 9.

72. See Weslager: *The Delaware Indians,* 424–25. There is some doubt about the role of Journeycake, who was later on accused of fraud by some tribal members. See letter dated February 9, 1874, from James Ketchum and Henry Tiblow to W.P. Adair. See also a letter from Superintendent Enoch Hoag to Commissioner of Indian Affairs Edward P. Smith (March 24, 1974). National Archives, M234, roll 63.
73. See Weslager: *The Delaware Indians,* p. 424–25.
74. See Cherokee Agent John B. Jones to Commissioner of Indian Affairs Ely S. Parker, April 4 1867, National Archives, M234, roll 104.
75. Captain Anderson Sarcoxie and others to the Commissioner of Indian Affairs Nathaniel G. Taylor, June 13 1867, National Archives, M234, roll 275.
76. Letter from Agent John Pratt to Superintendent Tomas Murphy, dated August 6, 1867. National Archives, M234, roll 278.
77. Ibid.
78. Exhibit D accompanying a letter from Agent John Pratt to Superintendent Thomas Murphy, 6 February 1868, National Archives, M234, roll 279 (the original letter to Ross is dated 9 December, 1866).
79 Letter from various Delaware councilors to Acting Commissioner of Indian Affairs Charles Mix, dated November 8, 1867. National Archives, M234, roll 278.
80. While the lands were not sold right away considerable pressure was applied to make the Delawares move.
81. General James Blunt to Commissioner of Indian Affairs Nathaniel G. Taylor, February 27 1868, National Archives, M234, roll 279.
82. Ibid.
83. Superintendent Thomas Murphy to Acting Commissioner of Indian Affairs Charles Mix, June 6 1868, National Archives, M234, roll 279.
84. Ibid.
85. Fall Leaf and others to Commissioner of Indian Affairs, [March-April 1868], National Archives, M234, roll 279. Fall Leaf and other resisted the move to the Cherokee Nation for a while but eventually had to give in as well.
86. Petition by Captain Anderson Sarcoxie and others to the Commissioner of Indian Affairs Nathaniel G. Taylor, June 13 1867, National Archives, M234, roll 278.
87. The sheriffs, Jacob Easy and John Buffalo, went around to collect the signatures but apparently no one really kept track of who had contacted whom. Thus a few people signed twice or even thrice, unaware of what kind of an impact this would have on them. This gave various government officials, among them Agent John Pratt, the opportunity to discard the document as invalid. See Agent John Pratt to Superintendent Thomas Murphy, February 6 1868, National Archives, M234, roll 279.
88. Petition by Captain Anderson Sarcoxie and others to the Commissioner of Indian Affairs Nathaniel G. Taylor, June 13 1867, National Archives, M345, roll 278.

Notes to Chapter Three

89. Ibid. Agent Pratt did not forward the petition until he was specifically ordered to do so by the Commissioner of Indian Affairs. When no response arrived, Sarcoxie wrote to the Commissioner directly to inquire if he had received the letters. See letter from Chief Anderson Sarcoxie to the Commissioner of Indian Affairs Nathaniel G. Taylor, July 8 1867, National Archives, M234, roll 278.
90. James Simons to the Commissioner of Indian Affairs, [c. July-December 1869], National Archives, M234, roll 280.
91. For the position of Fall Leaf see the letter from various Delawares to the Department of the Interior, February 2 1864, National Archives, M234, roll 276.
92. The numbers were affirmed by Thomas Murphy from the Neosho Agency. See Tomas Murphy to Superintendent Enoch Hoag, July 15 1870, National Archives, M234, roll 280.
93. For James Simon, see a letter, January 1 1863, accompanied by a memorial of the chiefs, from Agent F. Johnson to Commissioner of Indian Affairs William P. Dole, National Archives, M234, roll 276.
94. See James Simons and others to unknown recipient, January 25 1871, National Archives, M234, roll 280.
95. Charles Journeycake and others to Commissioner of Indian Affairs William P. Dole [1861], National Archives, M234, roll 275.
96. Ibid.
97. See for instance John Connor and others to Superintendent Thomas Murphy, August 5 1866, or Charles Journeycake and others to Acting Commissioner Charles Mix, November 8 1867, National Archives, M234, rolls 277 and 278.
98. See Carrigan and Chambers: *Administrative Termination*, p. 4.
99. Ibid.
100. For a more detailed discussion, see Claudia Haake: "Delaware Identity in the Cherokee Nation," *Indigenous Nations Studies Journal*, Spring 2003, p. 19–45.
101. Fall Leaf and others to the Commissioner of Indian Affairs William P. Dole, February 2 1864, National Archives, M234, roll 276.
102. Charles Journeycake to Commissioner of Indian Affairs William P. Dole, May 2 1863, National Archives, M234, roll 276.
103. Letter from various Delawares to Commissioner of Indian Affairs William P. Dole, undated but probably from 1860. National Archives, M234, roll 275.
104. Ibid. Also Letter dated February 26, 1964 from Fall Leaf, J.W. Armstrong, and Ben Simon, some of the band chiefs, to Commissioner of Indian Affairs William P. Dole. National Archives, M234, roll 276.
105. See also Hauptmann: *Fires*, p. 31f. From 1863 onward, Fall Leaf's involvement in the Civil War decreased, probably because of the precarious situation at home.
106. Weslager: *Delaware Indians*, p. 424.
107. See Weslager: *Delaware Indians*, p. 425.

108. See letter (May 21, 1868) from Acting Commissioner Charles Mix to Agent John Pratt. National Archives, M21, roll 86. The matter of expenses was difficult though, as delayed payments by the railroad affected the tribe. See for instance a letter from John Connor and Charles Journeycake to Agent Pratt, dated September 29, 1867. National Archives, M234, roll 278.
109. Letter dated October 17, 1867, from Agent John Pratt to Acting Commissioner of Indian Affairs Charles Mix. National Archives, M234, roll 278.
110. Pratt, a Baptist minister, in general did not facilitate matters for the Delawares. Probably in an attempt to 'civilize' and Christianize them, he frequently abused his influence by meddling in tribal affairs. And he seems to have shared the confusion about where in the Cherokee Nation the Delawares could settle without losing their tribal organization. (See letter (February 6, 1868) from Agent John Pratt to Superintendent Tomas Murphy. National Archives, M234, roll 279.) Furthermore, Delaware Charles Journeycake, himself a minister and a crucial figure in the removal, was his son in law. He was considered one of the modernists and seemingly not very well liked. His ascendancy to chief was probably at least partly due to white intervention, too.

    See also Newcomb: *Acculturation*, p. 109.
111. The Cherokees ratified the Articles of Agreement on June 13, 1867. The Delawares did not do so. See Carrigan and Chambers: *Administrative Termination*, p. 16.
112. See letter (June 6, 1868) from Superintendent Tomas Murphy to Acting Commissioner Charles Mix. National Archives, M234, roll 279. Superintendent Murphy also seems to have been under the misconception that the Delawares would not be able to keep their tribal organization intact east of the 96th meridian.
113. Letter [fall 1869] from Fall Leaf and others to General James Blunt. National Archives, M234, roll 280.
114. Ibid.
115. Letter from Commissioner of Indian Affairs Nathaniel G. Taylor to Superintendent Tomas Murphy, dated May 4, 1867. National Archives, M21, roll 86.
116. This group numbered about 200 people. See letter from Commissioner of Indian Affairs Nathaniel G. Taylor to Agent Tomas Murphy. National Archives, M21, roll 86.
117. Letter from Commissioner of Indian Affairs Taylor to Secretary of the Interior Orville H. Browning. National Archives, M348, roll 17.

    See also letters dated March 5 and March 6, 1868, both by Commissioner of Indian Affairs Nathaniel G. Taylor and addressed to Secretary of the Interior Orville H. Browning. National Archives, M348, roll 17.
118. Newcomb: *Acculturation*, p. 101.
119. There was also individual violence, coming from the settlers and squatters, as the files in the National Archives amply prove.
120. Letter (June 7, 1869) from Agent John Pratt to Superintendent Enoch S. Hoag. National Archives, M234, roll 279.

121. At this time, the Delawares still believed they had purchased the land in question with only one restriction—that they could not alienate it without the permission of the Cherokee Nation.
122. It seems like this river was also known as the Caney River. See Weslager: *Delaware Indians*, p. 428. Occasionally, the name Grand River is also found. In fact, the Neosho and the Spring River form the Grand River. For the numbers, see a letter dated July 15, 1870 from Agent Tomas Murphy to Superintendent Enoch S. Hoag. National Archives, M234, roll 280.
123. They became American citizens either with allotment, or in 1924 with the passage of the Indian Citizenship Act that also allowed Indians for the first time to vote in national elections. Occasionally Indians had been made citizens even before this date.
124. Weslager: *Migration*, p. 442.
125. See Weslager: *Migration*, p. 442f.
126. Barry Goldwater quote taken from Vine Deloria, Jr.: *We Talk, You Listen. New Tribes, New Turf*, n.p.: Macmillan, 1970, p. 49.
127. I use the word 'similar,' since Chief Justice John Marshall had described the position of Indian tribes towards the United States as one resembling that of a ward to its guardian. For more details on Indian wardship, see Felix Cohen: *Handbook of Federal Indian Law*, Buffalo: Hein, 1988 (Washington, D.C.: United States Government Printing Office, 1941).

NOTES TO CHAPTER FOUR

1. They paid $1 per acre for what was later determined to be only a life estate. The Cherokee lands west of the 96th meridian in fee simple sold for 70 cents. The same year, 1866, the Creeks sold their lands to the United States for 30 cents and the Seminoles for 15 cents per acre. The Choctaws and Chickasaws sold theirs for five cents only.
2. Cherokee-Delaware Agreement, April 8 1867, in Adams: *Legends*, p. 55.
3. Letter from various Delawares to the Commissioner of Indian Affairs, dated June 13, 1867. National Archives 234, roll 278.
4. Ibid.
5. Ibid.
6. Ibid.
7. Ibid.
8. Their desire for such an unbroken stretch of land to settle on was recorded in article 4 of their treaty of 1866.
9. Weslager: *Westward Migration*, p. 230.
10. Letter from various Delawares to the Commissioner of Indian Affairs, dated June 13, 1867. National Archives 234, roll 278.
11. One example is the agreement between the Cherokees and the so-called Loyal Shawnee.
12. Article 15 of the Cherokee Treaty of 1866.
13. See article 16 of the Cherokee Treaty of 1866.
14. Delaware treaty of 1866, article 15.

15. Letter from various Delawares to the Commissioner of Indian Affairs, dated June 13, 1867. National Archives 234, roll 278.
16. Article 4 of the Delaware Treaty of 1866.
17. See Letter (November 24, 1871) from John Connor to Columbus Delano, Secretary of the Interior. National Archives, M234, roll 280.
18. In a letter to Captain Sarcoxie (November 13, 1868), Lewis Downing regretted to hear that the Delawares were not satisfied in the Cherokee Nation but would not allow them to settle west of the 96th meridian, claiming they would then only experience more hardships. University of Oklahoma, Western History Collection, 3/198.
19. Even the ones who had removed early were not content and, among other things, complained about the exorbitant prices charged by merchants. See letter (March 10, 1869) from John Connor to Agent Thomas Murphy. National Archives, M21, roll 89.
20. Letter dated March 10, 1869, by Commissioner of Indian Affairs Taylor to Superintendent Thomas Murphy. National Archives, M21, roll 89.
21. Letter (February 2, 1870) from John Connor to Commissioner of Indian Affairs Ely S. Parker. National Archives, M234, roll 280.
22. Letter dated July 22 1870 from Superintendent Enoch S. Hoag to Commissioner of Indian Affairs Ely S. Parker. National Archives, M234, roll 280.
23. See letter (July 2, 1870) from Agent Mitchell from the Neosho Indian Agency to Superintendent Enoch S. Hoag. National Archives, M234, roll 280.
24. Letter dated July 22 1870 from Superintendent Enoch S. Hoag to Commissioner of Indian Affairs Ely S. Parker. National Archives, M234, roll 280.
25. Ibid. Various government officials report on partiality shown by Cherokee officers to Cherokee offenders. See for instance letter (July 1, 1871) from Special Agent Mitchell to Superintendent Enoch S. Hoag. National Archives, M234, roll 280.
26. Letter (July 22, 1870) from Superintendent Enoch S. Hoag to Commissioner of Indian Affairs Ely S. Parker. National Archives, M234, roll 280.
27. Ibid.
28. Ibid.
29. When the last Delawares moved to Oklahoma there were only 985 names on the official enrollment list drawn up by the Delaware agent in February of 1867. This list derived its main importance from the fact that it established membership in the main body of the Delawares and thus the birthright for future generations.

    The case of James Simons is presented in various letters, by him and others, to their agent or to the Commissioner of Indian Affairs. See primarily National Archives, M234, roll 278, M234, roll 280 and M234, roll 866.
30. See letter (July 1, 1871) from Special Agent Mitchell to Superintendent Enoch S. Hoag. National Archives, M234, roll 280. Another letter claims that even six lots were sold by one single person in this manner. See also letter (April 4, 1871) from Cherokee Agent Jones to Commissioner of Indian Affairs Ely S. Parker. National Archives, M234, roll 104.

Notes to Chapter Four 233

31. See letter (July 1, 1871) from Special Agent Mitchell to Superintendent Enoch S. Hoag. National Archives, M234, roll 280.
32. Letter (July 2, 1870) from James Simons and others to Superintendent Enoch S. Hoag. National Archives, M234, roll 280.
33. See Articles of Agreement (May 26, 1871). National Archives, M234, roll 280. The language contained therein does not indicate any involvement of government officials or trained lawyers but it cannot be ruled out either.
34. The numbers are being affirmed by Agent Thomas Murphy from the Neosho Agency. See letter July 15, 1870) from Agent Thomas Murphy to Superintendent Enoch S. Hoag. National Archives, M234, roll 280.
35. Ibid.
36. See letter (February 22, 1871) from Superintendent Enoch S. Hoag to Commissioner of Indian Affairs Ely S. Parker. National Archives, M234, roll 280.
37. Simons in a letter [1869] to the Commissioner of Indian Affairs. See National Archive, M234, roll 280.
38. See letter (January 25, 1871) from James Simons and others to unknown recipient. National Archives, M234, roll 280.
39. Ibid.
40. Ibid.
41. See letter from James Simons to the Commissioner of Indian Affairs [1869], National Archives, M234, roll 280, letter from Captain Fall Leaf to General James Blunt [1869], National Archives, M234, roll 280, letter (June 22, 1871) from Superintendent Enoch S. Hoag to Commissioner of Indian Affairs Ely S. Parker. National Archives, M234, roll 280, and letter (July 1, 1871) from Special Agent Mitchell to Superintendent Enoch S. Hoag. National Archives, M234, roll 280.
42. Letter (January 25, 1871) from James Simons and others to unknown recipient. National Archives, M234, roll 280.
43. See letter (June 22, 1871) from Superintendent Enoch S. Hoag to Commissioner of Indian Affairs Ely S. Parker. National Archives, M234, roll 280.
44. Letter (July 1, 1871) from Special Agent Mitchell to Superintendent Enoch S. Hoag. National Archives, M234, roll 280.
45. Ibid.
46. Letter (January 25, 1871) from James Simons and others to unknown recipient. National Archives, M234, roll 280.
47. Letter (July 1, 1871) from Special Agent Mitchell to Superintendent Enoch S. Hoag. National Archives, M234, roll 280.
48. See letter (July 31, 1871) from Secretary of the Interior Columbus Delano to the Commissioner of Indian Affairs. National Archives, M234, roll 280.
49. Ibid.
50. Ibid.
51. Judging from a letter (April 6, 1871), it was Charles Journeycake who called the Agents' attention to the secession in the first place. See let-

ter (April 4, 1871) from Cherokee Agent John Jones to Commissioner of Indian Affairs Ely S. Parker. National Archives, M234, roll 104. As already indicated, Journeycake cannot be called a traditional chief in the strict sense of the word. See the introductory chapter on the Delawares.

52. Weslager: *Migration*, p. 229 claims they returned after one year. The sources seem to indicate a somewhat longer absence, indicating the first to secede in 1869 and the last returning in 1871. See letter (July 31, 1872) from Superintendent Enoch S. Hoag to Commissioner of Indian Affairs Francis A. Walker, about the destitute situation the Neoshos found themselves in one year after moving back. National Archives, M234, roll 61.
53. Letter (July 31, 1872) from Superintendent Enoch S. Hoag to Commissioner of Indian Affairs Francis A. Walker. National Archives, M234, roll 61.
54. See letter (July 31, 1872) from Superintendent Enoch S. Hoag to Commissioner of Indian Affairs Francis A. Walker. National Archives, M234, roll 61.
55. See Letter (July 25, 1873) from James Simons and others to Superintendent Enoch S. Hoag. National Archives, M234, roll 61.
56. Ibid.
57. See for instance letter (April 26, 1873) from Superintendent Enoch S. Hoag to Commissioner of Indian Affairs Smith. National Archives, M234, roll 62.
58. Ibid.
59. Weslager: *Westward Migration*, p. 229. See also Newcomb: *Acculturation*, p. 106.
60. See letter (October 20, 1871) from Charles Journeycake to Superintendent Enoch S. Hoag. National Archives, M234, roll 280. Hoag's letter to Secretary Delano may have been in response to this one.
61. Letter (October 30, 1871) from Superintendent Enoch S. Hoag to Secretary of the Interior Columbus Delano. National Archives, M234, roll 280.
62. See National Archives, M234, roll 870. (Letter from Charles Journeycake to Indian Agent Sylvester Marston, May 7, 1878)
63. See National Archives, M234, roll 870. In the same letter as mentioned above, Charles Journeycake talks about the murder of Wilson Sarcoxie by Cherokee Eben Brown. See also a letter from Agent S. Marston to Commissioner Ezra Hayt from May 9, 1878. National Archives, M234, roll 870. But there are also earlier cases of murders committed against Delawares and by Cherokees. See National Archives, M234, roll 866. Here, various Delawares in an undated letter lay out the situation to Secretary of the Interior Columbus Delano. While they complain mostly about one specific case, the wording suggests that others have taken place. Yet another conflict resulting in death is sketched in a letter dated August 8, 1870, from Agent Craig to Commissioner Smith. In this case, a young Delaware is attacked by a Cherokee and happens to kill him in self-defense. The Agent reports the Cherokee to be a member of one of

Notes to Chapter Four

the bad families settling in the immediate neighborhood of the Delawares and continuously causing trouble there. See National Archives, M234, roll 103.

64. See various communications in 1877. National Archives, M234, primarily roll 866.
65. Petition from various Delawares to Secretary of the Interior Columbus Delano. National Archives, M234, roll 866. While the petition itself is not dated, the roll it is on is made up of correspondence from 1876 and 1877. A letter from the Commissioner of Indian Affairs, written in February 1877, already refers to the wording and contents of this petition. See letter (May 7, 1877) from Commissioner of Indian Affairs to Secretary of the Interior. National Archives, M234, roll 866.
66. Ibid.
67. Ibid.
68. Ibid.
Former head chief John Connor had died in 1871, shortly after Anderson Sarcoxie had passed away. In 1872 John Connor had been succeeded by his brother James, probably in part due to an intervention by the Central Superintendency. Assistant Chiefs were Charles Journeycake and James Simons. See also Carrigan and Chambers: *Administrative Termination*, p. 21.
69. Petition from various Delawares to Secretary of the Interior Columbus Delano. National Archives, M234, roll 866.
70. See Carrigan and Chambers: *Administrative Termination*, p. 20.
71. Letter (November 3, 1873) from Superintendent Enoch S. Hoag to Acting Commissioner of Indian Affairs H.R. Clum. National Archives, M234, roll 62.
72. Letter (October 9, 1868) from Acting Commissioner of Indian Affairs Charles Mix to Agent Thomas Murphy. National Archives, M21, roll 88.
73. See letter (February 12, 1877) from Agent S. Marston to Commissioner of Indian Affairs John Q. Smith. National Archives, M234, roll 867. Cana is also found in the spelling of Caney.
74. Ibid.
75. Carrigan and Chambers: *Administrative Termination*, p. 20.
76. Ibid.
77. Ibid, p. 25.
78. The Delawares kept speaking their language even after that. In Oklahoma that language was Unami, whereas the Canadian Delawares spoke Munsee. See Ives Goddard: "The Delaware Language, Past and Present"; in Herbert Kraft (ed.): *A Delaware Indian Symposium*, Harrisburg: The Pennsylvania Historical and Museum Commission, 1974.
79. See Carrigan and Chambers: *Administrative Termination*, p. 24.
80. This becomes all too apparent looking at the letters from Agent Pratt and others, reporting on the destruction brought about by squatters and others and how the Delawares suffered from the effects. See National Archives, M234, especially rolls 274–278.

81. Letter (June 13, 1867) from various Delawares to the Commissioner of Indian Affairs. National Archives, M234, roll 278. This is but one example for the application of the term 'nationality.' For others see the correspondence by Fall Leaf and Anderson Sarcoxie, quoted above.
82. I think it is possible that the friction developed along the lines of older problems but am not able to determine this from the sources available.
83. Several documents on M234, rolls 103 and 104, also talk about cooperation between the Cherokees and the Delawares when it came to arresting the perpetrators of arson. See National Archives, M234, rolls 103 and 104.
84. See letter (February 17, 1874) from W. P. Adair to Commissioner of Indian Affairs Edward P. Smith. National Archives, M234, roll 63. Adair, a Cherokee, pronounced the Delawares as a tribe or nation to be at an end, in connection to payment purposes and Cherokee control.
85. See Peter d'Errico: "American Indian Sovereignty: Now You See It, Now You Don't"; http://www.nativeweb.org/pages/legal/sovereignty.html (May 15, 2005), now at http://www.umass.edu/legal/derrico/nowyouseeit.html.

NOTES TO CHAPTER FIVE

1. See Carrigan and Chambers: *Administrative Termination,* p. 32.
2. The document was signed by the Commissioner of Indian Affairs in 1962. Not once was an organization for claims purposes mentioned.
3. See Carrigan and Chambers: *Administrative Termination,* p. 1.
4. In October 1978, Delaware Chairman Bruce Townsend, an attorney by profession, was replaced by someone less experienced, making the tribe more vulnerable.
5. For instance, the tribe could not retrieve artifacts it had loaned to various institutions under the Native American Graves and Repatriation Act.
6. The Delaware Tribal Child Development Mission was open not only to Delaware children, but in part also to other Native American children and children of different ethnic heritage.
7. For more details on the maintenance of Delaware culture, at least until the 1950s, see Newcomb: *Acculturation,* especially page 106–128.
8. For a personal account on the dolls see Lynette Perry and Manny Skolnick: *Keeper of the Delaware Dolls,* Lincoln and London: University of Nebraska Press, 1999. For the Doll Dance and other ceremonies and events, see also Carrigan and Chambers: *Administrative Termination,* p. 23ff.
9. The term Powwow is derived from an Algonquian word referring to shamans and their curing ceremonies. In the twentieth century it refers to 'the creative expression of Indian identity.' Today's powwows are not usually tribally exclusive.
10. Grumet: *The Lenapes,* p. 27.

NOTES TO CHAPTER SIX

1. Indeed, Marc Alan Sills in 1992 noted: "To this point in time, apparently no one has attempted to write either a comprehensive history or contemporary analysis of Indian policy in Mexico." See Marc Alan Sills: *Ethnocide and Interaction Between States and Indigenous Nations: A Conceptual Investigation of Three Cases in Mexico,* Ann Arbor: UMI, 1992, p. 339. For an outline of colonial Indian treatment see Charles Gibson: "Indian Societies Under Spanish Rule"; in: Leslie Bethell (ed.): *The Cambridge History of Latin America, Volume II—Colonial Latin America,* Cambridge: Cambridge University Press, 1987, and primarily p. 381–384 for possible explanations for the lack of studies. In 1997, Enrique Florescano's *Etnia, Estado y Nación. Ensayo sobre las identidades colectivas en México* has been published, somewhat remedying the situation. Christian F. Feest has conducted a brief comparison between US and Mexican Indian policy, which highlights certain aspects but is not comprehensive. See Christian F. Feest: "Die Indianerpolitik Mexikos und der USA, 1830–1930"; in: Friedrich Edelmayer, et al. (eds.): *Die vielen Amerikas. Die neue Welt zwischen 1800 und 1930,* Frankfurt: Brandes und Apsel, 2000, p. 89–104. R. David Edmunds, in his article „Native Americans and the United States, Canada, and Mexico," in Philip J. Deloria and Neal Salisbury (eds.): *A Companion to American Indian History,* Oxford: Blackwell, 2002, p. 397–421, has admirably compared the three countries' treatment of their Indian populaces. Yet in spite of this recent work on the subject, a comprehensive history of Mexican Indian policy is still lacking, with the possible exception of Guillermo Floris Margadant's 1980 article cited below.
2. With Independence all the Indians inside of Mexico became citizens, with all the rights and duties connected to that status, at least nominally. For questions of status, see Luis Villoro: "En torno al derecho de autonomía de los pueblos indígenas"; in: Fernando Benítez et al.: *Cultura y derechos de los pueblos indígenas de México,* Mexico City: Dirección de Publicaciones, Archivo General de la Nación, Fondo de Cultura Económica, 1996, especially p. 167.
3. For the idea of the 'raza cósmica,' see José Vasconcelos: *The Cosmic Race— La raza cósmica* (bilingual edition) Baltimore and London: Johns Hopkins University Press, 1997.
4. There were also some 'slip-ups' post-Independence when the abstract goal pursued by the state turned out to be very difficult from the reality and thus making it necessary to have some legal provisions specifically for Indians.
5. See Anthony Pagden: *Lords of All the World. Ideologies of Empire in Spain, Britain and France c. 1500—c. 1800,* New Haven and London: Yale University Press, 1995, p. 68f. See also Patricia Seed: *American Pentimento. The Invention of Indians and the Pursuit of Riches,* Minneapolis: University of Minnesota Press, 2001, p. 57f.
6. The papal bull 'Sublimis Deus' had in 1537 declared the Indians to be human beings and capable of reason.

For a discussion of the intellectual problems connected with the conquest, see Lewis Hanke: *The First Social Experiments in America. Study in the Development of Spanish Indian Policy in the Sixteenth Century*, Cambridge: Harvard University Press, 1935, especially p. 3–25 and also David J. Weber: *Bárbaros. Spaniards and Their Savages in the Age of Enlightenment*, New Haven and London: Yale University Press, 2005, p. 3.

7. See Seed: *American Pentimento*, p. 115 and 118. (Seed emphasizes the importance of the *reconquista*.)
8. Guillermo Floris Margadant: "Official Mexican Attitudes Toward the Indians: An Historical Essay," *Tulane Law Review*, 1980, Vol. 54, p. 966.
9. See Renate Pieper and Iris Luetjens: "Die Entwicklung der Indianergemeinden"; in: Horst Pietschmann (ed.): *Handbuch der Geschichte Lateinamerikas, Volume I*, Stuttgart: Klett-Cotta, 1994, p. 578. See also Horst Pietschmann: *Die staatliche Organisation des kolonialen Iberoamerika*, Stuttgart: Klett-Cotta, 1980, p. 176.
10. Eric Wolf: *Europe and the People Without History*, Berkeley: University of California Press, 1997, p. 142.
11. See Frederick C. Turner: *The Dynamic of Mexican Nationalism*, Chapel Hill: University of North Carolina Press, 1968, p. 25. See also Wolfgang Gabbert: "Soziale Ungleichheit und Indianismus auf der Halbinsel Yukatan," in Ellen Schriek and Walter Schmuhl: *Das Andere Mexico.Indigene Voelker von Chiapas bis Chihiuahua*, Gießen: Focus, 1997, p. 98.
12. See Floris: Official Mexican Attitudes, p. 968. See also Wolfgang Gabbert's comparable argument in Wolfgang Gabbert: *Becoming Maya. Ethnicity and Social Inequality in Yucatán Since 1500*, Tucson: The University of Arizona Press, 2004.
13. Weber: *Bárbaros*, p. 3.
14. James D. Cockroft: *Mexico. Class Formation, Capital Accumulation and the State*, 2nd edition, New York: Monthly Review Press, 1990, p. 9.
15. See Hans-Joachim König: "Barbar oder Symbol der Freiheit? Unmündiger oder Staatsbürger?—Indiobild und Indianerpolitik in Hispanoamerika"; in: Hans-Joachim König, Wolfgang Reinhard, Reinhard Wendt (eds.): *Der Europäische Beobachter außereuropäischer Kulturen. Zur Problematik der Wirklichkeitswahrnehmung*, Berlin: Zeitschrift für Historische Forschung Volume 7, 1989, p. 100.
16. See Pagden: *Lords of All the World*, p. 91.
17. William B. Taylor: *Drinking, Homicide, and Rebellion in Colonial Mexican Villages*, Stanford: Stanford University Press, 1979, p. 160.
18. On difficulties of definition with regards to the *encomienda*, see Horst Pietschmann: *Staat und staatliche Entwicklung am Beginn der spanischen Kolonisation Amerikas*, Münster: Aschendorff, 1980, p. 82. In the most common form of the *encomienda*, the master, the *encomendero*, was entitled to Indian labor in exchange for the duty of protection and instruction in the Christian doctrine. See Horst Pietschmann (ed.): *Handbuch der Geschichte Lateinamerikas, Volume II*, Stuttgart: Klett-Cotta, 1992, p. 579. See also Charles Gibson: *The Aztecs Under Spanish Rule*, Stanford: Stanford University Press, 1964, p. 58.

19. It was legally discontinued in 1542. The loss of lives within the system was largely due to diseases, but was not helped by the hardships suffered in the *encomienda;* while it was considerable, it is hard to quantify.
20. Floris: Official Mexican Attitudes, p. 973.
21. See Gibson: *Aztecs Under Spanish Rule,* p. 197 and p. 211. See Rik Hoekstra: *Two Worlds Merging. The Transformation of Society in the Valley of Puebla, 1570–1640,* Amsterdam: CEDLA, 1993, p. 231.

    However, this resettlement and the classification to go with it also often changed indigenous settlement structures. In this manner, the *pueblos de indios,* like labor policies such as the *repartimiento,* also served to form or reinforce communities, as well as their loyalties and allegiances. As most of the policies and measures explored above were rooted in or based on communities, their assimilative power was limited but they facilitated exploitation in the name and with the help of Christianity.
22. The Leyes Nuevas also prohibited the new allocation of *encomiendas.* Existing ones were to be reduced to an 'appropriate' size. The laws also did away with slavery for good (earlier on, a few exceptions had applied). See Pieper and Luetjens: Indianergemeinden, p. 581.
23. Seed: *American Pentimento,* p. 83.
24. Edward Holland Spicer (ed.): *Cycles of Conquest. The Impact of Spain, Mexico, and the United States on the Indians of the Southwest, 1533–1960,* Tucson: University of Arizona Press, 1962, p. 335.
25. See Gibson: *Indian Societies,* p. 407, Sills: *Ethnocide,* p. 266, and Pietschmann: *Staat und staatliche Entwicklung,* p. 59.
26. See Horst Pietschmann: "Die iberische Expansion im Atlantik und die kastilisch-spanische Entdeckung und Eroberung Anerikas"; in: Horst Pietschmann (ed.): *Handbuch der Geschichte Lateinamerikas, Volume I,* Stuttgart: Klett-Cotta, 1994, p. 242. See also Seed: *American Pentimento,* p. 84.
27. Gibson: *Indian Societies,* p. 407. For instance, what could be called hunting territories were assumed to be vacant and annexed by the Spaniards. The same was the case with communal areas.
28. María Teresa Vázquez Castillo: *Land Privatization in Mexico. Urbanization, Formation of Regions, and Globalization in Ejidos,* New York: Routledge, 2004, p. 22.
29. See Gibson: *Indian Societies,* p. 408.
30. See Frans J. Schryer: "Ethnic Identity and Land Tenure Disputes in Modern Mexico"; in: John E. Kicza: *The Indian in Latin American History. Resistance, Resilience, and Acculturation* (Jaguar Books on Latin America), Wilmington: Scholarly Resources, 1993, p. 207.
31. Weber: *Bárbaros,* p. 5.
32. See Weber: *Bárbaros,* p. 8.
33. See Pietschmann: *Staat und staatliche Entwicklung,* p. 92.
34. Integrative and assimilative attempts, Weber argues, had their origins in Enlightenment thought. See Weber: *Bárbaros,* p. 5.

    A fair part of the descendants of the Indians was, through the process of *mestizaje* (race blend through miscegenation but, significantly, also a process of cultural and social change), taken out of the traditional societies and more or less integrated primarily into the rural classes.

35. See Turner: *Mexican Nationalism*, p. 31. See also Enrique Krauze: *Mexico. Biography of Power. A History of Modern Mexico, 1810–1996*, New York: Harper Collins, 1997, p. 222, and Leonel Durán: "Las culturas indígenas de México y su proceso de cambio e identidad"; in: José Alcina Franch (ed.): *Indianismo e indigenismo en América*, Madrid: Alianza Editorial, 1990, p. 242.

    While not all Indians showed interest in the cause, those who did participate in the movement seem to have done so mainly due to their resentment of the discrimination they had experienced by Spain. See John E. Kicza: "Introduction"; in: John E. Kicza: *The Indian in Latin American History. Resistance, Resilience, and Acculturation* (Jaguar Books on Latin America), Wilmington: Scholarly Resources, 1993, p. xxi.

36. There were always exceptions and different policies as well, as for instance Augustín de Iturbide's treatment decision to exempt Indians Nations residing in Mexico from paying sales taxes or duties. See Weber: *Bárbaros*, p. 268.

37. "At the beginning of Independence, the insurgents tried to suppress the stratified and racist society of the hispanic era, which had separated the *repúblicas de indios* from the rest of colonial society"; Patricia Galeana: "Historia y perspectivas del indigenismo mexicano"; in: Fernando Benítez et al.: *Cultura y derechos de los pueblos indígenas de México*, Mexico City: Dirección de Publicaciones, Archivo General de la Nación, Fondo de Cultura Económica, 1996, p. 380.

38. Edmunds: Native Americans, p. 412.

39. Not every leader of the Independence movement(s) subscribed to the rhetoric of wanting to uplift the Indians.

40. Gabbert: *Becoming Maya*, p. 37.

41. Weber: *Bárbaros*, p. 265.

42. In the sense that these laws had pertained to all Indians this policy had in essence not been that dissimilar to British attempts at around the same time. However, the content of these laws was at times quite divergent to those of other colonial powers.

43. For an illustration of the sometimes limited understanding of citizenship see Alexander Dawson: *Indian and Nation in Revolutionary Mexico*, Tucson: University of Arizona Press, 2004, p. xix.

    Due to this problem, there is still no legal / juridical definition of 'Indian' in Mexico although the *Comisión Nacional para el Desarollo de los Pueblos Indígenas* (CDI) uses one but also seems to rely on self-identification. Thus today, the estimates about the number of indigenous Mexicans vary widely. See Wolfgang Gabbert: "Vom Land der Mestizen zur multi-ethnischen Nation." Staatspartei und Indianer im nachrevolutionären Mexico,' in: Dietmar Dirmoser et al. (eds.): *Die Wilden und die Barbarei*, Münster: LIT, 1992, p. 33.

44. See Rodolfo Stavenhagen: *Derecho indígena y derechos humanos en América Latina*, Mexico City: IIDH, 1988, p. 29.

45. Kicza: *Introduction*, p. xxi.

46. In the United States of America, the policies aimed at Natives in general have had a somewhat homogenizing influence, especially in the 20th century. (In the United States (and under British rule before it), Indian policy also created the category of the Indian but resettlement, land reductions, boarding schools and other measures especially in the twentieth century gave rise to pan-Indianism which in turn filled that abstract category with some meaning for the Natives. This so far has not been the case in Mexico although especially (seasonal) migration to the US has given birth to some broader networks.) In Mexico, however, the specific policies of the Realpolitik type had a contrary effect to that of the United States. They in themselves were an admission of failure as obviously it had not been possible to turn all Indians into Mexicans. Yet, instead of achieving the aim of Mexicanizing the Indians, the occasions when the government felt forced to what I have called Realpolitik, to acknowledge that Indian or Mestizo communities were still different from others, turned out to reinforce rather than eliminate those differences. While in the United States, Indian Policy created Indians, in Mexico, the isolated instances of 'Indian' policies created and/or reinforced diverse Indian villages/communities.
47. Weber: *Bárbaros,* p. 277.
48. Seed: *American Pentimento,* p. 152.
49. See Josefina Zoraida Vázquez: "Políticas indigenistas en la historia mexicana"; in: Fernando Benítez et al.: *Cultura y derechos de los pueblos indígenas de México,* Mexico City: Dirección de Publicaciones, Archivo General de la Nación, Fondo de Cultura Económica, 1996, p. 289–294, but especially p. 291–292.
50. See König: *Barbar oder Symbol der Freiheit?,* p. 109. See also Edmunds: Native Americans, p. 412.
51. See Rodolfo Stavenhagen: *Derecho indígena,* p. 23.
    The new laws also neglected the sense of identity which still prevailed in many traditional groups, and which was often reinforced through the collective ownership of their lands, which now came under increasing threat. Therefore identities were tied to villages rather than tribes.
52. According to Floris, "despite its negative attitude toward 'dead hand' control, article 8 of the famous 'Lerdo Law' of June 25, 1856, opened up the possibility of saving the collectively owned land from the *desamortización* movement. But a dangerous contradiction between article 8 and article 27 of the constitution of the following year (1857) created an ambiguous atmosphere and again exposed the land to the dangers of *desamortización.*" (Floris: Official Mexican Attitudes, p. 977.)
53. As María Teresa Vázquez has pointed out, "the *ejido* land tenure system existed prior to the 1910 Mexican Revolution under a different form. In early colonial times, Spaniards included *ejidos (exidos)* in their planning of cities and towns. Those *ejidos* were land grants for the use of city populations organized by Spanish colonizers. Later, this territorial organization also included Indigenous towns and cities. The colonial *ejidos* included, in addition to individual land grants for the members of a particular city or town, lands for common use or *propios* and *dehesas.*" (Vázquez: Land Privatization, p. 22.)
54. Spicer: *Cycles,* p. 336.

55. Spicer: *Cycles*, p. 336. See also Florescano: *Etnia*, p. 392.
56. Spicer: *Cycles*, p. 338.
57. Cockroft: *Mexico*, p. 76.
58. Edmunds: Native Americans, p. 413.
59. John Coatsworth: "Railroads, Landholding and Agrarian Protest in the Early Porfiriato," *The Hispanic American Research Review*, Volume 54, February 1974 p. 66.
60. See Floris: Official Mexican Attitudes, p. 978. See Galeana: Historia y perspectivas, p. 380.
61. See Jack Autrey Dabbs: "The Indian Policy of the Second Empire"; in: Thomas E. Cotner (ed.): *Essays in Mexican History*, Westport: Greenwood Press, 1958, p. 113–126. See also Feest: Indianerpolitik, p. 94.
62. As Alexander Dawson has pointed out, "the idea of assimilation has a problematic history in Mexico, where beliefs about racial inferiority raised serious doubts about the prospect of assimilating indigenous peoples." (See Dawson: *Indian and Nation*, p. 4.)
63. See Florescano: *Etnia*, p. 487.
64. See Alan Knight: "Racism, Revolution, and *Indigenismo*: Mexico, 1910–1940"; in: Richard Graham (ed.): *The Idea of Race in Latin America, 1870–1940*, Austin: University of Texas Press, 1990, p. 78f.
65. Floris: Official Mexican Attitudes, p. 980.
66. Knight: Racism, p. 79.
67. Shelley Bowen Hatfield: *Chasing Shadows. Indians Along the United States—Mexico Border, 1876—1911*, Albuquerque: University of New Mexico Press, 1998, p. xi.
68. See Feest: Indianerpolitik, p. 94. Deportation was a measure occasionally also used in colonial times. See Spicer: *Cycles*, p. 339. Yet it never reached the scale removal had in the United States.
69. Gabbert: *Becoming Maya*, p. 40.
70. Taylor: Mexican Village Uprisings, p. 133.
71. Another, even stricter law was passed in 1894, the Federal Water Law. That version permitted individuals to find lands not yet surveyed and thus to have a claim towards those lands. This also applied to *ejidal* lands not distributed to individuals. See Vázquez: Land Privatization, p. 24.
72. Taylor: Mexican Village Uprisings, p. 134.
73. See Alan Knight: *The Mexican Revolution, Volumes I and II*, Lincoln and London: University of Nebraska Press, 1986, p. 7. See also König: Barbar oder Symbol der Freiheit?, p. 112. Edmunds also explains that the Porfiriato paid little attention to Indians, except as laborers. See Edmunds: Native Americans, p. 413.
74. Friedrich Katz: "The Liberal Republic and the Porfiriato, 1867–1910"; in: Leslie Bethell (ed.): *Mexico Since Independence*. Cambridge: Cambridge University Press, 1991, p. 94.
75. Kicza: Introduction, p. xxiii.
76. Vázquez: *Land Privatization*, p. 29.

77. See David A. Brading: "Nacionalismo y estado en Hispanoamerica"; in: Juan Bosco Amores et. al.: *Iberoamérica en el siglo XIX. Nacionalsimo y dependencia,* Pamplona: Ediciones Eunate, 1995, p. 74.
78. Vázquez: *Land Privatization,* p. 29.
79. See Ute Schüren: „'Land ohne Freiheit'—Mexikos langer Abschied von der Agrarreform," in Karin Gabbert et al. (eds.): *Land und Freiheit (Lateinamerika. Analysen und Berichte),* Bad Honnef: Horlemann 1997, p. 33–65, particularly p. 35.
80. Vázquez: *Land Privatization,* p. 30.
81. Ibid, p. 33. For a number of those exceptions or methods of circumvention see Vázquez, p. 33–34.
82. Jean Meyer: "Revolution and Reconstruction in the 1920s"; in: Leslie Bethell (ed.): *Mexico Since Independence,* Cambridge: Cambridge University Press, 1991, p. 233.
83. See Feest: Indianerpolitik, p. 96.
84. Sills: *Ethnocide,* p. 278.
85. See Meyer: Revolution and Reconstruction, p. 216.
86. Meyer: Revolution and Reconstruction, p. 235.
87. See Schüren: 'Land ohne Freiheit,' p. 35.
88. Ibid, p. 37.
89. Ibid, p. 39.
90. Dawson: *Indian and Nation,* p. 126.
91. Ibid, p. 72–73.
92. However, none of its successor institutions ever again had the same power, funding, responsibilities, and freedom.
93. Dawson analyzes the intentions, thrust, and success of a number of such efforts yet all of these were very-small scale in comparison with what the United States did and thus failed to create pan-Indianism on the same scale as they did there. There seems to have been a strong emphasis on the teaching of Spanish throughout (even though there was a varying tolerance of indigenous languages), but technical and agricultural skills were also often taught. See Dawson: *Indian and Nation,* 2004.
94. See Dawson: *Indian and Nation,* p. 103.
95. Ibid, p. 123.
96. Gabbert: *Becoming Maya,* p. 99.
97. Ibid, p. 100.
98. See Dawson: *Indian and Nation,* p. 85.
99. Ibid, p. xix.
100. See Schüren: 'Land ohne Freiheit,' p. 43.
101. Vázquez: *Land Privatization,* p. 33. For a number of those exceptions or methods of circumvention see Vázquez, p. 58.
102. Ibid.
103. See Schüren: 'Land ohne Freiheit,' p. 44.
104. INI has since been replaced by the *Comisión Nacional para el Desarrollo de los Pueblos Indígenas* (CDI).

105. However, as Schüren points out, such at the surface conciliatory measures were paired with repression and even murder, indicating that attitudes had not really changed. See Schüren: 'Land ohne Freiheit,' p. 45–46.
106. Vázquez: *Land Privatization*, p. 63.
107. Schryer: *Ethnic Identity and Land Tenure*, p. 208.
108. And for this they were better prepared than ever before because, as a result of repeated attempts and efforts to modernize the indigenous sector through education, a new social group had developed among the Indians, the formally educated ones.
109. See Schüren: 'Land ohne Freiheit,' p. 50.
110. During the presidency of Miguel de la Madrid, Salomón Nahmad Sitton was made head of INI. He was considered a radical and had previously taken Indians' complaints very seriously. The steps he took after his appointment were supposed to counteract the effects of internal colonialism and patronizing authoritarianism. Among other measures, he replaced some INI officials with Indians. After only six months, Nahmad was removed from office under charges of corruption. His successor, Miguel Limón Rojas, contented himself with merely maintaining the status quo. But at least some steps had been taken away from assimilation and integration and towards participation and pluralism. This was achieved in part by Indian demands, which forced the state to reconsider its concepts and policies.
111. See Schüren: 'Land ohne Freiheit,' p. 51.
112. Vázquez: *Land Privatization in Mexico*, p. 2.
113. Vázquez: *Land Privatization*, p. 2. See also Schüren: 'Land ohne Freiheit,' p. 59.
114. See Schüren: 'Land ohne Freiheit,' p. 58.
115. Ibid, p. 58–59.
116. Dawson: *Indian and Nation*, p. 158.
117. Most recently, the failure of Indian policy in Mexico became evident with the January 1, 1994 uprising of the *Ejército Zapatista de Liberación Nacional* (Zapatista National Liberation Army) in Chiapas. Even though the rhetoric focusing mainly on indigenous rights was not among the original demands of the movement, Sub-Comandante Marcos has since demanded the recognition of the political and cultural rights of Mexico's 10 million indigenous people.
118. Dawson: *Indian and Nation*, p. 59.
119. Floris: Official Mexican Attitudes, p. 964.
120. Ibid.
121. Ibid, p. 965.
122. See Ellen Schriek and Walter Schmuhl: "Vorwort," in Ellen Schriek and Walter Schmuhl: *Das Andere Mexico.Indigene Voelker von Chiapas bis Chihuahua*, Gießen: Focus, 1997, p. 9.
123. As Gabbert has determined for Yucatán, "'indígena' has primarily remained a technical term, used and spread by institutions like INI, and is only rarely employed in everyday discourse." See Gabbert: *Becoming Maya*, p. 114 and Gabbert: "Soziale Ungleichheit und Indianismus auf der Halbinsel Yukatan,"

p. 98. Correspondingly, Shriek and Schmuhl have emphasized reasons not to identify as *indígena*. See Schriek and Schmuhl: "Vorwort," p. 7.

NOTES TO CHAPTER SEVEN

1. I use the terms 'Yaquis' and 'Yoeme' interchangeably and for variation. Traditionally, the Yaquis refer to themselves as Yoeme but have usually been referred to by the outside world as Yaquis. Yet even today, when more and more tribes are called by the name they have traditionally used to refer to themselves, the Yaquis, on both sides of the Mexican-US border are still mainly referred to as Yaquis.
2. The term '*rancherías*' refers to scattered communities on average of perhaps 300 persons. See Edward Holland Spicer: *The Yaquis. A Cultural History*, Tucson, Arizona: University of Arizona Press, 1980, p. 30. For population numbers from 1500 to 1767 see Bernd Hausberger: *Für Gott und König. Die Mission der Jesuiten im kolonialen Mexiko*, Oldenbourg: Verlag für Geschichte und Politik, 2000, p. 71.
3. Both the nature and the extent of this native trade is largely unknown. See Evelyn Hu-DeHart: *Missionaries, Miners, and Indians: Spanish Contact with the Yaqui Nation of Northwestern New Spain, 1533–1820*, Tucson: University of Arizona Press, 1981, p. 11.
4. See Evelyn Hu-DeHart: *Yaqui Resistance and Survival: the Struggle for Land and Autonomy, 1821–1910*, Madison: University of Wisconsin Press, 1984, p. 12.
5. See Edward H. Spicer: "Mayos and Yaquis"; in: Edward Holland Spicer (ed.): *Cycles of Conquest. The Impact of Spain, Mexico, and the United States on the Indians of the Southwest, 1533–1960*, Tucson, Arizona: University of Arizona Press, 1962.
6. See Edward H. Spicer (ed.): *Perspectives in American Indian Culture Change*, Chicago: University of Chicago Press, 1961, p. 9.
7. Hu-DeHart: *Resistance*, p. 17.
8. The Yaquis wanted political as well as cultural separation. See Evelyn Hu-DeHart: "Peasant Rebellion in the Northwest: The Yaqui Indians of Sonora, 1740–1976"; in: Friedrich Katz (ed.): *Riot, Rebellion, and Revolution*, Princeton: Princeton University Press, 1988, p. 156.
9. See Hu-DeHart: *Resistance*, p. 19.
10. Contingents of Yaquis had been recruited at times. See Hu-DeHart: *Resistance*, p. 21.
11. Hu-DeHart: *Resistance*, p. 19.
12. See Hu-DeHart: *Resistance*, p. 24. The commanding generals viewed it as a matter of race, while a British commercial agent thought unfulfilled promises of citizenship and democracy the reason for the rebellion.
13. Ibid.
14. Ibid, p. 18.
15. Ibid, p. 29.
16. Ibid.
17. Ibid, p. 32ff.

18. Hu-DeHart: Peasant, p. 160.
19. Evelyn Hu-DeHart: "Yaqui Resistance to Mexican Expansion," in: John E. Kicza (ed.): *The Indian in Latin American History. Resistance, Resilience, and Acculturation,* Wilmington: Scholarly Resources, 1993, p. 143.
20. Hu-De Hart: Peasant, p. 160
21. Hatfield: *Chasing Shadows,* p. 7. This declaring the lands to be *terrenos baldíos,* empty, vacant lands, was done on the basis of the so-called *Ley Lerdo,* passed in 1856, but a fair amount of land had remained untouched until Díaz came to power.
22. Hu-DeHart: Yaqui Resistance to Mexican Expansion, p. 146.
23. See Hu-DeHart: *Resistance,* p. 113.
24. Hu-DeHart: Peasant, p. 163.
25. Especially during this time, more and more pueblos-in-exile were created. For the communities in the US see for instance Spicer and also Thomas R. McGuire: *Politics and Ethnicity on the Río Yaqui: Potam Revisited,* Tucson: University of Arizona Press, 1986.
26. Hu-DeHart: Peasant, p. 173.
27. Hu-DeHart: Yaqui Resistance to Mexican Expansion, p. 164.

NOTES TO CHAPTER EIGHT

1. Evelyn Hu-DeHart: "Development and Rural Rebellion: Pacification of the Yaquis in the Late *Porfiriato*"; in: *The Hispanic American Historical Review,* Volume 54, Durham: Duke University Press, 1974, p. 80.
2. Letter of the Secretario del Estado to the Prefecto de Guaymas (April 23, 1903). AHGES, tomo 1794 (1903).
   For one contemporary report on the Yaquis' work reputation, see Ramón Corral: *Obras histórias.* Hermosillo: Biblioteca Sonorense de Geografía e Historia, 1959, p. 200, and also Francisco P. Troncoso: *Las guerras con los tribus Yaqui y Mayo,* Mexico City: Instituto Nacional Indigenista, 1977, p. 44. See also INAH, Sonora 8, for a description of the *Yoeme* as the "verdadero pueblo trabajador." (Newspaper article; *La Constitución,* No. 7, Tomo XXI, Hermosillo, dated November 24, 1899.)
3. Every tomo in the AHGES makes a mention of raids.
4. The shortage of workers is mentioned repeatedly in the governmental correspondence. See for instance AHGES, tomo 1882 (1904).
5. See for instance AHGES, tomo 1700 (1902) and 1794 (1903). See also various references in newspaper articles as collected in INAH, primarily in the collection entitled Sonora 8. See also CONDUMEX, Colección Bernardo Reyes, Carpeta 34, Legajo 6738; and Acervos Históricos Universidad Iberoamericana, Colección Porfirio Díaz, L15. (Letter from Corral to Díaz, June 14, 1890)
6. "The so-called manzos are the worst of all in the region ... The Yaquis are moving around there, always looking for work, but instead of working they take note of what is going on ... and in the night they go and tell those who are in the mountains; telling them where they can rob and kill if necessary."

[C.H.] AHGES, tomo 1882 (1904), letter from a shop owner dated October 15.
7. Probably almost all male Yaquis still living in the Yaqui Valley could be considered rebels. They numbered five or six thousand. See Hu-DeHart: *Resistance*, p. 129.
8. See Hu-DeHart: *Resistance*, p. 131. The border to Arizona was strictly patrolled and the Americans involved in the attempt to keep guns and ammunition from the Yaquis. See for example AHGES, tomo 1794 (1903) or 1881 (1904).
9. See Hu-DeHart: *Resistance*, p. 129.
10. See for instance Acervos Históricos Universidad Iberoamericana, Colección Porfirio Díaz, L14 for a discussion of the conditions the soldiers encountered and complained about. (Letter from General Cervantes to Díaz, dated March 10, 1889)
11. INAH, Sonora 9. (Special newspaper article entitled "La Pacificación de la Tribu Yaqui," 1912.)
12. See AHGES, tomo 1700 (1902).
13. According to Evelyn Hu-DeHart this happened between 1895 and 1897. See Hu-DeHart: *Resistance*, p. 132. While there is not sufficient evidence to completely prove this wrong, there are some indications that the statement may not entirely hold true. The *Boletines Sanitarios* show slightly more women than men among the persons who had been there the longest. (Indeed, the ratio is 18 women to 8 men, looking at arrivals in the time between 1891 and 1902. (I have not found anyone arriving earlier.) And the deportee who had been on Yucatán the longest and could be found in the *boletines* was also a woman, more specifically two women. They had been on Yucatán since 1891. Among the men, Antonio Garcia, a soldier, had been on the peninsula the longest (of all the once who were reported in the *boletines*). He arrived in 1894. See AGEY, Poder Ejecutivo, Beneficiencia, 1911, Cajas 749 and 774 (Documents dated September 22 and May 13) and AGEY, Poder Ejecutivo, Beneficiencia, 1904, Caja 458. (Document dated June 18, 1904) It is possible, though not very likely, that just none of the earliest deported men did get sick and were hospitalized for Yellow Fever. And the individuals who had been there the longest were also women. Among the arrivals before 1900, there were two women in 1891, a man each in 1894 and 1898, and again two women in 1899. In 1900, seven female Yaquis could be found in the *boletines*, but only one man.
14. See Hu-DeHart: *Resistance*, p. 132.
15. See AHGES, tomo 1881 (1904), in a letter presumably from Rafael Izábal to Luis Torres, dated April 20.
16. See Hu-DeHart: *Resistance*, p. 138.
17. Hu-DeHart: *Resistance*, p. 138.
18. See Hu-DeHart: *Resistance*, p. 140–141.
19. As Evelyn Hu-DeHart points out, the rebels acted increasingly independent from each other. In this she sees a necessity of guerilla warfare. See Hu-DeHart: *Resistanc*e, p. 203.
20. Ibid, p. 144.

21. A circular with rules can be found in 1902. It supplied ten rules to be followed strictly, as well as an explanation of why these measures had become necessary. The main reason stated was the mixing and exchange of rebels and workers. See AHGES, tomo 1700 (1902).
22. See for instance AHGES, tomo 1632 (1901) or 1700 (1902). Literally translated the word means 'save conduct.'
23. See AHGES, tomo 1632 (1901).
24. See AHGES, tomo 1552 (1900). For documents on gun control see primarily AHGES, tomo 1552 (1900) and 1700 (1902).
25. See AHGES, tomo 1632 (1901).
26. See AHGES, tomo 1700 (1902).
27. There was, for instance, the trader from Guyamas who in 1903 complained about the weapons he had had in store since 1900, not permitted to sell them. He even offered to send them out of the country. There are two similar cases in the same year where limited concessions were made. See AHGES, tomo 1795 (1903).
28. See for instance the case of the Maytorenas who were caught smuggling Yaquis. See AHGES, tomo 2316 (1908). Complaints about the Maytorenas can be found as early as 1904. See AHGES, tomo 1882 (1904).
29. Hu-DeHart: *Resistance,* p. 156.
30. The railroads did use Yaqui labor but even they eventually had to suffer from the anti-Yaqui measures. First their workers were put under surveillance and then they and their families were sent to the state capital—ironically by train. There, the same destiny awaited them as did their fellow *Yoeme.* See for instance AHGES, tomo 2193 (1907).
31. "Even though we have been born here in Sonora" [C.H.] Typed copy of a letter dated April 25, 1904, presumably from the *nueve capitanes* and directed to the government. AHGES, tomo 1881 (1904).
32. "Because we are from here" [C.H.] Ibid.
33. "Even though they are not armed" [C.H.] Ibid.
34. "We don't know what blame we carry." [C.H.] Ibid.
35. See Letter dated May 5, 1904 (typed copy). AHGES, tomo 1881 (1904).
36. See AHGES, tomo 1881 (1904). In response, Izábal had a statement published in *El Imparcial* saying he considered the Yaquis "útil" and during the war had treated them humanely but had also been forced to castigate them severely. See AHGES, tomo 1881 (1904).
37. See AHGES, tomo 1881 (1904).
38. They also claim never to have harmed any passengers, presumably meaning travelers. See AHGES, tomo 1881 (1904).
39. AHGES, tomo 1881 (1904).
40. Most applications to return servants were turned down. One exception can be found in 1902, when a Yaqui upon request was sent back to his employer but was to be kept under surveillance. See AHGES, tomo 1700 (1902). At other times, not even the vouching of several people did achieve this. See AHGES, tomos 2077 (1906) and 2078 (1906).

41. Mention of deserters can be found in almost any of the early tomos (volumes) in the AHGES. See for instance tomos 1552 (1900), 1794 (1903), 2077 (1906), and 2078 (1906).
42. In 1908, Tórin reported 301 Yaqui inhabitants, Pótam 273, Bácum 46, Cócorit 201, Alamos 307, and Guaymas 1558. See AHGES, tomo 2315 (1908). The numbers that can be found in Hu-DeHart: *Resistance,* p. 178 differ from the ones above. This would second her opinion about the unreliability of the numbers in the reports.
43. See for instance AHGES, tomos 1881 (1904), 1984 (1905), 2077 (1906), 2078 (1906), 2193 (1907), 2313 (1908), 2663 (1911) (for the time span until 1911).
44. See AHGES, tomo 1882 (1904). The letter in question was sent by the Secretarío del Estado.
45. This assumption is backed by an instruction found in 1908, when Governor Luis Torres says to leave sick Yaquis behind in the deportation. See AHGES, tomo 2315 (1908). One deportee with a contagious disease might have spoiled the entire shipment.
46. See for instance AHGES, tomo 1881 (2904).
47. See Hu-DeHart: *Resistance,* p. 167f.
48. AHGES, tomo 1881 (1904).
49. See AHGES, tomos 1881 (1904), 1984 (1905), 2078 (1906), 2313 (1908).
50. "He did not want to say anything and preferred to die." [C.H.] AHGES, tomo 2314 (1908).
51. See AHGES, tomo 1881 (1904). And even those who stayed were often kept specifically to work.
52. Ibid. Hence it was hard to recruit Yaquis as messengers as a letter dated April 24 by G.S. Mills, a negotiator, shows.
53. See AHGES, tomos 1881 (1904) and 1882 (1904). Unfortunately, the data are not as rich in other years, except for 1908.
54. See AHGES, tomos 2313 (1908), 2314 (1908), 2315 (1908), and 2316 (1908).
55. Oaxaca is mentioned only once and without any reference to a specific number of Yaquis. This impression is tentatively confirmed by the published memories of Yaquis. Only one is about the deportation to Oaxaca. See Juan Silverio Jaime León: *Testimonios de una mujer yaqui,* Mexico City: Conaculta, 1988. (And even this book mentions Yucatán often.) In Oaxaca, the Valle Nacional was the destination of the deportees. This deep canyon was also called the Valle de la Muerte (Valley of Death). See Krauze: *Mexico,* p. 222.
56. See AHGES, tomo 2195 (1907). In one case, two men who had fought against the rebels had the Prefecto of Ures inquiring on their and their families behalf. No answer is on file.
57. See AHGES, tomo 1881 (1904).
58. See AHGES, tomo 1882 (1904).
59. See Knight: Racism, p. 79.

60. See AHGES, tomo 2195 (1907). In my opinion, this was done because the Yaquis were in need of clothing. The clothes of the dead children were left behind.
61. See Telegram (April 9, 1908) from the police at Estación Torres. AHGES, folder with typewritten copies of various letters, 1908–1910.
62. AHGES, tomo 2195 (1907). In this case it was Prefect Felles of Ures who used the expression.
63. See Hu-DeHart: *Resistance,* p. 180. Many officials, for instance Secretary Alberto Cubillas, were of the opinion that only the Yaquis' elimination from Sonora could bring peace to the state. See CONDUMEX, Colección Ramón Corral, Carpeta 1/3, Legajo 30. (Letter from Alberto Cubillas to Ramón Corral, September 1908)
64. Hu-DeHart: *Resistance,* p. 180. She is referring to Olegario Molina, Ramón Corral, Luis Torres, and Rafael Izábal. See also Raquel Padilla Ramos: *Yucatán, fín del sueño yaqui,* Hermosillo: Gobierno del Estado de Sonora, 1995, p. 105. Similarly, Gilbert Joseph points to Olegario Molina's business connections. See Gilbert M. Joseph: "Rethinking Mexican Revolutionary Mobilization: Yucatán's Seasons of Upheaval, 1909–1915," in Gilbert M. Joseph and Daniel Nugent (eds.): *Everyday Forms of State Formation. Revolution and the Negotiation of Rule in Modern Mexico,* Durham and London: Duke University Press, 1994, p.140–141.
65. See AHGES, tomos 2319 (1908), 2077/78 (1906), 2193 (1907).
66. See John Kenneth Turner: *Barbarous Mexico,* Austin: University of Texas Press, 1969, p. 38.
67. See AHGES, tomo 1984 (1905), especially a letter dated October 31.
68. Raquel Padilla is of the same opinion. See Padilla: *Fín,* p. 65.
69. I have found one case in which the officials ask who is to receive the money coming out of a cattle sale. The original owner had been deported and his wife along with him. No answer is on file.
70. "For the purpose of guarding the Yaqui Indian prisoners of war" [C.H.] AHGES, tomo 1881 (1904). This happened in response to a request by the prefect of Guaymas.
71. See AHGES, tomo 2077/78 (1906). The warship in question was the 'canonero Tampico' and it was supposed to return for another shipment of Yaquis once this trip had been concluded. Two non-military ships were also mentioned as taking contingents of Yoeme.

    See also Jane Holden Kelley: *Yaqui Women. Contemporary Life Histories,* Lincoln and London: University of Nebraska Press, 1978. The memories of Chepa Moreno (p. 126–153) talk about a small boat taking them the first part of the voyage.
72. AHGES, tomo 2193 (1907). Other mentionings of ships of that type can be found in AHGES, tomo 2319 (1908). If the first leg of the voyage was usually conducted by means of a warship that would explain why Yucatecan Yaquis entertained the hope that a warship would return them to their home.
73. "Sufficient to complete/fill one boat trip." [C.H.] AHGES, tomo 2316 (1908). For more on the expenses, see Hu-DeHart: *Resistance,* p. 112.
74. See AHGES, tomo 3253 (1918).

75. These working captives earned between 11 and 25 centavos on the *haciendas*. See AHGES, tomo 2314 (1908).
76. See AHGES, tomo 2077/78 (1906).
77. See Turner: *Barbarous,* p. 38.
78. See Padilla: *Fín,* p. 115—118 and 130f.
79. The total number of deportees from the Yaqui tribe has never been officially tabulated. It is also next to impossible to estimate the total number of Yaquis at the eve of the deportation, due to wide dispersal, wars, and a generally high mobility. Contemporary estimates put their number at about 30,000.

    See Hu-DeHart: *Resistance,* chapter 6, for a more detailed discussion of these figures.
80. In the Sonoran sources, I have found no case at all. However, Raquel Padilla Ramos has tracked down at least one case of escape enroute to Yucatán. See Padilla: *Fín,* p. 132f.
81. See AHGES, tomo 2316 (1908).
82. See several references in AHGES, tomo 2315 (1908). They probably only received these vaccinations because they were a valuable commodity.
83. See Hu-DeHart: *Resistance,* p. 182.
84. The name is also found in the spelling of Buli.
85. See AHGES, tomo 2315 (1908).
86. "En seguida manifestaron que les trajeron las familias de ellos que estaban en Yucatán y se les manifestó que despues de sometidos podían solicitarlo del Gobierno, el que resolvería lo conveniente, con lo que también quedaron conformes." AHGES, tomo 2315 (1908).
    See also Hu-DeHart: *Resistance,* p. 184.
87. See AHGES, tomo 2315 (1908) for attempts to secure the time needed for such an endeavor. *Parientes* is the term generally used by the Yaquis to refer to other *Yoeme*. It implies kinship.
88. See AHGES, tomo 2315 (1908).
89. See AHGES, tomo 2316 (1908).
90. See AHGES, tomo 2316 (1908).
91. See for instance Rosalio Moisés, with William Curry Holden and Jane Holden Kelley: *A Yaqui Life. The Personal Chronicle of a Yaqui Indian,* Lincoln and London: University of Nebraska Press, 1971, p. 27.
92. See for instance AHGES, tomos 2313 (1908), and 2315 (1908), as well as folder with copies.
93. See list included in AHGES, tomo 2193 (1907).
94. AHGES, tomo 2316 (1908).
95. See AHGES, tomo 2195 (1907). Prefect Felles inquired about this but the response to his query is not on file.
96. See AHGES, tomo 2316 (1908).
97. See AHGES, tomo 2315 (1908).
98. See AHGES, tomo 2315 (1908).
99. See Hu-DeHart: *Resistance,* p. 188.
100. See AHGES, tomo 2315 (1908).
101. See Hu-DeHart: *Resistance,* p. 190.

102. Traditionally, decisions were made after a discussion in a council of all Yaquis. This practice had been revived by Cajeme, and Bule seems to have intended to use it as well. At least he was advised in a letter from May 24, 1908 not to bring all the Yaquis from the *pueblos* and the *haciendas* ("no pueden venir todos los yaquis de los pueblos y de las haciendas como querían"). AHGES, tomo 2316 (1908). In a letter to military commander Luis Medina Barrón, Bule stated that all he needed to do was to get the Yaquis together ("yo los voy á juntar"). Letter dated September 6, 1908. AHGES, 2316 (1908). Additionally, see a reference to the problem in a letter to the president. Acervos Históricos Universidad Iberoamericana, Colección Porfirio Díaz, L33, 9474. (Letter from Coronel José González to Díaz, July 4, 1908) See also José Velasco Toro: *Los Yaquis: Historia de una activa resistencia,* Xalapa: Editorial UV, 1988, p. 34.

    Additional problems were caused when those Yaquis who were upon Bule's request supposed to serve as intermediaries between the *pacíficos* and the rebels were arrested and scheduled for deportation to Yucatán. Thus, the remaining rebels were hesitant to meet the government representatives. See AHGES, tomo 2316 (1908)

103. "Pidieron que se les permitiera á los que fueron deportados á Yucatán últimamente que regresaran; á esto contestó el Señor Gobernador que el regreso de los de Yucatán depende de la conducta que éstos observen aquí." AHGES, tomo 2316 (1908).

    See also CONDUMEX, Colección Ramón Corral, Carpeta 1/3, Legajo 4. (Letter from Alberto Cubillas, Secretarion, to Ramón Corral, May 4, 1908)

104. According to a 1908 letter from the Sonoran governor, the latter permitted the "Yaqui deportado Silverio Bustamante" to come back to Sonora after about ten years of exile. He had been in Mérida and had always displayed a good conduct. See AHGES, tomo 2315 (1908).

    As already mentioned, I have found evidence of only one returning group. In 1912, 40 men, women and children came home from Yucatán, having traveled at least part of the way by ship. See AHGES, tomo 2782 (1912). Rosalio Moisés reports on the return of two women from Yucatán in 1907 who were deported again in 1909 but turned lose in Mexico City that time around. See Moisés: *A Yaqui Life,* p. 27.

105. Hu-DeHart: *Resistance,* p. 197.
106. For the story of such a return see Jaime: *Testimonios.*

NOTES TO CHAPTER NINE

1. The exception being a brief outbreak of hostilities in 1911 when the throws of the Mexican Revolution had already reached Yucatán and may have inspired or encouraged the Yaquis. See Raquel Padilla Ramos: *Progreso y Libertad. Los Yaquis en la Víspera de la Repatriación,* Mérida: Universidad Autónoma de Yucatán (tesis de maestría—ms), 2002, p. 133–187 (chapter IV).
2. I am using the expression 'deportee' even after the Yaquis have been on Yucatán for a while because I think they never really got used to being there and thus continued to feel like deportees or displaced persons.

3. See Spicer: *The Yaquis,* p. 102. Velasco reports the 1910 census to have found 2,757 Yaquis on Yucatán. However, Spicer states that reportedly in the early 1930s, no traces of Yaquis could be found on Yucatán. See Velasco: *Los yaquis* p. 38, and Spicer: *The Yaquis,* p. 103.
4. Fixed destinations are mentioned in many years. Haciendas and their owners are also mentioned but it is not clear if these destinations were fixed from the outset. In many cases it also becomes evident, that the Yaquis did not necessarily remain in one place only, even though many did.
See for instance AGEY, Poder Ejecutivo, Beneficiencia, 1909, Caja 650. See also Padilla: *Fín,* p. 88.
5. See Hu-DeHart: *Resistance,* p. 180.
6. See Padilla: *Fín,* p. 102f and 126ff. See also Turner: *Barbarous,* p. 38. Spicer quotes a price of $65 on delivery. See Spicer: *The Yaquis,* p. 102. (The price is probably in pesos.) Velasco gives the same number. See Velasco: *Los Yaquis,* p. 38, as does Figueroa. See Alejandro Figueroa Valenzuela: *Identidad étnica y persistencia cultural. Un estudio de la sociedad y de la cultura de los yaquis y de los mayos,* Mexico City: Centro de Estudios Sociológicos, El Colegio de México, 1992, p. 67. In addition, he speaks of the money being given to the Secretaría de Guerra y Marina and the captors. Friedrich Katz reports that a Colonel received 65 pesos per head; 10 went to him and 10 to the ministry. Katz: Liberal Republic, p. 92. Neither Padilla nor I have found any evidence for this in Yucatecan or Sonoran archives yet.
7. See Padilla: *Fín,* p. 150ff and Florescano: *Etnia,* p. 471. See also AGEY, Poder Ejecutivo, Gobernación, 1910, Caja 697.
8. AGEY, Poder Ejecutivo, Milicia, 1908, Caja 600. However, it could also mean belonging to a place.
9. In the archives the contract can be found under the year 1916. At this time, it was forwarded to the State Governor, Salvador Alvarado, as an example for the cruelties committed by the Díaz régime. In the accompanying letter it is emphasized that these conditions had been remedied. "El régimen Constitucionalista, ha procurado, consecuentemente con su amplio programa de reinvidicaciones, que los obreros y jornaleros de campo en general recobren sus derechos de ciudadanos libres, conculcados por la nefasda Dictadura felizmente derrocada," boasting that the new government had given these workers back their constitutional rights . (AGEY, Poder Ejecutivo, Gobernación, 1916, Caja 515. (3/14/1900))
10. Ibid. "Families belonging to the rebellious Indians of the Rio Yaqui who have been taken prisoners of war" [C.H.] Ibid.
Since families were usually broken up, it is surprising to find this phrasing in the contract. However, since it is only one example and probably an early one, this may have been amended in later years. It is also possible that none of the contracting parties understood families in the sense of father, mother, and children but rather as a group of male and female adults with children, not necessarily their own.
11. AGEY, Poder Ejecutivo, Gobernación, 1916, Caja 515. (3/14/1900)
12. In later years, an increasing sparseness of news about the Yaquis could also be at least partially explained with the fact that the officials had other, to

them more pressing things on their minds. Thus they probably did not fight them as much and also recorded less of what was going on.

13. "They will not accept peace unless their condition is met that all whites withdraw and leave the Rio [Yaqui] completely free" [C.H.] AHGES, tomo 2663 (1911).
14. "We're not hostile towards no one unless there's a reason" [C.H.] AHGES, tomo 3389 (1916). The document itself, a machine-written copy of a letter from the Yaquis, is dated 1913.
15. "Our fight is limited exclusively to re-conquer our rights and our lands taken away through brute force" [C.H.] Ibid. Similar demands were still made in 1918, when, under yet another government, they again talked about 'derechos,' about rights. See AHGES, tomo 3253 (1918). And in 1922 they attacked American settlers and asked them to give up their lands. See AHGES, tomo 3546 (1922). In 1924 a resident Spaniard complained that Yoeme had occupied parts of his lands. See AHGES, tomo 3713 (1924). This suggested that they were still protecting their rights and the lands they claimed for themselves.
16. See AHGES, tomo 2950 (1913).
17. Hu-DeHart: *Resistance*, p. 205.
18. See Jaime León: *Testimonios*, p. 7 and 8.
19. The Yellow Fever is a disease contracted and spread through the bite of a mosquito. The first symptoms are fever, headaches, backaches, and nausea. The disease reduces the number of the white blood cells and causes hemorrhages. It is also known as Black Vomit ('vómito prieto') because the patients in an advanced stage of the disease start to bleed from the nose and mouth. In its final stage, the patient turns yellow, as in hepatitis. Natives of Yucatán are generally immune to the disease because they are in the fetal state inoculated through the mother. The incubation time is about 10 to 17 days.
20. "The great health problem of our state"[C.H.] AGEY, Poder Ejecutivo, Gobernación (2), 1913, Caja 851.
21. AGEY, Poder Ejecutivo, Beneficiencia, 1914, Caja 463.
22. They were also checked for vaccination marks and to see if the vaccine had taken. See for example AGEY, Poder Ejecutivo, Beneficiencia, 1908, Cajas 599 and 600.
23. See AHGES, tomo 2315 (1908).
24. In an attempt to contain and exterminate the disease, a number of details were recorded concerning the Yaquis' long voyage to Yucatán. In some instances, other destinations of the ships taking them to Yucatán were given. This information can be found in at least some of the documents counting the incoming persons not immune to the Yellow Fever. The *boletines* usually also supplied the name of the ship but only rarely the origin of the passengers. There are a few mentionings of 'yaquis' or 'jornaleros yaquis' (Yaqui workers). Sometimes as few as 12 were aboard, while at other times the number came to well over four hundred. In some instances, the Yaquis were listed after the passengers, as if they were a commodity more than human beings. At other times, the native province, city or town is mentioned, along with the marital status, sex and age of

the diseased person. Also generally among the information given on these *boletines* or of letters similar in nature are the occupation of the sick person and the *hacienda* he or she works or worked on. Sometimes the time they have been away from their native province is mentioned. (In these *Boletines Sanitarios,* names and places of origin more often than not misspelled.) And there is the added insecurity of representativity. Some Yaquis may have been in greater danger for contracting the disease, for a variety of reasons. No group representative of all exiled Yoeme could be expected to get sick. A fair number of the *boletines* probably did get lost over the years, and the information included therein along with them.

25. As to the ones who did make it onto the records, one of the problems is that of multiple mentioning. Some did get sick various times over the years; others seemingly checked themselves into the hospital again and again, even over a short period of time. See the case of María Yoquihua, AGEY, Poder Ejecutivo, Beneficiencia, 1912, Caja 791. (Various documents of that caja)
26. Presumably either because the diseased person did not identify as Yaqui or because the writer of the *boletín* did not consider it necessary to record that information.
27. AGEY, Poder Ejecutivo, Beneficiencia, 1900–1902, Caja 358. (Document dated July 30, 1901)
28. AGEY, Poder Ejecutivo, Beneficiencia, 1902, Caja 376. (Document dated October 11, 1902)
29. Most of the identifications as Yaquis are tentative, relying on typical names and places of origin. Only in a fraction of the cases individuals were identified as Yaquis. The names are given in the spelling found in the sources. Spicer points out that many Yaquis in this time of danger abandoned their typical surnames in favor of more Spanish-sounding ones. See Spicer: *The Yaquis,* p. 102.
30. See AGEY, Poder Ejecutivo, Beneficiencia, 1907, Caja 562. (Document dated May 12, 1907)
31. The expression 'su tierra' is used in almost all the cases uniformly. In my judgement, it cannot be properly translated and is more conclusive than any translation into 'country' or 'land' could ever be as these terms lack the connectedness to the earth/soil.
32. See AGEY, Poder Ejecutivo, Beneficiencia, 1907, Caja 562. (Document dated May 13, 1907)
33. AGEY, Poder Ejecutivo, Beneficiencia, 1907, Caja 562. (Document not dated) The expression 'directly' is applied various times over the years and probably only means that the Yoeme in question were traveling without any unnecessary stops on the way.
34. See AGEY, Poder Ejecutivo, Beneficiencia, 1907, Caja 562. (Documents dated May 25, May 28, July 30 and 31)
35. Many of the sick soldiers were members of the Cepeda Peraza battalion. For more information see Knight: *Mexican Revolution,* p. 248.
36. See AGEY, Poder Ejecutivo, Beneficiencia, 1902, Caja 376. (Document dated October, 11, 1902)

37. This impression is confirmed by the memories recorded by J Kelley: *Yaqui Women*, the memories of Chepa Moreno and Dominga Ramírez, p. 126–153 and 154–196.
38. Turner mentions the following route: Guaymas, San Blas, Tepic, San Marcos, México, Veracruz. Turner: *Barbarous*, p. 44. Some alternatives can be found in Padilla: *Fín*, p. 128. Some Yaquis were also sent to the states of Campeche and Quintana Roo; or to other parts of the republic.
39. See for instance AGEY, Poder Ejecutivo, Beneficiencia, 1907, Cajas 562, and 566.
40. See Kelley: *Yaqui Women*, the memories of Chepa Moreno and Dominga Ramírez, p. 126–153 and 154–196. See also AGEY Fondo Justicia 1905, caja 557 (the case will be examined later in the chapter).
41. In 1911 and 1912, 99 Yaquis from the *boletines* stated to be residents of Mérida. Only ten still mentioned a *hacienda*. (The four cases that could be found in 1911 are all adults, two women and two men. See AGEY, Poder Ejecutivo, Beneficiencia, 1911, Cajas 749 and 774. (Documents dated May 13, July 1, and August 14 and 22, 1911)) Of the six cases in 1912, three were minors, all of them born on the *haciendas* mentioned as place of residence. (See AGEY, Poder Ejecutivo, Beneficiencia, 1912, Caja 791. (Documents dated May 15, August 10, and December 9, 1912)) As the youngest of these children was not even a year old and the oldest still only five, they would certainly go to wherever their parents went.
42. While the evidence is circumstantial and the name not uncommon this seems like too much of a coincidence.
43. She shows up on the *boletines* of July 15, 20, and 22.
44. See Kelley: *Yaqui Women*, the memories of Chepa Moreno and Dominga Ramírez, p. 126–153 and 154–196 for the difficulties in making a living.
45. Next to nothing is known about the conditions in the hospital-sections for those under the suspicion of suffering from Yellow Fever. We do know, however, that the patients were strictly separated. Otherwise, I can only speculate that the diseased persons were given a place to sleep and maybe some food while they remained hospitalized. It is often unclear what became of the patients after they were diagnosed. Some were discharged immediately in spite of suffering from a serious disease; others remained only to then vanish from the sources. Few ever resurface, usually dead.
46. See Padilla: *Progreso y Libertad*, especially chapters III, V and VI as well as Kelley: *Yaqui Women*, the memories of Chepa Moreno and Dominga Ramírez, p. 126–153 and 154–196.
47. As a general rule, I have used the spelling found in the Yucatecan sources. Where it varied throughout the documents I have favored the most common way of spelling displayed there. More often than not, the Yaqui names found in the court documents are corruptions of Sonoran names, which must have sounded very alien to Yucatecan ears more accustomed to Mayan names.

    Not all documents mentioned here clearly identify the persons mentioned therein as Yaquis but the ones that do not do so usually supply ample circumstantial evidence, e.g. place of birth or typical names.

48. Archivo General del Estado de Yucatán (AGEY), Fondo Justicia, 1908, Caja 704. Later in the document, Bacasena is also called a servant of the finca Cancachén, of which Casáres was the proprietor. The finca's name in other places has been given as Cacanchén.
49. "They would ordinarily heal in a period of not more than fifteen days and without endangering the life" [C.H.] AGEY, Fondo Justicia, 1908, Caja 704.
50. There is some confusion about the names of those involved and some evidence suggests that Villanueva and Valencia may have been the same person.

    A few of the cases explored here have also been analyzed with a different focus in another article, Claudia Haake: "Two Stories: Yaqui Resistance in Sonora and Yucatan" in: Nikolaus Böttcher and Bernd Hausberger (eds.): *Poder y resistencia en la historia de América Latina,* Berlin/Frankfurt a. M.: Ibero-Amerikanisches Institut/Vervuert, 2005.
51. The name of the hacienda may have been Tanihl. See Kelley: *Yaqui Women,* p. 163.
52. She is said to be 40 or 44 years old—the information in the document varies.
53. See AGEY, Fondo Justicia, 1908, Caja 704.
54. As in the previous case there seems to be some confusion about the names of those involved, probably because the typical Yaqui names sounded more than strange to Yucatecan ears. First, the defendant was referred to as Francisca Flores until she explicitly stated her name to be Francisca Loor Ségua. In the Yaquis' language, 'sewa' means flower, and so does 'loor.' So it is possible that the confusion stemmed from a mere repetition of her name on the part of Francisca, once in Yaqui and once in Spanish.
55. " . . . le fué á dar su merecido." AGEY, Fondo Justicia, 1908, Caja 704.
56. In addition to the criminal cases mentioned, there are cases of orphaned Yaquis. However, these cases include hardly any information on the children at all and are dedicated mainly to finding a legal representative for them. Sometimes the name and native town of the mother is included, but this confirms only the Yaqui identity of the children.
57. AGEY, Justicia, 1912, Caja 870. The documents are in part badly damaged by water and fungi. No other case mentions the word Yaqui as many times as this one.
58. Ibid. "I am going to screw the Yaqui; I am going to kill him."[C.H.] Here, the document is very ambiguous. It could also have been Buitimea making this utterance. Yet in that case he would have initiated the fight himself, which most likely would have resulted in a much shorter sentence for Alvarado.
59. AGEY, Justicia, 1912, Caja 870.
60. See Padilla: *Progreso y Libertad,* p. 156.
61. "Están fuera de la finca . . . los referidos Yaquis." AGEY, Justicia, 1912, Caja 881. Indeed, Luz Giosa may have been among those who left the haciendas in 1912, making their way to Mérida. With all probability, these Yaquis, set free by the Revolution, were trying to escape the fincas and, maybe, to return to their native Sonora. Apparently, other Yaquis were also missing from the same finca.
62. It is unclear for how long he was incarcerated.
63. "Of Yaqui origin" [C.H.] AGEY, Justicia, 1912, Caja 881.

64. This name seems to have been puzzling the court. He is also referred to as Mamado Marcelino.
65. In this context, another reference is made to Josefa being Yaqui, "ciendo de la familia Yaqui." See AGEY, Justicia, 1912, Caja 881.
66. "Large and continuous cups of aguardiente" [C.H.] AGEY, Justicia, 1912, Caja 881. Flora was the only one among the people involved about whom we do not know if she was a Yaqui or even just from Sonora. About her, it is only said that she was 40 years old, married, and did domestic work. See AGEY, Justicia, 1912, Caja 881.
67. See Gabbert: *Becoming Maya*, p. 44.
68. See Kelley: *Yaqui Women*, especially p. 136.
69. See Padilla: *Progreso y Libertad*, p. 133–187, on a possible gender component to contacts between Yaquis and non-Yaquis on the haciendas. Her evidence suggests that women were more likely to establish such contacts because of the nature of their work. See also Kelley: *Yaqui Women*, p. 126–153 and 154–196.
70. While the revolutionary armies arrived on Yucatán quite late, some effects of the events taking place elsewhere would have been felt beforehand. See for instance Joseph: Rethinking Mexican Revolutionary Mobilization, p. 161.
71. See Kelley: *Yaqui Women*, chapters on Chepa Moreno and Dominga Martínez, about the few instances Yaquis managed to practice their traditions on the haciendas, p. 126–153 and 154–196.
72. Padilla believes to have found some evidence suggesting infanticide. See Padilla: *Progreso y Libertad*, chapter IV (p. 133–187). The evidence I have discovered is too scarce to support or discredit this theory. Holden Kelley also hints at high infant mortality without suggesting infanticide. See also Kelley: *Yaqui Women*, p. 126–153 and 154–196.
73. See AGEY, Justicia, 1911, Cajas 830 and 831.
74. Given the presumably comparatively smallish number of Yaquis on haciendas it seems likely that the two men must have known each other. See also Kelley: *Yaqui Women*, chapters on Chepa Moreno and Dominga Martínez (p. 126–153 and 154–196) for descriptions of Yaqui communities on Yucatecan haciendas.
75. According to Yaqui memories as found in Holden Kelley's book, alcohol was available quite cheaply. See also Kelley: *Yaqui Women*, especially p. 138. See also Gabbert: *Becoming Maya*, p. 44.
76. Apart from the cases mentioned here, a few others indicate alcohol abuse, including some related to Yellow Fever (in AGEY, Beneficiencia, various years).
77. See AGEY, Justicia, 1911, Cajas 833.
78. The evidence can neither prove nor reject the theory that maybe the two men fought over Andrea Machilea. It is equally possible that Andrea had had previous dealings with Canto, possibly of an amorous nature.
79. In some cases, like the one of Antonio Alvarez, it could not be determined if the other involvees were of Yaqui origin as the documents gave no clues. (Alvarez was not the victim of a crime but had suffered a broken foot when a carriage ran over it when he and his friends were on the way to the station

to go to town, possibly to leave their hacienda for good.) See AGEY, Fondo Justicia, 1911, Caja 845.
80. An exception is posed by the memories chronicled in Jane Holden Kelley's book. However, these are the memories of women who were only children at the time whereas the court cases discussed here record the experiences of adult Yaquis.
81. Gabbert: *Becoming Maya*, p. 44.
82. The possibility that struggles did occur cannot be ruled out entirely. Minor matters were probably never known outside the haciendas. Padilla has identified some minor incidents—though mostly after the outbreak of the Revolution. See Padilla: *Progreso y Libertad*, p. 133–187.
83. Other traditions could sometimes be maintained though were also sometimes oppressed. See Padilla: *Progreso y Libertad*, p. 169 also Kelley: *Yaqui Women*, p. 126–153 and 154–196.
84. See Gabbert: *Becoming Maya*, p. 44. Furthermore, special living arrangements sometimes were in place especially for unmarried workers. See also Joseph: Rethinking Mexican Revolutionary Mobilization, p.158.
85. Hu-DeHart: *Resistance*, p. 205. (Most sources used by Hu-DeHart come from archives in Mexico City; one of which included a collection of materials from archives in other parts of the country—though not from Yucatán.) While families were not necessarily broken up when leaving Sonora, this could happen once they arrived in Yucatán. See Padilla: *Progreso y Libertad*, p. 63.
86. See Figueroa: *Identidad étnica y persistencia cultural*, primarily p. 379. Figueroa mentions culture and tradition in addition to territory, elements I would see as part of what I have referred to as community. See Figueroa 1992, p. 382. Spicer hints at the importance of land but primarily emphasized community in his examination of Yaqui identity. However, I believe that his discussion of the importance of the Eight Towns to an extent mirrors my argument here since he emphasizes their importance for the navigation of spiritual and sacred space. See Edward Holland Spicer: *The Yaquis*, chapter 6 (p. 287–332).
87. This significance is what Raquel Padilla Ramos hints at when spelling 'tierra' with a capital 'T' when it comes to the Yaquis. See Padilla: *Progreso y Libertad*, p. 5. See also Figueroa: *Identidad étnica y persistencia cultural*, p. 353 for the importance of land for the Yaquis.
88. In the cases examined here there is some evidence for Yaquis leaving the haciendas. In one instance, Luz Giosa, the wife of the defendant Fidencio Alvarado Fodo, cannot be summoned for a statement because she, like several others, has left the hacienda. This happened at about the same time that María de la Luz Flores attacked her partner because he had threatened to leave her and to return to his country by himself. These cases took place on different haciendas.

Evidence from other sources, records kept in an attempt to curb outbreaks of Yellow Fever, supports this. There, large numbers of Yaquis are identified as residents of Mérida. See various cajas in AGEY, Poder Ejecutivo / Gobernación in the years 1902—1914.

89. See Padilla: *Progreso y Libertad,* primarily p. 90–132. See also Kelley: *Yaqui Women,* chapters on Chepa Moreno and Dominga Martínez (p. 126–153 and 154–196).
90. See Padilla: *Progreso y Libertad,* primarily p. 133–187.
91. There is little evidence about how many made it back to Sonora or how they did this. I have found only one reference to Yaquis returning from their Yucatecan exile. A group of 40 Yaquis, men, women, and children, in 1912 came back to Sonora via Mazatlan on the steamship 'Pesqueira.' They were at first furnished with the barest necessities and then told to find work to finance themselves. It is unclear who paid for their passage home. See various correspondences in June of 1912, mainly by governor Maytorena, in AHGES, tomo 2782 (1912). Other evidence suggests that Yaquis returned on foot. See Jaime: *Testimonios,* p. 11–13.

    Padilla found a group of 500 being sent to Veracruz on a warship. See Padilla: *Progreso y Libertad,* p. 90. For the unresolved mysteries of the Yaquis' return see Padilla: *Progreso y Libertad,* p. 92 and 94. The stories found in Jane Holden Kelley's book are rather vague but nonetheless indicate that it was possible and probably not uncommon to return to Sonora. See Kelley: *Yaqui Women,* p. 126–153 and 154–196.
92. See AHGES, tomo 2315 (1908) and AHGES, tomo 2316 (1908).
93. See AHGES, tomo 2315 (1908).

NOTES TO CHAPTER TEN

1. See Velasco: *Los Yaquis,* p. 45f. These three leaders and their men formed the core of General Salvador Alvarado's forces. These two thousand men later became part of Obregón's army. Bule died very early on in the conflict. Urbalejo and Morales continued to fight for Alvaro Obregón, even though Urbalejo temporarily went over to the side of Pancho Villa. As Alan Knight once put it, Urbalejo was "essentially an Urbalejista." Knight: *The Mexican Revolution,* p. 311.

    Some other Yaquis were recruited by Colonel Fructuoso Méndez. The hard-core rebels held out even during the revolution and gave their allegiance to no one. See Hu-DeHart: *Resistance,* p. 208.
2. Spicer: *The Yaquis,* p. 227.
3. See Velasco: *Los Yaquis,* p. 43. In the AHGES, there are numerous indications that Sibalaume acquired great fame as a rebel leader. See for instance AHGES, tomos 2950 (1913) as well as 2783 and 2782 (both 1912). In 1911, tomo 2663, there is even one reference to "el famoso Sibalaume."
4. See Spicer: *The Yaquis,* p. 227. Velasco lists the return of the deportees among the things promised. See Velasco: *Los Yaquis,* p. 43. Sibalaume after the fall of Madero resumed his rebellion from the sierra.
5. Knight: *The Mexican Revolution,* p. 337.
6. See Spicer: *The Yaquis,* p. 229.
7. Spicer: *The Yaquis,* p. 227.

8. This happened in 1914 and 1915, while Urbalejo was fighting with Villa and Morales with Obregón.
9. Spicer: *The Yaquis*, p. 228. See also Hu-DeHart: *Resistance*, p. 208.
10. See Knight: *The Mexican Revolution*, p. 373.
11. See Hu-DeHart: *Resistance*, p. 209.
12. See Spicer: *The Yaquis*, p. 232.
13. See Hu-DeHart: Peasant Rebellion, p. 167.
14. See Hu-DeHart: *Resistance*, p. 210f. See also Spicer: *The Yaquis*, p. 232ff.
15. See Hu-DeHart: *Resistance*, p. 211. See also Spicer: *The Yaquis*, p. 232ff.
16. Spicer: *The Yaquis*, p. 235.
17. Hu-DeHart: *Resistance*, p. 212.
18. Hu-DeHart: Peasant Rebellion, p. 170.
19. See Hu-DeHart: Peasant Rebellion, p. 170, and also Hu-DeHart: *Resistance*, p. 217.

NOTES TO CHAPTER ELEVEN

1. Gary B. Nash: *Red, White, and Black. The Peoples of Early North America*, 3rd edition, Englewood Cliffs: Prentice Hall, 1992, p. 116. Fittingly, when their first contacts tool place, the Yaquis repelled a Spaniard on a slave raid and lived peacefully with another one who had no such objectives.
2. Ibid.
3. Nash: *Red*, p.143.
4. Patricia Nelson Limerick: *The Legacy of Conquest. The Unbroken Past of the American West*, New York and London: Norton, 1987, p. 216.
5. Also more generally it was seen as perfectly acceptable to bring Christianization to the Natives in return for their labor and land. Similarly, in the United States civilization efforts and treaty-making for the longest time were not viewed as incompatible. Both philosophies included a rationale of exchange that was not so very dissimilar.
6. As already mentioned, strictly speaking there was no 'pre-removal time' for the Delawares.
7. At the same time, the slavery question was also violently 'discussed' and created a situation from which the Indians suffered badly.
8. The question of the legal status had been determined by the decision of the U.S. Supreme Court in person of Chief Justice Marshall in 1932 during the Cherokee fight against removal following the Indian Removal Act of 1830 within the federal court system (Worcester vs. Georgia). He declared the Indians to be 'domestic dependent nations' and therefore like a ward to the United States, their guardian.

    See among others Remini: *The Legacy of Andrew Jackson*, and Robert F. Berkhofer: *The White Man's Indian*, New York: Knopf, 1978.
9. The first of the land cession treaties which eventually cost the Delawares their lands in Kansas took place in 1854 and assigned 80 acres of land to each member of the Delaware tribe. One ratified in 1860 gave preference to railroad companies in the land purchase and also gave them perpetual

right of way. The treaty of 1861 arranged in more detail the sale of land to railroad companies and methods of payment. And finally, the treaty of 1866 arranged for the permanent removal of the Delawares from Kansas to Indian Territory. This was also the last treaty between the Delawares and the United States.

10. Treaty between the USA and the Cherokee nation, 1866. See Chares J. Kappler: *Indian Affairs, Laws and Treaties, Volumes I-III,* Washington, Government Printing Office, 1904: *Affairs,* p. 947.
11. It has often been said that assimilation and extermination were the only measures practiced with regards to Native Americans. Yet removal was used as a substitute or also as a preceding step for both.
12. Padilla: *Fín,* p. 130. The total number of deportees from the Yaqui tribe has never been officially tabulated. Estimates for the period between 1902 and 1908 range from 8,00 to about 15,000, amounting to one-fourth or even one-half of the entire population when estimating the Yaquis to number 30,000 on the eve of the deportations which is probably an optimistic figure. It is also next to impossible to estimate the total number of Yaquis at the eve of the deportation, due to wide dispersal, wars, and a generally high mobility. Contemporary estimates put their number at about 30,000. See Hu-DeHart: *Resistance,* chapter 6, for a more detailed discussion of these figures.
13. Maybe cases like the one won for the Cherokee Freedmen and along with them for the Delawares and the Shawnees by Milton S. Turner in 1888 encouraged the Delawares to use this option for themselves. Turner won for his clients, the Cherokee Freedmen, a pro rata share of some land proceeds of the Cherokees. Others to profit from this decision were the Shawnees and Delawares incorporated in the Cherokee Nation. See National Archives, M574, roll 81.
14. The Sonoran Governor in a letter to General Salvador Alvarado (August 13, 1913) states that it would be very convenient to incorporate the Yaquis in their forces, "pues de esa manera se logrará no solo aumentar nuestro efectivo de combate sino tambien evitar que sigan dando guerra en los Pueblos del Rio." See AHGES, tomo 2950 (1913).
15. See Kelley: *Yaqui Women,* the memories of Chepa Moreno and Dominga Ramírez, p. 126–153 and 154–196.
16. See Ingrid Kummels: "Von 'Indianern' und 'indigenen Völkern.' Episoden aus der Geschichte Mexikos"; in: Ellen Schriek and Hans-Walter Schmuhl (eds.): *Das andere Mexiko. Indigene Völker von Chiapas bis Chihuahua,* Gießen: Focus, 1997, p. 22.

NOTES TO CHAPTER TWELVE

1. Richard N. Adams: „Strategies of Ethnic Survival in Central America"; in: Greg Urban and Joel Sherzer (eds.): *Nation-States and Indians in Latin America,* Austin: University of Texas Press, 1991, p. 189.
2. On philanthropic attitudes regarding removal, see Bernhard W. Sheehan: *Seeds of Extinction. Jeffersonian Philanthropy and the American Indian,* Chapel Hill: University of North Carolina Press, 1973, chapter IX.
3. See Sheehan: *Seeds,* p. 272.

4. Sheehan: *Seeds*, p. 270.
5. Reginald Horsman: *The Origins of Indian Removal, 1815–1824*, Michigan State University Press, 1969, p. 17.
6. I would like to make it clear that this should under no circumstances be considered a comparison of the Indian policies of the two states. I will limit myself to taking a closer look at some aspects relevant to the course of the history of the Yaquis and Delawares, pointing out similarities and dissimilarities. For a comparison of Indian policy in the two countries, see Feest: Indianerpolitik, p. 89–104.
7. Nash: *Red*, p. 297.
8. In fact, the resemblance is so great that I feel inclined to believe that General Diéguez may have been aware of the statement attributed to General Philip Sheridan. Quote taken from Ward Churchill: *Fantasies of the Master Race. Literature, Cinema and the Colonization of American Indians*, San Francisco: City Lights, 1998, p. 178.
9. 'The best Yaqui is a dead Yaqui.' Quote taken from Figueroa: *Identidad étnica*, p. 71. Also quoted in Knight: Racism, p. 83.
10. Hatfield: *Chasing Shadows*, p. xii.
11. At least not after the intensive fur trade had ceased. Even then the Indians had worked on their own and merely traded the fruits of their efforts. Later on, they mostly mattered as consumers of trade goods.
12. Thomas R. Berger: *A Long and Terrible Shadow. White Values, Native Rights in the Americas Since 1492*, 2nd edition, Seattle: University of Washington Press, 1991, p. 74.
13. Ibid.
14. This at least seemed to have been the case when they sued for a share of moneys awarded the Delaware tribe. But the fact that a group of people, formerly Delaware tribal members, was still identifiable should serve as an indication that some sense of community prevailed.
15. Hatfield: *Shadows*, p. 69.
16. See Florescano: *Etnia*, p. 493.
17. Figueroa: *Identidad*, p. 102.
18. I suspect the weighting of 'race' v. 'land' may have shifted once both states— as well as their Natives—had run out of the latter.
19. This is not dissimilar to Michael Green's conclusion about the Creek. "The only cement necessary was a uniform dedication to the land. Each side could tolerate how differently the other chose to use the land as long as they could agree that the land was patrimony of all." (Michael D. Green: *The Politics of Indian Removal. Creek Government and Society in Crisis*, Lincoln and London: University of Nebraska Press, 1985, p. 72)
20. General Blunt to Commissioner of Indian Affairs Nathaniel G. Taylor, February 27 1868, National Archives, M234, roll 279.
21. Ibid.
22. Superintendent Thomas Murphy to the Acting Commissioner of Indian Affairs Charles Mix, June 6 1868, National Archives, M234, roll 279.
23. Fall Leaf and others to Commissioner of Indian Affairs, [March-April 1868], National Archives, M234, roll 279. Fall Leaf and other resisted the

move to the Cherokee Nation for a while but eventually had to give in as well.
24. Petition by Captain Anderson Sarcoxie and others to the Commissioner of Indian Affairs Nathaniel G. Taylor, June 13 1867, National Archives, M234, roll 278.
25. The sheriffs, Jacob Easy and John Buffalo, went around to collect the signatures but apparently no one really kept track of who had contacted whom. Thus a few people signed twice or even thrice, unaware of what kind of an impact this would have on them. This gave various government officials, among them Agent John Pratt, the opportunity to discard the document as invalid. See Agent John Pratt to Superintendent Thomas Murphy, February 6 1868, National Archives, M234, roll 279.
26. Petition by Captain Anderson Sarcoxie and others to the Commissioner of Indian Affairs Nathaniel G. Taylor, June 13 1867, National Archives, M345, roll 278.
27. Ibid. Agent Pratt did not forward the petition until he was specifically ordered to do so by the Commissioner of Indian Affairs. When no response arrived, Sarcoxie wrote to the Commissioner directly to inquire if he had received the letters. See Chief Anderson Sarcoxie to the Commissioner of Indian Affairs Nathaniel G. Taylor, July 8 1867, National Archives, M234, roll 278.
28. James Simons to the Commissioner of Indian Affairs, [c. July-December 1869], National Archives, M234, roll 280.
29. Charles Journeycake and others to Commissioner of Indian Affairs William P. Dole, undated, National Archives, M234, roll 275.
30. See for instance John Connor and others to Superintendent Thomas Murphy, August 5 1866, or Charles Journeycake and others to Acting Commissioner Charles Mix, November 8 1867, National Archives, M234, rolls 277 and 278.
31. See Carrigan and Chambers: *Administrative Termination*, p. 4.
32. Ibid.
33. For a more detailed discussion, see Haake: Delaware Identity, p. 19–45.
34. See Fall Leaf and others to the Commissioner of Indian Affairs William P. Dole, February 2 1864, National Archives, M234, roll 276.
35. Charles Journeycake to Commissioner of Indian Affairs William P. Dole, May 2 1863, National Archives, M234, roll 276.
36. They moved to lands west of 96° longitude. The numbers are being affirmed by Thomas Murphy from the Neosho Agency. See Murphy to Superintendent Enoch Hoag, July 15 1870, National Archives, M234, roll 280.
37. See Carrigan and Chambers: *Administrative Termination*, p. 19.
38. It is not clear if this petition ever made it to Congress.
39. For a more detailed discussion, see Haake: Delaware Identity.
40. Typed copy of a letter dated April 25, 1904, presumably from the nueve capitanes and directed to the government. AHGES, tomo 1881 (1904).
41. Maybe these results were of an accidental nature rather than the fruits of cunning plans as they seem like by-products of different governmental strategies more than separate plans.

42. Cornell and Hartmann: *Ethnicity and Race,* p. 150.
43. Thomas Hylland Eriksen: *Ethnicity and Nationalism. Anthropological Perspectives,* London and Boulder: Pluto, 1993, p. 33. Eriksen also allows for outside pressures as a factor in the ascription of ethnic identity.
44. George De Vos and Ida Romanucci-Ross: "Preface"; in: George De Vos and Ida Romanucci-Ross (eds.): *Ethnic Identity. Cultural Continuities and Change,* 2nd edition, Chicago and London: University of Chicago Press, 1982, p. ix.
45. Adams: *Strategies of Ethnic Survival,* p. 193.
46. The Yaqui communities in the United States, however, did not dissolve upon the outbreak of the Mexican Revolution and persist to this day, having gained federal recognition.
47. Knight: *Racism,* p. 84.
48. Kicza: Introduction, p. xi.
49. Stuart Hall: "Who Needs Identity?"; in: Stuart Hall and Paul DuGay (eds.): *Questions of Cultural Identity,* London: Sage, 1996, p. 4.
50. Deloria: *We Talk, You Listen,* p. 13.
51. Cornell and Hartmann: *Ethnicity,* p. 80.
52. Adams: Strategies of Ethnic Survival, p. 200.
53. Deloria: *Custer,* p. 16.
54. Duane Champagne: "Change, Continuity, and Variation in Native American Societies as a Response to Conquest"; in: William B. Taylor and Franklin Pease (eds.): *Violence, Resistance, and Survival in the Americas: Native Americans and the Legacy of Conquest,* Washington and London: Smithsonian Institution Press, 1994, p. 214.
55. Donald L. Fixico: *The Invasion of Indian Country in the Twentieth Century. American Capitalism and Tribal Natural Resources,* Niwot, CO: University of Colorado Press, 1988, p. xviii.
56. John Kicza: Introduction, p. xi.
57. See M. Annette James: "Federal Identification Policy: A Usurpation of Indigenous Sovereignty in North America," in: M. Annette James: *The State of Native America,* Boston: South End, 1992.
58. See Nagel: *American Indian Ethnic Renewal,* p. 71.
59. Fixico: Federal and State Policies, p. 391.
60. Cornell and Hartmann: *Ethnicity,* p. 111.
61. Ibid, p. 110.
62. Ibid.
63. Linda Gordon: *The Great Arizona Orphan Abduction,* Cambridge: Harvard University Press, 1999, p. 314.
64. Adams: Strategies of Ethnic Survival, p. 191.
65. I do not suggest that the prey in question should therefore be thankful for the predator's attacks.

NOTES TO CHAPTER THIRTEEN

1. Colin G. Calloway (ed.): *After King Philip's War. Presence and Persistence in Indian New England,* Hanover and London: University Press of New England, 1997, p. 12.

2. Seed: *American Pentimento*, p. 3.
3. Horsman: *Indian Removal*, p. 18.
4. See White: Using the Past, p. 235. He views this to be the case at least until the twentieth century.
5. See Stephen Cornell: *The Return of the Native. American Indian Political Resurgence*, Oxford: Oxford University Press, 1988, p. 41.
6. Seed: *American Pentimento*, p. 6.
7. Tim Alan Garrison: *The Legal Ideology of Removal. The Southern Judiciary and the Sovereignty of Native American Nations*, Athens and London: The University of Georgia Press, 2002, p. 21.
8. "As secretary of war, Calhoun gave federal treaty agents the authority to use 'subterfuge and fraud' to obtain Indian cessions; time after time, the federal government's treaty commissioners strictly followed those directions." (Garrison: *Legal Ideology*, p. 24.)
9. Horsman: *Indian Removal*, p. 1.
10. Seed: *American Pentimento*, p. 5.
11. Dorothy V. Jones: *License for Empire*, Chicago: University of Chicago Press, 1982, p. 121f.
12. Reginald Horsman: *Expansion and American Indian Policy, 1783–1812*, Michigan State University Press, 1967, p. 173.
13. Horsman: *Expansion*, p. 173.
14. Horsman: *Indian Removal*, p. 9.
15. Ibid, p. 17f.
16. Ibid, p. 16.
17. Tim Garrison has traced the impact of such conflicts on the southern judiciary and has shown how this, in turn, affected the southern removal policy. See Garrison: *Legal Ideology*, especially p. 8.
18. Brian W. Dippie: *The Vanishing American: White Attitudes and U.S. Indian Policy*, Lawrence: University of Kansas Press, 1982, p. 24.
19. Augie Fleras and Jean Leonard Elliott: *The Nations Within. Aboriginal-State Relations in Canada, the United States, and New Zealand*, Toronto: Oxford University Press, 1992, p. 2.
20. Anya Peterson Royce: *Ethnic Identity. Strategies of Diversity*, Bloomington: Indiana University Press, 1982, p. 58.
21. Sills: *Ethnocide*, p. 341.
22. Paula Mitchell Marks: *In a Barren Land. American Indian Dispossession and Survival*, New York: William Marrow and Company, 1998, p. 376.
23. Royce: *Ethnic Identity*, p. 61.
24. Adams: Strategies of Ethnic Survival, p. 192.
25. Fleras and Elliott: *Nations Within*, p. 2. See also Berger: *Shadow*, p. xi.
26. Means: *Fear*, p. 421.
27. Rhys Isaac: "Inclusive Histories," in Stuart Macintyre (ed.): *The Historian's Conscience. Australian Historians on the Ethics of History*, Melbourne University Press, 2004, p. 69.
28. This is somewhat surprising as Natives had been used in a positive manner when it came to justify the country's striving for independence. (The

mistreatment of the indigenous population was cited among the reasons that necessitated the country to break away from Spain.) In the Declaration of Independence of the United States, however, Natives were only mentioned as something the king had failed to protect the colonists from and thus in a rather negative manner.

29. Ward Churchill: "Perversions of Justice: Examining US Right to Occupancy in North America," in Ward Churchill: *Perversions of Justice. Indigenous Peoples and Angloamerican Law*, San Francisco: City Lights, 2003, p. 1.
30. Ann Curthoys: "Constructing National Histories," in Bain Attwood and S. G. Foster (eds.): *Frontier Conflict. The Australian Experience*, Canberra: National Museum of Australia, 2003, p. 199.
31. Alice B. Kehoe: "Maintaining the Road of Life"; in: William B. Taylor and Franklin Pease (eds.): *Violence, Resistance, and Survival in the Americas: Native Americans and the Legacy of Conquest*, Washington and London: Smithsonian Institution Press, 1994, p. 204.
32. White: Using the Past, p. 218.
33. Seed: *American Pentimento*, p. 173.
34. White: Using the Past, p. 227.
35. Jack P. Greene: *The Intellectual Construction of America. Exceptionalism and Identity from 1492 to 1800*, Chapel Hill: University of North Carolina Press, 1993, p. 15.
36. Jan Kociumbas: "Performances: Indigenisation and Postcolonial Culture," in Hsu-Ming Teo and Richard White (eds.): *Cultural History in Australia*, Sydney: University of New South Wales, 2003, p. 140.
37. Ibid, p. 136.
38. Limerick: *Legacy of Conquest*, p. 18.
39. Berger: *Shadow*, p. xii.
40. Deloria: *Custer*, p. 50.
41. Michel-Rolph Trouillot: *Silencing the Past. Power and the Production of History*, Boston: Beacon, 1992, p. 26.
42. David William Cohen: *The Combing of History*, Chicago: University of Chicago Press, 1994, p. 244.
43. White: Using the Past, p. 224.
44. Horsman: *Indian Removal*, p. 18.
45. Dipesh Chakrabarty: *Provincializing Europe. Postcolonial Thought and Historical Difference*, Princeton and Oxford: Princeton University Press, 2000, p. 250.
46. See David Wilkins: *American Indian Sovereignty and the U.S. Supreme Court. The Masking of Justice*, Austin: University of Texas Press, 1997.
47. David Lowenthal: "Identity, Heritage, and History," in John R. Gillis (ed.): *Commemorations: The Politics of National Identity*, Princeton: Princeton University Press, 1994, p. 50.
48. Renato Rosaldo: "Imperialist Nostalgia," in *Representations*, No. 26, Special Issue: Memory and Counter-Memory (Spring, 1989), 107–122, p. 108.

Bibliography

LIST OF ARCHIVES

(Unless further specified, various collections of the archive in question have been used. Detailed information will be given in the footnotes. Abbreviations as given below.)

USA:

United States National Archives
Western History Collection, Oklahoma University

Mexico:

AHGES—Archivo Historico General del Estado de Sonora
AGEY—Archivo General del Estado de Yucatán
CONDUMEX—Centro de Estudios de Historia Mexicana: Colección Ramón Corral; Colección Bernardo Reyes
INAH—Instituto Nacional de Antropología e Historia
Acervos Históricos Universidad Iberoamericana: Colección Porfirio Díaz

SOURCES CONSULTED

Abel, Annie Heloise: *The American Indian as Slaveholder and Secessionist,* Lincoln and London: University of Nebraska Press, 1992 (Cleveland: Clark, 1915).
———. *The American Indian in the Civil War, 1862–1865,* Lincoln and London: University of Nebraska Press, 1992 (Cleveland: Clark, 1919).
Acosta, Roberto: *Apuntes historicos Sonorenses: La conquista temporal y espiritual del Yaqui y del Mayo,* Mexico City: Aldina, 1949.
Adams, Richard C.: *Legends of the Delaware Indians and Picture Writing,* edited and with an introduction by Deborah Nichols, New York: Syracuse University Press, 1997.

Adams, Richard N.: „Strategies of Ethnic Survival in Central America"; in: Greg Urban and Joel Sherzer (eds.): *Nation-States and Indians in Latin America*, Austin: University of Texas Press, 1991, p. 181–206.
Alcina Franch, José (ed.): *Indianismo e indigenismo en América*, Madrid: Alianza Editorial, 1990.
Anderson, Benedict: *Imagined Communities. Reflections on the Origin and Spread of Nationalism*, 7th edition, London and New York: Verso, 1996.
Anderson, H. Allen: "The Delaware and Shawnee Indians and the Republic of Texas, 1820–1845"; in: *Southwestern Historical Quarterly* 94, October 1990, p. 231–60.
Anderson, Terry L.: *Sovereign Nations or Reservations? An Economic History of American Indians*, San Francisco, California: Pacific Research Institute for Public Policy, 1995.
Barfield, Thomas (ed.): *The Dictionary of Anthropology*, Oxford: Blackwell, 1997.
Barth, Fredrik (ed.): *Ethnic Groups and Boundaries*, Bergen: Allen & Unwin, 1969.
Becker, Felix: "Indianermission und Entwicklungsgedanke unter spanischer Kolonialherrschaft"; in: Inge Buisson and Manfred Mols (eds.): *Entwicklungsstrategien in Lateinamerika in Vergangenheit und Gegenwart*, Paderborn: Schöningh, 1983, p. 44–65.
Benítez, Fernando et al. (eds.): *Cultura y derechos de los pueblos indígenas de México*, Mexico City: Dirección de Publicaciones, Archivo General de la Nación, Fondo de Cultura Económica, 1996.
Berger, Thomas R.: *A Long and Terrible Shadow. White Values, Native Rights in the Americas Since 1492*, 2nd edition, Seattle: University of Washington Press, 1991.
Berkhofer, Robert F.: *Salvation and the Savage*, Lexington: University of Kentucky Press, 1965.
———. *The White Man's Indian: Images of the American Indian from Past to Present*, New York: Knopf, 1978.
Berlandier, Jean Luis: *The Indians of Texas in 1830*, Washington: Smithsonian Institution Press, 1969.
Bernecker, Walther L. et al. (eds.): *Handbuch der Geschichte Lateinamerikas, Volume II*, Stuttgart: Klett-Cotta, 1992.
Bethell, Leslie (ed.): *The Cambridge History of Latin America, Volume II—Colonial Latin America*, Cambridge: Cambridge University Press, 1984.
———(ed.): *Mexico Since Independence*, Cambridge: Cambridge University Press, 1991.
Bieder, Robert E.: *Science Encounters the Indian, 1820–1880. The Early Years of American Ethnology*, Norman: University of Oklahoma Press, 1986.
Bird, S. Elizabeth: *Dressing in Feathers. The Construction of the Indian in American Popular Culture*, Boulder: Westview Press, 1996.
Blum, John M. (ed.): *The National Experience. A History of the United States*, 3rd edition, New York: Harcourt, Brace, Jovanovich Inc., 1973.
Bordewich, Fergus M.: *Killing the White Man's Indian. Reinventing Native Americans at the End of the Twentieth Century*, New York: Doubleday, 1996.
Brading, David A.: "Nacionalismo y estado en Hispanoamerica"; in: Juan Bosco Amores et. al: *Iberoamérica en el siglo XIX. Nacionalismo y dependencia*, Pamplona: Ediciones Eunate, 1995, p. 55–77.

Brasser, T. J. C.: "The Coastal Algonkians: People of the First Frontiers," in: Eleanor Burke Leacock and Nancy Oestreich Lurie (eds.): *North American Indians in Historical Perspective*, New York: Knopf, 1971.

Brinton, Daniel Garrison: *The Lenape and their Legends*, Philadelphia: D.G. Brinton, 1885.

Brøstedt, Jens, Jens Dahl, Andrew Gray, Hans Christian Gulløv, Georg Henriksen, Jørgen Brøchner Jórgensen, and Inge Kleivan (eds.): *Native Power. The Quest for Autonomy and Nationhood of Indigenous Peoples*, Bergen / Oslo / Stavanger / Tromsø: Universitetsforlaget AS, 1985.

Brown, Kathleen M.: "The Anglo-Algonquian Gender Frontier"; in: Nancy Shoemaker (ed.): *Negotiators of Change*, New York, NY: Rutledge, 1995, p. 26–48.

Brysk, Alyson: *From Tribal Village to Global Village. Indian Rights and International Relations in Latin America*, Stanford: Stanford University Press, 2000.

Buisson, Inge and Manfred Mols (eds.): *Entwicklungsstrategien in Lateinamerika in Vergangenheit und Gegenwart*, Paderborn: Schöningh, 1983.

Burton, Jeffrey: *Indian Territory and the United States, 1866–1906: Courts, Government, and the Movement for Oklahoma Statehood*, Norman: University of Oklahoma Press, 1995.

Cadwalader, Sandra L. and Vine Deloria, Jr. (eds.): *The Aggressions of Civilization. Federal Indian Policy Since the 1880s*, Philadelphia: Temple University Press, 1984.

Caffrey, Margaret M.: "Complimentary Power: Men and Women of the Lenni Lenape"; in: *American Indian Quarterly*, Volume 24, Number 1, 2000, p. 44–63.

Calhoun, Craig (ed.): *Social Theory and the Politics of Identity*, Oxford: Blackwell, 1994.

———. "Social Theory and the Politics of Identity," in Craig Calhoun (ed.): *Social Theory and the Politics of Identity*, Oxford: Blackwell, 1994.

Calloway, Colin G. (ed.): *New Directions in American Indian History*, Norman and London: University of Oklahoma Press, 1987.

———. (ed.): *After King Philip's War. Presence and Persistence in Indian New England*, Hanover and London: University Press of New England, 1997.

———. *First Peoples. A Documentary Survey of American Indian History*, Boston and New York: Bedford, 1999.

Carrigan, Gina and Clayton Chambers: *A Lesson in Administrative Termination: An Analysis of the Legal Status of the Delaware Tribe of Indians*, n.p., 1994 (unpublished manuscript).

Castile, George Pierre: *To Show Heart. Native American Self-Determination and Federal Indian Policy, 1960–1975*, Tucson: University of Arizona Press, 1998.

Castile, George Pierre and Robert L. Bee (eds.): *State and Reservation. New Perspectives on Federal Indian Policy*, Tucson and London: University of Arizona Press, 1992.

Chaat Smith, Paul and Robert Allen Warrior: *Like a Hurricane. The Indian Movement From Alcatraz to Wounded Knee*, New York: The New Press, 1996.

Chalk, Frank and Kurt Jonassohn: *The History and Sociology of Genocide. Analyses and Case Studies*, New Haven and London: Yale University Press, 1990.

Champagne, Duane: *Social Order and Political Change. Constitutional Governments Among the Cherokee, the Choctaw, the Chickasaw, and the Creek,* Stanford: Stanford University Press, 1992.

———. *Chronology of Native North American History. From Pre-Columbian Times to the Present,* Detroit / Washington, D.C. / London: Gale Research Inc., 1994.

———. "Change, Continuity, and Variation in Native American Societies as a Response to Conquest"; in: William B. Taylor and Franklin Pease (eds.): *Violence, Resistance, and Survival in the Americas: Native Americans and the Legacy of Conquest,* Washington and London: Smithsonian Institution Press, 1994, p. 208–225.

———. "American Indian Studies Is for Everyone"; in: Devon A. Mihesuah (ed.): *Natives and Academics. Researching and Writing About American Indians,* Lincoln and London: University of Nebraska Press, 1998, p. 181–186.

———(ed.): *Contemporary Native American Cultural Issues,* Walnut Creek, CA / London / New Delhi: Alta Mira Press, 1999.

Chakrabarty, Dipesh: *Provincializing Europe. Postcolonial Thought and Historical Difference,* Princeton and Oxford: Princeton University Press, 2000.

Chenaut, Victoria and María Teresa Sierra (eds.): *Pueblos indígenas ante el derecho,* México City: Centro de Investigaciones y Estudios Superiores en Antropología Social, 1995.

Churchill, Ward: *Since Predator Came: Notes From the Struggle For American Indian Liberation,* Littleton, CO: Aigis, 1995.

Clendinnen, Inga: *Aztecs: An Interpretation,* New York: Cambridge University Press, 1991.

Clifton, James (ed.): *Being and Becoming Indian. Biographical Studies of North American Frontiers,* Chicago: Dorsey Press, 1989.

———(ed.): *The Invented Indian. Cultural Fictions and Government Policies,* New Brunswick and London: Transaction, 1990.

Clinton, Robert N., Nell Jessup Newton and Monroe E. Price: *American Indian Law. Cases and Materials,* 3rd edition, Charlottesville, VA: Michie, 1991.

Coatsworth, John: "Railroads, Landholding and Agrarian Protest in the Early Porfiriato," *The Hispanic American Research Review,* Volume 54, February 1974, p.48–71.

Cockroft, James D.: *Mexico. Class Formation, Capital Accumulation and the State,* 2nd edition, New York: Monthly Review Press, 1990.

Cohen, David William: *The Combing of History,* Chicago: University of Chicago Press, 1994.

Cohen, Felix S.: *Handbook of Federal Indian Law,* Buffalo: Hein, 1988 (Washington, D.C.: United States Government Printing Office, 1941).

Coleman, Michael C.: "Nothing Compares to Comparison"; in: *American Indian Quarterly* 22 (Winter / Spring 1998), Nos. 1 & 2, p. 116–121.

Cornell, Stephen: *The Return of the Native. American Indian Political Resurgence,* Oxford: Oxford University Press, 1988.

Cornell, Stephen and Douglas Hartmann: *Ethnicity and Race: Making Identities in a Changing World,* London: Pine Forge Press, 1998.

Corral, Ramón: *Obras histórias,* Hermosillo: Biblioteca Sonorense de Geografía e Historia, 1959.

Corrigan, Philip: "State Formation"; in: Joseph, Gilbert M. and Daniel Nugent (eds.): *Everyday Forms of State Formation. Revolution and the Negotiation of Rule in Modern Mexico,* Durham and London: Duke University Press, 1994, p. xvii-xix.

Cotner, Thomas E. (ed.): *Essays in Mexican History,* Westport: Greenwood Press, 1958.

Crowe, Charles (ed.): *The Age of Civil War and Reconstruction, 1830–1900,* 2nd edition, Homewood, Illinois: Dorsey, 1975.

Curthoys, Ann: "Constructing National Histories," in Bain Attwood and S. G. Foster (eds.): *Frontier Conflict. The Australian Experience,* Canberra: National Museum of Australia, 2003, p. 185–200.

D'Errico, Peter: "Introduction. Native Americans in American Politics"; in: Jeffrey D. Schultz, Kerry L. Haynie, Anne M. McCulloch, Andrew L. Aoki (eds.): *Encyclopedia of Minorities in American Politics. Volume 2—Hispanic Americans and Native Americans,* Phoenix: Oryx, 2000, p. 569–580.

———. "American Indian Sovereignty: Now You See It, Now You Don't" (inaugural lecture at the American Indian Civics Project at Humboldt State University, Arcata, CA, USA, October 24, 1997); http://www.nativeweb.org/pages/legal/sovereignty.html (April 2001), now at http://www.umass.edu/legal/derrico/nowyouseeit.html

Dabbs, Jack Autrey: "The Indian Policy of the Second Empire"; in: Thomas E. Cotner (ed.): *Essays in Mexican History,* Westport: Greenwood Press, 1958, p. 113–126.

Dabdoub, Claudio: *Historia del Valle del Yaqui,* Mexico City: Manuel Porrúa, 1964.

Davis, Mary B. (ed.): *Native America in the Twentieth Century. An Encyclopedia,* New York and London: Garland, 1994.

Davis, Robert and Mark Zannis: *The Genocide Machine in Canada: The Pacification of the North,* Montréal: Black Rose Books, 1973.

Dawson, Alexander: *Indian and Nation in Revolutionary Mexico,* Tucson: University of Arizona Press, 2004.

De Vos, George: "Ethnic Pluralism: Conflict and Accommodation"; in: George De Vos and Ida Romanucci-Ross (eds.): *Ethnic Identity. Cultural Continuities and Change,* 2nd edition, Chicago and London: University of Chicago Press, 1982, p. 5–34.

De Vos, George and Ida Romanucci-Ross: "Preface"; in: George De Vos and Ida Romanucci-Ross (eds.): *Ethnic Identity. Cultural Continuities and Change,* 2nd edition, Chicago and London: University of Chicago Press, 1982, p. vii-viii.

De Vos, George and Ida Romanucci-Ross (eds.): *Ethnic Identity. Cultural Continuities and Change,* 2nd edition, Chicago and London: University of Chicago Press, 1982.

De Vos, George and Ida Romanucci-Ross: "Ethnicity: Vessel of Meaning and Emblem of Contrast"; in: George De Vos and Ida Romanucci-Ross (eds.): *Ethnic Identity. Cultural Continuities and Change,* 2nd edition, Chicago and London: University of Chicago Press, 1982, p. 363–390.

Debo, Angie: *And Still the Waters Run,* Princeton: Princeton University Press, 1940.

———. *The Road to Disappearance,* Norman: University of Oklahoma Press, 1941.

Dedrick, John M. and Eugene H Casad: *Sonora Yaqui Language Structures,* Tucson: University of Arizona Press, 1999.
Deloria, Philip J. and Neal Salisbury (eds.): *A Companion to American Indian History,* Oxford: Blackwell, 2002.
Deloria, Vine Jr.: *We Talk, You Listen. New Tribes, New Turf,* n.p.: Macmillan, 1970.
———. "Congress in its Wisdom: The Course of Indian Legislation"; in: Sandra L. Cadwalader and Vine Deloria, Jr. (eds.): *The Aggressions of Civilization. Federal Indian Policy Since the 1880s,* Philadelphia: Temple University Press, 1984, p. 106–148.
———. *Custer Died for Your Sins. An Indian Manifesto,* 3rd edition, Norman and London: University of Oklahoma Press, 1989.
———. *God Is Red. A Native View of Religion,* 2nd edition, Golden, CO: North American Press, 1992.
———. *Red Earth, White Lies. Native Americans and the Myth of Scientific Fact,* Golden, CO: Fulcrum, 1997.
———. *For This Land. Writings on Religion in America,* New York and London: Routledge, 1999.
———. *Spirit and Reason. The Vine Deloria, Jr. Reader,* Golden, Colorado: Fulcrum, 1999.
Deloria, Vine Jr. and Clifford Lytle: *American Indians, American Justice,* 8th edition, Austin: University of Texas Press, 1997.
Deloria, Vine Jr. and Clifford M. Lytle: *The Nations Within. The Past and Future of American Indian Sovereignty,* Austin: University of Texas Press, 1984.
Deloria, Vine Jr. and Raymond J. DeMallie (comps.): *Documents of American Indian Diplomacy: Treaties, Agreements, and Conventions, 1775–1979,* Norman: University of Oklahoma Press, 1999.
Dening, Greg: *Performances,* Chicago: University of Chicago Press, 1996.
Dippie, Brian W.: *The Vanishing American: White Attitudes and U.S. Indian Policy,* Lawrence: University of Kansas Press, 1982.
Dirmoser, Dietmar et al. (eds.): *Die Wilden und die Barbarei,* Münster: LIT, 1992.
Durán, Leonel: "Las culturas indígenas de México y su proceso de cambio e dentidad"; in: José Alcina Franch (ed.): *Indianismo e indigenismo en América,* Madrid: Alianza Editorial, 1990.
Edelmayer, Friedrich et al. (eds.): *Die vielen Amerikas. Die neue Welt zwischen 1800 und 1930,* Frankfurt: Brandes und Apsel, 2000.
Edmunds, R. David: „Native Americans and the United States, Canada, and Mexico"; in: Philip J. Deloria and Neal Salisbury (eds.): *A Companion to American Indian History,* Oxford: Blackwell, 2002, p. 397–421.
Elliott, J. H.: "The Spanish Conquest"; in: Leslie Bethell (ed.): *The Cambridge History of Latin America,* Cambridge: Cambridge University Press, 1987, p. 1–58.
Eriksen, Thomas Hylland: *Ethnicity and Nationalism. Anthropological Perspectives,* London and Boulder: Pluto, 1993.
Fabila, Alfonso: *Las tribus yaqui de Sonora; su cultura y anhelada autodeterminación,* Mexico City: Departamento de Asuntos Indígenas, 1940.
Feest, Christian F.: "Die Indianerpolitik Mexikos und der USA, 1830-1930"; in: Edelmayer, Friedrich et al. (eds.): *Die vielen Amerikas. Die neue Welt zwischen 1800 und 1930,* Frankfurt: Brandes und Apsel, 2000, p. 89–104.

Fellman, Michael: *Citizen Sherman. A Life of William Tecumseh Sherman,* Lawrence: University Press of Kansas, 1995.
Figueroa Valenzuela, Alejandro: *Identidad étnica y persistencia cultural. Un estudio de la sociedad y de la cultura de los yaquis y de los mayos,* Mexico City: Centro de Estudios Sociológicos, El Colegio de México, 1992.
Figueroa Valenzuela, Alejandro: *Por la tierra y por los santos. Identidad y persistencia cultural entre yaquis y mayos,* Mexico City: Consejo Nacional para la Cultura y las Artes, 1994.
Fixico, Donald L.: *Termination and Relocation. Federal Indian Policy, 1945—1960,* Albuquerque: University of New Mexico Press, 1986.
——. *The Invasion of Indian Country in the Twentieth Century. American Capitalism and Tribal Natural Resources,* Niwot: University of Colorado Press, 1988.
——. *Rethinking American Indian History,* Albuquerque: University of New Mexico Press, 1997.
——. "Ethics and Responsibilities in Writing American Indian History"; in: Devon A. Mihesuah (ed.): *Natives and Academics. Researching and Writing About American Indians,* Lincoln and London: University of Nebraska Press, 1998, p. 84–99.
——. "Federal and State Policies and American Indians"; in: Philip J. Deloria, and Neal Salisbury (eds.): *A Companion to American Indian History,* Oxford: Blackwell, 2002, p. 379–396.
Fleras, Augie and Jean Leonard Elliott: *The Nations Within. Aboriginal-State Relations in Canada, the United States, and New Zealand,* Toronto: Oxford University Press, 1992.
Florescano, Enrique: *Etnia, estado y nación. Ensayo sobre las identidades colectivas en México,* México City: Aguilar, 1997.
Floris Margadant, Guillermo: "Official Mexican Attitudes Toward the Indians: An Historical Essay," *Tulane Law Review,* 1980, Vol. 54, p. 964–986.
Fogelson, Raymond D.: "Perspectives on Native American Identity"; in: Russell Thornton (ed.): *Studying Native America. Problems and Prospects,* Madison: University of Wisconsin Press, 1998, p. 40–59.
Forbes, Jack D.: *Wapanakamikok Language Relationships: An Introductory Study of Mutual Intelligibility Among the Powhatan, Lenape, Natick, Nanticoke, and Otchipwe Languages,* Davis: University of California, 1972.
——. *Tribes and Masses. Explorations in Red, White and Black,* Davis: DQ University Press, 1978.
——(ed.): *The Indian in America's Past,* Englewood Cliffs: Prentice Hall, 1964.
Foreman, Grant: *Indian Removal. The Emigration of the Five Civilized Tribes of Indians,* Norman: University of Oklahoma Press, 1932.
Fried, Morton H.: *The Notion of Tribe,* Menlo Park, CA: Cummings, 1975.
Gabbert, Wolfgang: "'Vom Land der Mestizen zur multi-ethnischen Nation.' Staatspartei und Indianer im nachrevolutionären Mexico"; in: Dietmar Dirmoser et al. (eds.): *Die Wilden und die Barbarei,* Münster: LIT, 1992, p. 33–47.
——. „Soziale Ungleichheit und Indianismus auf der Halbinsel Yukatan," in: Ellen Schriek and Hans-Walther Schmuhl (eds.): *Das andere Mexiko. Indigene Völker von Chiapas bis Chihuahua,* Gießen: Focus 1997, p. 96–113.

———. Becoming Maya. Ethnicity and Social Inequality in Yucatán Since 1500, Tucson: The University of Arizona Press, 2004.
Galeana, Patricia: "Historia y perspectivas del indigenismo mexicano"; in: Fernando Benítez et al. (eds.): Cultura y derechos de los pueblos indígenas de México, Mexico City: Dirección de Publicaciones, Archivo General de la Nación, Fondo de Cultura Económica, 1996, p. 379–398.
Garrison, Tim Alan: The Legal Ideology of Removal. The Southern Judiciary and theSovereignty of Native American Nations, Athens and London: The University of Georgia Press, 2002.
Gibson, Charles: The Aztecs Under Spanish Rule, Stanford: Stanford University Press, 1964.
———. "Indian Societies Under Spanish Rule"; in: Leslie Bethell (ed.): The Cambridge History of Latin America, Volume II—Colonial Latin America, Cambridge: Cambridge University Press, 1987, p. 381–419.
———. The Nahuas After the Conquest. A Social and Cultural History of the Indians of Central Mexico, Sixteenth Through Eighteenth Centuries, Stanford: Stanford University Press, 1992.
Gillis, John R. (ed.): Commemorations: The Politics of National Identity, Princeton: Princeton University Press, 1994.
Goddard, Ives: "The Delaware Language, Past and Present"; in: Herbert Kraft (ed.): A Delaware Indian Symposium, Harrisburg: The Pennsylvania Historical and Museum Commission, 1974, p. 103–110.
Gonzalez, Mario and Elizabeth Cook-Lynn: The Politics of Hallowed Ground. Wounded Knee and the Struggle for Indian Sovereignty, Urbana and Chicago: University of Illinois Press, 1999.
Gordillo, Gustavo: Campesinos al asalto del cielo: una reforma agraria con autonomía, Mexico City: Siglo Veintiuno Editores, 1988.
Gordon, Linda: The Great Arizona Orphan Abduction, Cambridge: Harvard University Press, 1999.
Gouy-Gilbert, Cécile: Une résistance indienne: les Yaquis du Sonora, Lyon: Fédérop, 1983.
Green, Leslie Claude: The Law of Nations and the New World, Edmonton: University of Alberta Press, 1989.
Green, Michael D.: The Politics of Indian Removal. Creek Government and Society in Crisis, Lincoln and London: University of Nebraska Press, 1985.
Greenblatt, Stephen: Marvelous Possessions. The Wonder of the New World, Chicago: University of Chicago Press, 1991.
———(ed.): New World Encounters, Berkeley / Los Angeles / Oxford: University of California Press, 1993.
Greene, Jack P.: The Intellectual Construction of America. Exceptionalism and Identity from 1492 to 1800, Chapel Hill: University of North Carolina Press, 1993.
Grossman, George S.: "Indians and the Law"; in: Colin G. Calloway (ed.): New Directions in American Indian History, Norman and London: University of Oklahoma Press, 1987, p. 97–126.
Grumet, Robert S.: The Lenapes, New York and Philadelphia: Chelsea House Publishers, 1989.

Bibliography

Haake, Claudia: "Identity, Sovereignty and Power: the Cherokee-Delaware Agreement of 1867, Past and Present," *American Indian Quarterly*, vol. 26, no. 3, 2002, 418–35.

———. "Delaware Identity in the Cherokee Nation," *Indigenous Nations Studies Journal*, vol. 3, no. 1, 2003, 19–45.

———. "Two Stories—Yaqui Resistance in Sonora and Yucatán," in Nikolaus Böttcher and Bernd Hausberger (eds), *Poder y resistencia en la historia de América Latina*, Berlin/Frankfurt a. M.: Ibero-Amerikanisches Institut/Vervuert, 2005, p. 345–366.

Hall, Stuart: *Formations of Modernity*, Cambridge: Polity Press, 1992.

———. "Who Needs Identity?"; in: Stuart Hall and Paul DuGay (eds.): *Questions of Cultural Identity*, London: Sage, 1996, p. 1–17.

———. *Cultural Studies. Ein politisches Theorieprojekt. Ausgewählte Schriften 3*, Hamburg: Argument Verlag, 2000.

Hall, Stuart and Paul DuGay (eds.): *Questions of Cultural Identity*, London: Sage, 1996.

Handler, Richard: "Is 'Identity' a Useful Cross-Cultural Concept?," in John R. Gillis (ed.): *Commemorations: The Politics of National Identity*, Princeton: Princeton University Press, 1994.

Hanke, Lewis: *The First Social Experiments in America. Study in the Development of Spanish Indian Policy in the Sixteenth Century*, Cambridge: Harvard University Press, 1935.

Harring, Sidney L.: *Crow Dog's Case. American Indian Sovereignty, Tribal Law, and United States Law in the Nineteenth Century*, Cambridge: Cambridge University Press, 1994.

Hartz, Louis: *The Founding of New Societies. Studies in the History of the United States, Latin America, South Africa, Canada, and Australia*, New York: Harcourt, 1964.

Hatfield, Shelley Bowen: *Chasing Shadows. Indians Along the United States—Mexico Border, 1876—1911*, Albuquerque: University of New Mexico Press, 1998.

Haupt, Heinz-Gerhard and Jürgen Kocka (eds.): *Geschichte und Vergleich. Ansätze und Ergebnisse international vergleichender Geschichtsschreibung*, Frankfurt: Campus Verlag, 1996.

Haupt, Heinz-Gerhard and Jürgen Kocka: "Historischer Vergleich: Methoden, Aufgaben, Probleme. Eine Einleitung"; in: Heinz-Gerhard Haupt and Jürgen Kocka (eds.): *Geschichte und Vergleich. Ansätze und Ergebnisse international vergleichender Geschichtsschreibung*, Frankfurt: Campus, 1996, p. 9–45.

Hauptmann, Laurence: *Between Two Fires: American Indians in the Civil War*, New York: Free Press, 1995.

Hausberger, Bernd: *Für Gott und König. Die Mission der Jesuiten im kolonialen Mexiko*, Oldenbourg: Verlag für Geschichte und Politik, 2000.

Heideking, Jürgen: *Geschichte der USA*, Tübingen and Basel: Francke, 1996.

Hernández Silva, Héctor Cuauhtémoc: *Insurgencia y autonomía. Historia de los pueblos yaquis, 1821–1910*, Mexico City: Ciesas, 1996.

Hernández, Fortunato: *Las razas indígenas de Sonora y la Guerra del Yaqui*, Mexico City: J. de Elizalde, 1902.

Hirschfelder, Arlene and Martha Kreipe de Montaño: *The Native American Almanac. A Portrait of Native America Today*, New York: Macmillan, 1996.

Hoekstra, Rik: *Two Worlds Merging. The Transformation of Society in the Valley of Puebla, 1570–1640*, Amsterdam: CEDLA, 1993.

Hoffecker, Carol E. (ed.): *New Sweden in America*, Newark: University of Delaware Press, 1995.

Holden, William Curry: *Studies of the Yaqui Indians of Sonora, Mexico*, Lubbock: Texas Technological College, 1936.

Holt, Barry and Gary Forrester: *Digest of American Indian Law: Cases and Chronology*, Littleton, CO: Rothman, 1990.

Horsman, Reginald: *Expansion and American Indian Policy, 1783–1812*, Michigan State University Press, 1967.

———. *The Origins of Indian Removal, 1815–1824*, Michigan State University Press, 1969.

Hosen, Frederick E.: *Rifle, Blanket and Kettle. Selected Indian Treaties and Laws*, Jefferson, NC and London: McFarland, 1985.

Hoxie, Frederick: *A Final Promise: The Campaign to Assimilate the Indians, 1880–1920*, Lincoln: University of Nebraska Press, 1984.

——— (ed.): *Encyclopedia of North American Indians. Native American History, Culture, and Life from Paleo-Indians to the Present*, Boston and New York: Houghton Mifflin, 1996.

Hu-DeHart, Evelyn: "Development and Rural Rebellion: Pacification of the Yaquis in the Late *Porfiriato*"; in: *The Hispanic American Historical Review*, Volume 54, Durham: Duke University Press, 1974, p. 72–93.

———. *Missionaries, Miners, and Indians: Spanish Contact with the Yaqui Nation of Northwestern New Spain, 1533–1820*, Tucson: University of Arizona Press, 1981.

———. *Yaqui Resistance and Survival: the Struggle for Land and Autonomy, 1821–1910*, Madison: University of Wisconsin Press, 1984.

———. "Peasant Rebellion in the Northwest: The Yaqui Indians of Sonora, 1740–1976"; in: Friedrich Katz (ed.): *Riot, Rebellion and Revolution*; Princeton: Princeton University Press, 1988, p. 141–175.

———. "Yaqui Resistance to Mexican Expansion"; in: John E. Kicza (ed.): *The Indian in Latin American History. Resistance, Resilience, and Acculturation* (Jaguar Books on Latin America), Wilmington: Scholarly Resources, 1993.

———. *Adaptación y resistencia en el yaquimi: los yaquis durante la colonia*, Tlapan: Ciesas, 1995.

Hurtado, Albert and Peter Iverson: *Major Problems in American Indian History*, Lexington, Mass., and Toronto: Heath, 1994.

Isaac, Rhys: "Inclusive Histories," in Stuart Macintyre (ed.): *The Historian's Conscience. Australian Historians on the Ethics of History*, Melbourne University Press, 2004, p. 66–75.

Iverson, Peter: *"We Are Still Here." American Indians in the Twentieth Century*, Wheeling, Il: Harlan Davidson, 1994.

Jaime León, Juan Silverio: *Testimonios de una mujer yaqui*, Mexico City: Conaculta, 1988.

Jaimes, M. Annette (ed.): *The State of Native America. Genocide, Colonization, and Resistance,* Boston: South End Press, 1992.

Joe, Jennie R.: "Gender and Culture: American Indian Women in Urban Societies"; in: William B. Taylor and Franklin Pease (eds.): *Violence, Resistance, and Survival in the Americas: Native Americans and the Legacy of Conquest,* Washington and London: Smithsonian Institution Press, 1994, p. 249–265.

Johansen, Bruce: *Wasi'chu. The Continued Indian Wars,* New York: Monthly Review, 1979.

———. *Debating Democracy, Native American Legacy of Freedom,* Santa Fe: Clear Light, 1998.

Jones, Dorothy V.: *License for Empire,* Chicago: University of Chicago Press, 1982.

Joseph, Gilbert M.: "Rethinking Mexican Revolutionary Mobilization: Yucatán's Seasons of Upheaval, 1909–1915"; in: Joseph, Gilbert M. and Daniel Nugent (eds.): *Everyday Forms of State Formation. Revolution and the Negotiation of Rule in Modern Mexico,* Durham and London: Duke University Press, 1994, p. 135–169.

Joseph, Gilbert M. and Daniel Nugent (eds.): *Everyday Forms of State Formation. Revolution and the Negotiation of Rule in Modern Mexico,* Durham and London: Duke University Press, 1994.

Joseph, Gilbert M. and Daniel Nugent: "Popular Culture and State Formation in Revolutionary Mexico"; in: Joseph, Gilbert M. and Daniel Nugent (eds.): *Everyday Forms of State Formation. Revolution and the Negotiation of Rule in Modern Mexico,* Durham and London: Duke University Press, 1994, p. 3–23.

Josephy, Alvin (ed.): *America in 1492. The World of the Indian Peoples Before the Arrival of Columbus,* New York: Knopf 1992.

Josephy, Alvin M. and Joane Nagel (eds.): *Red Power. The American Indians' Fight for Freedom,* 2nd edition, Lincoln and London: University of Nebraska Press, 1992.

Kaplan, Marcos: *Formación del estado nacional en América Latina,* Santiago de Chile: Editorial Universitaria, 1969.

Kappler, Charles J.: *Indian Affairs, Laws and Treaties, Volumes I-III,* Washington, Government Printing Office, 1904.

Katz, Friedrich (ed.): *Riot, Rebellion and Revolution;* Princeton: Princeton University Press, 1988.

———. "The Liberal Republic and the Porfiriato, 1867–1910"; in: Leslie Bethell (ed.): *Mexico Since Independence.* Cambridge: Cambridge University Press, 1991, p. 49–124.

Kehoe, Alice B.: "Maintaining the Road of Life"; in: William B. Taylor and Franklin Pease (eds.): *Violence, Resistance, and Survival in the Americas: Native Americans and the Legacy of Conquest,* Washington and London: Smithsonian Institution Press, 1994, p. 193–225.

Kelley, Jane Holden: *Yaqui Women: Contemporary Life Histories,* Lincoln: University of Nebraska Press, 1978.

Kicza, John E.: *The Indian in Latin American History. Resistance, Resilience, and Acculturation* (Jaguar Books on Latin America), Wilmington: Scholarly Resources, 1993.

———. "Introduction"; in: John Kicza (ed.): *The Indian in Latin American History. Resistance, Resilience, and Acculturation* (Jaguar Books on Latin America), Wilmington: Scholarly Resources, 1993, p. xi-xxvi.

Kinietz, Vernon: *Delaware Culture Chronology*, Indianapolis: Indiana Historical Society, 1946.

Knight, Alan: *The Mexican Revolution, Volumes I and II*, Lincoln and London: University of Nebraska Press, 1986.

———. "Racism, Revolution, and *Indigenismo:* Mexico, 1910–1940"; in: Richard Graham (ed.): *The Idea of Race in Latin America, 1870–1940*, Austin: University of Texas Press, 1990, p. 71–113.

Kociumbas, Jan: "Performances: Indigenisation and Postcolonial Culture," in Hsu-Ming Teo and Richard White (eds.): *Cultural History in Australia*, Sydney: University of New South Wales, 2003, p. 127–140.

Kohn, Rita and W. Lynwood Montell: *Always a People, Oral Histories of Contemporary Woodland Indians,* Bloomington and Indianapolis: Indiana University Press, 1997.

König, Hans-Joachim: "Barbar oder Symbol der Freiheit? Unmündiger oder Staatsbürger?—Indiobild und Indianerpolitik in Hispanoamerika"; in: Hans-Joachim König, Wolfgang Reinhard, Reinhard Wendt (eds.): *Der Europäische Beobachter außereuropäischer Kulturen. Zur Problematik der Wirklichkeitswahrnehmung,* Berlin: *Zeitschrift für Historische Forschung* Volume 7, 1989, p. 97–118.

König, Hans-Joachim, Wolfgang Reinhard, and Reinhard Wendt (eds.): *Der Europäische Beobachter außereuropäischer Kulturen. Zur Problematik der Wirklichkeitswahrnehmung,* Berlin: *Zeitschrift für Historische Forschung* Volume 7, 1989.

Kößler, Reinhard and Tilman Schiel (eds.): *Nationalstaat und Ethnizität,* 2nd edition, Frankfurt am Main: IKO Verlag, 1995.

Kraft, Herbert C.: *The Lenape: Archaeology, History, and Ethnography,* Newark: New Jersey Historical Society, 1986.

———(ed.): *A Delaware Indian Symposium,* Harrisburg: The Pennsylvania Historical and Museum Commission, 1974.

———(ed.): *The Lenape Indian. A Symposium,* South Orange, NJ: Archaeological Research Center Seton Hall University, 1984.

Krauze, Enrique: *Mexico. Biography of Power. A History of Modern Mexico, 1810–1996*, New York: Harper Collins, 1997.

Kummels, Ingrid: "Von 'Indianern' und 'indigenen Völkern.' Episoden aus der Geschichte Mexikos"; in: Ellen Schriek and Hans-Walter Schmuhl (eds.): *Das andere Mexiko. Indigene Völker von Chiapas bis Chihuahua,* Gießen: Focus, 1997, p. 11–32.

Kuper, Leo: *Genocide. Its Political Use in the Twentieth Century,* New Haven, London: Yale University Press, 1981.

Lagarda Burgos, Sergio D.: *Conflictos que ha suscitado la tenencia de la tierra en el Valle del Yaqui* (Ph.D. diss.), Mexico City: Ciudad Universitaria, 1961.

Landers, Jane: *Black Society in Spanish Florida,* Urbana: University of Illinois Press, 1999.

Lang, James: *Conquest and Commerce. Spain and England in the Americas,* New York: Academic Press, 1975.

Leacock, Eleanor Burke and Nancy Oestreich Lurie (eds.): *North American Indians in Historical Perspective*, New York: Knopf, 1971.
Limerick, Patricia Nelson: *The Legacy of Conquest. The Unbroken Past of the American West*, New York and London: Norton, 1987.
Limerick, Patricia Nelson, Clyde A. Milner II, and Charles E. Rankin (eds.): *Trails. Toward a New Western History*, Lawrence: University Press of Kansas, 1991.
Lowenthal, David: "Identity, Heritage, and History," in John R. Gillis (ed.): *Commemorations: The Politics of National Identity*, Princeton: Princeton University Press, 1994.
Lyden, Fremont J. and Lyman H. Legters (eds.): *Native Americans and Public Policy*, Pittsburgh: University of Pittsburgh Press, 1992.
Lyons, Oren, John C. Mohawk et al.: *Exiled in the Land of the Free. Democracy, Indian Nations, and the U.S. Constitution*, Santa Fe: Clear Light, 1991.
Macintyre, Stuart (ed.): *The Historian's Conscience. Australian Historians on the Ethics of History*, Melbourne University Press, 2004.
MacLeod, William C.: *The American Indian Frontier*, London: Dawsons, 1968.
———. "The Family Hunting Territory and Lenápe Political Organization"; in: *The American Anthropologist*, Vol. 24, No. 4, October-December, 1922, p. 448–463.
Maihold, Günter: *Identitätssuche in Lateinamerika. Das indigenistische Denken in Mexiko* (Forschungen zu Lateinamerika), Saarbrücken: Breitenbach, 1986.
Marks, Paula Mitchell: *In a Barren Land. American Indian Dispossession and Survival*, New York: William Marrow and Company, 1998.
Martin, Calvin (ed.): *The American Indian and the Problem of History*, Oxford: Oxford University Press, 1987.
———. "The Metaphysics of Writing Indian-White History"; in: Martin, Calvin (ed.): *The American Indian and the Problem of History*, Oxford: Oxford University Press, 1987, p. 27–34.
Mathes, Valerie Sherer: *The Indian Reform Letters of Helen Hunt Jackson, 1879–1885*, Norman: University of Oklahoma Press, 1998.
Matthiessen, Peter: *In the Spirit of Crazy Horse*, New York: Penguin, 1992.
McDonnell, Janet A.: *The Dispossession of the American Indian, 1887–1934*, Bloomington and Indianapolis: Indiana University Press, 1991.
McGuire, Thomas R.: *Politics and Ethnicity on the Río Yaqui: Potam Revisited*, Tucson: University of Arizona Press, 1986.
McNickle, D'Arcy: *Native American Tribalism. Indian Survivals and Renewals*, London: Oxford University Press (Institute of Race Relations), 1973.
Means, Russell, with Marvin J. Wolf: *Where White Man Fear to Tread. The Autobiography of Russell Means*, New York: St. Martin's Press, 1995.
Merrell, James H.: *Into the American Woods. Negotiators on the Pennsylvania Frontier*, New York and London: Norton, 1999.
Meyer, Jean: "Revolution and Reconstruction in the 1920s"; in: Leslie Bethell (ed.): *Mexico Since Independence*, Cambridge: Cambridge University Press, 1991, p. 201–240.
Mihesuah, Devon A. (ed.): *Natives and Academics. Researching and Writing About American Indians*, Lincoln and London: University of Nebraska Press, 1998.

Miller, Jay, Colin G. Calloway, and Richard A. Sattler: *Writings in Indian History, 1985–1990*, Norman: University of Oklahoma Press, 1995.
Mirafuentes Galván, José Luis: "Colonial Expansion and Indian Resistance in Sonora: The Seri Uprisings in 1748 and 1750"; in: William B. Taylor and Franklin Pease (eds.): *Violence, Resistance, and Survival in the Americas: Native Americans and the Legacy of Conquest*, Washington and London: Smithsonian Institution Press, 1994, p. 101–123.
Moisés, Rosalio, with Jane Holden Kelly and William Curry Holden: *A Yaqui Life. The Personal Chronicle of a Yaqui Indian*, Lincoln and London: University of Nebraska Press, 1971.
Morris, C. Patrick: "Termination by Accountants: The Reagan Indian Policy"; in: Fremont J. Lyden and Lyman H. Legters (eds.): *Native Americans and Public Policy*, Pittsburgh: University of Pittsburgh Press, 1992, p. 63–84.
Nabokov, Peter (ed.): *Native American Testimony. A Chronicle of Indian-White Relations From Prophecy to the Present, 1492—1992*, New York: Viking, 1991.
Nagel, Joane: *American Indian Ethnic Renewal. Red Power and the Resurgence of Identity and Culture*, New York and Oxford: Oxford University Press, 1996.
Nash, Gary B.: *Red, White, and Black. The Peoples of Early North America*, 3rd edition, Englewood Cliffs: Prentice Hall, 1992.
Newcomb, William W., Jr.: *The Culture and Acculturation of the Delaware Indians*, Ann Arbor: University of Michigan Press, 1956.
Olavarría, María Eugenia: *Símbolos del desierto*, Mexico City: Universidad Autónoma Metropolitana, 1992.
Osterhammel, Jürgen: "Transkulturell vergleichende Geschichtswissenschaft"; in: Heinz-Gerhard Haupt and Jürgen Kocka (eds.): *Geschichte und Vergleich. Ansätze und Ergebnisse international vergleichender Geschichtsschreibung*, Frankfurt: Campus Verlag, 1996, p. 271–313.
Padden, Robert: *The Hummingbird and the Hawk: Conquest and Sovereignty in the Valley of Mexico, 1503–1541*, New York: Harper & Row, 1970.
Padilla Ramos, Raquel: *Yucatán, fín del sueño yaqui*, Hermosillo: Gobierno del Estado de Sonora, 1995.
——. *Progreso y Libertad. Los Yaquis en la Víspera de la Repatriación*, Mérida: Universidad Autónoma de Yucatána (tesis de maestría—ms), 2002.
Pagden, Anthony: *The Fall of Natural Man. The American Indian and the Origins of Comparative Ethnology*, Cambridge: Cambridge University Press, 1982.
——. *Lords of All the World. Ideologies of Empire in Spain, Britain and France c. 1500—c. 1800*, New Haven and London: Yale University Press, 1995.
Patch, Robert W.: *Maya and Spaniard in Yucatan, 1648–1812*, Stanford: Stanford University Press, 1993.
Perry, Lynette and Manny Skolnick: *Keeper of the Delaware Dolls*, Lincoln and London: University of Nebraska Press, 1999.
Pevar, Stephen L.: *The Rights of American Indians and Their Tribes*, New York: Puffin Books, 1997.
Philp, Kenneth R.: *Termination Revisited. American Indians on the Trail to Self-Determination, 1933–1953*, Lincoln and London: University of Nebraska Press, 1999.

Pieper, Renate and Iris Luetjens: "Die Entwicklung der Indianergemeinden"; in: Horst Pietschmann (ed.): *Handbuch der Geschichte Lateinamerikas, Volume I*, Stuttgart: Klett-Cotta, 1994, p. 575–596.

Pietschmann, Horst: *Staat und staatliche Entwicklung am Beginn der spanischen Kolonisation Amerikas*, Münster: Aschendorff, 1980.

———(ed.): *Handbuch der Geschichte Lateinamerikas, Volume I*, Stuttgart: Klett-Cotta, 1994.

Pommersheim, Frank: *Braid of Feathers. American Indian Law and Contemporary Tribal Life*, Berkeley / Los Angeles / London: University of California Press, 1995.

Prevost, Tony Jollay: *The Delaware & Shawnee Admitted to Cherokee Citizenship and the Related Wyandotte & Moravian Delaware*, Bowie, MD: Heritage Books, 1993.

Price, Monroe E. and Robert N. Clinton: *Law and the American Indian. Readings, Notes, and Cases*, 2nd edition, Charlottesville, VA: Michie, 1973.

Priest, Loring B.: *Uncle Sam's Stepchildren. The Reformation of United States Indian Policy, 1865–1887*, New York: Octagon, 1969.

Prucha, Francis Paul: *American Indian Policy in the Formative Years. The Indian Trade and Intercourse Acts, 1790–1834*, Cambridge: Harvard University Press, 1962.

———. *Lewis Cass and American Indian Policy*, Detroit: Wayne State University Press, 1967.

———. *Documents of United States Indian Policy*, Lincoln: University of Nebraska Press, 1975.

———. *American Indian Policy in Crisis: Christian Reformers and the Indian, 1865–1900*, Norman: University of Oklahoma Press, 1976.

———. *Indian Policy in the United States. Historical Essays*, Lincoln: University of Nebraska Press, 1981.

———. *Indian-White Relations in the United States. A Bibliography of Works Published 1975–1980*, Lincoln: University of Nebraska Press, 1982.

———. *The Great Father. United States Government and the American Indians (Volume I and II)*, Lincoln: University of Nebraska Press, 1984.

———(ed.): *The Indians in American Society. From the Revolutionary War to the Present*, Berkeley: University of California Press, 1985.

———(ed.): *Americanizing the American Indians. Writings by the "Friends of the Indian," 1880–1900*, Cambridge: Harvard University Press, 1973.

Remini, Robert: *The Revolutionary Age of Andrew Jackson*, New York: Perennial, 1976.

———. *Andrew Jackson, 3: The Course of American Democracy, 1833–1845*, Baltimore: Johns Hopkins University Press, 1984.

———. *The Legacy of Andrew Jackson*, Baton Rouge: Louisiana State University Press, 1988.

Robbins, Rebecca L.: "Self-Determination and Subordination. The Past, Present, and Future of American Indian Governance"; in: M. Annette Jaimes (ed.): *The State of Native America. Genocide, Colonization, and Resistance*, Boston: South End Press, 1992, p. 87–121.

Rosaldo, Renato: "Imperialist Nostagia," in *Representations*, No. 26, Special Issue: Memory and Counter-Memory (Spring, 1989), p. 107–122.

Royce, Anya Peterson: *Ethnic Identity. Strategies of Diversity,* Bloomington: Indiana University Press, 1982.
Sark, Elmer J.: *100 Years in Oklahoma. Treaty Delaware—Cherokee Indians 1867,* n.p., n.d.
Schriek, Ellen and Hans-Walter Schmuhl (eds.): *Das andere Mexiko. Indigene Völker von Chiapas bis Chihuahua,* Gießen: Focus, 1997.
Schryer, Frans J.: "Ethnic Identity and Land Tenure Disputes in Modern Mexico"; in: John E. Kicza: *The Indian in Latin American History. Resistance, Resilience, and Acculturation* (Jaguar Books on Latin America), Wilmington: Scholarly Resources, 1993, p. 171–196.
Schultz, Jeffrey D., Kerry L. Haynie, Anne M. McCulloch, Andrew L. Aoki (eds.): *Encyclopedia of Minorities in American Politics. Volume 2—Hispanic Americans and Native Americans,* Phoenix: Oryx, 2000.
Seed, Patricia: *Ceremonies of Possession in Europe's Conquest of the New World, 1492–1640,* Cambridge: University of Cambridge Press, 1995.
———. *American Pentimento. The Invention of Indians and the Pursuit of Riches,* Minneapolis: University of Minnesota Press, 2001.
Sheehan, Bernhard W.: *Seeds of Extinction. Jeffersonian Philanthropy and the American Indian,* Chapel Hill: University of North Carolina Press, 1973.
Shoemaker, Nancy (ed.): *Negotiators of Change. Historical Perspectives of Native American Women,* New York: Rutledge, 1995.
Sills, Marc Alan: *Ethnocide and Interaction Between States and Indigenous Nations: A Conceptual Investigation of Three Cases in Mexico,* Ann Arbor: UMI, 1992.
Smith, E. B. (ed.): *Indian Tribal Claims Decided in the Court of Claims of the United States,* Washington, D.C.: University Publications of America, n.d. (compiled in 1947).
Smith, Jean Edward: *John Marshall—Definer of a Nation,* New York: Holt and Company, 1996.
Sollors, Werner: *The Invention of Ethnicity,* Oxford: Oxford University Press, 1989.
Speck, Frank Gouldsmith: *A Study of the Indian Big House Ceremony,* Harrisburg: Pennsylvania Historical Commission, 1931.
Spicer, Edward Holland: *Potam, a Yaqui Village in Sonora,* Menasha: n. p., 1954.
———. *A Short History of the Indians of the United States,* New York: Van Nostrand Reinhold Co., 1969.
———. *The Yaquis: A Cultural History,* Tucson: University of Arizona Press, 1980.
———. *The American Indians,* Cambridge: Harvard University Press, 1982.
———. *People of Pascua,* Tucson: University of Arizona Press, 1988.
———. (ed.): *Perspectives in American Indian Culture Change,* Chicago: University of Chicago Press, 1961.
———. (ed.): *Cycles of Conquest. The Impact of Spain, Mexico, and the United States on the Indians of the Southwest, 1533–1960,* Tucson: University of Arizona Press, 1962.
Stannard, David E.: *American Holocaust. Columbus and the Conquest of the New World,* New York and Oxford: Oxford University Press, 1992.
Stavenhagen, Rodolfo: *Derecho indígena y derechos humanos en América Latina,* México City: El Colegio de México, 1988.

———. *The Ethnic Question. Conflicts, Development, and Human Rights*, Tokyo: United Nations University Press, 1990.

———. *Ethnic Conflicts and the Nation-State*, New York: St. Martin's, 1996.

Stavenhagen, Rodolfo and Diego Iturralde: *Entre la ley y la costumbre. El derecho consuetudinario indígena an América Latina*, México City: Instituto Indigenista Interamericano, 1990.

Stiffarm, Lenore A. and Phil Lane: "The Demography of Native America. A Question of American Indian Survival"; in: M. Annette Jaimes (ed.): *The State of Native America. Genocide, Colonization, and Resistance*, Boston: South End Press, 1992, p. 23–53.

Takaki, Ronald: *Iron Cages. Race and Culture in Nineteenth-Century America*, London: Athlone Press, 1980.

———. *Strangers from a Different Shore. A History of Asian Americans*, Boston, Toronto, London: Little, Brown and Co., 1989.

———. *A Different Mirror. A History of Multicultural America*, Boston: Brown, Little and Company, 1993.

Taussig, Michael: "The Legacy of Conquest"; in: William B. Taylor and Franklin Pease (eds.): *Violence, Resistance, and Survival in the Americas. Native Americans and the Legacy of Conquest*, Washington DC: Smithsonian Institution Press, 1994, p. 269–284.

Taylor, Theodore W.: *The Bureau of Indian Affairs*, Boulder, CO: Westview Press, 1984.

Taylor, William B.: *Drinking, Homicide, and Rebellion in Colonial Mexican Villages*, Stanford: Stanford University Press, 1979.

———. "Patterns and Variety in Mexican Village Uprising"; in: John E. Kicza: *The Indian in Latin American History. Resistance, Resilience, and Acculturation* (Jaguar Books on Latin America), Wilmington: Scholarly Resources, 1993.

Taylor, William B. and Franklin Pease (eds.): *Violence, Resistance, and Survival in the Americas: Native Americans and the Legacy of Conquest*, Washington and London: Smithsonian Institution Press, 1994.

Thornton, Russell: *American Indian Holocaust and Survival. A Population History Since 1492*, Norman and London: University of Oklahoma Press, 1987.

———(ed.): *Studying Native America. Problems and Prospects*, Madison: University of Wisconsin Press, 1998.

———. "The Demography of Colonialism and 'Old' and 'New' Native Americans"; in: Russell Thornton (ed.): *Studying Native America. Problems and Prospects*, Madison: University of Wisconsin Press, 1998, p. 17–39.

Todorov, Tzvetan: *The Conquest of America. The Question of the Other*, Norman: Oklahoma University Press, 1999.

Toqueville, Alexis de: *Democracy in America. Volume 1,* New York: Random House Vintage Classics, 1990 (New York: Langley, 1840).

Trabulse, Elías: "Los orígenes científicos del indigensimo actual"; in: Fernando Benítez et al. (eds.): *Cultura y derechos de los pueblos indígenas de México*, Mexico City: Dirección de Publicaciones, Archivo General de la Nación, Fondo de Cultura Económica, 1996, p. 77–101.

Trenkwalder Schoenenberger, Regula: *Lenape Women, Matriliny and the Colonial Encounter, Resistance and Erosion of Power (c. 1600–1876): An Excursus in Feminist Anthropology*, Bern and New York: P. Lang, 1991.
Tresierra, Julio C.: "Mexico: Indigenous Peoples and the Nation-State"; in: Donna Lee Van Cott: *Indigenous Peoples and Democracy in Latin America*, New York: St. Martin's Press, 1994, p. 187–210.
Tronosco, Francisco P.: *Las guerras con los tribus Yaqui y Mayo*, Mexico: Instituto Nacional Indigenista, 1977.
Trouillot, Michel-Rolph: *Silencing the Past. Power and the Production of History*, Boston: Beacon Press, 1995.
Turk, James F.: "Before Penn: Swedish Colonists in the Land of the Lenape"; in: *Journal of American History* 76, December 1989, p. 849–851.
Turner, Frederick C.: *The Dynamic of Mexican Nationalism*, Chapel Hill: University of North Carolina Press, 1968.
Turner, John Kenneth: *Barbarous Mexico*, Austin: University of Texas Press, 1969.
Underhill, Ruth Murray: *Red Man's America: A History of the Indians of the United States*, Chicago: n.p., 1971.
Urban, Greg and Joel Sherzer (eds.): *Nation-States and Indians in Latin America*, Austin: University of Texas Press, 1991.
Van Cott, Donna Lee (ed.): *Indigenous Peoples and Democracy in Latin America*, New York: St. Martin's Press, 1994.
Vasconcelos, José: *The Cosmic Race—La raza cósmica* (bilingual edition), Baltimore and London: Johns Hopkins University Press, 1997.
Vázquez Castillo, María Teresa: *Land Privatization in Mexico. Urbanization, Formation of Regions, and Globalization in Ejidos*, New York: Routledge, 2004.
Velasco Toro, José: *Los Yaquis: Historia de una activa resistencia*, Xalapa: Editorial UV, 1988.
Veliz, Claudio: *The New World of the Gothic Fox. Culture and Economy in English and Spanish America*, Berkeley: University of California Press, 1994.
Villa, Eduardo W.: *Historia del Estado de Sonora*, Hermosillo: Gobierno del Estado de Sonora, 1984.
Villoro, Luis: "En torno al derecho de autonomía de los pueblos indígenas"; in: Fernando Benítez et al. (eds.): *Cultura y derechos de los pueblos indígenas de México*, Mexico City: Dirección de Publicaciones, Archivo General de la Nación, Fondo de Cultura Económica, 1996, p. 161–184.
Wade, Peter: *Race and Ethnicity in Latin America*, London and Chicago: Pluto, 1997.
Waldman, Carl: *Encyclopedia of Native American Tribes*, New York: Facts on File, 1988.
Wallace, Anthony F.C.: *Teedyuscung. King of the Delawares, 1700–1763*, Philadelphia: University of Pennsylvania Press, 1949.
Wallace, Anthony F.C.: *The Long Bitter Trail. Andrew Jackson and the Indians*, New York: Hill and Wang, 1993.
Walliman, Isidor and Michael Dabkowski (eds.): *Genocide and the Modern Age. Etiology and Case Studies of Mass Death*, New York and London: Greenwood, 1987.

Bibliography

Washburn, Wilcomb E.: *The Indian and the White Man,* New York: New York University Press, 1964.

———. *The American Indian and the United States. A Documentary History,* volumes I-IV, New York: Random House, 1973.

———. *Red Man's Land / White Man's Law,* 2nd edition, Norman: University of Oklahoma Press, 1995.

Weber, David J.: *Bárbaros. Spaniards and Their Savages in the Age of Enlightenment,* New Haven and London: Yale University Press, 2005.

Weber, Max: *Wirtschaft und Gesellschaft. Grundriss der verstehenden Soziologie,* 5th edition, Tübingen: J. C. B. Mohr, 1972.

Weeks, Philip: *Farewell, My Nation. The American Indian and the United States, 1820–1890* (The American History Series), Wheeling, IL: Harlan Davidson, 1990.

Wells, Alan and Gilbert M. Joseph: *Summer of Discontent, Seasons of Upheaval. Elite Politics and Rural Insurgency in Yucatan, 1876–1915,* Stanford: Stanford University Press, 1996.

Weslager, Clinton Alfred: *Dutch Explorers, Traders, and Settlers in the Delaware Valley, 1609–1644,* Philadelphia: University of Pennsylvania Press, 1961.

———. *The English on the Delaware: 1610–1682,* New Brunswick: Rutgers University Press, 1967.

———. *The Delaware Indians. A History,* New Brunswick: Rutgers University Press, 1972.

———. *The Delaware Indian Westward Migration: With Texts of two Manuscripts, 1821–22, Responding to General Lewis Cass's Inquiries about Lanape Culture and Language,* Wallingford: Middle Atlantic Press, 1978.

———. *The Delawares: A Critical Bibliography,* Bloomington: Indiana University Press, 1978.

———. *New Sweden on the Delaware: 1638–1655,* Wilmington: Middle Atlantic Press, 1988.

Wessel, Carola: *Delaware-Indianer und Herrnhuter Missionare im Upper Ohio Valley,* Tübingen: Max Niemeyer, 1999.

White, Richard: *The Middle Ground: Indians, Empires, and Republic in the Great Lakes Region, 1650–1815,* New York: Cambridge University Press, 1991.

———. "Using the Past. History and Native American Studies"; in: Russell Thornton (ed.): *Studying Native America. Problems and Prospects,* Madison: University of Wisconsin Press, 1998, p. 217–243.

Wilkins, David E.: *American Indian Sovereignty and the U.S. Supreme Court, The Masking of Justice,* Austin: University of Texas Press, 1997.

Williams, Robert A., Jr.: *The American Indian in Western Legal Thought. The Discourses of Conquest,* New York and Oxford: Oxford University Press, 1990.

Wilson, James: *The Earth Shall Weep, A History of Native America,* New York: Grove, 1998.

Wolf, Eric R.: *Sons of the Shaking Earth: The People of Mexico and Guatemala—Their Land, History, and Culture,* Chicago: University of Chicago Press, 1974.

———. *Europe and the People Without History,* Berkeley / Los Angeles / London: University of California Press, 1982.

Wright, Muriel H.: *A Guide to the Indian Tribes of Oklahoma,* Norman: University of Oklahoma Press, 1951.
Wright, Ronald: *Stolen Continents. The Americas Through Indian Eyes Since 1492,* Boston / New York / London: Houghton Mifflin, 1992.
Wunder, John R. (ed.): *Native Americans and the Law. Contemporary and Historical Perspectives on American Indian Rights, Freedoms, and Sovereignty,* New York and London: Garland, 1996.
Zaraida Vázquez, Josefina: "Políticas indigenistas en la historia mexicana"; in: Fernando Benítez et al. (eds.): *Cultura y derechos de los pueblos indígenas de México,* Mexico City: Dirección de Publicaciones, Archivo General de la Nación, Fondo de Cultura Económica, 1996, p. 289–294.
Zavala Castro, Palemón: *El Indio Tetabiate y la nación de los Ocho Pueblos del Río Yaqui,* Hermosillo: Gobierno del Estado de Sonora, 1991.
Ziontz, Alvin J.: "Indian Litigation"; in: Sandra L. Cadwalader and Vine Deloria, Jr. (eds.): *The Aggressions of Civilization. Federal Indian Policy Since the 1880s,* Philadelphia: Temple University Press, 1984, 150–183.

Index

A
Alcatraz, occupation of, 24, 220n. 55
Alemán Valdes, Manuel, 101
Allotment, 20, 182; *see also Dawes General Allotment Act, see also Burke Act*
Alvarado, Salvador, 260n. 1
American Indian Movement (AIM), 18, 24
American Indian Religious Freedom Act (1978), 26
American Revolution, 12
Anderson, William (Delaware chief), 35–37
Apaches, 18, 111, 117, 183
Articles of Agreement (between Cherokees and Delawares, 1867), 61, 79–80, 169
    as grounds for termination / loss of federal recognition, 77, 80–82
    Delaware opposition to, 53–56, 64–73
    negotiations of, 48–49, 62
    revised version, 50, 62–63, 76
    signing of, 50–52, 63, 72, 175–176, 186
Assimilation, 23, 196, 203, 207–209
    as US objective, 12, 20, 179–182, 195, 200–202, 206
    as Mexican objective, 183
Avila Camacho, Manuel, 101

B
Banderas, Juan (Yaqui), 112–115, 165, 214n. 10
Battle of Fallen Timbers (1794), 34
Battle of Tippecanoe (1811), 36
Broncos (active Yaqui rebels), 118, 129, 136, 172
    collaboration with pacificos/mansos, 122–123, 167, 170
Bureau of Indian Affairs (BIA), 6, 80, 205
    budget of, 22
    Delaware termination, 77, 80
    establishment of, 14
    investigation of, 26
    policy of, 21
    rhetoric of, 20
Bule, Luis (Yaqui), 135–137, 155, 157,
    attempts to call council of all Yaquis, 252n. 102, 135, 189
    accepting peace conditions, 173, 189
    death of, 260n. 1
Buli, Luis, *see Luis Bule*
Burke Act (1906), 20, 219n. 35

C
Cajeme (Yaqui leader), 115–118, 121–122, 252n. 102
Calles, Plutarco Elías, 99–100, 159
Cárdenas, Lázaro, 99–105, 160
Carlisle Industrial School, 19
Carranza, Venustiano, 97–98, 158–159
Castañeda, Carlos, 4
Cheyenne, 17
Cherokee Nation cases, 15, 216n. 8, 261n. 8
Cherokee Nation v. Georgia (1831), 14, 216n. 8
Cherokee
    conflicts with Georgia, 15
    degree of civilization, 180, 185
    Delawares selecting Cherokee lands, 45, 48, 225n. 20

289

Delawares settling on Cherokee lands, 57, 67
enmities with Delawares, 58, 77, 80–82, 163, 175, 188
in Civil War, 47, 50, 65
internal conflicts, 17
removal of, 15, 66, 186
reorganization, 80
Trail of Tears, 15
Civil Rights Act (1866), 18–19, 165, 218n. 22
Civil War, 47, 50, 65, 179, 184, 218n. 22
Code Talkers, 22
Collier, John, 21
Comisión Nacional para el Desarollo de los Pueblos Indígenas, 205, 240n. 43,
Composición de tierras, 88
Connor, John (Delaware chief), 38, 53–54, 67, 71, 73, 186
Constitution of 1917 (Mexico), 98
    Article 27, 98–99
    Article 123
    reforms of 1992, 102–103, 105
Cooper, James Fenimore, 4
Corral, Ramón, 128
Curtis Act (1898), 80
Custer, George Armstrong, 18

D

Dawes General Allotment Act (1887), 20, 80, 218n. 32
Delawares
    clans, 29, 38, 54, 74, 221n. 6
    constitution and bylaws, 80
    Delaware Business Committee, 75, 80
    Delaware Tribe of Western Oklahoma, 82
    early contacts with Europeans, 30–33
    early social organization, 29–30, 221nn. 3, 7
    enrollment list for removal, 52, 57, 232n. 29
    in US Civil War, 46–47
    intermarriage with Cherokees, 75
    intrusions by Iroquois/Haudenosaunee, 31–32, 222nn. 11, 12, 15
    Moravian missionaries, 35, 223n. 16; see also Moravians
    number of removing Delawares, 52, 55, 57, 68, 232n. 29
    Quakers, 32
    seceding or wild Delawares; see Neosho Delawares
    temporary regaining of federal recognition, 81
    traditionalists v. modernists, 53–56, 73–76, 185–187, 236n. 82
Departamento Autónomo de Asuntos Indígenas, 100–101
Díaz, Porfirio, 6, 95, 97, 157, 184
    Veto against Yaqui deportations, 117, 130
    government of (Porfiriato), 96, 121, 160, 174
    fight against Yaquis, 119, 128, 140, 171–172, 183, 196
Díaz Ordaz, Gustavo, 102
Doctrine of Discovery, 11
Downing, Lewis (Cherokee chief), 67

E

Echeverría Alvarez, Luis, 102–103
Ejidos, 93, 96, 99–101, 103, 241n. 53
Encomienda, 87–89, 238n. 18, 239nn. 19, 22
Espinosa, Luis (Yaqui), 137–138, 142, 157–160, 174

F

Fall Leaf, Captain (Delaware), 47
    opposition to treaties, 56
    opposition to removal, 49–50, 53–56, 68, 73, 186, 188
Five Civilized Tribes Citizenship Act (1901), 219n. 36
Five Civilized Tribes/Nations, 17, 31, 48, 57, 168, 170
Fletcher v. Peck (1810), 14
Fourteenth Amendment, 19, 218n. 25

G

Gaming, 26
Geronimo, 18
Ghost Dance, 18
Gold Rush, 42
Grant, Ulysses S. 19
Great American Desert, 13, 16

H

Haudenosaunee, 32; see also Delawares, intrusions by
Huerta, Adolfo de la, 99–100, 159

I

Indian Appropriation Act (1851), 16

Index

Indian Child Welfare Act (1978), 25
Indian Citizenship Act (1924), 21
Indian Civil Rights Act (1968), 23–24, 218n. 25
Indian Claims Commission, 22, 206, 219n. 45
Indian Delegation Act (1946), 27
Indian Removal Act (1830), 15, 66, 170
   Delaware removal, 3, 5,
   Delaware removals prior to passage of, 37–38, 165
Indian Reorganization Act (1934), 21, 218n. 32
Indian Self-Determination Act (1975), 25
Instituto Nacional Indigenista, 101, 205, 243n. 104, 244n. 110
Izábal, Rafael, 124, 127, 133

J

Jackson, Andrew, 13, 15, 202, 214n. 13
Jefferson, Thomas, 13, 35, 214n. 13
Jesuits, 5–6, 108, 110
Johnson v. McIntosh (1823), 14, 211
Johnson, Andrew, 58
Journeycake, Charles (Delaware chief), 49, 186–188
   Articles of Agreement, 51–55, 72–73, 228n. 72
   ascendancy to chief, 38, 230n. 110
   death of, 75
Journeycake, Isaac (Delaware), 49, 51, 72
Juárez, Benito, 94

K

Kansas-Nebraska Act (1854), 43, 61, 76, 168, 217n. 20
Kaskaskias, 69, 71
Ketchum, Captain (Delaware chief), 38, 42
Klamath, 23

L

Laws of Burgos, 87
Ley Agraria (1915), 98
Ley Lerdo (1856), 93, 96, 241n. 52, 246n. 21
Leyes Nuevas; see New Laws
Lincoln, Abraham, 46
Little Bighorn, 18
Locke, John, 12
Longest Walk, 25
López Portillo, Adolfo, 102–103
Louisiana Purchase (1803), 13

M

Madero, Francisco, 157–158
Madison, James, 214n. 13
Madrid, Miguel de la, 102, 244n. 110
Maldonado, Juan; see Tetabiate
Manifest Destiny, 16
Mansos; see Pacíficos
Marshall, John, 14, 58, 231n. 127
Matus, Luis (Yaqui), 137, 159
Maximilian of Habsburg, 94
Menominee, 23
Meriam Report (1928), 21
Mexican Revolution, 85, 104
   as savior of Yaqui resistance, 3, 138, 140, 163, 174–177, 199
   on Yucatán, 155
   effects on Yaquis post-Revolution, 192, 196
Missionaries, 89; see also individual denominations
Molina, Olegario, 144
Monroe, James, 202, 214n. 13
Morales, Lino (Yaqui), 157–158, 159, 260n. 1
Moravians (Unitas Fratrum), 5, 33, 35, 165–166
Mori, Ignacio (Yaqui), 159–160

N

Native American Graves Protection and Repatriation Act (1990), 26
Neosho Delawares, 69–74, 83, 176, 188, 191
   duration of secession, 234n. 52
New Laws (1542–43), 88, 239n. 22
Nueve Capitanes (Yaquis), 128, 131

O

Oaxaca, 6, 119, 129, 134, 249n. 55
Obregón, Alvaro, 99–100, 158–159, 181, 260n. 1
One Drop Rule, 194
Osages, 37, 48, 58, 67, 71

P

Pacíficos (non-fighting Yaquis), 128–129, 131, 135–136, 170–172, 189
   collaboration with broncos, 122–123, 167, 170
Pan-Indianism, 20, 23
Pawnees, 38
Peace of Ortiz (with Yaquis, 1897), 124–125

Penn, William, 32
Peoria, 69–70
Plains Indian Wars, 18
Plan de Agua Prieta, 159
Plan de Guadalupe (1913), 97
Plan de Iguala (1821), 91
Pontiac, 33
Porfiriato; *see Díaz, Porfirio, government of*
Portes Gil, Emilio, 99
Pratt, John (Delaware agent), 48, 50, 57
   Articles of Agreement, 51–52
   influence on Delawares, 54–56, 187, 230n. 110

Q
Quakers, 32

R
Railroads
   US (and Delawares), 45–46, 261n. 9
   Mexico (and Yaquis), 127, 17, 258n. 30
Raza cósmica, 85, 237n. 3
Reforma, 93
Relocation (policy), 23, 182
Repartimiento, 87–88, 239n. 21
República de españoles, 88, 91
República de indios, 88, 91
Requerimineto, 87
Reyes, Bernardo, 125
Rodriguez, Abelardo, 99
Ross, John (Cherokee chief), 52
Roosevelt, Franklin Delano, 21
Ruíz Cortines, Adolfo, 101
Rurales, 129, 131
Reconstruction, 17, 18, 179, 184, 218n. 22

S
Salinas de Gortari, Carlos, 102
Sarcoxie, Anderson (Delaware), 48, 52–54, 56, 186
Sarcoxie, John (Delaware), 67, 73
Seminoles, 185
Shawnees, 43, 71, 223n. 21, 262n. 13
Sheridan, Philip, 18, 181
Sherman, William Tecumseh, 17
Sibalaume (Yaqui), 157, 260n. 3
Simon, Ben (Delaware), 45
Simons, James (Delaware), 45, 54, 68–71
Sioux, 17, 18, 25–26, 205
Six Nations; *see Haudenosaunee*
Squatters, 44, 168, 235n. 80
Stand Watie (Cherokee), 218n. 21

Sublimus Deus (papal bull of 1537), 237n. 6

T
Tecumseh, 35–36
Tenskwatawa, 35–36
Termination (policy), 22, 23, 182, 219n. 47
Terrenos baldíos, 90, 94, 96, 105, 246n. 21
Tetabiate (Yaqui leader), 124–126
Torres, Luis, 133, 136
Trail of Broken Treaties, 24
Trail of Tears, 15, 168; *see also individual tribes*
Treaties, 174, 217n. 12, 219n. 39
   treaty-making, 11, 12, 19
   Treaty of Greenville (1795), 34
   Treaty of Fort Pitt (with Delawares, 1778), 12, 33, 59, 213n. 7, 216n. 2
   Treaty of St. Mary (with Delawares, 1818), 223n. 18
   Treaty of 1829 (with Delawares), 37, 41
   Treaty of New Echota (with Cherokee, 1835), 15
   Treaty of 1854 (with Delawares), 61, 168, 261n. 9
   Treaty of 1860 (with Delawares), 44–46, 168, 225n. 28
   Treaty of 1861 (with Delawares), 45–46, 168, 261n. 9
   Treaty of 1866 (with Delawares), 47, 50–51, 59–63, 168–169, 261n. 9
      articles of, 53, 64–65
      negotiations of, 48
      post-removal impact on Delawares, 77
   Treaty of 1866 (with Cherokees), 48, 77, 169, 226n. 48
      articles of, 49, 50, 63–65, 80

U
Unitas Fratrum; *see Moravians*
Urbalejo, Francisco (Yaqui), 157, 260n. 1

V
Van Buren, Martin, 214n. 13
Vasconcelos, José, 85, 237n. 3
Villa, Francisco 'Pancho,' 97–98, 260n. 1

W
Wars
   French and Indian War (1754–1763), 32, 222n. 13

Spanish-American War (1846–1848), 16
United States Civil War; see Civil War
War of 1812, 36
World War I, 21, 22
World War II, 22, 82
Washington, George, 12
White Eyes (Delaware chief), 33, 165, 214n. 10
Worcester v. Georgia (1832), 15, 261n. 8
Wounded Knee
  1890, 18
  1973, 25, 220n. 58
Wyandots, 43

Y
Yaquis
  Conflict under Banderas, 111–115
  Conflict under Cajeme, 115–118
  Contract about captives in Yucatán, 141
  Early organization, 107–108
  Jesuit mission, 108–110, 115, 163, 166
  Ladino yaquis, 115
  Numbers of deportees, 130, 134–137, 145, 251n. 79
  Pascua Yaquis, 214n. 17
  Post-Revolutionary deportations, 133
  returnees from Yucatán, 260n. 91
  Revolt of 1740, 108–110, 166
  Slavery, rumors of, 133
  Yellow Fever, 135, 142–147, 254nn. 19, 24, 256n. 45
  Yucatecan court appearances, 147–154
Yaquimi, 107, 114–115, 118, 124, 128, 136
  protectiveness of, 110, 121–122
  ties to, 131, 140, 154, 158

Z
Zapata, Emiliano, 97–98